David A. Denyer

Israel's Apostasy
and
Restoration

Israel's Apostasy
and
Restoration

Essays in Honor of
Roland K. Harrison

Edited by
Avraham Gileadi

BAKER BOOK HOUSE
Grand Rapids, Michigan 49516

Printed in the United States of America.

Some Scripture quotations are from the King James Version of the Bible. Some Scripture quotations are from the Revised Standard Version of the Bible, copyrighted 1946, 1952, 1971, 1973, by the Division of Christian Education of the National Council of the Churches of Christ in the U.S.A. and used by permission.
Some Scripture quotations are from the Holy Bible: New International Version. Copyright © 1973, 1978, International Bible Society. Used by permission of Zondervan Bible Publishers.
Some Scripture quotations are from *The New English Bible*. The Delegates of the Oxford University Press and the Syndics of the Cambridge University Press 1961, 1970. Reprinted by permission.

Library of Congress Cataloging-in-Publication Data

Israel's apostasy and restoration.

1. Bible. O.T.—Criticism, interpretation, etc.
2. Bible. O.T.—Theology. 3. Harrison, R. K.
(Roland Kenneth) I. Harrison, R. K. (Roland Kenneth)
II. Gileadi, Avraham.
BS1110.I86   1987   221.6   88-22280
ISBN 0-8010-3830-8

TABLE OF CONTENTS

Foreword

Peter C. Craigie

In the spring of 1983, I was privileged to teach for a short time at Arthur Turner Training School, a small Anglican theological college in Pangnirtung, about 30 miles from the Arctic Circle on Baffin Island. In the Canadian Arctic, the word *spring* is something of a euphemism; with temperatures hovering around –30° C, I spent a good deal of time in the small library reviewing the reading material available to the Innuit theological students. I found two well-thumbed copies of Roland Harrison's *Introduction to the Old Testament*, a copy of his commentary of *Jeremiah and Lamentations*, and various similar works. All were well used, and I thought that perhaps, sometimes, a prophet may find honor even in the remoter reaches of his own country.

And yet Canada was not always home to Roland K. Harrison. He was born in Lancashire, England, on August 4, 1920. Despite a childhood marred by ill health, his sense of vocation and natural energy propelled him toward theological studies, which he pursued during the dark years of World War II. His primary academic qualifications (B.D., 1943; M.Th., 1947; and Ph.D., 1952) were all awarded by the University of London, England, and it is clear (with the benefit of hindsight) that a solid academic foundation was established for the years that were to follow. In the year of his first graduation, 1943, Harrison was ordained into the ministry of the Church of England, and he has continued to practice that ministry up to the present day in the Anglican Church of Canada.

After serving as a chaplain for two years at Clifton Theological College in Bristol, England (1947–49), Harrison moved to Canada and has remained there ever since. He began his academic teaching career at Huron College, an Anglican college affiliated with the University of Western Ontario in London, Ontario. Then as now, Huron combined both arts and sciences with divinity in a university setting, and the context seems to have set the lines of Harrison's subsequent career; he has had one foot (the best-known foot!) planted firmly in the academic world, the other set equally firmly in the ecclesiastical world. At Huron College, he was initially responsible for instruction in Greek and New Testament studies (1949–52), but in 1952 he was appointed to the Hellmuth

Professorship of Old Testament Studies and concurrently assumed the head-ship of the Department of Hebrew in the University of Western Ontario.

After eleven years at Huron College, Roland Harrison was called to fill the Chair of Old Testament at Wycliffe College, an Anglican college affiliated with the University of Toronto. Since 1960, he has taught Old Testament to a generation of theological students and has supervised the graduate work of numerous students preparing for advanced degrees. When one teaches in a college over a long period of time, it is never easy to assess the impact of one's work; students come and go, rarely to be heard from again. One perpetual source of delight to me has been in teaching continuing education courses for clergy in various parts of Western Canada; I frequently come across clergy (from various denominations) who have an unusual mastery of the contents of the Hebrew Bible coupled with an enthusiasm for studying the ancient scrip-tures. Time and time again, my questions to such clergy about where they learned their Old Testament have been met with the response: "I took Old Testament with Professor Harrison in Toronto years ago!" I mention this point because those of us in the academic world are frequently ignorant of the influ-ence that teaching can have on the lives and ministries of others. And a person who has made his mark on the academic world, as Professor Harrison has, cannot be measured in the academic world alone; he has also exerted a wide-spread influence over a whole generation of students, in Canada and else-where, who are not scholars, but for whom the Hebrew scriptures have become a part of daily life and ministry.

Above all else, however, it has been the steady stream of publications from Roland Harrison's pen that has made him well known to a wider audience. I have, I must confess, long since lost count of the numerous books that Harrison has published. To call him *indefatigable* is an understatement, and his productivity in scholarship is all the more remarkable in the light of an early life scarred by persistent ill health. I recall as a student reading his *History of Old Testament Times* (1957) and *The Dead Sea Scrolls* (1961). He has produced a multitude of works since then, ranging from "teach yourself" volumes on biblical archaeology and Hebrew to commentaries of Old Testa-ment books. But perhaps his best-known work is the enormous volume pub-lished in 1969, *Introduction to the Old Testament*.

In his *Introduction* (with its 1,215 pages), Harrison set himself the formi-dable task of providing an overview of the entire Old Testament in the context of life and culture of the ancient Near East (the field in which he had pursued his doctoral studies). In addition to the conventional reviews of the biblical books as such, Harrison provided extensive histories of biblical scholarship, reviews of archaeology, history, canon, religion, and theology. The *Introduc-tion* combined, to use an old-fashioned distinction, both *Einleitung* and *Einführung* in a single volume; it was useful as an introductory volume for students but also contained some original and penetrating insights for scholars who cared to tackle the major work.

In the preface to his *Introduction*, Harrison wrote that he had taken con-siderable pains not to "burke any issue," and it is a promise amply fulfilled in the book as a whole. His generally conservative approach, balanced by his training in Near Eastern studies, culminated in a volume that contains not only a distinctive and clearly enunciated perspective on the Old Testament but also a trenchant critique of "liberalism" and various literary–critical methods for which Professor Harrison has little sympathy. Perhaps the outspoken criticism and firm convictions expressed throughout the volume were among the reasons it found little support in certain areas of the scholarly world. The reviewer for the *Journal of Biblical Literature* (vol. 89, 1970, p. 227), for example, took a single page to describe, or perhaps caricature, the book; but Harrison's volume is too massive to reduce to any simple categorization. Harrison knew thoroughly what he criticized, and if his plain-spoken critique of much of contemporary scholarship was not well received in some quarters, it may be in part because he touched some sensitive nerves!

What some reviewers have taken to be a negative and reactionary tone in Harrison's writings cannot be found in the man himself. All those who know him are impressed, first and foremost, by Roland Harrison's enthusiasm for the Old Testament and by his cordial and gentlemanly personality. His is an infectious enthusiasm, and it helps explain the prolific output from Harrison's study: his love for the Old Testament and his awareness of its value for human life and faith have provided in part the urge to communicate its significance in writing. And his contributions have not been restricted to books *about* the Bible; he has also played a major role in the modernization of biblical translations, notably in the preparation of the New King James Bible. On the publication of the NKJV, Harrison's natural enthusiasm reached new peaks; here was a volume that not only conveyed the ancient text in modern speech but also sought to retain the cadences that had made the original King James Version so suitable for public reading in worship. There is nothing obscurantist or fundamentalist about Harrison's love for the KJV, both old and new; it is rather an appreciation for fine language, balanced by the recognition that the use of scripture in public worship calls for particular and unusual sensitivity on the part of the translator.

Inevitably, I suppose, one must ask to what extent R. K. Harrison has made an "original contribution" to Old Testament studies. His name is certainly not associated primarily with novel ideas or hypotheses, as are the names of Gottwald or Mendenhall, for example. Indeed, the conservative nature of his work tends to militate against novelty from the outset. Yet it is important to understand Harrison's conservatism in the proper light; he is conservative in his approach to *scripture* as such, without feeling particularly constrained by the traditional "conservative" approaches to scripture. Therefore, he can write in the preface to his *Introduction*: "The conclusions that appear in the book are tentative and amenable to modification in the light of whatever relevant factual information may emerge in the future." That is to say, Harrison is conservative in his thought, but he betrays little evidence of being hidebound by traditional conservative perspectives; he feels free to follow the evidence where it leads him but is rarely persuaded by what he considers to be the subjective trends of much of contemporary Old Testament scholarship.

For all that, there is an originality to Harrison's work that is rarely recognized. He maintained a staunchly conservative perspective when it was rare to do so in the academic world; and he remained firmly *in* the academic world, refusing the potential obscurantism of the fundamentalist wing and reading widely in contemporary scholarship, regardless of whether or not he found himself in sympathy with what he read. He did not simply repeat the accepted positions of the tradition he espoused but engaged directly in the scholarly task and worked out independently the reasons for the conclusions he reached. Thus, although Harrison may not be recalled by later generations as the founder of a particular school of thought, he may rightly be remembered as one who employed all the scholarly resources available to him to establish a scholarly position, despite the lack of common acceptance for that position in the scholarly community as a whole.

But perhaps one of the most significant roles Harrison played has been the encouragement he has given to a whole generation of theological students in the conservative tradition. Swamped by a mass of scholarly tomes whose methods they found both disturbing and difficult, students found that Harrison's books provided a new perspective. It was clear that one did not have to abandon scholarship if one wished to remain faithful to scripture. And simply knowing that there was someone "out there" who had thought through the difficulties of scholarship from a conservative perspective was a source of strength to many young students. Some followed Harrison's lead; others developed their own positions but were profoundly influenced by his works in the course of their intellectual development.

The approach of retirement has not in any sense diminished "R. K.'s" enthusiasm for his work. He merely thinks of the extra time available to him for writing, once he is released from the responsibilities of teaching. And his increasing involvement in the editorial aspects of publishing are providing him with a new opportunity for encouraging the next generation to become involved in publication and scholarship. Since 1968, he has been editor of the *New International Commentary on the Old Testament*, and nowadays he is involved with a multitude of other editorial projects. These are not simply responsibilities or tasks that must be done, but opportunities that Harrison has seized to encourage a new generation to participate in the study and proclamation of the substance of the Old Testament. The contributors to this volume in his honor, coming from a variety of traditions in various countries, are testimony in small part to the influence Harrison has had and continues to have.

I cannot end this brief appreciation without a word of personal thanks. For many years, I knew Professor Harrison only from correspondence, in which he was always prompt and helpful. And he was willing to take a risk with younger scholars; whether or not his confidence was justly deserved, it was always a source of encouragement, to me and to many others. But what I have appreciated most in R. K. Harrison is simply his love and enthusiasm for the Hebrew Bible; the scholar who does not love his topic rarely elicits enthusiasm in others, but Harrison has the gift of communicating his love of scriptures to others. It would be a little impertinent to suggest that Harrison would have made a good Hebrew prophet, yet there are elements of the prophet in his character: a deep love for the word of God, an outspoken statement of his views on truth, and an unwavering commitment to the service of fellow human beings. No single *Festschrift* can do full justice to the diverse talents of Roland K. Harrison, but this volume expresses in a small way the esteem in which many persons hold a significant writer and teacher of our times.

Peter C. Craigie passed away in 1985, not long after writing this tribute.

LIST OF CONTRIBUTORS

BATTENFIELD, JAMES R.   Grace Graduate School, Long Beach, California
BLOCK, DANIEL I.   Bethel Theological Seminary, St. Paul, Minnesota
BULLOCK, C. HASSELL.   Wheaton College, Wheaton, Illinois
CHRISTENSEN, DUANE L.   American Baptist Seminary/West, Berkeley, California
COLESON, JOSEPH E.   Western Evangelical Seminary, Portland, Oregon
CRAIGIE, PETER C.   University of Calgary, Alberta, Canada
DUMBRELL, WILLIAM J.   Moore Theological College, Sydney, Australia
GILCHRIST, PAUL R.   Covenant College, Lookout Mountain, Tennessee
GILCHRIST, PAUL R.   Covenant College, Lookout Mountain, Tennessee
GILEADI, AVRAHAM.   Brigham Young University, Provo, Utah
GREENSPAHN, FREDERICK E.   Center for Judaic Studies, University of Denver, Colorado
HOFFMEIER, JAMES K.   Wheaton College, Wheaton, Illinois
KRAUSE, ALFRED E.   Lake in the Hills, Illinois
LASOR, WILLIAM SANFORD.   Altadena, California
LUNDQUIST, JOHN M.   New York Public Library, New York, New York
MATTHEWS, VICTOR H.   Southwest Missouri State University, Springfield, Missouri
MCCREADY, WAYNE O.   University of Calgary, Alberta, Canada
MERRILL, EUGENE H.   Dallas Theological Seminary, Dallas, Texas
OSWALT, JOHN N.   Trinity Evangelical Divinity School, Deerfield, Illinois
RICKS, STEPHEN D.   Brigham Young University, Provo, Utah
SMITH, GARY V.   Bethel Theological Seminary, St. Paul, Minnesota
STUART, DOUGLAS K.   Gordon-Conwell Theological Seminary, South Hamilton, Massachusetts
WALTKE, BRUCE K.   Westminster Theological Seminary, Philadelphia, Pennsylvania
WATTS, JOHN D. W.   Southern Baptist Theological Seminary, Louisville, Kentucky
WOLF, HERBERT M.   Wheaton College, Wheaton, Illinois
YOUNGBLOOD, RONALD.   Bethel Theological Seminary/West, San Diego, California

Preface

This book represents something of an experiment, an attempt to go beyond what normally constitutes a *Festschrift*. By way of honoring one under whose tutelage I learned how scholarship and faith in the word of God should edify one another, I acted on the rather bold premise that this *Festschrift* could not only have a unifying theme but that, in order to attain thematic unity, its topics could be predetermined and assigned to individual scholars. To my surprise, the response was dramatic. This reflected the high esteem in which Roland K. Harrison is held. Had it been another who was honored by such an attempt, the result might have been chaotic.

Even so, the book did not materialize without formidable challenges. (I report this to forewarn any who might attempt a similar endeavor.) After delineating an area of study and germinating a number of topics—the bulk of which were to comprise new areas of research—I had the task of matching topics and contributors. To be sure, someone other than I might have been more successful. I knew personally almost none of the contributors, nor they me. But what I lacked in persuasive power was more than offset by their enthusiasm to honor Professor Harrison. There was something that united us; a match was made.

In fairness to these scholars, I should mention that the topics assigned to them did not always reflect areas of study already familiar to them. This was due not merely to the limitations of subject matter but to the innovative nature of many of the topics; a goal of this *Festschrift* was to break new ground in biblical scholarship. Thus, with few exceptions, none of the scholars was fully in his own element. Apart from two who wrote on their own topics, all agreed to write on the topics assigned to them. This was a labor of love.

It is to their immense credit, therefore, that the scholars contributing to this volume have evidenced such expertise in dealing with central and peripheral aspects of Israel's apostasy and restoration in the light of prophetic thought. While other scholars might have executed their task as well or better, I am personally gratified by the sublime blend of faith and scholarship that has made these contributions a success. In this, Professor Harrison himself has set a high standard. We therefore dedicate this work to him.

Avraham Gileadi

1

From Egypt to Canaan:
A Heroic Narrative

Frederick E. Greenspahn

Stories about heroes appear in many cultures. Although these tales differ widely from one another, each reflecting the character and values of the society that preserves it, such tales frequently manifest a common, cyclical pattern: the hero ventures forth, encountering trials in the course of which some boon is acquired before he finally returns to his place of origin.[1] Their commonality is not, however, restricted to the broad outline of such tales but extends also to detailed components. As a result, it has proven possible to construct an outline of the prototypical heroic narrative. J. Campbell calls this the "monomyth" and describes it in the following terms:

> The mythological hero, setting forth from his common day hut or castle, is lured, carried away, or else voluntarily proceeds to the threshold of adventure. There he encounters a shadow presence that guards the passage. The hero may defeat or conciliate this power and go alive into the kingdom of the dark (brother-battle, dragon-battle; offering, charm), or be slain by the opponent and descend in death (dismemberment, crucifixion). Beyond the threshold, then, the hero journeys through a world of unfamiliar yet strangely intimate forces, some of which severely threaten him (tests), some of which give magical aid (helpers). When he arrives at the nadir of the mythological round, he undergoes a supreme ordeal and gains his reward. The triumph may be represented as the hero's sexual union with the goddess-mother of the world (sacred marriage), his recognition by the father-creator (father atonement), his own divinization (apotheosis) or again—if the powers have remained unfriendly to him—his theft of the boon he came to gain (bride-theft, fire-theft): intrinsically it is an expansion of consciousness and therewith of being (illumination, transfiguration, freedom). The final work is that of the return. If the powers have blessed the hero, he now sets forth under their protection (emissary); if not, he flees and is pursued (transformation flight, obstacle flight). At the return threshold the transcendental powers must remain behind; the hero re-emerges from the kingdom of dread (return, resurrection). The boon that he brings restores the world (elixir).[2]

To be sure, not every heroic narrative contains all of these elements; still, there is sufficient conformity to justify using this outline for purposes of comparison to derive deeper insights into individual examples.

The earliest-known tale of this sort is the story of Gilgamesh. Although its roots are Sumerian, the weaving together of originally separate tales seems to have taken place within the Babylonian culture.[3] The fact that the individual episodes antedate their incorporation into a larger epic strengthens the importance of the extent to which the overall structure, as it now exists, follows the monomythic pattern. It is important to recognize that although he may be partly divine, the hero—in this case Gilgamesh—is not a god.[4] Indeed, such characters' heroism lies precisely in their ability, or at least their effort, to overcome human limitations. Though he fails to accomplish his goal, Gilgamesh is different at the end of his adventures from what he had been at their start. The success of his venture is, therefore, a very personal and ultimately lonely achievement. He "who knew all things"[5] has learned something new; his transformation results from this newly gained insight.

BIBLICAL PARALLELS

Biblical characters do not readily fit this heroic pattern. The Bible's heroes reflect values which were, understandably, quite different from the "honour and martial courage" characteristic of ancient Greece and Mesopotamia.[6] In fact, those who come closest to this common heroic mold are precisely those who seem most at odds with the general tenor of biblical ideals. For example, Samson's bravery and lust are reminiscent of classical heroic traits, as is his personal feud with the Philistines, yet he almost systematically violates the various tenets of his Nazarite status.[7] It is not surprising, therefore, that, in contrast to the other judges, he is credited with having been able only to "*begin* saving Israel from the hand of the Philistines" (Judg 13:5; italics added).[8]

For our purposes, it is important to observe that the Samson tale conforms superficially to the cyclical structure of the heroic pattern: he descends to Philistia (*wayyēred*, Judg 14:1), where most of the action occurs, until he is brought back for burial in his native land (*wayya'ălû* . . . *'ôtô*, Judg 16:31).[9] Of course, Samson returns only after his death—which is not exactly a heroic accomplishment but is a further demonstration of the ways in which this narrative plays with and modifies the heroic model. The Joseph narrative also contains heroic features: the hero is brought down to Egypt (*hûrad*, Gen 39:1), where he remains until the Israelites bring his corpse with them at the time of the Exodus (*he'ĕlû*, Josh 24:32).[10] Narrative symmetry thus links the Exodus with the patriarchs and serves as a framework for the Joseph story. But again, the fact that Joseph returns only after his death makes it difficult to call this a heroic transformation.

There are biblical tales in which geographic symmetry does correspond to the hero's returning in some way changed: Abraham comes back to Canaan after having obtained food in Egypt (Gen 12:10–13:1), while both Moses and Elijah flee to the desert, where they encounter God before returning to their people (Exod 2:15–4:28; 1 Kgs 19).

Perhaps the clearest case is Jacob's sojourn in Haran, the description of which is bounded by two visions. In the first vision, he learns of God's continuing presence (Gen 28:10-22), while the second results in his being given the name *Israel* (Gen 32:25-33). The importance attached to names in the Bible suggests that Jacob's new name reflects a dramatic transformation in his personality: the journey bracketed by these experiences is devoted to his encounter with Laban during which the deceitful boy is himself subjected to deception and Rebecca's son is transformed into the husband of Leah and Rachel. Jacob, who had fled his brother's anger, is now able to confront Esau with humility (Gen 33:3); he who had struggled with his brother must now contend with the rivalries of his own sons. Still, despite its geographical and narrative symmetry, even this account is relatively brief, conveying little of the adventure one expects in a heroic narrative.

For the most part such stories resemble the monomyth only because they are geographically cyclical, their primary events taking place outside of the initial and final setting. The Hebrew Bible does, however, contain one important narrative in which the adherence to this pattern is far more substantial— the description of Israel's experience in Egypt.[11]

THE EXODUS AS MONOMYTH

Campbell has pointed out the relationship between the monomyth and the Exodus.[12] For him, the story begins with Joseph's descent into the pit (it could as well have started with the journey into Egypt, since that too is called a descent[13]) and concludes with the achievement of freedom. While this perspective demonstrates the narrative's clearly cyclical structure, proceeding from Canaan through Egypt and back to Canaan again, it fails to account for many other elements of the monomyth. For example, the geographic cycle should reflect a narrative symmetry, yet Israel's entrance into Egypt has little of the drama that is so obvious when they depart. Furthermore, the groups involved in these two journeys are far from identical: the children of Israel *(bĕnê yiśrā'ēl)* who descend into Egypt are Jacob's twelve sons (Exod 1:1-5), while those who return are a collection of tribes numbering in the hundreds of thousands (Exod 12:37). Even if one were to respond that this is precisely the kind of transformation appropriate for such a tale, the fact remains that the Bible virtually ignores the time spent in Egypt, which structurally should constitute the ordeal and thus the center of the monomyth.[14]

These problems can, however, be easily resolved if we posit that the monomyth begins in Egypt rather than in Canaan. The cursory treatment of the centuries-long Egyptian sojourn then ceases to matter, since it is not part of the epic at all. Moreover, the Exodus encompasses only one generation, with the result that those involved in the "return" are more comparable to the *bĕnê yiśrā'ēl*, "sons of Israel," with whom the story began. The implication that crossing the sea was the threshold *into* adventure accords well with the fact that such borders are often represented by bodies of water.

This approach places the "adventure" in the wilderness rather than in Egypt. While the hazards of oppression are not to be minimized,[15] biblical literature consistently portrays the desert as a frightening place. Inhabited only by demons and dangerous animals,[16] it is ṣimmāʾôn ("thirsty") and ʾereṣ gĕzērâ ("a cut-off land"), terms which lend credence to its conceptualization as a place of death.[17] The images of darkness and lament often used to describe it are precisely those applied to the underworld,[18] an equation found in other Near Eastern cultures as well.[19] It is thus appropriate that the Bible ascribes Israel's survival to divine protection, which provided water in a dry land and food in a place where no plants grow.[20]

The biblical Israelites certainly regarded the desert period as far more threatening than their oppression in Egypt. Repeatedly they complain that they were safer and more comfortable as Egyptian slaves than they are in the wilderness.[21] Although intended to illustrate the obstinacy of this people who had become more accustomed to serving Pharaoh than God,[22] such statements also demonstrate that, from the Israelite perspective, both Egypt and Canaan were lands of settlement, places where people could survive. It was the uninhabited desert that posed a threat to their existence. The allegation that Moses had brought them "out of a land flowing with milk and honey in order to kill [them] in the desert . . . without bringing [them] to a land flowing with milk and honey or giving [them] a field and vineyard to possess" (Num 16:13–14) is not, therefore, entirely ironic.[23] For such people, freedom was more of an ordeal than slavery.

Thus, Israel's adventure does indeed begin after they crossed the sea and left the security of Egypt behind. Water often symbolizes death in biblical and ancient Near Eastern literature,[24] so that the desert again constitutes a realm of danger and adventure, separated from lands of sustenance and security. Israel's crossing demonstrates her ability to pass a border guarded by the forces of chaos.

The major difficulty with this approach is the problem of symmetry: the monomyth should conclude with the hero's return to the place from which he began. Israel, of course, does not go back to Egypt; instead, the Bible describes her conquest of a new land. While this might seem to support the inclusion of Israel's descent into Egypt within the monomythic structure, it is not a necessary interpretation. Although Egypt and Canaan are not geographically identical, we have already seen hints that these settled lands were viewed similarly. There are further indications that the entrance into Canaan can be viewed as a return, albeit not literally, to slavery.

That there is an overall parallel between the crossing of the sea and of the Jordan River is well known; the Bible itself points out the analogy.[25] The leaders associated with these two passages are also depicted similarly, as the Book of Joshua recognizes (Josh 1:5, 17; 3:7, 14). Moses is told to remove his shoes when he first encounters God on holy ground; subsequently he performs a circumcision, splits a body of water, and sends out spies, two of whom report back favorably (Exod 3–4, 14; Num 13). For Joshua, the sequence is reversed: before crossing the Jordan, he sends out two spies, next the river is parted, after which he circumcises the Israelites, and then removes his shoes in response to a vision on holy ground (Josh 2–5). He too reveals God's law to Israel from a mountain top and celebrates a Passover (Josh 5:10–11; 8:30–35). To the extent that Joshua is presented as a lesser reflection of Moses, the entrance into Canaan emerges as a mirror image of the exodus from Egypt.

The climax of the heroic tale comes in union with the deity, which can be expressed in a variety of ways. Although Israel's transformation had already begun in Egypt, as signalled by the shift in those who bear the names of Jacob's sons from individuals to tribes, it was in the desert that these tribes were shaped into Israel and there, the Bible implies, that they first met God and became partners in his covenant (for example, Deut 32:10). In terms of Campbell's scheme, which speaks of "the hero's sexual union with the goddess–mother" and "recognition by the father–creator," one might recall biblical references to the fact that Israel, who is sometimes depicted as God's offspring (Exod 4:22),[26] comes to be called by God's name (Num 6:27; 2 Chr 7:14), and that the covenant is often represented as a marriage between them.[27] The observation that Israel experienced an "expansion of consciousness and therewith of being" at Sinai is thus both literally and symbolically true.[28] Sinai serves as the apotheosis for the Exodus as monomyth. Israel's encounter with God created an explicitly new level of awareness to accompany the transition from the old, slave-born generation to a younger, desert-bred group less inhibited by the experience of Egypt and more ready to become truly Israel.

IMPLICATIONS

The fact that the exodus narrative follows this basic pattern does not imply that it was borrowed or even consciously shaped. The monomyth is not a template, but an abstraction based on a large number of unrelated accounts. That a variety of tales fit this format, therefore, has no relevance with regard to their origin. Still, the degree to which the description of the exodus–conquest conforms to so widespread a format should not be surprising. The monomythic structure is found in central and highly charged heroic tales. For ancient Israel there was no more important event than the Exodus. From a quantitative perspective, it dominates the Bible's historiographic literature, encompassing four of the Pentateuch's five books.[29] God is repeatedly described as the one who brought Israel out of the land of bondage. Moreover, the covenant, which plays a central role in biblical thought, has its locus and justification in this event, as do several major holidays, making it the key moment in Israelite theology.

That the exodus–conquest is told in accordance with the monomythic pattern emphasizes the thematic unity of the account in its present form. This is not to claim that the story was written at one time by one author. Heroic tales can have complex prehistories. As noted above, the Epic of Gilgamesh, the oldest-known narrative of this type, is itself the combination of originally separate traditions. Amalgamating such materials can be a creative process, as in the present case in which the final configuration is clearly responsible for much of the story's impact. In fact, depending on how one dates the union of the exodus and conquest traditions, this may be the earliest example of such a heroic narrative after the Gilgamesh Epic itself.[30] Even if the symmetrical structure is as late as the Deuteronomist, the biblical account would still be among the oldest-known narratives of this type.

The similarities between the biblical exodus and other heroic narratives must not obscure the existence of certain salient differences between them. Most obvious is the fact that, as we have already seen, the protagonist in such accounts is usually an individual whose heroic stature results from his confrontation with forces more powerful than himself.

In the Bible, however, the central role is given over to the people Israel as a whole. This group orientation, which permeates many different strata of biblical tradition,[31] reflects the national character of the Hebrew Bible. This is not to suggest that Israel was idealized, any more than Gilgamesh or Odysseus can be taken as moral exemplars; but neither do Israel's shortcomings detract from her centrality. God may be the mover of history and final arbiter of right and wrong, but it is Israel, her failures and accomplishments, who occupies center stage.[32] Even her sins are important.

In fact, Israel's sinfulness serves as a major theme of this narrative. Longing to return to Egypt, worshiping the golden calf at the moment of revelation, rejecting the opportunity to invade Canaan — these are Israel's wilderness activities. They all share in their denial of the divinely sanctioned nature of the exodus–conquest and thus demonstrate not only Israelite obstinacy but also her rejection of God himself, along with the divinely mandated and supported mission. Israel is a strange kind of hero, a renegade who demands attention through negativity in order to sabotage the assigned task.[33]

We can thus see how the structure of a major biblical narrative conforms to a pattern widely attested throughout the world. The centrality of the exodus in Israelite thought is illustrated as much by the way in which it is presented as by the frequency of allusions to it. At the same time, deviations from the pattern — the focus on an entire people and their negative depiction — reflect much that is characteristically Israelite. For ancient Israel to have produced such an account, in which she herself plays the central and negative role, is remarkable testimony to the nature of this people's self-perception.

NOTES

1. This tripartite structure may derive from seasonal myths or even rites of passage (separation, initiation, return) (see Joseph Campbell, *The Hero with a Thousand Faces* [New York:

Pantheon, 1948], 30; and G. R. Levy, *The Sword from the Rock* [London: Faber and Faber, 1953], 13).

2. Campbell, *Hero*, 245–46. The term *monomyth* was first used, albeit quite differently, by James Joyce in *Finnegan's Wake* (New York: Viking, 1939), 581.

3. S. N. Kramer, "The Epic of Gilgamesh and Its Sumerian Sources: A Study in Literary Evolution," *JAOS* 64 (1944): 7–23; see also J. H. Tigay, *The Evolution of the Gilgamesh Epic* (Philadelphia: University of Pennsylvania, 1982), esp. 242–43.

4. The narrative is clear that immortality was reserved for the gods (compare Gen 3:22), which, in context, cannot include Gilgamesh (see R. C. Thompson, *The Epic of Gilgamesh, Text, Transliteration, and Notes* [Oxford: Clarendon, 1930], 27 and 53, for the Old Babylonian version [III iv.6–7 and X iii.3–4]. According to the Assyrian version, Utnapishtim's becoming like a god is equivalent to his gaining immortality [XI.3–4]; Thompson, *Epic of Gilgamesh*, 60).

5. *Ša kullati idû* (I i.2; Thompson, *Epic of Gilgamesh*, 11).

6. G. S. Kirk, *The Songs of Homer* (Cambridge: Cambridge University Press, 1962), 57.

7. See J. Blenkinsopp, "Structure and Style in Judges 13–16," *JBL* 82 (1963): 65–76.

8. The fact that the classical heroic type is most closely approximated by a Danite judge may not be accidental (compare E. Margalit, "Hahaqbālâ Bên Sippûr Šimšôn Lěsippûrê Gôyê Hayyam Hā'ēgē'î," *Beth Mikra* 11 [1966]: 122–30; and Y. Yadin, "And Dan, Why Did He Remain in Ships [Judges V, 17]," *AJBA* 1 [1968]: 9–23).

9. See A. Kariv, "Ḥîdat Šimšôn Ûpišrâ," *Karmelit* 10 (1963): 30–37.

10. I am grateful to Avraham Gileadi for drawing this point to my attention.

11. Several of the previously mentioned narratives which also conform to this structure may have been modelled on the exodus account (see Joseph Campbell, *The Masks of God: Occidental Mythology* [New York: Viking, 1964], 130; F. M. Cross, *Canaanite Myth and Hebrew Epic* [Cambridge: Harvard University Press, 1973], 191–94; and U. Cassuto, *A Commentary on the Book of Genesis* [Jerusalem: Magnes, 1964], 2:334–36).

12. Campbell, *Masks of God*, 137–38.

13. Gen. 39:1; the verb *yrd* is often used for travel to Egypt; see Gen. 12:10; 26:2; 37:25; 42:3; 43:7, 15; 46:3–4.

14. Campbell's approach does have the advantage of the Joseph story's corresponding to the hero's being "lured to the threshold of adventure" (Campbell, *Hero*, 245), which fits Joseph's observation to his brothers that "it was not you who sent me here, but God" (Gen 45:8; compare 50:20).

15. The use of death symbolism to describe Egypt is pointed out by J. Ackerman, "The Literary Context of the Moses Birth Story," in *Literary Interpretations of Biblical Narratives*, ed. K. R. R. Gros Louis, with J. S. Ackerman and T. S. Warshaw (Nashville: Abingdon, 1974), 84.

16. For example, Lev. 16:10; Deut. 8:15; Isa. 21:1; Jer. 2:6; Mal. 1:3.

17. Lev. 16:22; Deut. 8:15; compare Jer. 17:6.

18. Deut. 32:10; Jer. 2:6, 31; Job 24:19; see also J. Pedersen, *Israel, Its Life and Culture* (London: Oxford University Press, 1926), I–II, 453–65.

19. See A. Haldar, *The Notion of the Desert in Sumero-Accadian and West Semitic Religions* (UUÄ 1953:3; Uppsala: A. B. Lundequistska, 1953), 11–12, and passim, as well as A. J. Wensinck, *The Ocean in the Literature of the Western Semites* (Amsterdam: Johannes Muller, 1918), 44–53.

20. See Deut. 8:15–16; Jer. 2:2–6; Ps. 107:4–6.

21. For example, Exod. 16:3; Num. 11:5; 14:3; 16:3–4; 20:5; and by implication in Exod. 17:3.

22. A. Ahuviah points out that Israel escaped Egyptian slavery in order to serve God (" *)a'āleh)etkem mē'ōnî miṣrayim* [Exod. 3:17]," *Beth Mikra* 23 [1978]: 301–3; see also Exod. 10:8, 24, 26).

23. Exod. 16:3 contains a more detailed statement of their "recollection" of life in Egypt.

24. See Wensinck, *The Ocean;* H. G. May, "Some Cosmic Connotations of *Mayim Rabbim* 'Many Waters,' " *JBL* 74 [1955]: 9–21.

25. For example, Josh. 4:23; see A. R. Hulst, "Der Jordan in den alttestamentlichen Überlieferungen," *OTS* 14 (1965): 179–84.

26. For the semi-divine status of the hero, see also Hesiod's description of the heroic age in *Works and Days* LCL (Cambridge: Harvard University Press, 1936), 12–15.

27. Campbell, *Hero*, 245; also 109–71; compare Jer. 2:2 and Hosea 2.

28. This was the same mountain where Moses had first learned the divine name, although somewhat earlier (Exod 6:1–3).

29. Genesis and Joshua, which incorporate the preparation for and culmination of the Exodus, could also be included here.

30. Which tradition influenced the description of the other, and thus by what period the two stood as brackets around a distinct desert period, is not entirely clear (see R. de Vaux, *The Early History of Israel* [Philadelphia: Westminster Press, 1978], 384–88).

31. See H. Wheeler Robinson, *Corporate Personality in Ancient Israel* (Philadelphia: Fortress Press, 1964).

32. Compare Campbell, *Masks of God*, 138: "Whereas elsewhere the principle of divine life is symbolized as a divine individual (Dumuzi–Adonis–Attis–Dionysos–Christ), in Judaism it is the People of Israel whose mythic history thus serves the function that in other cults belongs to an incarnation or manifestation of God."

33. See M. E. Harding, *Psychic Energy, Its Source and Its Transformation*, Bollingen 10, 2d ed. (New York: Pantheon Books, 1963), 55, 296. I am grateful to Carl Raschke for the comparison.

2

Golden Calves and the "Bull of Jacob": The Impact on Israel of Its Religious Environment

John N. Oswalt

The issue of Israel's distinction from or connection to the Near Eastern culture around it has been one of significant interest at least since the first great archaeological discoveries of the last century. In its initial form the discussion centered on the connections, with numerous efforts to show the essential similarities between the thought of Israel and that of her neighbors.[1] Later, largely through the influence of W. F. Albright and his students, the pendulum began to swing in the opposite direction, although this did not by any means represent a thoroughgoing shift of the whole scholarly community.[2] One of the most influential writers expressing this changed point of view is G. E. Wright. He maintains that in spite of some superficial similarities, Israel's fundamental perspectives were quite different from those of her neighbors. He says, "The two faiths rest on entirely different foundations. The religion of Israel suddenly appears in history, breaking radically with the mythopoeic approach to reality."[3] Among the differences in perspective that Wright saw as fundamental are monotheism, iconoclasm, rejection of magic and fertility ritual, and concern for history.[4] Other writers who espouse this or a similar point of view are W. F. Albright,[5] Y. Kaufmann,[6] C. H. Gordon,[7] and J. Bright.[8] These writers of the 1940s through the early 1960s helped to establish something of a consensus that whatever Israel's religion was, it was not simply another of the religions of the ancient Near East. It was, in a real sense, unique.

This consensus, however, was fragile enough to begin to crumble when the first questions were raised against it. As early as 1967, B. Albrektson presented evidence that he believed showed the ancient Near Eastern religions to be much more historically based than was believed earlier. He asserts, "This much at any rate is clear, that the Old Testament idea of historical events as divine revelation must be counted among the similarities, not among the distinctive traits: it is part of the common theology of the ancient Near East."[9]

H. W. Saggs makes a thoroughgoing attempt to assert that Israel was not distinct from her environment. In a recent work, Saggs discusses the areas of creation, history, good and evil, communication with the divine, and universalism. In each case he presents evidence that he believes shows similar concepts in both Israel and the ancient Near East.[10] Without going so far as to say that Israel's religious concepts were borrowed from neighboring religions, as writers a century ago might have said,[11] Saggs insists that it is inappropriate to talk of any *essential* differences between the two complexes of thought. Although there are differing emphases, they are part of the same whole.[12]

While it may not be said that Saggs's point of view represents a new consensus among biblical scholars, it is still probably fair to say that it is the opinion of a majority. In this light it is incumbent on any who—as I do—still consider Old Testament religion unique to present other evidence. This paper will seek to review such evidence and to restate the argument in the light of contemporary concerns and points of view.

BASIC PARAMETERS

First, it must be said that the biblical evidence calls forth two assertions countering extreme views on this subject. On the one hand, Old Testament religion and culture did not exist in a vacuum but reflected numerous similarities to neighboring religions and cultures. Some examples of these similarities are substitutionary sacrifice, prophets speaking for a god, temple structure, the style and structure of religious literature, the use of case structures for law codes, and the concepts of ritually clean and unclean. These make it plain that whatever Israel was, she was not an isolated phenomenon growing up in separation from the peoples around her.

On the other hand, one must assert with equal clarity that Israel was not merely another culture of the ancient Near East. Whatever may be said about the weaknesses of Wright's approach,[13] his basic observations remain trenchantly correct: Israel alone stands apart from her neighbors in her monotheism, iconoclasm, her rejection of magic and nature myth, and her assertion that adherence to YHWH's will rather than to a magically contrived continuity with natural cycles is the key to life. These differences are of a fundamental and radical nature. They strike at the very heart of a people's view of existence and therefore cannot be gainsaid.

To be sure, as Albrektson and Saggs have well demonstrated, one cannot say that the surrounding cultures neither entertained such ideas nor experimented with them; they did. The Egyptian king Ikhnaton attempted to reduce all gods to one and to limit his representation to the sun-disc. The Assyrian emperors, as well as other monarchs, saw their gods as intervening regularly in history on their behalf. Not infrequently, concepts reflecting a highly ethical and nonmanipulative religion appear in the religious literature of Israel's neighbors, as for instance in the Egyptian hymns to Amon-Re or the Mesopotamian prayers of lament.

However, the appearance of these and other similarities to Hebrew thought are exceptions to the rule. In contrast, Israelite literature represents these ideas as being at the heart of her thought from the beginning of Israel's existence. Furthermore, any deviation from these doctrines was seen as an aberration that was abhorred and eradicated as quickly as possible. What Israel's neighbors rose to occasionally and persevered in with difficulty, Israel took as the norm, denying the validity of any other experience or manner of thought.

In effect, the highest attainment of Israel's neighbors was the starting level for Israel. That her neighbors sometimes thought in monotheistic ways and that Israelites sometimes worshiped other gods must not obscure the fact that of all nations of the ancient Near East, Israel was alone in having a pervasively monotheistic outlook. No other nation or culture attained this level across its whole society; Israel maintained it for at least a millennium and a half. By the same token, it must not be said that because Israel's neighbors frequently conceived of their gods as operating within history, and the Israelites sometimes referred to YHWH in the language of myth, that the two concepts of deity were essentially similar. Israel's God was not to be known by speculating on the continuities between himself and the natural cycles. Nor were his forays into human history merely occasional and unrelated instances of guidance or deliverance. Rather, the whole of Israel's experience was understood in relation to a consistent, overarching divine purpose that was revealed in a persistent yet creative involvement in the behavior of his people.[14]

ORIGINS OF ISRAEL'S RELIGION

It is sometimes averred that the remarkable coherence of Israel's religious beliefs was the result of a continual rewriting of Israel's traditions in which later developed beliefs were imposed on earlier writings and any contrary material in those writings was expunged.[15] In addition to the fact that no concrete evidence of this process can be adduced (such as earlier manuscripts showing theological or conceptual alterations to texts), it does not explain the origin of the ideas which flowed with such power as to create the rewriting of a whole tradition. Why should this radical rewriting happen in this culture alone? The forces of syncretism and universalism were everywhere at work in the Persian and Hellenistic periods. Why did they produce such a fantastic result in one country only, and why in that one? Without dismissing the possibility of some rewriting (although Israel's insistence that it was through the historical process that God is revealed raises some questions about how much rewriting her own principles would allow), there must have been a commitment to one God, who cannot be identified with nature, far back in Israel's history. This is the only way to explain her thoroughly conceptualized religious understanding. Without a deep and pervasive base on which to build, the process of rewriting is not a sufficient explanation for the unparalleled result.[16]

THE BULL CULT

A specific example of the ideas I am discussing is the phenomenon of the bull cult in Israel. All over the ancient world, wherever cattle were raised, the bull was the symbol of potency, fecundity, and power.[17] This was true in Mesopotamia, Persia, Egypt, Canaan, Anatolia, Greece, and Rome. Whatever other natural principle the great god of the time might be identified with, he was also understood as a bull. So Amon-Re, the Egyptian sun-god, was a bull; so were Baal, the Canaanite storm god, and Asshur, the Assyrian storm god.[18] In this environment it would be remarkable if some part of this concept did not creep into Israelite thinking. That it did so recurrently is an established fact. The premier example of this, of course, was that of the golden calves in the Sinai wilderness (Exod 32). However, that was neither the first nor last instance in which YHWH was identified with or described as a bull. The idols of the Northern Kingdom, almost certainly understood to be Yahwistic, were bulls (1 Kgs 12:25–30); and the fact that Jonathan, a grandson of Moses, was the first priest of the idol cult that continued in Dan from the time of the Judges until the exile suggests that the Levitical family may originally have been in some special way connected with the bull cult (Judg 18:30–31).[19]

All of this suggests that throughout Israel's history, from exodus to exile, there was a nearly continuous worship of YHWH as a bull. Given the environment in which Israel existed, this fact is hardly surprising. What is surprising is the thorough condemnation of this practice in the biblical text (note Hosea's sarcastic comment, "Men kiss calves!" [Hos 13:2]). Once again the question must be asked, What explains this violent reaction? But before pursuing that line I will consider another piece of data.

Alongside occurrences of bull worship in the Yahwistic setting, there also existed a group of references that seem to refer to YHWH as a bull. However, the denotation of the term in question is not at all clear. Hebrew *ʾăbîr*, which AV translates as "mighty One" or "mighty *God*,"[20] is evidently a cognate of *ʾabbîr*, which is most frequently translated as "bull."[21] Brown, Driver, and Briggs note that *ʾăbîr* has been taken as a construct form of *ʾabbîr*. However, if that is the case, it is a variant form, for *ʾabbîr* itself appears as a construct (1 Sam 21:8; Ps 22:13).

But *ʾabbîr* is something of a boundary word. Unlike *par*, which refers solely to the physical bull, *ʾabbîr* refers to the characteristics of the bull, in particular, its might. Thus, especially in Hebrew poetry, it may be used of the bull itself (Ps 50:13). More frequently, however, it refers to "mighty (bullish) ones," either divine (Ps 68:30) or human (Isa 34:7). The term *ʾăbîr*, if indeed it is a cognate of *ʾabbîr*, is removed from *bull* one step further and concentrates solely on the attribute of might. Significantly, the term is used only of YHWH. G. von Rad suggests that it is an appellation stemming from Israelite prehistory and the "religion of the fathers."[22] If that is so, its biblical usage makes it plain that the phrase no longer has any reference to the concrete bull but has become solely descriptive;[23] in that context also fall the analogous expressions "Fear of Isaac" (Gen 31:42, *paḥad yiṣḥāq*) and "Pride of Jacob" (Amos 8:7, *gěʾôn yaʿăqōb*).

TRANSCENDENCE

We must ask, therefore, what is it that accounts for Israel's official rejection of the bull cult and its careful distinction of essence and description in its usage of *ʾăbîr?* The answer lies in Israel's concept of the divine transcendence. Whereas Israel's neighboring religions stressed the continuity of all things with each other, even those that were superficially alike, Hebrew religion stressed that God was distinct from his creation and discontinuous with it. Whereas the gods of the nations were understood to be an integral part of the psycho–socio–physical world, such identification was specifically forbidden to the Hebrews. In many ways this is the profoundest insight of Hebrew religion. Whatever God is, he is not the world around us. Nature may reflect him and may point to him, but the contemplation of nature is not, in and of itself, a contemplation of God. Nor is nature the best evidence of God's character. The best revelation of God, say the Hebrews, is found in his ongoing involvement with those who seek to know and do his will.[24]

It is similarly important to note that Israel did not merely substitute divine identity with history for divine identity with nature. God was not the historical process for the Hebrews. As with nature, history revealed God but was not God. Evidence of this distinction appears in two related concepts: (1) God's foreknowledge, as revealed in the prophets (if he is the process, he cannot know in advance how he himself will develop—this is a particular defect of process theology); and (2) his personal involvement with his people. Taken together, these two pervasive ideas of the Hebrew Bible show that, in Israel's view, God transcended history as much as he did nature.

Whence Transcendence?

The concept technically known as transcendence—that God is separate from his creation—is one that has great implications for the character of Hebrew religion. But before pursuing those implications, I must consider the origin of transcendence. For example, whence came this rejection of divine identity with nature and the assertion that God was seen especially in and through historical experience? Perhaps the most common answer given today is the one I already alluded to: these are late concepts whose formulation by the Hebrews is a historical accident on par with the discovery of the wheel or fire. These concepts were then systematically superimposed on earlier Israelite traditions that had been, in essence, very similar to the religious traditions of the Canaanites.

Yet, this solution begs the question, as a study of Canaanite literature will make very clear. It would be impossible at a late date, say 500–400 B.C., to superimpose biblical theology on an essentially Canaanite religious structure and produce what we now have in the Hebrew Bible. The differences between the two literatures are too vast for a mere superimposition of a new theology to account for them. A complete rewriting of Israelite literature would have been required, a project that, so far as I know, no one suggests took place approaching that late date.

But, one might protest, this kind of suddenness is not what is being suggested. In fact, what is envisioned is the kind of process that J. Wellhausen so brilliantly put forth in his JEDP theory a hundred years ago. The keystone idea of this theory is that Hebrew religious thought developed through a dialectic that carried the culture through some six or eight hundred years of development. Thus revision was more or less constant from the time of the settling of the tribes in the land until postexilic times. According to this approach, there was no sudden imposition of new ideas, but a process of growth, one with many fits and starts to be sure, but a process nonetheless.

While this suggestion might solve the difficulties of the late-revision approach, it comes no nearer to solving the original question: whence came the distinctive shape of Hebrew religion? For, as Wright showed thirty years ago in an argument that has never been refuted, the growth metaphor is not an adequate explanation for Hebrew religion.[25] In particular, it does not explain why these ideas should have had the power in this one culture to displace the common views of the surrounding environment. Furthermore, the discoveries of Saggs, Albrektson, and others that the concepts of divine creation, God working in history, the unity of deity, etc., were not unique to Israel only strengthens the case. Why should these ideas have had so little impact on those cultures, indeed, have surfaced like bubbles and promptly disappeared, but on the other hand become the unique worldview of Israel?[26]

Transcendence Vs. Continuity

The answer to this latter question is, in my way of thinking, a critical one. There was one concept present in Israel which became the ruling one; it determined the shape of all others. And because it was not present in Israel's neighbors, its absence became, among them, the determining factor. That concept—transcendence—was the idea that God was other than the psychophysical order of the universe; he was not accessible in or through it, and it was impossible to manipulate him by manipulating it. This was the concept that always "de-mythed" Israel's religious imagery. On the other hand, it was the absence of this concept that always doomed Israel's neighbors' best thought, plunging it back into mythology.

Fundamentally, the question is an epistemological one: how could God be known? Israel's neighbors believed God could be known directly, through immediate participation in the natural order.[27] For Israel, divine knowledge was mediated from outside the natural order, hence the important role of the Hebrew prophets. Israelite theology could not escape the transcendence of God because its expressions of God were always exclusivist. For Israelites to call

God a rock was not to say that he *was* a rock; transcendence broke the link between image and reality. This fact is seen even more clearly in the phrase, "the Mighty One of Jacob." Whatever the origins of the term *ʾăbîr*, God is nowhere considered to *be* a bull; the term was reduced to a descriptor — it does not speak of essence.

Thus it was that the representation of God as a bull was forbidden and looked upon as an abomination when it occurred. For the Hebrew people, fresh from Egypt with its inclusivist theology, it was not a problem to conceive of Moses worshiping a nonvisible YHWH on the mountain while they worshiped a visible YHWH in the valley. But Moses understood fully that unless the link between Creator and creation was broken, it would become impossible in any ultimate sense to maintain God's unity and exclusiveness, and his immunity to magic, all of which were central to the new faith. In a real sense, the incident of the golden calves was the final episode among the exodus events in the conflict between Egyptian and Israelite theology. At that point, as it was to do again and again — for the battle was not over — Israelite theology prevailed.

EMERGENCE OF THE CONCEPT

If we accept the position of M. Noth that there is no good reason to believe Moses ever existed, let alone that he was the central figure in a struggle between exclusivist and inclusivist faiths,[28] what then? Whence came this doctrine of divine transcendence that was to exercise such a determining force on the shape and content of the emerging Hebrew tradition?[29] Here we touch on the center of the problem. If we accept that the Hebrew Bible and its theology are the result of a long process of continual rethinking and revision, whereby an ultimate result was achieved that made Israel's religion quite different from the religions around it, then we must ask, What guided that process? What ruling concept approved the incorporation of some practices and ideas and resulted in the eventual rejection of others? If that concept was not there from the beginning, when and why did it emerge?

Obviously I will nominate transcendence as an explanation. This alone can account for the amazing absence of human male figures of deity in all the archeological strata of Israelite occupations. This alone could make Israelite kings separate from, and subordinate to, their prophets. But when did this concept emerge? Surely it must have been earlier than the late preexilic age, as many scholars maintain today. By that time, too many of the traditions would already have received their determinative shape. Wholesale revision would have been impossible. Could it have emerged in the early monarchy? Certainly the Israelite traditions would have been much less fixed at that time. Wellhausen would have insisted that Israel was henotheistic at that point, not monotheistic. What Wellhausen would have agreed to was that the concept of covenant faithfulness was at the heart of the earliest material. Covenant was a ruling concept.

With that much we can agree, as does Wright. But whence came the covenant? Why did the Hebrews use this form to express their relation to God, instead of some of the readily available religious forms of their neighbors? Instead of coming from a religious milieu, the covenant seems to find its only comparison in political treaties between a king and a vassal nation. Why should the Hebrews use this form for religious purposes? Examination of some of the elements of the covenant suggests some reasons: (1) prohibition of recognition of or service to any other king; (2) the right of the king to make absolute prohibitions; and (3) the resting of the relationship on trust and obedience rather than on ritualistic manipulation. In other words, these elements and the form in which they appeared were admirably suited for the expression of the doctrine of transcendence.

Now, we must ask, Did the existence of this doctrine require the use of the covenant form, or did the use of the covenant form give rise to the doctrine? Surely the former is correct. There is no reason why the Hebrews should have abandoned the well-worn religious forms of their neighbors without a compelling doctrinal reason to do so. On the other hand, if the Hebrews had indeed come to a radically new conception of God, there was every reason for them to look for new ways whereby this concept could be expressed.

Thus I would argue that transcendence was fundamental to Israel's thinking from Sinai onward.[30] It was this concept that again and again gave determinative shape to what emerged as Israelite thought and culture. Without the existence of this concept, what did emerge is unintelligible. This is not to say that the society as a whole adopted and held to this idea. But it is to say that its power was such as to continually defeat those who consciously or unconsciously supported the idea of continuity with the society's inclusivist tendencies. In sum, unless transcendence had been there from the beginning, it is hard to imagine its having later gained such power, especially since continuity was the ruling principle among all of Israel's neighbors.

There is one final argument in favor of transcendence having been the dominant thought in Israel from that nation's beginning as a people. That is the extreme difficulty of this concept's evolving into existence. As noted above, when elements of the idea, such as divine unity or exclusiveness, are conceived within the context of continuity, they always die aborning, because any divine principle that is a part of this universe cannot at the same time be distinct from it. Furthermore, such austere concepts do not lend themselves to the kind of utility or divine concerns (or the lack thereof) that most religions seek.[31] In Egypt in the fourteenth and thirteenth centuries B.C., in the religion of Amon-Re (not that of Aton), these ideas emerged, but they could not be maintained without moving from the conceptual base of continuity to that of transcendence, a move the Egyptians could not make. According to the Hebrew Bible, Israel made that move, not out of superior intellect, but as a result of direct revelation from God. I maintain that if transcendence is not allowed at this early date — Sinai — then whenever it appeared it could only have been by revelation at that time. One does not grow from continuity to transcendence. One must make a leap. When did that leap occur, if not at Sinai?

CONCLUSION

Israel was affected by her neighbors. She borrowed their culture, technologies, and patterns of speech. Yet she had an internal compass that continually guided this borrowing according to a consistent set of principles. Thus, she may have a king, but not a deified king; she may have sacrifice, but not for the purpose of feeding God; she may have a tripartite temple, but there is no representation of God in the cella; she may refer to God as "Rider in the Clouds," an epithet of the Canaanite Baal, but he is never the storm, as Baal is; she may call him "Bullish one of Jacob," but he is not a bull. What is that compass? I have argued that it is the concept of divine transcendence, a principle that in one form or another must have guided Israel from its beginnings, for it had enough power to reassert itself again and again in Israel's darkest hours. Whence that principle? Discovered? No, received; received, as Israel insists, from the transcendent One himself.

NOTES

1. Compare, for example, the creation epic, Enuma Elish, with the Genesis creation account.
2. See, for instance, the works of Martin Noth, who would argue that any supposed distinction between the two is merely rewriting based upon later reflection.
3. G. Ernest Wright, *The Old Testament against Its Environment* (London: S.C.M. Press, 1950), 28–29.
4. Ibid., 20–29.
5. W. F. Albright, *From the Stone Age to Christianity*, 2d ed. (Garden City, N.Y.: Doubleday, 1957).
6. Yehezkel Kaufmann, *The Religion of Israel from Its Beginnings to the Babylonian Exile*, trans. Moshe Greenberg (New York: Schocken, 1976).
7. C. H. Gordon, *The Ancient Near East*, 3d ed. (New York: W. W. Norton, 1965).
8. John Bright, *A History of Israel*, 3d ed. (Philadelphia: Westminster Press, 1981).
9. Bertil Albrektson, *History and the Gods* (Lund, Sweden: Gleerup, 1967), 114.
10. See, for example, H. W. Saggs, *Encounter with the Divine in Mesopotamia and Israel* (United Kingdom: Athlone Press, 1978), 63: "It is therefore not legitimate to accept that there is a basic difference between the Israelite and Mesopotamian views of the divine powers."
11. Note, for example, Franz Delitzsch, *Babel and Bible* (New York: G. P. Putnam's & Sons, 1903), esp. 67.
12. Saggs, *Encounter with the Divine*, 187–88.
13. John William Rogerson (*Myth in Old Testament Interpretation* [Berlin: Walter de Gruyter, 1974], 85–100) believes that Wright depends too heavily on what Rogerson feels are the faulty analyses of the primitive mind by Ernst Cassirer, *Mythical Thought*, vol. 2 (*The Philosophy of Symbolic Form*, trans. Ralph Manheim [New Haven: Yale University Press, 1955]);

and Henri Frankfort (*The Intellectual Adventure of Ancient Man* [Chicago: University of Chicago Press, 1946]). However, a reading of Wright will make it plain that most of Wright's work is taken up with an analysis of biblical data and, despite references to Frankfort, is not nearly so dependent upon these as Rogerson maintains.

14. Thus, even when Israel used images from mythical traditions, her sense of history was so strong that the images were taken out of the milieu of myth and thoroughly historicized. So, Isa. 51:9–10 refers to the Red Sea crossing, not to a supra-temporal, supra-mundane creation as did the original myth (see my "The Old Testament and the Myth of the Dragon," *EVQ* 49 [1977]: 163–72).

15. See, for example, *Old Testament Form Criticism*, ed. John H. Hayes (San Antonio, Tex.: Trinity University Press, 1974), 70.

16. Note Wright's cogent argument on this point (*Old Testament against Its Environment*, 60–68).

17. Compare *The Interpreter's Dictionary of the Bible*, ed. George Arthur Buttrick (New York: Abingdon Press, 1962), 1:473–74, 488–89.

18. See J. B. Pritchard, *The Ancient Near East in Pictures* (Princeton, N.J.: Princeton University Press, 1954), 170, 177, for further illustrations.

19. Albright's widely accepted suggestion (*Stone Age*, 299ff.) that the bulls were only considered to be pedestals upon which the invisible YHWH stood is not supported by the text (1 Kgs 12:28, 32). Furthermore, it is plain that even if such a fine distinction had ever been proposed by Jeroboam or his theologians it would have been moot. The vast majority of the people would have worshiped what they saw. In contrast, the twelve bulls bearing the bronze "sea" in front of the temple (1 Kgs 7:25) would much less likely (though not impossibly) have become objects of worship.

20. The occurrences are in Gen. 49:24; Ps. 132:2, 5; Isa. 1:24; 49:26; 60:16. All except Isa. 1:24 refer to ʾăbîr yaʿăqōb. That instance is ʾăbîr yiśrāʾel.

21. See, for example, Pss. 50:13; 68:30; Isa. 34:7; Jer. 50:11.

22. Gerhard von Rad, *Old Testament Theology*, trans. D. Stalker (New York: Harper, 1962), 1:7, 167.

23. LXX is interesting at this point. Three times it translates ʾăbîr simply as *theos*, "God" (Ps 132:2, 5; Isa 60:16); once as *ischuos*, "strength" (Isa 49:26); and once as *dunastos*, "strength" (Gen 49:24). The reference in which *Israel* is used instead of *Jacob* (Isa 1:24) appears to be taken to refer to the hosts of Israel.

24. Compare Albrektson, *History and the Gods*, 119.

25. Wright, *Old Testament against Its Environment*, esp. chap. 1.

26. The Egyptian and Mesopotamian systems of thought were inclusivist. If there existed one personal and consistent God of the universe who chose to reveal himself through history, it would be surprising that these great cultures had not surfaced ideas like this at some point or other. That these highly developed cultures never succeeded in integrating such ideas into their systems is a point to which Albrektson and Saggs give insufficient attention, in my view.

27. Ironically, it is Hebrew religion that first made secularism possible, for in the pagan mind-set, all was sacred because all was God.

28. Martin Noth, *The History of Israel*, trans. Stanley Godman (New York: Harper, 1958), 134–36.

29. To be sure, Noth does not deny that some event took place at Sinai with some portion of the people who were to become Israel. However, he is unable to determine the nature or content of that event (ibid., 134).

30. See Wright, *Old Testament against Its Environment*, 29, for a similar position.

31. Note Aristotle's "Unmoved Mover," a unitary, immaterial force—a being which cannot have concern for its creations. This idea is the best that sheer human logic can produce as an emergent doctrine.

3

YHWH's Refutation of
the Baal Myth through
the Actions of Elijah and Elisha

James R. Battenfield

In what ways did YHWH refute the Baal myth? This question has proved to be an intriguing one for Bible exegetes and theologians; and scholars of diverse points of view have sifted through the subject for many years. Since the discoveries of the cuneiform tablets at Ras Shamra-Ugarit, much has been written on the conflict between YHWH and Baal, with particular emphasis on the Elijah/Elisha narratives.[1] L. Bronner's dissertation at the University of Pretoria in 1964 focused precisely on this topic.[2] Especially helpful have been a work of G. Fohrer,[3] an article by F. C. Fensham,[4] and literary studies by O. H. Steck[5] and R. L. Cohn.[6]

Not every passage in the Elijah/Elisha narrative cycles is equally pertinent to the present investigation. Passages that will be examined are 1 Kgs. 16:29–32; 17:1–7, 8–24; 18:1–15, 16–46; 19:1–9a, 9b–18; 2 Kgs. 1:1–18; 2:1–18, 19–22; 3:1–27; 4:1–7, 8–37. These pericopes will be taken up in their present biblical order. The main corpus of interest, however, will be 1 Kings 17–19. From a literary standpoint, these three chapters are framed by what critical scholars term "deuteronomic" material in chapter 16 and a war account not directly related to the Elijah corpus in chapter 20.[7] However, as indicated, the content of 1 Kgs. 16:29–32 is part of the Elijah story.

Ugaritic parallels are of great significance in this study. The parallels generally include motifs of (1) nature, that is, rain, fire, and agriculture; (2) life, healing, and death; and (3) a miscellaneous group of topics scattered throughout these literary cycles.[8]

BAAL'S MYTHS AND YHWH'S REFUTATIONS

Historical Introduction — 1 Kgs. 16:29–32

These verses — 1 Kgs. 16:29–32 — form the beginning of the YHWH-versus-Baal complex. They introduce King Ahab (874–853 B.C.) and provide a literary hinge — the phrase *YHWH God of Israel* (v 33) connects this section with the beginning of chapter 17 (compare v 1).[9] Ahab was the son of Omri, who reigned twelve years in Israel, six of those years from his limited royal residence at Tirzah (16:23). A civil war raged in Israel for four years.[10] Omri had the allegiance of the army. Tibni, the son of Ginath (vv 21, 22), controlled the ruling class, but Omri prevailed and became king. Although scholars feel the characters in the royal succession are in place sequentially, "the chronology of this period is under vexed dispute."[11]

Whatever the absolute dates of the events, Ethbaal of Tyre watched the civil war in Israel with more than a passing interest. He had been King of Tyre since about 887 B.C. and was on good terms with both Ben-Hadad I of Aram–Damascus and with Israel; the Tyre–Israel alliance dated from circa 875–870 B.C..[12] A marriage was arranged between Ahab, Omri's son, and Jezebel, Ethbaal's daughter; the marriage took place circa 878–872 B.C.[13] Ahab and Jezebel's political and cultural influence over a twenty-year span cannot be underestimated in studying the lives of Elijah and Elisha, considering the excitement that surrounded these two prophets in Israel. The stage was set for a contest between YHWH and Baal.

Elijah Fed by Ravens — 1 Kgs. 17:1–7

This passage begins with Elijah's oath or promise to Ahab concerning an impending drought: "As YHWH, the God of Israel, lives, whom I serve, there will be neither dew nor rain in the next few years except at my word" (v 1, NIV). In Ugaritic mythology the theme of drought entailed the defeat of Baal by the god Mot, or Death. Death brought aridity and sterility to the earth when Baal entered the entrails of Mot, as the following text illustrates:

> Baal will enter his inward part,
> yea descend into his mouth,
> like a single olive,
> the produce of the earth,
>   and the fruit of the trees.
> Sore afraid was the mighty one, Baal,
> filled with dread, the Rider of the Clouds.[14]

Miracles involving nature appear prominently in both the Elijah and Elisha narratives. Elijah's declaration stands significantly at the head of chapters 17 and 18. It signals a contest in which YHWH challenges not only the power but even the existence of Baal in the hearts of the people of the Northern Kingdom. To withhold rain is to render Baal unable to perform his alleged role as the great storm-god of Semitic lore. Many passages can be summoned to show Baal's fundamental connection with rainfall. An example:

> To the earth Baal rained,
> and to the fields the Mighty One, the Lovely One.[15]

The motif of rain at Ugarit tied into the story of Baal obtaining a house for himself. This house had a window in it. From this window it was believed that rain fell on the inhabitants of Ugarit:

> Let a window be opened in the house,
> an aperture in the midst of the palace,
> and let a cleft be opened in the cloud.[16]

To the Ugaritians, Baal was supremely the "rain god." That YHWH controlled all nature was early challenged by Canaanite mythology. The Canaanites deified nature and its forces, as have many world religions before and since. Baal, the main active god of the Ugaritic pantheon, was given several titles in Ugaritic literature: (1) *zbl b'l arṣ*, "Prince, Lord of Earth"; (2) *aliyn b'l*, "the Mighty One, Baal"; (3) *hd* "Hadad" — Addu of the Babylonians — which has to do with Baal's role as a rain/storm god; (4) *'ly n'm*, "the Mighty One, the Lovely One"; and (5) *rkb 'rpt*, "The Rider in the Clouds." Several major texts that deal with rain and natural forces include these names. C. F. A. Schaeffer, who excavated at Ras Shamra for about fifty years, has described Baal this way:

> The most remarkable of the divinities of the Ras Shamra pantheon was Baal. His identity with the Phoenician Hadad, the Syrian–Hittite Teshub, and Seth or Sutekh of the Egyptians seems indisputable. These are merely different names for the same divinity, who, like Baal of Ras Shamra, is described as a god of the heights, storms, and rains. In the texts Baal makes his voice heard in the clouds, he shoots forth lightning, and sends the beneficent rain. He is a god in the prime of life, and has a graceful and athletic figure, as is shown on the great Ras Shamra stele, where he is seen brandishing a club and holding in his left hand a stylized thunderbolt ending in a spear-head.[17]

On the stele the spear's shaft looks like a plant of some kind, linking the god with vegetation; also depicted under Baal's feet are what are probably the waters of the earth or subterranean waters, perhaps both. The total picture is one of a nature god par excellence.

Precisely what place 1 Kgs. 17:1–7 has in the overall story of Elijah is difficult to say. Why must the prophet go into the Jordan Valley and be fed by ravens? Elijah was to hide himself, and ravens leave no tracks. There is something to say for the idea that the raven experience helped Elijah to prepare for the spiritual perils that lay before him. Whatever the reason, Elijah and the ravens obeyed YHWH's command. A command to "sustain" (*ṣiwwîtî lĕkalkelkā*, v 4) was given to the ravens. But the brook dried up; the prophesied drought was beginning to take effect in the lowlands. J. Gray thinks that "ravens" (*hā'ōrĕbîm*) should be read as "Arabs" (*hā'arābîm*).[18] This unnecessarily takes much of the miraculous out of the account and is not based on any versional support. Elijah has seen YHWH's miraculous provision. From the desert he will go to the seacoast and the spiritual warfare that awaits him.

The Widow at Zarephath — 1 Kgs. 17:8–24

This story, consisting of two distinct scenes, has not received enough attention from scholars who describe the YHWH-versus-Baal contest. Elijah was instructed by YHWH to move again, now to Zarephath in the territory of Sidon. Literary links abound, connecting this story to the "raven" episode. *şiwwîtî lĕkalkelkā* (vv 4, 9) has been noted; "dwell" *(wayyēšeb)* is found in verses 5 and 9; "bread" *(leḥem)* of verse 6 is repeated in verse 11; "rain" *(gešem)* appears in both verse 7 and verse 14.[19] The present study will not dwell further on such literary matters. The placement of these terms, however, is not accidental; in a sense, the widow was taking the place of the ravens in sustaining YHWH's prophet.

One might say that when Elijah obeyed YHWH, then the woman obeyed Elijah. She and her son were at the point of death, preparing their last meal. The fact that Elijah had to sustain the widow and boy points not only to YHWH as provider for the needy but also as one who "trained" his prophet, as it were, to be obedient to him. Flour and oil signify life; they are the two common staples in any ancient, as well as modern, Near Eastern household.

As mentioned, in the Ras Shamra stele, Baal's spear contains a plant or sacred tree. In Ugaritic letters Baal, *zbl bʿl arṣ*, "the Prince, Lord of the Earth," was also referred to as *bn dgn, Son of Dagan. Dgn* means "corn" or "food-stuffs."[20] The well-known Dagan was not a fish deity, as scholars formerly thought; rather, he was certainly a vegetation god, and Baal as "son of Dagan" shared this agrarian reputation, as the stele shows. W. F. Albright said years ago that Dagan "was worshiped all through the Euphrates Valley as far back as the twenty-fifth century B.C.,"[21] and the discoveries at Ebla in Syria have more than confirmed Albright's assertion. P. Matthiae reports: "The Ebla pantheon was markedly polytheist. Some five hundred divinities are mentioned in the texts. The principal god of the city seems to have been Dagan."[22] Ada (= Adad) was also represented as the equivalent of Baal by the people of Ebla.

In Ugaritic literature the death and revival of Baal was clearly tied to the agriculture of the people. The goddess Anat, consort to Baal, in resuscitating her companion, had to overcome Mot, the god of death and sterility. The battle was described in agricultural terminology:

> She seized Mot;
>   with a sword she crushed him,
> with a pitchfork she winnowed him,
>   with fire she burned him,
> with millstones she ground him;
>   in the field she planted him
> in order that the birds might eat his remnants,
>   in order that the fowl might consume his portion,
> Remnant called to remnant.[23]

The verbs in this passage have great significance. When Mot died, fertility returned to the earth. Bronner says, "Anat's treatment of Mot shows that he suffered vicariously the fate of corn, and by his suffering made possible the revival of corn."[24]

In the story of 1 Kgs. 17:8ff., opposition to the popular beliefs about Baal among the population of Zarephath is implied in Elijah's directions to the widow. YHWH had spoken: these food supplies shall not be exhausted until the heaven-sent drought is concluded—a sign of YHWH's faithful provision through Elijah.

A time lapse of unspecified length occurs between verses 16 and 17, separating the two stories whose settings are at Zarephath. The woman's son falls ill and stops breathing. "There was not breath left in him" (v 17b). Gray claims that the child did not really die and that the use of the verb *ḥāyâ* in verse 22 indicates "revived" rather than something akin to "came alive again."[25]

The whole point of the story, however, seems to be paramountly a demonstration that YHWH, not Baal, has the power of life over death. The woman's resentment toward Elijah (v 18) is replaced by a confession affirming that the prophet is truly from YHWH (v 24). These two contrasting attitudes frame a fine chiasmus from verse 18 to the end of the chapter.[26] YHWH has again shown his power by raising the widow's son. Baal was not only helpless; he was nonexistent. YHWH alone is God.

Elijah and Obadiah — 1 Kgs. 18:1–15

Three years of drought pass. The presentation of Elijah to Ahab is to be the occasion of YHWH sending rain on the land to demonstrate his authority over all nature. Ahab must see this sign of power. Will he lay aside his worship of Baal and the influence of his wife, Jezebel, or will he persist in his paganism? The Obadiah narrative must be included in the Elijah corpus to show something of the severity of the famine brought on by the drought. The king and his house steward, Obadiah, have been reduced to searching for pasture for their animals. The grave, life-and-death consequences implicit in 18:1–15 are a prelude to the contest which follows on Carmel.

Elijah on Mount Carmel — 1 Kgs. 18:16–46

The encounter between Elijah and Ahab is occasioned by their exchange of accusations. Each accuses the other of being a "troubler" *('ōkēr)* of Israel (vv 17–18). Elijah equates Ahab's troubling or disturbing the Northern Kingdom with his forsaking of the commandments of YHWH and with his going after the *baalim*. This "troubling" is apostasy, or backsliding, a retreat from or turning of one's back on revealed truth in preference to a man-made pagan religion.

In verse 20 the movement of the story speeds up. Assembling the prophets on Mount Carmel may have taken several days at the very least. Elijah poses the first and most primary question: "How long will you limp on two crutches?" His question evidently opposes syncretism, the indiscriminate worship of YHWH and Baal together. The challenge is simple and pointed: "If YHWH is God, go after him; but if Baal, go after him" (v 21). The contest itself, beginning at verse 23, is a direct challenge to Baal's existence.

In the sight of all, Elijah wants to ensure there is no trickery: let the devotees of Baal choose a bull, let the preparations be equal. It is abundantly implied that either god has an equal chance to respond. Importantly, it is the

god who will answer *by fire*—that will be God. A real miracle is therefore
necessitated, an actual entry of YHWH or Baal into the human sphere, a physical, graphic, dramatic display of divine power. The god who acts will be vindicated; the one who does not will be refuted.

In Ugaritic literature the claim is also made that Baal has power over fire.
Among other portrayals, the spear in Baal's left hand on the Ras Shamra stele
is said to denote lightning;[27] hence the fire of Elijah's proposal at Carmel is
most counter to the Baal myth. Many other forms of testing might have been
chosen. A strange text, yet one worth citing in full, has to do with Baal and
fire:

> Fire is set on the house,
>   flame on the palace.
> Behold, a day and a second;
>   fire eats into the house,
> flame into the palace.
>   A third, a fourth day;
> fire eats into the house,
>   flame into the palace.
> A fifth, a sixth day;
>   fire eats into the house,
> flame [in the midst of the pala]ce.
>   Behold, on the seve[nth] d[ay];
> the fire departs from the house,
>   the flame from the palace.
> Silver turns from blocks,
>   gold is turned from bricks.[28]

Bronner is in error in attributing this particular fire to Baal. Baal did not
originate the fire; Kothar-wa-Ḥasis, the builder of Baal's house, did. Baal's
house was tested, reinforced, and completed by fire as the culmination of the
building process.[29] Baal was literally "at home" with fire.

The dancing of Baal's prophets around their altar has provoked a good bit
of discussion among scholars, notably R. de Vaux.[30] By verse 27, it is obvious
that Baal is not answering his prophets, although much time and effort has
been expended to summon him. The debunking of Baal, the subject of this
essay, is reported frankly, even humorously, while the Israelites watch. That
the Baal prophets cut themselves is also analogous to various religious frenzies
in which the letting of blood was supposed to signify the issuing forth of the
life substance itself. The prophets of Baal have had nearly all day in which to
get their god to respond, but without result.

By Mosaic prescription (see Exod 24:4), Elijah repairs the altar using twelve
stones, emblematic of the united kingdom of north and south (YHWH's theo-
cratic ideal), and without chicanery he prays to the God of his fathers: "Answer
me, O YHWH, answer me, in order that this people may know that you, O
YHWH, are God, and that you are turning their heart back again" (v 37). A
dignified, whole burnt offering of a young bullock replaces the fanatic display
of the pagan priests.

Then comes the amazing climax: fire miraculously falls—like lightning
from a cloudless sky! And it consumes everything. Baal is often pictured on

plaques and reliefs as the storm-god with a lightning bolt in his hand, but emphatically, Baal is no god. The Israelites' amazed reaction, "YHWH, he is God" (v 39), is followed immediately by Elijah's command to exterminate the prophets of Baal (see Exod 32:36). Such was the harsh reality of the conflict of that day. Jezebel had many of the prophets of YHWH killed (v 4). The struggle was not one of political expediency or religious preference only; it was to the death, so violently opposed were the two competing systems.

Refocusing the power of this object lesson on Ahab, Elijah commands the king to "go up, eat and drink," YHWH's drought having concluded. His fire is now to be followed by a downpour, because He is the god of fire, storm, life, and death. Verse 41 answers the promise of verse 1. The scene moves to the top of Carmel. YHWH of the storm is coming! The sky blackens and the rain comes, a triumphant victory for YHWH! Cohn remarks that Elijah's running ahead of Ahab's chariot to Jezreel (v 46) symbolizes a return to Israelite normalcy: "king follows prophet."[31]

Elijah Flees to Horeb — 1 Kgs. 19:1–9a

Enter Jezebel, the patroness of Baal! It is she who has been the real power behind the throne. She is understandably enraged over Elijah's having the Baal prophets slain. She swears by the "gods" that she will kill Elijah. The disillusioned prophet flees to the south at a time when one wonders how he could fear anything, given the victory at Carmel. Is it fear, however, or frustration that occasions Elijah's flight? The text of verse 3 begins with "and he saw" *(wayyar')*, not "and he feared" *(wayyîrā')*, the reading of the Septuagint. The present writer submits that Elijah *saw* the situation: Jezebel had in no way repented upon hearing Ahab's account of the miracle on Mount Carmel, so Elijah, in frustration, "went to (care for) his soul," heading toward the wilderness.

Cohn observes: "But the author uses Elijah's despair for his own purpose, to demonstrate the sovereignty of YHWH despite his prophet's resignation."[32] Not without significance, Mount Horeb lies at the opposite extremity of arable Syro–Palestine, poles apart from Mount Ṣaphon (Casius) of Ugaritic lore, which is in the north of Syria.[33]

YHWH Appears to Elijah — 1 Kgs. 19:9b–18

The word of YHWH comes to Elijah, signaling a revelatory encounter is to take place. From Elijah's standpoint, the contest on Mount Carmel was outward and physical and resulted in the death of Baal's prophets. Here at Horeb the struggle between YHWH and Baal is an inward, theophanic display. Scholars have long pointed out that this account parallels Moses' experiences in Exodus 32–34.[34] F. M. Cross uses the phrase "direct dependence" in comparing 1 Kgs. 19:9–14 with Exod. 33:17–23; 34:6–8. Like Elijah, Moses enters "the cave" *(hammĕ'ārâ)* of Exod. 33:21–22, at Horeb.

An exciting yet mysterious scene follows. Cross sees a real polemic against Baal in this nineteenth chapter, particularly in three theophanic significations of Baal, the Canaanite storm-god: the "great and strong (storm-)wind," the "(earth-)quaking," and the "fire" (vv 11–12).[35] Each of these events violently makes its presence felt to Elijah at the cave door. But YHWH, though he cosmically controls each, shows his beleaguered prophet that He is not *in* any of these lethal weather-god manifestations.

Instead, the surprise climax comes in the affirmation that YHWH is to be equated with the *qôl děmāmâ daqqâ*, that is, "the silent sound," the "still small voice" in the AV, which Cross calls the "imperceptible whisper." However one chooses to translate the phrase, this much is evident: "YHWH was not immanent in the storm. The *qōl Ba'l*, the thunderous voice of Ba'l, has become the . . . imperceptible whisper."[36] R. B. Coote believes that the silence, in contrast to the previous thunder, was a sign that YHWH would allow his prophet, who wanted death, to live. In a very interesting article J. Lust retranslates the *qôl děmāmâ daqqâ* to read "a roaring and thunderous voice."[37] His reasons seem well founded, and the subject deserves further study.

The message that Elijah is to receive (vv 15–19) and the mission he is to perform—these are perhaps the more pressing features of the encounter with YHWH. The menace of Baalism needed swift judgment. The faithful of Israel are being offered a new beginning in following YHWH. Elijah's mission is to anoint Hazael of Syria and Jehu of Israel and also to pass on his mantle to his successor Elisha.[38]

The culmination of 1 Kings 19 is Elijah's calling of Elisha, son of a wealthy family (twelve oxen; 1 Kgs 19:19), as signified by Elijah's casting his mantle over his protege.

YHWH's Judgment on Ahaziah — 2 Kgs. 1:1–18

Elijah's role in the YHWH-versus-Baal contest continues into the Second Book of Kings. This first pertinent section encompasses three elements that impinge on the present theme: a name of Baal, a strong theological confession, and a reference to fire. There is a god of the Philistine city of Ekron called Baal–Zebub. This epithet is proof that Baal was venerated at an old city–state of the Shephelah long after Ugarit's demise. Baal–Zebub meant "Lord of Flies," bringing pestilence to mind. The very name Baal–Zebub was in itself a slurring of Baal's reputation.

YHWH enters the scene in the person of his angel. The statement of verse 3 is relentlessly anti-myth, anti-Baal, and anti-idolatry: "Is it because there is no God in Israel that you are going to inquire of Baal–Zebub, the god of Ekron?" Otherwise, only verses 10–12 touch significantly on the present theme: YHWH is the God of natural elements, viz., fire. Bronner summarizes: "The various Biblical passages where Elijah enlisted the aid of fire to prove that God rules over all these forces, aimed to undermine a popular belief that Baal had dominion over this element."[39]

Elijah Taken up to Heaven — 2 Kgs. 2:1–18

Several motifs analogous to Ugaritic literature are evident in two of the three narrative portions of 2 Kings 2. In verse 8, Elijah, again after the pattern of Moses in Exodus 14, strikes the waters of the Jordan with his cloak to part them, and he and Elisha cross over on dry ground. At Ugarit, Baal's most serious rival was called *zbl ym*, "Prince Sea," or *ṭpṭ nhr*, "Judge River."[40] Attention needs to be focused on verse 11, the famous "chariot of fire" episode. Elijah knows that YHWH is going to take him to heaven (v 2). The verbs *lāqaḥ* and *nāśāʾ* are used in the Hebrew Bible for taking or carrying a prophet to God (Pss 49:16; 73:24; compare 2 Kgs 2:16). But what was intended by the *mode* of Elijah's being taken? Gen. 5:24 records the ultimate in simplicity regarding God's "taking" a man to himself: Enoch "was not" *(ʾênennû)*, "for God took him." Elijah could be taken any number of ways. But "a chariot of fire" is YHWH's chosen conveyance — evidently to refute Baalism. For of Baal it was said,

> Seven years may Baal withhold,
> eight, the Rider of Clouds![41]

Healing of the Water — 2 Kgs. 2:19–22

This short pericope concerns Elisha's making the water wholesome at Jericho. In the Ras Shamra stele, cited previously, Baal is depicted as (1) treading on the earth and (2) ruling over the waters on and beneath the earth (thus also over underground springs and fountains). This depiction is natural enough with reference to popular Canaanite belief. Joshua's famous curse on Jericho (Josh 6:26) is evidently terminated by Elisha's casting salt into the spring there, purifying the water. The salt perhaps symbolizes cleansing and separation from past corruption; the miracle belongs to YHWH in refutation of Baal's alleged supremacy over that most precious commodity — water.

Moab Revolts — 2 Kgs. 3:1–27

The water motif is further apparent in the narrative of Moab's revolt. The *maṣṣēbat habbaʿal*, "the sacred stone of Baal" (v 2, NIV), was probably a standing stone or pillar of some kind, quite commonly seen at archaeological sites today. The term is in the plural in the Septuagint, Syro-Hexapla, and Vulgate. Analogies are numerous. The statement about Jehoram (Joram), king of Israel, removing the *maṣṣebâ* of Baal, shows some conscientious eradication of Baal in the years 850–840 B.C., but the sins of Jeroboam I are still mentioned against King Jehoram.

Accompanying the water motif in this pericope is one concerning music. From the Aqht literature comes this citation:

> Even as Baal, when he gives life,
>   entertains the living,
> entertains and gives him to drink,
>   and the lovely one sings and croons over him
> and responds to him.[42]

In verse 15 Elisha says, "bring me a harpist." Commentators often say that a musical accompaniment to a prophetic utterance meant the prophet was in a state of ecstacy.[43] There is no reason, however, for saying such a thing, any more than asserting that Elijah has to self-induce ecstacy at Mount Carmel. He plainly does not. Taking parallels from modern dervish communities of the Near East, as was the habit of Robertson Smith and others, is anachronistic and farfetched.

Perhaps Elisha calls for music simply to shut out the excitement of the battle at hand and to concentrate on receiving his message from YHWH. There is no indication of frenzy. YHWH commands his people to make the valley full of ditches. The ditches are supernaturally filled with water, and eventually the victory goes to Israel. YHWH is in control of the waters of the earth. Moab's system of religion was Canaanite nature worship. This chapter also, then, interfaces with the present discussion.

The Widow's Oil—2 Kgs. 4:1–7

Like Elijah, Elisha performs miracles with oil and grain. Baal is called *bn dgn* and *zbl b'l arṣ*, as mentioned. These terms point out Baal's relation to vegetation and fertility. This miraculous increase of the oil supply and the similar oil miracle in 1 Kgs. 17:8–24 show that YHWH is God of the earth's produce.

The Shunammite's Son Restored to Life—2 Kgs. 4:8–37

A craving for progeny is amply documented from Ugarit; particularly was this so in the Aqht poetry, wherein it was written concerning Danel:

> Who has no son like his brothers,
>   even a root like his kinsmen.[44]

King Keret, known from Ugaritic texts, was bereaved of his entire family. The king slept; 'El appeared to him in a vision and told him to bring a sacrifice to the gods. Baal was the one who would answer Keret with the gift of a son; and the myth ends when Keret marries and fathers children.[45] In our pericope Elisha acts as a sort of intermediary for childbirth, analogous to Baal's role in the Ugaritic tablets. YHWH, not Baal, nor Elisha for that matter, grants the Shunammite a child. The child dies, bringing to mind the story of Elijah in 1 Kings 17. Prayer raises the child to life, illustrating not only that YHWH gives children, but that he can take them to himself or restore them to life.

AN ALTERNATIVE APPROACH

Judging from the texts under scrutiny, YHWH has refuted Baal at every turn, and done so resoundingly. The God of Israel stands supreme over paganism, so much so that the people of the Northern Kingdom are left without excuse in electing to follow Baal. Before summarizing the results of this investigation, however, I would like to suggest an alternative interpretive approach that bears significantly on this topic and that may help modify and clarify scholarly opinion on the subject of YHWH versus Baal.

To this point, the assessment of Canaanite and Israelite religion has been along traditional paths. However, a more refined historical approach may be taken. Is it correct to compare a ninth-century B.C. Palestinian/Phoenician setting—that of Elijah and Elisha—with a 1400–1200 B.C. Ugaritic milieu? Have scholars, enamored with the abundance of Ugaritic studies, been looking in the wrong time and place to find their best parallels to illustrate the contest of YHWH versus Baal in connection with the background of Elijah and Elisha?

The contribution of Fensham's article, previously referred to, is important in that he asks the question which scholars such as Bronner apparently did not ask: What is meant by "Baal," specifically in the ninth century B.C., and, more specifically, in 1 Kings 17–19? The answer to this simple question opens an expanded, fresh side to the discussion, and several proposed solutions will be aired.

First, the position of K. Galling, following A. Alt, is that the "Baal–Carmel" of the Romans is to be equated with the Baal of 1 Kings 17–19.[46] Using as his source the Periplus of Pseudo-Skylax, Galling cites a shrine built on Mount Carmel to Zeus (fourth century B.C.).[47] But what relation would Jezebel have sustained with a local Baal? Rather her Baal must have been Tyrian, considering that she was the daughter of the king of Tyre. That Baal was later to be equated with the Greek Zeus all will admit.

Second, O. Eissfeldt, with his characteristic thoroughness, believes that Baal–Shamem ("Lord of Heaven") is the Baal of 1 Kings 17–19.[48] M. Avi-Yonah must also be numbered with those who hold this view. To Avi-Yonah, Hadad = Baal–Shamem = Jupiter Heliopolitanus = Carmel; he concludes that the Baal of Carmel is identical with Hadad, the great god of the Syrians and Phoenicians, whose worship posed so formidable a threat to Israel in the ninth-century B.C.[49] Mulder, on the other hand, offers a variant view:

> The OT knows that the mountain tops are the dwelling place of this deity, and also that Baal is a god of heaven, since it frequently mentions him in connection with the host of heaven, the sun, the moon, and the symbols of the zodiac (2 K. 17:16; 21:3; 23:4f.; cf. Jer. 32:29). It is doubtful whether this justifies the view that he should be identified with Baal-shamem.[50]

So it does not seem Baal–Shamem should be equated too readily with the standard concept of Baal/Hadad from Ugarit and the Bible. Also quite at variance with Avi-Yonah is R. A. Oden, who makes a very substantial case instead for Baal–Shamem (the "father" figure of the Canaanite/Phoenician pantheon) equaling 'El, who occupied the same senior rank at Ugarit.[51] In this light, *habbě'ālîm* in 1 Kgs. 18:18 included several Baals; Baal–Shamem was one of them. Why is there the deliberate shift to the singular *habba'al* in verse 19? A specific, different Baal was intended, the one for which we are now searching.

Third, as discussed previously, one may opt for the view that we are dealing here with the second millennium B.C. Baal, the youthful champion of the Ugaritic pantheon. Bronner indeed makes a significant contribution in singling out Ugaritic motifs concerning Baal relative to our Kings narratives. However, sometimes her points of comparison seem less than compelling. If we date the *terminus ad quem* of Ugaritic literature to circa 1200 B.C., we are at least three hundred years earlier than the time of Elijah. But if we exchange the anachronistic Ugaritic concept of Baal for a ninth-century tradition that would be known and practiced in Samaria and Mount Carmel, which would be more accurate: Baal–Shamem or another Baal?

Fourth, there seems to be a growing tendency among scholars to identify the most prominent Baal of 1 Kings 17–19 with Baal–Melqart of Tyre, and included under the term *bě'ālîm* in this context may be the Phoenician/Sidonian deity Eshmun as well. As in the view of Alt and Galling, a good bit of our information on Melqart and Eshmun comes from times later than those of Elijah. Perhaps we can now say that this deficiency is being overcome, and a tracing of the careers of these two deities is becoming a little more secure. What was rather out of reach for Bronner may be within reach today. We begin, however, with Albright's comments of 1942:

> Some confusion has been caused by Alt's contention that the Baal of Elijah's crusade was the local Baal of Carmel and by Eissfeldt's view that it was not the Tyrian Melcarth but Baal-shamem, the Syrian "Lord of Heaven." Both interpretations are partly correct: Alt is clearly right in stressing the antiquity and importance of the sanctuary of Baal on Mount Carmel; Eissfeldt is emphatically correct in protesting against the current scholarly belief that the "Baals" of the Old Testament were merely local vegetation deities and in stressing the cosmic sweep of Baal's power, but there is nothing concrete to justify his identification of the Baal against which Elijah contended with Baal-shamem. It is quite possible that the Israelites identified the Canaanite Baals with which they came into contact with Baal-shamem, perhaps following Canaanite usage, but this view is only one of several possibilities. We do not yet know to what extent the Canaanites themselves syncretized their various Baals. On the other hand, Eissfeldt is not warranted in suggesting that the Tyrian Baal was a deity of local rather than cosmic significance, since all high gods possessed cosmic scope and cosmic functions among the Canaanites. . . . The decisive proof that the Baal cult that was propagated by the Tyrian princess Jezebel was really Baal of Tyre is furnished by a comparison of 1 Kgs 18:19, which mentions 450 prophets of Baal and 400 prophets of Asherah, with the Ugaritic epic of Keret, lines 198, 201, which refer to the goddess "Asherah of the Tyrians." Many other references to Asherah in the books of Kings, once together with Baal (II Kings 23:4), suggest that *the Canaanite Baal of the Israelite Monarchy was formally identified with the Tyrian Baal, though it is still quite impossible to say just how this Baal differed in myths and attributes from the great storm-god of the second millennium* [italics added]. In view of the enormous commercial influence and cultural prestige of Tyre and its nearness to Israel, there is nothing at all surprising in the diffusion of the cult of its principal deity through Israel.[52]

Keret, lines 198, 201, does refer to *)aṭrt ṣrm*, "Asherah of Tyre," and *)elt ṣdynm*, "Goddess of Sidon."[53]

A principal early advocate of this fourth and last identification that we are considering was de Vaux. He discusses fully the identity of the Baal of 1 Kings 18, and he has made a good case for Baal–Melqart with a fair, even-handed working of the sources.[54] Part of de Vaux's case admittedly is based on later sources, which may be enumerated in this way: Josephus, referring to the work of Menander (342–292 B.C.), states that Hiram of Tyre built new shrines for Heracles and Astarte.[55] In another context, Josephus says virtually the same thing but adds, "and he [Hiram] was the first to celebrate the awakening of Heracles."[56]

This "awakening" may have had to do with the idea of Melqart–Heracles as a fertility god;[57] it seems that, among other things, Melqart was a vegetation deity who had to be awakened each spring from his winter hibernation.[58] Was an attempt to effect this "awakening" the reason for the frantic gyrations of the prophets of Baal in 1 Kings 18? If one subscribes to this reasoning for Melqart, the answer is yes.

Fortunately, pre-Roman evidence is available in defense of the Baal–Melqart identification. A well-attested Aramaean stele from the ninth-century B.C. — and thus contemporary with Elijah — was discovered at Breğ north of Aleppo. Barhadad dedicated the stele to Melqart.[59] De Vaux explains:

> The god is seen wearing a conical hat and a Syrian loincloth; on his shoulder he carries an open-wrought ax. He is therefore a warrior god, but since this characteristic is common to all the chief Syrian gods, it tells us little about his personality.[60]

The text of this votive stele reads as follows: "The stele, which Bar[ha]dad, the son of [?] king of Aram, set up for his lord, for Melqart, because he had made a vow and he had hearkened to his voice."[61] Barhadad had made the vow and heard the king's supplications. E. Lipiński comments on this text relative to the history of religions:

> This is an Old Aramaic votive inscription for Melqart, the chief god of Tyre, also called "Baal of Tyre." . . . The inscription dates from the last decades of the ninth century BC and is the earliest evidence so far for the worship of the god Melqart. . . . The Melqart stele is evidence for the cult of this god, who is really native to Tyre, in Aramaean territory. I Kings 16.31f. (cf. I Kings 18.16–40; II Kings 10.18–27) bears witness to the establishment of a similar cult in the northern kingdom of Israel; the Baal of Jezebel, the daughter of the king of Tyre, can only have been the Baal of Tyre.[62]

It seems, at any rate, that a growing number of respected scholars are involved in making the Baal–Melqart–Heracles connection, namely, Albright, de Vaux, and now H. Gese, R. du Mesnil du Buisson, and Lipiński.

Another important piece must be added to the puzzle. R. Borger published the inscriptions of Esarhaddon in 1956.[63] A treaty there inscribed was made between Esarhaddon of Assyria and "Baal of Tyre." There follows a list of gods in the order, Baal–Shamem, Melqart, Eshmun. The text is a little late for our purpose, dating to 677 B.C.,[64] but it remains significant. Certainly Melqart was linked to Eshmun. Later traditions show that Eshmun was a healing deity, identified with the earlier Adonis of Byblos and the later Asklepios. The royal name Eshmunazar (II) probably translates "Eshmun has helped." The earliest attestation of Eshmun is in the treaty of Esarhaddon, just cited. The god is associated with Melqart in fertility, particularly that of land and crops.[65]

In Byblos, Tyre, and Sidon, then, we have a kind of triad datable to the fourth century B.C. — if we take the three to be Melqart–Heracles, Asteria–Astarte, and Zeus.[66] Du Mesnil du Buisson puts it another way: The triad of Tyre is possibly the mother–goddess Europe (Asherat), the father–god Zeus (Baal–Shamem) and the son Heracles (Melqart, Baal of Tyre).[67] The only remaining problem is the fact that we are not very well informed about the name Melqart or about the god's attributes in the time of Elijah.[68]

Alexander the Great wished to sacrifice to Heracles in his temple at Tyre.[69] On taking the maritime city stronghold in 332 B.C., he achieved that desire. From Tyre, the cult of Melqart spread with the expansion of Phoenician colonization. Especially noteworthy are the citations showing that Melqart–Heracles was associated with vegetation, and emphatically with fire, on high places such as those at Carthage, and at Cadiz, Spain, the ancient Gades.[70] Gese and du Mesnil du Buisson have convincingly traced Melqart–Heracles and Eshmun–Asklepios into Roman times.

In discussing the culture of the Phoenicians, D. Baramki identified Aliyan with Eshmun, noting that sculpture of this god dates back to the Early Bronze period.[71] This statement points to a considerable timespan for the veneration of Eshmun far in advance of Elijah's time. And the name Aliyan is well documented at Ugarit, as in the honorific *aliyn b'l*.[72] This name is tantamount to saying Eshmun–Baal or Eshmun–Melqart. W. W. G. Baudissin, in his massive study of Adonis and Eshmun, discusses Eshmun–Melqart at some length.[73] S. V. McCasland points out that Asklepios was one of the most popular gods of the Hellenistic period.[74] And outside Greece, it can be shown that Asklepios was worshiped in Phoenicia through identification with the important Phoenician deity Eshmun.

Further, McCasland affirms: "It seems probable therefore that wherever the Phoenician god Eshmun was worshipped, whether at home or in the colonies, during the Hellenistic period his cult was absorbed by Asklepios. This also indicates that Eshmun himself was a healing deity."[75] In Palestine in the first-century A.D., the worship of the healing god Asklepios was centered in Tiberias, Neapolis, and Ascalon. The hot springs at Tiberias are called Al Hammam today; in ancient times they were called Hammath.[76] Myths built up over the passing of time about the healing wonders of hot springs in Palestine associated with Asklepios, whose Phoenician forerunner was Eshmun.

Eshmun possibly is attested in the Hebrew Bible. In 2 Kgs. 17:30 we read: "The men from Babylon made Succoth–Benoth, the men from Cuthah made Nergal, and the men from Hamath made Ashima" (NIV).[77] Ashima is the *'ăšîmā'* of the Masoretic Text. Baumgartner spells it with a final *hē*.[78] R. Dussaud, among many others, also relates Eshmun to Adonis.[79] Certainly the men of Syrian Hamath would have been interested in Eshmun of nearby Phoenicia.

A less secure reference may be the *ašmat* of Amos 8:14.[80] The absolute state of the noun would be *ašmâ*,[81] and the line in Amos might read: "they that swear by Eshmun of Samaria," rather than the traditional "they that swear by the guilt of Samaria." The former reading would imply that Eshmun worship was still infesting the Northern Kingdom approximately one hundred years after Elijah.

CONCLUSION

What can be said in conclusion about YHWH's refutation of the Baal myth in light of the foregoing discussion? There seems to be no reason why Jezebel's Tyrian version of Baal, that is, Baal–Melqart, cannot be shown to answer to the attributes of Baal generally, as the latter has been customarily identified throughout the ancient Near East.

During the crucial ninth century B.C. in Israel, YHWH, ever demonstrating his love to his errant people, sought to wean them from the superstitions of their nature-worshiping neighbors by giving them graphic object lessons dramatized by the actions of Elijah and his successor, Elisha. Though temporary battles were won, such as the shining example at Mount Carmel, the net effect of Elijah's and Elisha's ministry, humanly speaking, was failure. Israel persisted in her backslidden state until, in 722 B.C., YHWH gave the Israelite North into the hands of the vicious Assyrians; the demise of the Southern Kingdom was not long in following in 586 B.C..

If there is any truth to the idea that Baal–Melqart and especially Baal–Eshmun were supposed to have powers of healing, this assumption casts the two stories of 1 Kings 17 in much fuller light. It is most significant that Elijah, following YHWH's command, went to Zarephath of Sidon to interact with the widow and her son. Even more absorbing is to theorize that the flour and oil miracle of Elijah may have refuted the popular Phoenician concept of Baal–Melqart as a vegetation deity having alleged powers over agriculture; and that Elijah's raising of the boy may have been in direct opposition to the mythical reputation of Baal–Eshmun, the "healer" of Sidon. In this light, the contest of YHWH versus Baal becomes just as crucial in 1 Kings 17 as in chapter 18. Perhaps chapter 17 is more pivotal in light of Elijah's career: the prophet was fresh from his desert experience with the ravens, and Zarephath was his first challenge.

Perhaps more than Jezebel's religious tenacity can now be seen in the 1 Kings 18 situation. If a specifically Tyrian Baal was her champion deity, then a political or even familial nationalism (or devotion to the god of her father Ethbaal) figured as much in her fanatical killing of YHWH's prophets as any "religious" allegiance alone. Power must have been supreme to her; witness the way she engineered the death of Naboth (1 Kgs 20). Baal–Melqart may be said to have possessed the powers that scholars have attributed to "Baal" all along. The geographical proximity of Carmel to Phoenicia seems also better served in the Melqart view.

In 1 Kings 19, particularly in the theophany at Sinai, YHWH sought to refute the general Canaanite Baal concept by demonstrating his power over natural forces to the frustrated Elijah, about to be replaced by a successor.

Baal–Zebub of Ekron was the Baal of 2 Kgs. 1:1–18. This fact helps establish the ground upon which we posit a Baal–Melqart for Tyre. The general Baal concept of the Bronze Age was becoming more and more diffused in the Iron Age, and gods were attached increasingly to geographical regions, cities, and even local shrines. The same might be said for 2 Kgs. 2:1–18; but in 1:19–22 we have a pericope that suggests Eshmun–Asklepios (the water motif in 2 Kgs 3 is not concerned with healing, so it may be discounted here). The story of the widow's oil of 2 Kgs. 4:1–7 is reminiscent of 1 Kgs. 17:7ff.; likewise 2 Kgs. 4:8–37 is analogous to 1 Kgs. 17:17ff. YHWH used Elisha to refute Baal–Eshmun's healing reputation, just as he used Elijah earlier.

In the ninth-century B.C., YHWH conclusively refuted the Baal myth through the actions of Elijah and Elisha. After these two superlative prophetic figures passed from the scene, however, Israel's idolatrous apostasy reasserted itself, as history affirms. But YHWH would refute Baal again in succeeding generations.

NOTES

1. See Gunnar Östborn, *Yahweh and Baal* (Lund, Sweden: Gleerup, 1956).
2. Published as Leah Bronner, *The Stories of Elijah and Elisha as Polemics against Baal Worship*, Pretoria Oriental Series, 6 (Leiden, Netherlands: Brill, 1968).
3. Georg Fohrer, *Elia*, Abhandlungen zur Theologie des Alten und Neuen Testaments, 53 (Zurich: Zwingli, 1957).
4. F. C. Fensham, "A Few Observations on the Polarisation between Yahweh and Baal in I Kings 17–19," *ZAW* 92 (1980): 227–36.
5. Odil Hannes Steck, *Überlieferung und Zeitgeschichte in den Elia-Erzählungen*, WMANT 26 (Neukirchen–Vluyn, West Germany: Neukirchener, 1968).
6. Robert L. Cohn, "The Literary Logic of 1 Kings 17–19," *JBL* 101 (1982): 333–50.
7. Ibid., 334.
8. Bronner, *Stories*, 54.
9. Alexander Rofé, "Classes in the Prophetical Stories: Didactic Legenda and Parable," *SVT* 26 (Leiden, Netherlands: Brill, 1974), 148, n. 4; see also Cohn, "Literary Logic," 335, n. 4.
10. H. J. Katzenstein, *The History of Tyre: From the Beginning of the Second Millennium B.C.E until the Fall of the Neo-Babylonian Empire in 538 B.C.E* (Jerusalem: Schocken, 1973), 142.
11. James A. Montgomery and H. S. Gehman, *A Critical and Exegetical Commentary on the Books of Kings*, ICC (Edinburgh: Clark, 1951, 1976), 284.
12. Katzenstein, *History of Tyre*, 137–38.
13. Ibid., 144.
14. *KTU* 1.5, II:3–7 (= *UT* 67), as cited in M. Dietrich, O. Loretz, and J. Sanmartin, *Die keilalphabetischen Texte aus Ugarit* (Neukirchen–Vluyn, West Germany: Neukirchener, 1976).
15. *KTU* 1.16, III:5–6 (= *UT* 126).
16. *KTU* 1.4, VII:17–19 (= *UT* 51).

17. Claude F. A. Schaeffer, *The Cuneiform Texts of Ras Shamra Ugarit*, Schweich Lectures, 1936 (London: Oxford, 1939), 63–64, and pl. xxxii, fig. 2.
18. John Gray, *I & II Kings: A Commentary*, 2d ed. rev., in OTL (Philadelphia: Westminster, 1970), 378, n. d.; compare Cohn, "Literary Logic," 335, n. 6.
19. Cohn, "Literary Logic," 335.
20. Ludwig Koehler and Walter Baumgartner, eds., *Lexikon in Veteris Testamenti Libros* (Leiden, Netherlands: Brill, 1958), 203.
21. William F. Albright, *Archaeology and the Religion of Israel*, 5th ed. (1942; reprint, Baltimore: Johns Hopkins, 1968), 74.
22. Paolo Matthiae, *Ebla: An Empire Rediscovered* (Garden City, N.Y.: Doubleday, 1981), 187.
23. *KTU* 1.6, II:30–37 (= *UT* 49).
24. Bronner, *Stories*, 80.
25. Gray, *Kings*, 381, 383.
26. As nicely illustrated by Cohn, "Literary Logic," 336.
27. Schaeffer, *Cuneiform Texts*, pl. xxxii, fig. 2.
28. *KTU* 1.4, VI:22–35 (= *UT* 51).
29. Bronner, *Stories*, 60–61; compare Cyrus H. Gordon, *Ugarit and Minoan Crete* (New York: Norton, 1967), 62–63.
30. Roland de Vaux, "The Prophets of Baal on Mount Carmel," chap. 13 of *The Bible and the Ancient Near East* (Garden City, N.Y.: Doubleday, 1971), 240; see also Leonard Greenspoon, "The Origin of the Idea of Resurrection," in *Traditions in Transformation*, ed. Baruch Halpern and Jon D. Levenson (Winona Lake, Ind.: Eisenbrauns, 1981), 316–18, whose comments on 1 Kings 18, particularly verse 27, are most cogent.
31. Cohn, "Literary Logic," 341.
32. Ibid., 342.
33. Bronner, *Stories*, 137.
34. Frank M. Cross, *Canaanite Myth and Hebrew Epic* (Cambridge, Mass.: Harvard University Press, 1973), 193–94.
35. Ibid., 194.
36. Ibid.
37. Johan Lust, "Elijah and the Theophany on Mount Horeb," in *La Notion biblique de Dieu: le Dieu de la Bible et le Dieu des philosophes*, ed. J. Coppens et al., Bibliotheca ephemeridum theologicarum lovaniensium, vol. 41 (Gembloux, Belgium: Louvain University Press, 1976), 99.
38. See the concise treatment of the whole story in Robert B. Coote, "Yahweh Recalls Elijah," in *Traditions in Transformation*, 115–20, esp. 119–20.
39. Bronner, *Stories*, 62.
40. Ibid., 128–29.
41. *KTU* 1.19, I:43–44 (= *UT* 1 Aqht), plus numerous other examples.
42. *KTU* 1.17, VI:30–32 (= *UT* 2 Aqht).
43. Notably Gray, *Kings*, 486–87, who cites also W. Robertson Smith, *The Prophets of Israel*, 2d ed. (London: Black, 1912), 391–92.
44. *KTU* 1.17, I:18–19 (= *UT* 2 Aqht); see also *KTU* 1:17, I:27–34 (= *UT* 2 Aqht), a lengthy but representative passage on the duties of a son toward his father.
45. See John Gray, *The Krt Text in the Literature of Ras Shamra*, 2d ed. (Leiden, Netherlands: Brill, 1964).
46. K. Galling, "Der Gott Karmel und die Ächtung der fremden Götter," in *Geschichte und Altes Testament* (Alt Festschrift), in Beiträge zur historischen Theologie, 16 (Tubingen, West Germany: Mohr, 1953), 105–25; see also Albrecht Alt, "Das Gottesurteil auf dem Karmel," in vol. 2 of *Kleine Schriften zur Geschichte des Volkes Israel*, 3 vols. (Munchen, West Germany: Beck'sche, 1953), 2:135–49.
47. Galling, "Karmel," 110.
48. See Otto Eissfeldt, "Ba'alšamēm und Jahwe," *ZAW* 57 (1939): 1–31.

49. M. Avi-Yonah, "Mount Carmel and the God of Baalbek," *IEJ* 2 (1952): 124.
50. J. C. de Moor and M. J. Mulder, "Ba'al," in *TDOT*, ed. G. J. Botterweck and Helmer Ringgren (Grand Rapids, Mich.: Wm. Eerdmans, 1977): 2:198.
51. R. A. Oden, Jr., "Ba'al Šamēm and 'Ēl," *CBQ* 39 (1977): 472–73.
52. Albright, *Archaeology and the Religion of Israel*, 156–59; compare Eissfeldt, "Ba'alšamēm," 19ff.
53. See in addition the comments of Gray, *KRT Text*, 16, 55–56.
54. R. de Vaux, "Les prophètes de Baal sur le mont Carmel," in *BibOr* (1967), 485ff., published for the first time in *Bulletin de Musée de Beyrouth* 5 (1941): 7–20. The material can now be found in English in "The Prophets of Baal," in de Vaux, *The Bible and the Ancient Near East*, 238–51.
55. *Against Apion* 1.18; compare H. St. J. Thackeray, trans., "Against Apion," in *Josephus* in Loeb Classical Library (London: Heinemann, 1926), 1:210–11.
56. *Antiquities* 8.144–46; compare H. St. J. Thackeray and Ralph Marcus, trans., "Antiquities of the Jews," in *Josephus* in Loeb Classical Library (London: Heinemann, 1934), 5:648–51.
57. See also the discussion of S. A. Cook, *The Religion of Ancient Palestine in the Light of Archaeology*, in Schweich Lectures, 1925 (London: Oxford, 1930), 135–37.
58. Fensham, "A Few Observations," 229.
59. See Maurice Dunand, "Stèle araméenne dédiée à Melqart," *Bulletin du Musée de Beyrouth* 3 (1939): 65–76; see also James B. Pritchard, *The Ancient Near East in Pictures* (Princeton, N.J.: Princeton University Press, 1954), 170, pl. 499. W. F. Albright, "A Votive Stele Erected by Ben-Hadad I of Damascus to the God Melcarth," *BASOR* 87 (1942): 23–29, felt that he had identified Bar/Ben-Hadad of 1 Kgs. 15:18, but de Vaux, "Prophets of Baal," 239, n. 12, deems this impossible.
60. De Vaux, "Prophets of Baal," 239–40; see also Hartmut Gese, "Die Religionen Altsyriens," in *Die Religionen der Menschheit*, (10/2), ed. C. M. Schröder (Stuttgart: Kohlhammer, 1970), 195–96; also discussing the stele in much the same way is Robert du Mesnil du Buisson, *Nouvelle études sur les dieux et les mythes de Canaan*, Études préliminaires aux Religions orientales dans l'Empire romain, 33 (Leiden, Netherlands: Brill, 1973), 45.
61. H. Donner and W. Röllig, *Kanaanäische und Aramäische Inschriften*, 2d ed., 3 vols. (Wiesbaden, West Germany: Harrassowitz, 1966), 1:37, text #201; 2:203–4.
62. E. Lipiński, "North Semitic Texts," in *Near Eastern Religious Texts Relating to the Old Testament*, ed. Walter Beyerlin, OTL (Philadelphia: Westminster, 1978), 229.
63. R. Borger, *Die Inschriften Asarhaddons Königs von Assyrien*, AfO, Beiheft 9 (Graz, Austria: im Selbstverlage des Herausgebers, 1956), 109.
64. Du Mesnil du Buisson, *Nouvelle études*, 45.
65. Gese, "Religionen," 189; note, however, the textual problem in *KAI* 14:17, whether the text reads *šd qdš* or *šr qdš*, "holy field," or "holy prince." On Eshmun, see S. Vernon McCasland, "The Asklepios Cult in Palestine," *JBL* 58 (1939): 221–27.
66. Gese, "Religionen," 193–94.
67. Du Mesnil du Buisson, *Nouvelle études*, 42.
68. Fensham, "A Few Observations," 230.
69. Herodotus (2.44) mentioned the temple of Heracles at Tyre (see A. D. Godley, trans., *Herodotus* in Loeb Classical Library [London: Heinemann, 1926], 1:330–31); on the temple at Hierapolis as a primary source for understanding pagan religious practices, see Harold W. Attridge and Robert A. Oden, *The Syrian Goddess (De Dea Syria) Attributed to Lucian* (Missoula, Mo.: Scholars Press, 1976), esp. 39–61.
70. Gese, "Religionen," 197; see Patrick D. Miller, Jr., "Fire in the Mythology of Canaan and Israel," *CBQ* 27 (1965): 256–61; see also A. García y Bellido, *Les Religions orientales dans l'Espagne Romaine*, Études préliminaires aux Religions orientales dans l'Empire romaine, 5, ed. M. J. Vermaseran (Leiden, Netherlands: Brill, 1967), esp. 152ff.
71. Dimitri Baramki, *Phoenicia and the Phoenicians* (Beirut: Khayats, 1961), 68.
72. See Cyrus H. Gordon, *Ugaritic Textbook*, AnOr, 38 (Rome: Pontifical, 1967), 426.

73. Wolf W. G. Baudissin, *Adonis und Esmun* (Leipzig, East Germany: Hinrichs'sche, 1911), 275–82.
74. McCasland, "Asklepios," 221.
75. Ibid., 222–23
76. Ibid., 224.
77. Gese, "Religionen," 190, n. 84; on the connections with the Sumerian underworld god Nergal, see Henri Seyrig, "Heracles-Nergal," *Syria* 24 (1947): 62–80, and Wathiq al-Salihi, "Hercules-Nergal at Hatra," *Iraq* 33 (1971): 113–15. In this passage Nergal (Melqart) is linked with Ashima (Eshmun) in Syria.
78. Walter Baumgartner, *Hebräisches und Aramäisches Lexikon*, 3d ed. (Leiden, Netherlands: Brill, 1967), 1:91.
79. René Dussaud, "les Religions des Hittites et des Hourrites, des Phéniciens et des Syriens," in *"Mana": Introduction a l'Histoire des Religions*, vol. 1, pt. 2 (Paris: Presses Universitaires de France, 1949), 366, 368, 394ff.
80. Gese, "Religionen," 190, n. 84.
81. Baumgartner, *Lexikon*, 93.

4

The Period of the Judges:
Religious Disintegration
Under Tribal Rule

Daniel I. Block

The designation of the historical period that began with the conquest of Canaan and ended with the establishment of the monarchy in Israel as the "era of the judges" is legitimized by later Hebrew reflection on this period. The author of the Book of Ruth fixes his delightful story "in the days when the judges judged" (1:1, *bîmê šĕpōṭ haššōpṭîm*). In the Nathan oracle (2 Sam 7:11), reference is made to the day on which YHWH commanded judges to be over his people Israel.[1] The celebration of the Passover under the direction of Josiah is described in 2 Kgs. 23:22 as unprecedented "since the days of the judges who judged Israel" *(mîmê haššōpṭîm ʾăšer šāpṭû ʾet yiśrāʾēl)*, a period here juxtaposed with "the days of the kings of Israel and the kings of Judah."

Unfortunately, apart from the enigmatic reference to Israel on the Merneptah Stela,[2] our knowledge of the period of the judges is dependent almost entirely on the biblical Book of Judges and the first chapters of 1 Samuel. Since the Book of Judges represents an intentional unit, and in view of the present limitations of space, my attempt to recapture the religious climate of the time will focus on this material.

Although modern scholars are sharply divided on the credence to be allowed for the biblical material covering the era,[3] this is all the information we have. In the study which follows, I will marshall what data may be gleaned from these sources to attempt to determine at least the Hebrew historian's understanding of the period. In so doing, I will seek to answer three questions: (1) What was the political climate in Israel in the Early Iron Age? (2) What was the spiritual condition of the nation at this time? (3) What role did the political leaders (the judges) play in these religious developments?

THE POLITICAL CLIMATE IN EARLY ISRAEL

Most recent studies of the Book of Judges have focused on two major issues: the nature of the judges' office and the nature of the tribal league which constituted Israel. In order to lay the ground for the sections which follow, these two matters require some attention here as well.

The Office of "Judge"

The Book of Judges appears to deal with two types of judges, frequently classified by scholars as "minor" and "major" judges. The names of five of the minor judges (Tola, Jair, Ibzan, Elon, Abdon) are provided in two short lists on either side of the Jephthah account (Judg 10:1–5; 12:8–15). With the exception of Tola, who is also identified as a "deliverer" (*wayyāqām . . . lĕhôšî(a)et yiśrā)ēl*, 10:1), these are presented simply as men who "judged Israel" (*wayyišpōṭ)et yiśrā)ēl*).[4] For all the major judges, with the exception of the enigmatic Shamgar (3:31), the narrator constructs his account of their exploits around the recurring cycle of apostasy–oppression–plea for divine aid–deliverance through the judge (see 2:10–3:6). Described in this way are Othniel (3:7–11), Ehud (3:12–30), Deborah and Barak (4:1–24), Gideon (6:1–8:28), and Jephthah (10:6–12:7).[5]

A. Malamat has rightly argued that the functional distinctions between the major and minor judges should not be too sharply drawn. The differences in the accounts derive primarily from the sources used by the narrator: family chronicles for the minor judges; folk narratives for the deliverer judges.[6] In any case, the reference to Bedan alongside Jerubbaal (Gideon), Jephthah, and Samuel, in 1 Sam. 12:11, indicates that our information on the judges is incomplete. They seem, however, to have fulfilled two roles—the administration of justice in Israel (see Judg 4:5; 1 Sam 7:15–17) and the deliverance of the people from external oppression, corresponding to the two terms "judge" (*šōpēṭ*) and "deliverer" (*môšîa(*), respectively.

A. Alt and M. Noth have argued that the minor judges represented men who held the central office in the twelve-tribe amphictyony.[7] Although this view has the advantage of recognizing the judges as more than local figures, the hypothesis remains purely conjectural. The texts leave no hints regarding the judges' ascent to power. In any case, this theory of early Israelite political organization has come under increasing criticism.[8] R. K. Harrison has suggested that the judges arose from the aristocratic ruling classes, and that descent from the *gibbôrê ḥayil* ("mighty men of valor") was of primary importance, Abimelech and Jephthah being the examples cited.[9] However, it appears this interpretation treats the expression *gibbôr ḥayil* too technically. Gideon's identification as such (Judg 6:12) seems to mean nothing more than "mighty warrior."[10] Furthermore, the expression is not applied to Abimelech, whom Malamat has demonstrated to have represented the antithesis of the norm.[11] As for Jephthah, the designation is applied to him, not his father (11:1), apparently as a retrospective impression of the man in the mind of the narrator.

Since the epochal work of M. Weber, the judges (especially the major ones) have been commonly treated as *charismatic* leaders, men (and women, for example, Deborah) endowed with extraordinary physical traits, raised in times of distress to bring relief to a weary people.[12] This interpretation is attractive, but it is significant that of all the judges named, only Gideon and Jephthah are identified as *gibbôr ḥayil*, surely a prerequisite to this view of charisma. The fact that Deborah was a prophetess may have been helpful in her judicial functions (4:4), but its value for delivering the nation is not obvious. Samson was a man of extraordinary strength, a trait necessary for his actions, but nowhere does the narrative suggest that this was the basis of his judgeship.

It may be argued that all these features qualified one for the office of judge, but *qualification* is distinct from *authorization*. The "Book of Saviors"[13] emphatically states in the preface (Judg 2:16, 18) as well as in the narratives of each of the major judges (save Shamgar, who appears to have been non-Israelite),[14] that the authorization of judges was a divine decision. YHWH raises up judges/deliverers (*wayyāqem yhwh šōpṭîm/môšia‛*, 2:16, 18; 3:9, 15); YHWH strengthens *(wayěḥazzēq)* Eglon (3:12; compare 16:28); YHWH gives the command to arm against Sisera (4:6); YHWH sends his angel *(mal'ak)* to call Gideon (6:11–40); YHWH plans Gideon's strategy (7:2–23); YHWH calls Samson before he is born (13:5) and stirs him to action (13:25, *wattāḥel*); YHWH's Spirit comes upon the judges (3:10; 11:29; 14:6, 19; 15:14) or clothes them (6:34). Indeed, apart from the Spirit of YHWH, Samson has neither the authority nor the power to act (16:20).

If the authorization and qualification for judgeship are perceived as being supernatural rather than natural gifts, then the designation of the judges as *charismatic* leaders is appropriate. But there can be no question that for the narrator, the deliverer judge and the citizenry, the official was a divine agent; he was imbued with the divine Spirit, and he was granted supreme authority in the society (see 10:13–14).[15]

The "Tribal League"

In spite of the demise of the amphictyonic theory of Israelite political structures in the Early Iron Age, the view that the nation constituted some sort of tribal confederacy/league persists.[16] It appears, however, that this interpretation requires considerable qualification. B. Lindars has argued convincingly that in the period of the judges there was no tribal *system* by which governmental affairs were handled.[17] This does not mean that the various tribes lacked a sense of cohesion. It is clear that the narrator perceived the tribes as one people. In fact, he goes out of his way to emphasize the point in several ways.

First, the frequency of the name "Israel" is higher in the Book of Judges than in any other book of the Hebrew Bible, including Exodus through Joshua, where the nation is purportedly operating as a unit, first under Moses, then under Joshua.[18] Second, the pan-Israelite expressions "all Israel" and "all the sons of Israel" occur in Judg. 8:27 and 2:4; 20:1, respectively. Gideon's forces are identified as the "men of Israel" (7:8, 23; 8:22), rather than by their tribal names (see also 9:55). Even Gideon is referred to as "the son of Joash, a man of Israel" (7:14). In the final chapters the same applies to the forces marshalled against the warriors of Benjamin.[19] Other pan-Israelite expressions occurring in the book include "the hand of Israel" (3:30; 11:21), "the camp of Israel" (7:15), "the misery of Israel" (10:16), "the daughters of Israel" (11:40), "the border of Israel" (19:29), "the inheritance of Israel" (20:6), and, repeatedly, "the sons of Israel."[20] Also noted are references to a person judging Israel, ruling over Israel, saving Israel, and in the final chapters, "There was no king in Israel."[21]

Further, in the book, YHWH's anger burns against Israel (2:14, 20; 3:8; 10:7); he tests Israel (2:22; 3:1, 4); ritual mourning becomes a custom in Israel (11:39); disgraceful acts are committed in Israel (20:6); wickedness is removed from Israel (20:13); events happen in Israel (21:3); a man is a priest to a family and tribe in Israel (18:19). Not only does the expression "the tribes of Israel" (šibṭê yiśrāʾēl) appear repeatedly in the last two chapters,[22] the actual tribes making up the nation are frequently identified by name.[23] In fact, the crisis in the final chapters arises with the prospect of one tribe being missing in Israel (21:3, lĕhippāqēd hayyôm miyiśrāʾēl šēbeṭ ʾeḥād), being cut off from Israel (21:6, nigdaʿ šēbeṭ ʾeḥād miyiśrāʾēl), and being blotted out from Israel (21:17, yimmāḥeh šēbeṭ miyiśrāʾēl). To lose Benjamin would render the nation incomplete.

It seems obvious that to the narrator, the Israel of this period represented one nation. However, this raises the question whether this was not a retrojection of later perceptions into an earlier era. In response it should be observed that (1) the above expressions are not restricted to the narrator's deuteronomistic comments; they appear in all segments of the book; (2) the definition of the land of Israel as "from Dan to Beersheba" seems to represent at least an early monarchy perspective;[24] (3) the archival judge lists (10:1–5; 12:8–15), which appear to be based on early sources, refer to Israel this way;[25] (4) the song of Deborah, dating back at least to the eleventh century B.C., uses the national name similarly,[26] even to the extent of listing many of the tribes.[27] It may be safely concluded, therefore, that the Israel that confronts us in the Book of Judges viewed itself as one nation.

Extra-biblical support for this interpretation may be provided by the reference to Israel on the Merneptah Stela from the thirteenth century B.C. Significantly, within the context of a series of Canaanite names, each containing the foreign land determinative, only Israel is referred to as a foreign people. Some have interpreted this as an indication that Israel was not yet permanently settled at the time.[28] However, the form may also recognize that in the case of Israel a primarily ethnic rather than geographic sense is intended; that is, the Egyptian king acknowledges Israel as a people, rather than a country, irrespective of settlement.

But this raises the problem of the basis on which this unity was perceived to have been founded. At the outset, there appears to have been a recognition of ethnic unity based on descent from a common ancestor. This may be hinted at by the frequent use of the warm, relational term, ʿam, "people," from a root signifying "paternal uncle," which often implies internal blood relationship.[29]

This connotation surfaces especially in the account of the marriage of Samson. Initially Samson's parents protest his marriage to the Philistine, pleading, "Is there no woman among the daughters of your relatives (ʾaḥêkā), or among all our people (běkol ʿammî), that you must take a wife from the uncircumcised Philistines?" (14:3). The woman speaks of her countrymen as "the sons of my people"[30] (běnê ʿammî, 14:16, 17). Ethnic distinction is clearly intended here. The same applies to the identification of the inhabitants of Laish as "a people quiet and secure" (18:27).[31]

The frequent use of the expression běnê yiśrāʾēl (61 times) in the book may point in a similar direction.[32] Significantly, when the servant proposes to his Levite master that they spend the night in Jebus, the latter responds, "We will not turn aside into the city of foreigners which is not of the sons of Israel" (ʿîr nokrî ʾăšer lōʾ mibnê yiśrāʾēl, 19:12), preferring to move on to Gibeah of Benjamin, considered to be of the běnê yiśrāʾēl, and therefore safe. Although the expression ʾāḥ ("brother") may be interpreted socio–politically in some contexts, that is, as a partner in an alliance,[33] in the opening annalistic summary of the conquest of the land, Judah and Simeon are treated as brothers (ʾaḥîm, Judg 1:3, 17). In the appendix, the sons of Israel treat the Benjamites as brothers (20:23, 28) and vice versa (20:13). The loss of the tribe of Benjamin is treated as the loss of a member of the family (21:6; see also 14:3; 18:14). The other side to this coin is the occasional reference in the book to the Patriarchs as the fathers of the Israelites (2:1, 12, 17). That the Israelites perceived themselves as a single family from early times seems clear.[34]

It has long been recognized that the tribes of Israel were closely linked religiously. YHWH was their national deity and had entered into a covenant with them at Sinai (see 5:5 and Deut 33:2–5), a covenant that required Israel's exclusive allegiance (Judg 2:1–2; 6:10; 10:13–14). For this reason YHWH is called "the God of Israel" (yhwh ʾĕlōhê yiśrāʾēl),[35] in contrast to the other gods, the gods of the surrounding peoples (ʾĕlōhîm ʾăḥērîm mēʾĕlōhê hāʿammîm ʾăšer sĕbîbôtêhem, 2:12). Elsewhere he is identified as Israel's deity by means of pronominal suffixes.[36] The nation, on the other hand, was recognized as "the people of God" (ʿam hāʾĕlōhîm, 20:2),[37] or "his people, Israel" (ʿammo yiśrāʾēl, 11:23).

How this theological unity was expressed by the tribes during this time is not clear. In spite of the vast amount of ink used to describe the role of the central shrine, the place where the ark presumably rested,[38] neither the Book of Judges nor the early chapters of 1 Samuel indicate that the Israelites convocated regularly, or even once, at a central shrine to worship YHWH or that the tribes held any religious festivals in common.[39] Our sources simply do not record how the consciousness of Israel's status as the people of YHWH was celebrated. If anything, they indicate that this was one of the major problems of the day (see below).

The frequent discussions of the amphictyony and the tribal league notwithstanding, evidence for a *politically* united nation during the period of the judges is scanty. The political term gôy[40] is applied to Israel only once in the Book of Judges, and never in 1 Samuel. The single occurrence in Judg. 2:20 is significant, however, in that it occurs in the speech of YHWH in which Israel's special status is being rejected. Inasmuch as she has abandoned her covenant deity, she has become a *gôy*, like all the other *gôyîm*.[41]

The nature of government in premonarchic Israel is not entirely clear. It appears from Judges 1 that political authority was transferred from the central figure to the separate tribes. This impression is confirmed by (1) the notice of foreign aggression directed against individual tribes (10:9); (2) the addressing of appeals for military aid to the other tribes (4:10; 6:35; 7:23-24); and (3) the reports of tribal responses to such appeals (5:14-18; 8:1; especially 12:1-6).

However, the process whereby decisions were made at the tribal level is nowhere defined. Obviously the elders *(zĕqēnîm)* would have been involved. The body of elders, which antedates the Exodus (see Exod 3:16, 18; 4:29), served primarily as representatives of the nation under Moses' and Joshua's leadership.[42] Later, however, in accordance with the deuteronomic legislation, they carried important executive functions—sitting at the gates of the cities resolving civil and judicial matters.[43] How the elders were promoted to this office is unknown, although seniority was surely a significant factor. The number of elders in the nation, or in any given tribe, for that matter, is also unknown. The seventy elders separated by Moses can hardly have represented any type of quota; the texts emphasize that these were selected *"from the elders of Israel* whom you know to be elders of the people and their officers" (Num 11:16, 24-25; compare Exod 24:1; italics added).

In the era of the judges it was natural that the crises precipitated by foreign invasions should become a concern of the elders. However, as the call of Jephthah illustrates, tribal interests tended to remain primary (Judg 11:5-11). Nevertheless, their impotence in the face of such threats is demonstrated by their elevation of Jephthah to the status of "head" *(rō᾽š*, 11:11) and "chief" *(qāṣîn*, 11:6).[44] Twice the narratives report the gathering of elders of all the tribes, once to determine the appropriate response to the decimation of the Benjamites (21:16; compare "chiefs of all the people" *[pînnôt kol hā῾ām]*, 20:2) and once to ask Samuel for a king (1 Sam 8:4). The latter text is especially instructive. On the one hand, they request an official who would assume responsibility for the military leadership of the nation against the Philistines, as well as take over their judicial roles (1 Sam 8:5, 19-20). On the other, the event demonstrates that this body did not have the authority to make such appointments. It is tempting to see here a recognition of Samuel as a prophet in the Mosaic tradition (compare Deut 18:18).

In addition to the elders, several other types of functionaries served the political process in Israel. Reference has already been made to Jephthah as a *head* and *chief.* The former term is applied to military leaders in this and later contexts.[45] However, several important references also assign judicial roles to holders of this office.[46] These men appear to have been appointed on the basis of their special abilities.[47] In the Book of Joshua occasional reference is made to "clerks" *(šōṭĕrîm*, Josh 8:33), a type of minor judge or subordinate civil officer.[48] Although this office probably continued into the period of the judges, it does not figure in the narratives.

Although the judges are described as having jurisdiction over Israel, and the entire nation appears before Gideon, asking him to be king and worshiping his ephod (Judg 8:22–28), and although the chiefs of all the people gather at Mizpah to discuss the fate of Benjamin (20:1–2), none of this signals a centralization or standardization of political power. They may represent aspirations in that direction, but aspirations should not be confused with reality. In fact, the absence of centralized authority seems to have been the quality of national life that most impressed the final editor of the Book of Judges.[49]

This national defect surfaced immediately after the passing of Joshua (Judg 1:1–36) and later precipitated the demand for a king in the face of the Philistine threat (1 Sam 8:4–9). In fact, the convocation before Samuel at Ramah by all the elders of Israel arose specifically out of a desire to remedy this deficiency. Inasmuch as the convocation at Mizpah in Judg. 20:1–2 had been concerned with how to deal with the Benjamite outrage, it was an *ad hoc* gathering whose ultimate function became military; it could hardly be classified as a typical political assembly of the nation's leaders. With the death of Joshua, a central unifying figure/symbol had disappeared (Judg 1:1).

The Book of Judges seems to describe a nation that is the opposite of what tribal confederacies are usually perceived to be. The narrator would have us recognize that in spite of the consciousness of ethnic and spiritual unity, the nation was determined to destroy itself. From a political standpoint, Israel was her own worst enemy. Consequently, she failed to deal decisively with the Canaanites (1:1–36);[50] her men hesitated to assume leadership even when it was thrust upon them (4:6–9, Barak; 6:1–40, Gideon). On the one hand, individual tribes and clans refused to get involved in times of national crisis (5:17; 21:9); on the other, when they were not asked to participate, jealousy threatened to cause self-destruction (8:1–2; 12:1–6, Ephraim in both instances).

When strong leadership did emerge, it patterned itself after the worst aspects of Canaanite city–state despotism (9:1–57, Abimelech),[51] or was preoccupied with personal advantage (11:8–11, Jephthah), or treated power as a private plaything, provoking the ire of enemies upon the nation and alienating countrymen (14:10–15:16, Samson). The climax (or perhaps nadir) and ultimate act of self-destruction occurs in chapter 20, when the holy war that should have been waged against the Canaanites is directed at one of their own tribes.[52]

THE RELIGIOUS CLIMATE IN EARLY ISRAEL

In view of Israel's political debacle in the pre-monarchic era, the narrator's negative evaluation of Israelite society in the absence of kingship, and the circumstances of the demand for a king in 1 Samuel 8, it is not surprising that some have understood the Book of Judges as an apology for the Davidic monarchy.[53] Although the later pro-Davidic stance of the books of Samuel and Kings would certainly support this thesis, it is not so clear that the compiler of the Judges material was that concerned about political structures. Even if the book provides a great deal of information on the political situation in Israel during the period of settlement, it seems that a fundamental hermeneutical error is committed if the book is used primarily for the reconstruction of political structures. Writing from a deuteronomic/prophetic perspective,[54] the narrator was much more concerned about the religious situation in the nation. The materials incorporated into the document have been selected and arranged to develop the thesis that in the aftermath of the death of Joshua the *religious* experience of Israel was disastrous. Evidence for this interpretation may be drawn from several sources.

The Prologue (Judg 1:1–2:5)

B. S. Childs has aptly observed that the function of the prologue in the Book of Judges is to highlight the disobedience of the Israel that succeeded the era of Joshua.[55] Not only has the nation been fractured politically, but spiritually she seems to be coming apart as well. Although the tone of the annalistic Judg. 1:1–36 appears relatively secular, there is a marked contrast between the presence of YHWH with Judah and Joseph on the one hand, and on the other with the remainder of the tribes, who refuse to apply the principle of the *ḥerem* to the Canaanites. Even if they enslave the natives, letting them live is a violation of the covenant (2:1–5; compare Deut 7:1–5). This text provides perspicuous evidence of the compiler's concerns.

The Introduction to the Book of Deliverers (Judg 2:6–3:6)

The introduction to the Book of Deliverers draws the same contrast between the fidelity of the nation during the time of the conquest and the infidelity of the settlement period, emphasizing that the apostasy was rooted in the failure of the nation to transmit the memory of YHWH's acts of deliverance to the next generation (2:10). Without the next generation's having a clear vision of YHWH's claim upon them, the pursuit of the Canaanite deities was a natural consequence. The emphasis here (and one that should not be overlooked in the succeeding accounts) is placed on YHWH's response to Israel's apostasy and the cyclic pattern of his initial anger, his delivering them into the hands of the enemy, his sensitivity to their cry for help, and his appointment of a savior–judge.

The oppressors of the nation represent YHWH's appointed tests of Israel's covenantal loyalty (2:21–3:1). The narrator emphasizes not only how quickly the spiritual disintegration set in (2:10), as well as the progressive intensification of Israel's apostasy with each succeeding cycle (2:17–19), but also the cause of the problem—intermarriage with the Canaanites (3:6) and failure to retain a fresh and vital memory of YHWH's saving acts (3:7). This thesis statement establishes the primarily religious focus of the narratives that follow.

The Introductions to the Deliverer Cycles
(Judg 3:7–16:31)

The concern with the fundamentally religious problem of the era is maintained with the prefatory comment before each of the deliverer cycles: "Now the sons of Israel did evil in the sight of YHWH" (3:7, 12; 4:1; 6:1; 10:6; 13:1). These evaluations formally serve to tie together the separate accounts, and to connect them with the thesis statement.

The Appendices (Judg 17:1–21:25)

The two appendices describing the origin of the Danite cult center (17:1–18:31) and the Benjamite scandal (19:1–21:25), although separate incidents, are linked internally by the presence of Levites in the accounts and externally by the narrator's evaluation of the period (17:6; 18:1; 19:1; 21:25). Apparently these events were selected for inclusion to illustrate further the disastrous effects of the cancerous apostasy on the nation.

The first account illustrates (1) the loss of personal integrity in an Ephraimite household (17:1–3); (2) the establishment of private cults antithetical to YHWH (17:4–5); (3) the shiftlessness and opportunism of the priestly class (17:7–13; 18:20); (4) the glibness with which Levites performed their duties (18:5–6); (5) the unscrupulous disrespect of the Danites toward the rights and feelings of their countrymen (18:17–20); and (6) the centrifugal tendency of tribes to act independently in religious matters (18:27–31).

The second appendix portrays the decadence of Israel even more graphically. Leaving aside the lack of spiritual mission on the part of the Levite (19:1), and the questionable morality of the concubine (19:2), the degeneracy of the Benjamites is cast against the backdrop of normal custom and hospitality. Whereas it was expected that an Israelite would feel insecure in a Canaanite city (19:12), the visiting party should have been received by its countrymen. However, the first hint of trouble is provided by an Ephraimite also living in the Benjamite community of Gibeah. This alien takes the Levite into his house to protect him from the natives. However, in terms obviously reminiscent of the divine visitors' experience in Sodom (Gen 19:1–11), the city residents demand homosexual relations with the guest. The response of the host is to protect his company and offer his daughter and the concubine to the people, the latter of whom is then ravished and left for dead. The cry of 19:30 is the appeal of the narrator, alerting the nation to its unprecedented decadence. The upshot of this event is the gathering of the elders of all Israel's tribes to Mizpah to deal with the rot in Benjamin. They declare holy war on this tribe after the manner of Israel's holy war against the Canaanites in chapter 1. The people have become their own worst enemies.

The narrator attributes the degeneracy of the nation to the lack of central authority, as well as to the individualization of society, an anarchy in which each man had become his own standard of morality (17:6; 21:25). The covenant principles embodied in the Decalogue have been completely forgotten; virtually every one of its terms has been violated. As at the conclusion to our discussion of the political climate in Israel, so here as well it may be observed that the narrator has brought his readers full circle. The spiritual condition of the people inhabiting the land of Canaan at the end of the settlement period is the same as it had been at the beginning. It has made no difference that the identity of that people has changed. In doing so the narrator has again demonstrated his primary concern. It is not the tracing of Israel's *political evolution*, but the recounting of her *spiritual devolution*. He has exposed the total Canaanization of Israelite society.

THE ROLE OF THE JUDGES
IN EARLY ISRAEL'S RELIGIOUS LIFE

Later reflection on the role of the judges in the context of increasing Israelite apostasy tended to idealize them as paragons of fidelity. Thus Ben Sirach writes:

> The judges also with their respective names,
>   those whose hearts did not fall into idolatry
>   and who did not turn away from the Lord—
> may their memory be blessed!
> May their bones revive from where they lie,
>   and may the name of those who have been honored
> live again in their sons! (Sir 46:11)

This compares with the view of the author of the Book of Hebrews, who includes Gideon, Barak, Samson, and Jephthah in his recitation of the heroes of faith in Israel's tradition (Heb 11:32). In the main, contemporary popular interpretation continues to read the Book of Judges through the eyes of these later idealists, rather than letting the redactor of the material speak for himself. An unbiased reading of the record causes one to wonder whether the judges were really saviors of the nation or part of the problem that plagued Israel. Upon closer examination, the picture painted of these personages is quite different from popular perceptions.

Othniel (Judg 3:7–11)

The account of Othniel is schematic in nature and tells us nothing about his personality, let alone his spiritual condition. The narrator emphasizes, on the other hand, his role as the agent of YHWH: "YHWH raised up a deliverer"; "the spirit of YHWH came upon him"; "YHWH gave Cushan-rishathaim into his power" (3:9–10). What additional information is provided is genealogical and statistical.

Ehud (Judg 3:12–30)

The account of Ehud's victory over the Moabites is longer than Othniel's, and his strategy is described in greater detail. However, apart from his comment, "Pursue them, for YHWH has given your enemies the Moabites into your hands" (3:28), not a hint of his personal faith is given. Even this statement is of such a general nature that it need not have been anything more than a rallying slogan. It is interesting that in 3:20 only the general title for the deity, Elohim, is used rather than YHWH. Although the editor makes no moralizing comment about Ehud's behavior, his treachery and brutality seem to be of a piece with Canaanite patterns. Again the emphasis of the narrative is on YHWH sending the oppressor (3:12) and his raising up a deliverer (3:15), not on Ehud's charismatic or spiritual qualification for the task.

Shamgar (Judg 3:31)

Shamgar's presence in the cycles of the judges is puzzling. The brevity of the account precludes a clear interpretation of his role. However, it has been recognized that, judging by his name, he was not even an Israelite.[56] But even if he was, his identification as "son of Anath" hardly commends him for his Yahwistic piety.[57] His presence here appears to confirm a dearth of qualified leadership within Israel. Although caution is advised in attempts to explain absence of information, the lack of heroic details in the account may reflect a certain embarrassment on the part of the author, or his sources, that the nation had to turn to outsiders for help.

Deborah and Barak (Judg 4:1–5:31)

Deborah may yet represent the exception that proves the rule. The narrator provides more hints of her spiritual commitment than for any other judge. Her prior roles as prophetess and judge (4:4) are reminiscent of Samuel (1 Sam 3:19–21; 7:15–17). She is aware of YHWH's, the God of Israel's, command to march against Sisera (4:6). She has confidence that YHWH will deliver Sisera into her hand (4:9; compare v 14). The Song of Deborah (chap. 5) is a clear testimony of praise to YHWH, who has given the victory. In contrast to Deborah stands Barak, appearing weak-willed and indecisive (4:8). He will not assume leadership without Deborah's presence, leading to the caustic comment that "YHWH will sell Sisera into the hands of a woman" (4:9).

Lindars has perceptively pointed out the "feminist" theme in this heroic narrative.[58] Although Sisera dies at the hands of another woman, Jael, this heightens the motif. But contemporary feminists may hardly adopt Deborah and Jael as normative models. Indeed the reverse is true. Although the idea of women in leadership is not offensive to the narrator, this passage again points out the degeneracy of the nation. In the absence of firm committed leadership from the men, YHWH will use women.

Gideon (Judg 6:1–8:35)

In himself, there is certainly nothing in Gideon that commends him for a leadership role in Israel. His father is a community leader in the Baal cult (6:25–27). Gideon himself is cynical of YHWH's interest in Israel (6:13). His use of the fleece to confirm YHWH's appointment of him as the deliverer from the Midianites smacks of forbidden augury (compare Deut 18:9–14) and in any case betrays a lack of confidence in YHWH (6:36–40). YHWH concedes to Gideon's fear with another dream omen (7:9–14). Also problematic are his fascination with the crescent amulets (symbols of the astral cults) of the Midianites (8:21), his subsequent apostasy, expressed by making the ephod a national cult symbol (8:24–27, 33),[59] his harem (8:30), and his taking a Shechemite concubine (8:31; compare 3:6). In spite of his pious comment, "I will not rule over you" (8:23), all of these actions suggest the opposite. He behaves like an oriental king, a status memorialized in the name of his son, Abimelech ("my father is king").

Although Gideon's father, Joash, bears one of the rare Yahwistic names of the period,[60] and although the aetiology offered for Gideon's other name, Jerubbaal, ostensibly reflects an anti-Baalistic polemic,[61] it is clear that in later times the name was interpreted negatively and the offensive theophore was replaced with bōšet ("shame").[62] It seems also that the narrator of the Book of Judges himself understood the name Jerubbaal as a syncretistic development, for in the account of Gideon's son (namely, Abimelech's abortive attempt at establishing himself as king in Shechem, after the pattern of Canaanite kings) Abimelech is consistently identified as the son of Jerubbaal rather than Gideon (9:1, 5, 16, 24, 28–29). The narrator seems to have read the story of Gideon's posterity in the light of Gideon's apostasy.

Jephthah (Judg 10:6–12:7)

The narrator's characterization of Jephthah as a "valiant warrior" (gibbôr ḥayil, 11:1) hardly commends him spiritually for the role of savior in Israel. Indeed, he was a most unlikely candidate for leadership, being the ostracized son of a harlot and a leader of a band of brigands in the mountains of Gilead (11:1–3). Although his bargaining with the Ammonites reflects political astuteness and an awareness of YHWH's actions in Israel's history (11:12–28), his negotiations with the leaders of Gilead are motivated by opportunistic ambition (11:9–11). His rash vow, preceding his battle with the Ammonites, sounds like the type of bargain foreigners would make with their gods (11:30–31).[63] Its fulfillment clearly caused him great personal anguish but need not have presented any great theological conflict—in view of his contacts with other child-sacrificing peoples.[64] In fact, he may have viewed this as a supreme demonstration of piety.[65]

Samson (Judg 13:1–16:31)

In Samson, Israelite impiety sinks to its nadir. Samson's parents do not appear to be very perceptive spiritually, as witnessed by their skeptical response to the birth announcement of the *mal'ak yhwh* ("angel of YHWH," 13:2–23). In the narrative they refer to YHWH by the general term *Elohim* (13:6, 8, 22). They refer to YHWH only after the angel had done so (13:23; compare v 16), but even then with some ignorance concerning YHWH's motives and methods. Their naming of their son Samson is also suspiciously syncretistic. It is difficult to dissociate the name from the cult of the solar deity, Shamash. Samson's association with Zorah, a mere two and one-half miles from the shrine of Beth-Shemesh, adds weight to this interpretation.[66] The name may be a shortened form of "Man of Shemesh."[67]

In his personal conduct Samson is anything but a model of faith and piety. He marries a Philistine, in deliberate rebellion against the wishes of his parents (14:1–4, and the divine prohibition?); he meddles with the enemy from whom he is to bring deliverance (14:10–19); he has an affair with the Philistine harlot (16:1–3) and with Delilah (16:4ff.); he fritters away his calling and divinely given talent, using it essentially to achieve selfish ends, rather than to liberate Israel. In the end, he appeals for one more demonstration of divine aid out of purely personal concern (16:28; compare 15:18). Like most of the other judges, Samson was an unlikely candidate for leadership in Israel. The narrator seems to stress that what accomplishments were achieved were all to YHWH's credit, produced in spite of, rather than because of, the man.[68]

CONCLUSION

It has become apparent that the role of the judges in arresting spiritual backsliding in Israel should not be overestimated. It is of great significance that not one of them is charged by YHWH to launch a crusade against idolatry in the nation, or to call the people back to YHWH. The only judge who engages in tasks like these is the last one, Samuel (1 Sam 7:1–11). This should probably be attributed to his prophetic role, rather than his functions as judge (see 1 Sam 3:19–21). In any case, this account is part of an entirely new narrative.

If a direct appeal for religious reform is ever made to the Israelites in the Book of Judges, the challenge is presented by an angel *(mal'ak)* of YHWH (Judg 2:1–5), a prophet *(nabi')* of YHWH (6:7–10), or by YHWH himself, without reference to an intermediary (10:10–16). It is never made by a judge. The role of the judges (especially of the deliverers) seems to have been primarily, if not exclusively, to relieve the pressure upon Israel from foreign nations whom YHWH had sent as agents of punishment. In other words, they were called upon to deal with the symptoms and effects of Israel's spiritual malaise, rather than with its underlying causes.

The human materials available for dealing with the foreign oppressors were raw indeed. The characters of the judges, far from being described as paragons of virtue and faith, tended to be the opposite. They were more often than not part of the spiritual problem rather than the solution (Deborah being the notable exception, but then she was a prophetess before she was a deliverer, 4:4). Nor should the judges be excused as following principles acceptable in an earlier day, but later rejected, or by appealing to some form of progressive revelation, or by accepting that they did what they thought was right.[69] If anything, the judges were the opposite of charismatic leaders—if by the expression we mean those naturally gifted and qualified for a task.

The Book of Judges is not so much a written commemoration of Israel's heroes in the Early Iron Age as a witness to YHWH's gracious determination to preserve his people, by answering their pleas and providing deliverance. It is within this context that the special activity of the Spirit (rûaḥ) of YHWH should be interpreted. Whereas in the case of Gideon the Spirit is said to have "clothed" (lābšâ) the man (6:34), this should not be interpreted too differently from every other instance in which the Spirit is described as having come/rushed upon its object.[70] This expression, reminiscent of Num. 24:3 (in which case Balaam, the Mesopotamian prophet, experiences the same phenomenon), does not presuppose any particular level of spirituality on the part of the recipient. To the contrary, this divine intrusion into human experience seems to graphically describe YHWH's arresting of men ill-disposed toward resolving Israel's problems and his equipping of them for the saving task.[71]

It seems that for too long the Book of Judges has been treated as a political document valued primarily for the data it provides on Israelite governmental institutions in the Early Iron Age. Our study suggests that the narrator's intentions were quite different. If he touched on Israel's pre-monarchic political institutions, this was merely to assist him in the development of his central thesis: Israel is in a sorry state of spiritual decline. With the abandonment of the covenant deity, YHWH, and the adoption of Canaanite cultic practices and theology came the absorption of prevailing moral and social values—in short, the Canaanization of Israelite society. The narrator's call is a prophetic call for renewal and recommitment to the covenant God; it is a reminder of the continuation of YHWH's gracious saving acts in Israel's history.

NOTES

1. MT has *šibṭê yiśrāʾēl* in verse 7, where the parallel text, 1 Chr. 17:6, has *šōpṭê yiśrāʾēl*. P. V. Reid, "*šbṭy* in 2 Samuel 7:7," *CBQ* 37 (1975): 17–20, has argued MT should be preserved, interpreting the phrase, "staff bearers of Israel," which makes good sense in conjunction with the command to "shepherd *(rʿh)* YHWH's people Israel" in the same verse.

2. See J. B. Pritchard, ed., *Ancient Near Eastern Texts Relating to the Old Testament*, 3d ed. (Princeton, N.J.: Princeton University Press, 1969), 378.

3. Representative of those who are cautious concerning the reliability of the biblical narratives are T. L. Thompson, *The Historicity of the Patriarchal Narratives: The Quest for the Historical Abraham*, BZAW 133 (Berlin: de Gruyter, 1974): 324–26; A. D. H. Mayes, "The Period of the Judges and the Rise of the Monarchy," in *Israelite and Judaean History*, ed. J. H. Hayes and J. M. Miller, OTL (Philadelphia: Westminster, 1977), 286–93. For more conservative approaches, see W. W. Hallo, "Biblical History in Its Near Eastern Setting: The Contextual Approach," in C. D. Evans et al., eds., *Scripture in Context: Essays on the Comparative Method* (Pittsburgh: Pickwick, 1980), 1–26; K. A. Kitchen, "The Old Testament in Its Context 3: From Joshua to Solomon," *TSFB* 61 (1971): 5–14; K. A. Kitchen, "The Old Testament in Its Context 6," *TSFB* 64 (1972): 2–10; R. K. Harrison, *Introduction to the Old Testament* (Grand Rapids, Mich.: Wm. Eerdmans, 1969), 680–94.

4. See H. W. Herzberg, "Die Kleinen Richter," *TLZ* 79 (1954): 285–90 (= *Beiträge zur Traditionsgeschichte und Theologie des Alten Testaments* [Gottingen, West Germany: Vandenhoeck & Ruprecht, 1962], 118–25); R. de Vaux, *The Early History of Israel*, trans. D. Smith (Philadelphia: Westminster, 1978), 752–59.

5. See de Vaux, *Early History of Israel*, 760–66. Samuel is appropriately included here.

6. A. Malamat, "The Period of the Judges," in *Judges*, ed. B. Mazar, in *World History of the Jewish People* (Givatayim, Israel: Jewish History Publications, 1971), 3:131. Hereafter referred to as *WHJP* III.

7. A. Alt, *Die Ursprünge des israelitischen Rechts* (Leipzig, East Germany: S. Hirzel, 1934), 31–33 (English translation, "The Origins of Israelite Law," in *Essays on Old Testament History and Religion*, trans. R. A. Wilson [Garden City, N.Y.: Doubleday, 1968], 130–320); M. Noth, *The History of Israel*, 2d ed. (New York: Harper & Row, 1958), 99–103; for variations of the view, see de Vaux, *Early History of Israel*, 752–53.

8. For discussion and bibliography, see B. Lindars, "The Israelite Tribes in Judges," in *Studies in the Historical Books of the Old Testament*, ed. J. A. Emerton, VTSup 30 (Leiden, Netherlands: E. J. Brill, 1979), 95–11; de Vaux, *Early History of Israel*, 695–715.

9. Harrison, *Introduction to the Old Testament*, 681.

10. See also J. A. Soggin, *Judges: A Commentary*, trans. J. S. Bowden, OTL (Philadelphia: Westminster, 1981), 115; for opposing view, see R. G. Boling, *Judges: A New Translation with Introduction and Commentary*, AB (Garden City, N.Y.: Doubleday, 1975), 131: "aristocrat."

11. A. Malamat, "Charismatic Leadership in the Book of Judges," in *Magnalia Dei: The Mighty Acts of God*, ed. F. M. Cross et al. (Garden City, N.Y.: Doubleday, 1976), 163–64.

12. See ibid., 152–68, for full discussion.

13. The expression translates "Retterbuch," applied by W. Richter to the main part of the book, here used of Judg. 2:16–16:31, with the exceptions of 10:1–5 and 12:8–15 (see W. Richter, *Traditionsgeschichtliche Untersuchungen zum Richterbuch*, BBB 18 [Bonn: P. Hanstein, 1963]; W. Richter, *Die Bearbeitung des "Retterbuches" in der deuteronomisticschen Epoche*, BBB 21 [Bonn: P. Hanstein, 1964]).

14. Judg. 3:31.

15. Compare later reflection in 2 Sam. 7:11 (= 1 Chr 17:10), "from the day that I commanded Judges to be over my people Israel."

16. See J. Bright, *A History of Israel*, 3d ed. (Philadelphia: Westminster, 1981), 162–82, who drops the term *amphictyony*, but replaces it with *tribal league*.

17. Lindars, *Israelite Tribes in Judges*, 95–112.

18. There are 184 occurrences in 9,884 words, or 1.86%. Compare the proportions for the remaining books of the Pentateuch and the Joshua–Kings corpus: Gen. 43:20611 (.002%), Exod. 170:16712 (1.02%), Lev. 74:11950 (.62%), Num. 238:16413 (1.45%), Deut. 72:14294 (.5%), Josh. 160:10051 (1.59%), 1 Sam. 151:13264 (1.14%), 2 Sam. 117:11036 (1.06%), 1 Kgs. 203:13140 (1.54%), 2 Kgs. 164:12280 (1.34%). The figures for the words in the

books are derived from E. Jenni and C. Westermann, eds., *Theologisches Handwörterbuch zum Alten Testament* (Zurich: C. Kaiser Verlag, 1979), 2:539.

19. Judg. 20:11, 17, 20 (2 times), 22, 33, 36, 38, 39 (2 times), 41, 42, 48; 21:1. As if to emphasize that the Benjamites were not to be considered less Israelite, their kinship to the remaining tribes is noted (20:13, 23).

20. *běnê yiśrā'ēl* 61 times. G. A. Danell's comment (*Studies in the Name Israel in the Old Testament* [Uppsala, Sweden: Appelbergs, 1946], 67), that the variation between *běnê yiśrā'ēl* and the simple form seems purely arbitrary needs some qualification. Although multiple member construct chains occur in Judg. 4:24 *(yad běnê yiśrā'ēl)* and 3:2 *(dōrōt běnê yiśrā'ēl)*, these are exceptional cases. (The longest construct chain involving the long form is found in Num 14:5, "all the assembly of the congregation of the sons of Israel").

21. Judg. 3:10; 4:4; 10:2, 3; 12:7, 8, 9, 11 (2 times), 13, 14; 15:20; 16:31; Judg. 9:22; 14:4 (the Philistines); Judg. 3:31; 6:14, 15, 32, 36; 10:1; 13:15; Judg. 17:6; 18:1; 19:1; 21:25, respectively. Compare the deliverer saving *běnê yiśrā'ēl* in Judg. 3:9.

22. Judg. 20:2, 10, 12; 21:5, 8, 15. See also 18:1.

23. The annalistic summary of the conquest in Judg. 1:1–36, lists under the *běnê yiśrā'ēl* Judah, Simeon, Benjamin, Joseph, Manasseh, Ephraim, Zebulun, Asher, Dan, and Naphtali. The only deliverer identified by tribe is Ehud, a Benjamite (3:15). The Deborah–Barak account in chapter 4 refers to Ephraim, Naphtali, and Zebulun. Gideon's forces *('îš yiśrā'ēl)* include men from Manasseh, Ashur, Zebulun, and Naphtali (6:35; 7:23). Ephraim is offended for not having been invited. In 10:9 the sons of Israel being afflicted by the Ammonites include Benjamin, Judah, and Ephraim. Gilead was also obviously included. In 20:1 all the *běnê yiśrā'ēl* are identified geographically as coming "from Dan to Beersheba and the land of Gilead." On this expression, see M. Soebø, "Grenzbeschreibung und Landideal im Alten Testament mit Besonderer Berücksichtigung der *min-'ad* Formel," *ZDPV* 90 (1974): 21–22. Soebø observes that the expression concerns above all else the people and land of Israel as a whole and unity.

24. The expression never appears after the division of the kingdom (see 1 Sam 3:20; 2 Sam 3:10; 17:11; 24:2,15; 1 Kgs 5:5; 1 Chr 21:2), except in 2 Chr. 30:5, where Hezekiah is apparently attempting to recapture pan-Israelite jurisdiction in his religious reforms, after the pattern of David's and Solomon's realms.

25. On the authenticity and antiquity of these lists, see de Vaux, *Early History of Israel,* 759.

26. Judg. 5:1, 3, 5, 7, 9. Note especially her self-designation as "mother in Israel," v. 7.

27. Included are Ephraim, Benjamin, Zebulun, Issachar, Reuben, Gilead, Dan, and Naphtali (5:14–19). These are to be compared with other early tribal lists, namely the Blessing of Jacob (Gen 49), and the Blessing of Moses (Deut 33), both of which name most of these tribes. On the dates of these texts, see F. M. Cross and D. N. Freedman, *Studies in Early Yahwistic Poetry, SBL Dissertations Series* 21 (Missoula, Mont.: Scholars Press, 1975), 5–7.

28. See R. J. Williams, *Documents from Old Testament Times* (London: Thomas Nelson & Sons, 1958), 140. B. Mazar, "The Exodus and Conquest," *WHJP* III, 3:81, agrees that Israel is mentioned as an ethnic group but suggests that a group of Israelite tribes had already settled in Canaan at the time.

29. See my discussion in *The Foundations of National Identity: A Study in Ancient Northwest Semitic Perspectives* (Ann Arbor, Mich.: University Microfilms, 1983), 1–83.

30. In Judg. 3:5–6 the narrator laments the breakdown of this ethnic distinction by the cohabitation and intermarriage of the Israelites with the Canaanites. See the appearance of both ideas in Gen. 34:15–16, "If you will become like us in that every male among you will be circumcised, then we will give our daughters to you, and we will take your daughters to ourselves, and we will live *(wěyāšabnû)* with you and become one people *('am 'eḥād)."*

31. *'am šōqēṭ ûbōṭēaḥ,* on which, see A. Malamat, "The Danite Migration and the Pan-Israelite Exodus–Conquest," *Bib* 51 (1970): 5–6.

32. See my discussion " 'Israel'–'sons of Israel': A Study in Hebrew Eponymic Usage," *Studies in Religion* 13 (1984): 3:301–26. A. Malamat observes that the expression "people of Israel"

('am yiśrā'ēl) first occurs in 2 Sam. 18:7; 19:14 (but compare the appositional phrase, "the people, Israel" [hā'ām yiśrā'ēl] in Josh 8:33) but that this represents the end of a progression of expressions, běnê yiśrā'ēl — 'am běnê yiśrā'ēl (Exod 1:9) 'am yiśrā'ēl ("The Proto-History of Israel: A Study in Method," in The Word of the Lord Shall Go Forth, ed. C. L. Meyers and M. O'Connor [Winona Lake, Ind.: Eisenbrauns, 1983], 304).

33. See 1 Kgs. 9:13, Hiram and Solomon; 1 Kgs. 20:32-33, Ahab and Benhadad. See also N. K. Gottwald, The Tribes of Yahweh: A Sociology of the Religion of Liberated Israel, 1250-1050 B.C.E. (Maryknoll, N.Y.: Orbis Books, 1979), 524: "'aḥîm may be relatives by descent or 'brothers' by political commitment."

34. See the Blessing of Jacob, Genesis 49.

35. Judg. 4:6; 5:3, 5; 6:8; 11:21, 23 (juxtaposed with Chemosh, the god of the Ammonites [sic]); 21:3.

36. "Your God" ('ĕlōhêkā), 6:26; "our God" ('ĕlōhênû), 10:10; 16:23, 24; "their God" ('ĕlōhêhem), 3:7; 8:34. Compare the reference to Dagon as "their god," that is, of the Philistines, in 16:23.

37. The expression occurs only here and 2 Sam. 14:13 ('am 'ĕlōhîm), but compare Ps. 47:10, 'am 'ĕlōhê 'abrāhām ("the people of the God of Abraham").

38. Noth, History, 95-96, believes the ark moved from Shechem to Bethel to Gilgal and finally to Shiloh.

39. See also Lindars, Israelite Tribes in Judges, 111. But see the reference to the celebration of the Passover in the period of the judges in 2 Kgs. 23:22.

40. See Block, Foundations of National Identity, 84-127 and 493-521.

41. See A. Cody, "When Is the Chosen People Called a Gôy?" VT (1964): 1-6.

42. See Exod. 12:21; 17:5-6; 18:12; 19:7; 24:1, 9; Lev. 4:15; 9:1; Num. 16:25; Deut. 27:1; 31:9, 28; Josh. 7:6; 8:10.

43. Deut. 19:12; 21:1-9, 18-21; 22:13-21; 25:1-10; compare Josh. 20:4. Ruth 4:1-12 provides the clearest picture of such civil procedures.

44. On the role of the elders, see R. de Vaux, Ancient Israel (New York: McGraw–Hill, 1965), 152-53.

45. For example, 2 Sam. 23:8-39; 1 Chr. 11:6, 10, 11, 15, 20, 42; 12:3, 14, 18, 20, 23, 32; 27:3. For a detailed discussion, see J. R. Bartlett, "The Use of the Word ראש as a Title in the Old Testament," VT 19 (1969): 1-3.

46. Deut. 33:2-5, 21: compare Num. 25:4-5; Job 29:25. For discussion, see Bartlett, "Use of the Word ראש," 4-7.

47. See also Bartlett (ibid.), 10. On the use of the term, see further, H. P. Müller, "ראש rō'š Kopf," in E. Jenni and C. Westermann, eds., Theologisches Handwörterbuch zum Alten Testament, 2:701-15.

48. The term is derived from a root meaning "to write." The extent to which scribal activity was involved in their work is unclear. For discussion, see de Vaux, Ancient Israel, 155; Bartlett, "Use of the Word ראש," 4, n. 3.

49. See the expression "In those days there was no king in Israel; everyone did that which was right in his own eyes" (Judg 17:6; 18:1; 19:1; 20:25); for discussion, see the W. J. Dumbrell, " 'In those days there was no king in Israel; every man did that which was right in his own eyes.' The Purpose of the Book of Judges Reconsidered," JSOT 25 (1983): 23-33.

50. Note the question posed to YHWH, "Who shall go up first?" (Judg 1:1), assuming from the outset independence of action.

51. On Abimelech as the antitheses of the charismatic leadership of the judges, see Malamat, "Charismatic Leadership," 163-64.

52. With an ironical touch, in Judg. 20:18 the narrator brings his readers full circle by having the Israelite tribes pose the same question they had raised earlier with reference to the Canaanites and framing YHWH's response as an echo of 1:1-2 (see also Boling, Judges, 286).

53. A. E. Cundall, "Judges—An Apology for the Monarchy?" Exp Tim 81 (1970): 178-81. See also the comment of the esteemed scholar in whose honor this essay is written, Introduction

        to the Old Testament, 692: "The purpose of the work was to show that a centralized hereditary kingship was necessary for the well being of the Covenant theocracy."

54. See the designation of the Joshua–Kings corpus as the Former Prophets in the Hebrew canon.

55. B. S. Childs, *Introduction to the Old Testament as Scripture* (Philadelphia: Fortress, 1979), 259.

56. For full discussion, see P. C. Craigie, "A Reconsideration of Shamgar Ben Anath (Judg 3:31 and 5:6)," *JBL* 91 (1972): 239–40; compare de Vaux, *Early History of Israel,* 823.

57. See Judg. 3:31; 5:6. The name *ben ʿānāt* has surfaced on an arrowhead apparently dating from the period of the judges (see F. M. Cross, "Newly Found Inscriptions in Old Canaanite and Early Phoenician Scripts," *BASOR* 238 [1980]: 6–7). For further discussion, see my " 'Israel'–'Sons of Israel,' " 3:301–26.

58. B. Lindars, "Deborah's Song: Women in the Old Testament," *BJRL* 65 (1983): 158–75.

59. See G. W. Ahlström, *Aspects of Syncretism in Israelite Religion* (Lund, Sweden: C. W. K. Gleerup, 1963), 14–24.

60. The name *yôʾāš* means "Yahweh is strong" (F. Brown, S. R. Driver, and C. A. Briggs, *A Hebrew and English Lexicon of the Old Testament* [Oxford: Clarendon Press, 1907], 219–20). The only other Yahwistic names from this period are Jotham (9:5), Micah/Micaiah (17:4), Jehonathan (18:30), Joel (1 Sam 8:2). For studies of these names, see M. Noth, *Die israelitischen Personennamen im Rahmen der gemeinsemitschen Namengebung* (Stuttgart: Kohlhammer, 1928), 101–3; Z. Zevit, "A Chapter in the History of Israelite Personal Names," *BASOR* 250 (1983): 1–16, esp. 3.

61. See Boling, *Judges,* 144, that for the narrator Jerubbaal "stands for God's accomplishment through this one historical savior," which hardly suits the present context.

62. Compare 2 Sam. 11:21, Jerubbesheth. Compare also Ishbaal/Ishbosheth, 1 Chr. 8:33; 9:39/ 2 Sam. 2:8, 10, 12, 15; 3:8, 14, 15; 4:5, 8, 12; Meribbaal/Mephibosheth, 1 Chr. 8:34; 9:40/2 Sam. 4:4.

63. Compare the following two selected from numerous similar Punic inscriptions:

      lrbt ltnt pn bʿl   To the lady, Tanit, the face of Baal
      wlʾdn lbʿl ḥmn   and the lord Baal-Hamon.
      ʾš ndr knmy   That which was vowed by *knmy*
      ʿbd ʾšmnʿmš   servant of *ʾšmnʿmš,*
      bn bʿlytn bʾsry   son of *Bʿlytn,* his child.
      tbrkʾ   May she bless him. (KAI 79:1–6)

      lrbt ltnt pn bʿl   To the lady, to Tanit, the face of Baal,
      wlʾdn lbʿl ḥmn   and the lord, Baal-Hamon.
      ʾš ndr mtnbʿl   That which was vowed by *Mtnbʿl,*
      ʾšt ʿbdmlqrt   the wife of *ʿbdmlqrt,*
      bn bʿlḥnʾ bn bdʿštrt the son of *bʿlḥnʾ,* the son of *Bdʿštrt,*
      k šmʿ qlʾ   because they (the deities)
                   heard her voice.
      ybrkʾ   May they bless her. (KAI 88:1–6)

64. Compare the king of Moab's sacrifice of his eldest son in a time of distress (2 Kgs 3:27). On the subject, see de Vaux, *Ancient Israel,* 441–46; G. C. Heider, *The Cult of Molek: A Reassessment, JSOTS* 43 (Sheffield, England: JSOT Press, 1985), and the popular treatment of L. E. Stager and S. R. Wolff, "Child Sacrifice at Carthage: Religious Rite or Population Control," *BAR* 10 (1984): 31–51.

65. On Jephthah, see P. Trible, "A Meditation in Mourning: The Sacrifice of the Daughter of Jephthah," *USQR* 36 Supplement (1981): 59–60.

66. See J. Gray, *Joshua, Judges and Ruth,* NCB (Greenwood, S.C.: Attic Press, 1967), 234–35, who argues that some of the Samson stories may represent historifications of a solar myth.

67. See Boling, *Judges,* 225. The significance of the *-wn* ending is unclear, but it may serve as a diminutive, hence "little sun" ("Sunnyboy!").

68. Note especially the ethically problematic (from the modern perspective) explanation of the narrator for Samson's interest in Philistine women (Judg 14:4).
69. See W. S. LaSor, D. A. Hubbard, and F. W. Bush, *Old Testament Survey: The Message, Form, and Background of the Old Testament* (Grand Rapids, Mich.: Wm. Eerdmans, 1982), 223: "as God himself recognized."
70. Compare Judg. 3:10; 11:29; 14:6, 19; 15:14; 1 Sam. 10:10; 11:6; 16:13.
71. The Samson narrative is especially instructive in that he does not get involved with the Philistines until after the Spirit of YHWH has begun to stir him (Judg 13:25).

5

The Prophets during the Monarchy:
Turning Points in Israel's Decline

William Sanford LaSor

When I first began Old Testament studies, some scholars held that the prophets were God's "advisors to the kings."[1] If we accept the view that Samuel was the last of the judges and the first of the prophets,[2] then we can say that the office of prophet began about the same time as the beginning of the monarchy. It is also true that the prophetic office ceased, for a while, soon after the end of the kingdom of Judah. These statements, as we shall see, must be examined carefully.

There were, of course, prophets before the time of Samuel. The term is used of Abraham (Gen 20:7), Moses (Deut 34:10; Hos 12:13), and others. The Hebrew canon contains the Former Prophets, suggesting that some relationship between those writings and the writings of the Latter Prophets was seen by those who collected the canonical scriptures. Then, there is the curious statement that "he who is now called a prophet was formerly called a seer" (1 Sam 9:9), possibly a gloss, but at any rate suggesting that the term *prophet* had come into a new period of usage with Samuel.[3]

But if there was some kind of newness of the prophetic office with Samuel and the rise of the monarchy, there was also a clear-cut distinction between the Former and the Latter Prophets. This distinction is not merely chronological. An important difference between them is found in two facts: (1) the prophets prior to the eighth century B.C. were primarily advisors to the kings, whereas those from Amos on were often bypassing the kings and going to the people; and (2) the eleventh- through ninth-century B.C. prophets, while they may have left us some literary remains (for example, Samuel), did not put their prophetic messages into written form in the manner attributed to the eighth-through sixth-century B.C. prophets.

The Book of Samuel is quite distinct from the Book of Jeremiah or even, more obviously, Amos. The book called Samuel was attributed to Samuel,[4] and it does contain some accounts of his life and ministry. It was considered canonical and therefore was believed to be inspired. It is not history, although it contains much historical material; rather, it is a theological interpretation of history. But the works of the Latter Prophets differ in that (1) they give little historical material—sometimes none (for example, Joel); and (2) they consist largely of the prophetic utterances of the prophets (Jonah is a notable exception). The Book of Amos is composed largely of the preaching of Amos; the Book of Samuel differs markedly in this respect.[5]

The questions I will consider here, briefly stated, are these: What caused the difference between the Former Prophets and the Latter Prophets? What happened early in the eighth century B.C. that resulted in the prophetic works of Amos, Hosea, Micah, and Isaiah, as well as the prophets that followed? Obviously, it was not the division of the monarchy into the Northern and Southern Kingdoms (Israel and Judah), for that occurred in the latter part of the tenth century (ca. 931 B.C.). Nor was it the fall of Samaria (722 B.C.), although this is certainly related to the primary cause.

For the cause, we must turn to the prophet Amos, because he is generally considered to be the earliest of the Latter Prophets.[6] These statements will serve our purpose: "You only have I known of all the families of the earth; therefore I will punish you for all your iniquities" (Amos 3:2). "Because I will do this to you, prepare to meet your God, O Israel!" (4:12). "The end has come upon my people Israel" (8:2).

The people as a whole are addressed. While the kings were regularly addressed by the Former Prophets, and found wanting, they were not the sole cause of the present condition. In now by-passing the king, Amos not only remonstrates against the monarchy but against the source of the trouble: violation of the Sinai covenant by the people as a whole.

The context of Amos' prophecy must be examined. This shows that YHWH has been long-suffering with his people. The refrain, "yet you did not return to me," repeated five times (4:6–11), recalls various acts of YHWH whereby he sought to call his people to repentance—but they did not return to him. The bill of particulars of YHWH's judgment on Israel (2:6–16) rehearses some of the mighty acts of YHWH on Israel's behalf. Finally, YHWH's patience has almost reached its limit. Israel, a harlot wife like Gomer, has been cast out and is "not my people" (Hos 1:9). Samaria will be a "heap in the open country," and her idols will be laid waste, "for from the hire of a harlot she gathered them, and to the hire of a harlot they shall return" (Mic 1:6–7). Israel, the Northern Kingdom, the "Oholah" of Ezekiel's metaphor of two sisters (Ezek 23:4), has reached the point of no return. The Sinai covenant has been broken irrevocably.

AN ELECT PEOPLE AND TASK

To understand the prophecy of YHWH's judgment, we must first understand the prophetic concept of Israel. This people was not just another of the nations of the world. If we attempted to study the biblical history of Israel in the same way that we might study the history of other nations, we would continually run into problems that have no solution. The efforts of nineteenth-century scholars to group the ancient Near East into a whole, and to study the development of Israel as part of the development of the entire region, failed — and the failure was due to refusing to accept the biblical position that Israel was in a very real sense "God's people."[7]

This was Amos' view: "You only have I known of all the families of the earth" (Amos 3:2). Obviously, the verb *know* does not refer to knowledge about, for the omniscient God of the prophets knew all about Damascus, Gaza, Tyre, Edom, the Ammonites and Moabites, Assyria, and Babylonia. He brought the Philistines from Caphtor, and the Syrians from Kir (9:7). The verb *know* involves an intimacy, a relationship similar to that of a husband who *knows* his wife with the resulting production of "seed."

The biblical concept of Israel was traced back to the Abrahamic promise, "I will make of you a great nation . . . and by you all the families of the earth will be blessed" (Gen 12:2–3). What was meant by "the descendants of Abraham" (called "seed" in a number of passages) became a moot question. Some held that only those physically descended from Abraham, specifically through Isaac and Jacob, were Abraham's seed. But the Israelites who were delivered from Egypt by YHWH were a mixed multitude (Exod 12:38). The "sojourner" was also a part of Israel, subject to the laws of Israel's God (20:10). Descendants of gentile mothers were counted among the Israelites, of whom were the Midianite Zipporah, mother of Moses' son Gershom (2:21–22), and Ruth the Moabitess who gave rise to the line of David (Ruth 4:17).[8]

When the Israelite nation was founded (as I understand the Exodus–Sinai event), YHWH told Moses to say to the people, "Now therefore, if you will obey my voice and keep my covenant, you shall be my own possession among all peoples; for all the earth is mine, and you shall be to me a kingdom of priests and a holy nation" (Exod 19:5–6). There are three points here: (1) the Lord of all the earth explicitly singles out Israel to be his own possession; (2) he declares that Israel is to be a kingdom of priests; and (3) Israel is to be a holy nation.

Of all the nations of the world, Israel was to be the singular possession of YHWH. This can be seriously misinterpreted, and has been. It can be looked upon as an end in itself. If so viewed, God can be accused of favoritism. Why should one people be chosen and the others ignored or, worse, damned? But there is a complementary statement, namely that Israel was to be a kingdom of priests. What is a priest? By common definition, it is a mediator, a person who stands between God and the sinner, who presents the sinner's offering of repentance to God and who makes God's pardon known to the sinner. But if Israel is the priest, to whom does Israel minister? Obviously, to the nations of the world. In other words, Israel's election is to bring the nations (Gentiles) to God. This was the original plan in the call of Abraham (Gen 12:3), and its fulfillment is projected more specifically in some prophecies of Isaiah (Isa 61:6; 66:20–21).

How was Israel's mediation to be accomplished? Israel was to be a holy nation. Again, if we limit our interpretation to secular meanings of words, we might conclude that Israel was to be a separated people, set apart — that is the basic meaning of the root *qdš*—and walled off from the rest of the world. That, apparently, was the original meaning of the term translated "Pharisees." That, according to a popular but mistaken etymology, is the meaning of *ekklēsia*, "church."[9] But *holy* must be defined by its biblical point of reference. YHWH told Moses to tell the people of Israel, "You shall be holy; for I YHWH your God am holy" (Lev 19:2). The biblical meaning of the term must therefore be derived from studying YHWH himself.

In a sense, YHWH *is* separated from the world. He is in heaven, and we are on earth (Eccl 5:2). YHWH is also separated from sin and every kind of immorality. He is the standard of righteousness, and whatever is not found in him or does not proceed from him is not good. Therefore his people must be righteous. But this separation of God from the world is again not an end, but a means. The heavens are high above the earth, and that is a measure of his *ḥesed*, his covenant love. The east is separated from the west, and that is a simile of how far he removes our transgressions from us (Ps 103:11–12). Wherever we find the concept of the election of God's people, we find that it is ultimately redemptive. His people are chosen to bring the nations to him (Isa 49:5–6; 56:6–7).

ISRAEL'S RESPONSE

Against this background we must consider the sins of Israel. Ezekiel presents Israel's history in allegorical form, using the figures of a faithless wife and two daughters (Ezek 16:3–63). The figure of an unfaithful wife is also used in Hosea (chap. 2), Isaiah (50:1), and Jeremiah (2:1–3; 3:1–5). But the best way to comprehend Israel's faithlessness is to survey the material in the Pentateuch and the Former Prophets.

The miraculous deliverance of the Israelite tribes from Egyptian bondage was scarcely three months old, and Moses was still on the Mount, receiving instructions from YHWH, when the people made the golden calf (Exod 32:1–10). It was clearly an apostasy, a rejection of YHWH and a turning to the gods of Egypt (Exod 32:4, 8; Ezek 20:8). Possibly it was also an orgy, evidenced by the difficult statement in Exod. 32:25.[10] The intercession of Moses provided YHWH with the occasion to manifest his grace (Exod 32:31–32; 33:12–17). This was not the first indication of Israel's dissatisfaction with YHWH's deliverance. At the Sea of Reeds, the children of Israel had wanted to return to Egypt (14:11–12). They complained about the bitter water at Marah (15:23–24). They murmured about having no food (16:3) and not enough water (17:3). One must admit that the choosing of Israel was not based on Israel's merit, but solely on YHWH's grace.

After the apostasy of worshiping the golden calf and its terrible consequences, the people again showed their rebellious and stubborn nature. They complained about the manna and demanded meat (Num 11:4–6); YHWH gave them quails (11:31–32). Twelve men were sent to spy out the land of Canaan that YHWH had promised to give them. On their return, ten of them reported on the difficulties (13:27–29), and the people longed to be back in Egypt (14:1–4). Again, Moses' intercession saved the people from destruction (14:11–25; compare Ezek 20:8–17).

When we consider the events that happened in a single generation,[11] the contrast between the constant goodness of YHWH and the complaints, rebellions, and faithlessness of his people is almost incredible. Indeed, some students of the Bible have found it incredible and have attempted to rewrite or revise the stories. A people who had witnessed the deliverance from Egypt, the parting of the Red Sea, the thunderings at Sinai, the gifts of manna and quails, the terrible judgments at Sinai and on Kohath and his fellows in rebellion, as well as the miraculous victories over the Amalekites, Sihon king of the Amorites, and Og king of Bashan—how could they fail to give to YHWH total and cordial submission?

Again there was apostasy. "Israel yoked himself to Baal of Peor" (Num 25:3). While the Israelites were encamped at Shittim, the people bowed down to the gods of the Moabites and played the harlot with the daughters of Moab (25:1–2). Twenty-four thousand Israelites were struck down with the plague (25:1–9; Deut 4:3). The event was etched deeply in Israel's memory (Ps 106:28–31; Hos 9:10). "What happened from Shittim to Gilgal" refers to "the saving acts of YHWH" (Mic 6:5; compare Josh 3:1–4:24). But Shittim and Gilgal also called to mind the sins of Israel (Hos 4:15; 9:15; 12:11; Amos 4:4; 5:4).

Gilgal was the Israelites' first encampment after crossing the Jordan and entering the land of Canaan (Josh 4:19). It was the scene of the circumcision of the generation born in the wilderness (5:2) and of the first Passover observed in the land (5:10). It was the place where the ark was located until it was transferred to Shiloh (18:1).[12] Saul was crowned king at Gilgal (1 Sam 11:14–15). David was received back as king at Gilgal after the death of Absalom (2 Sam 19:40). Gilgal had become a cult center (see 1 Sam 15:21), dating probably from the entrance into Canaan, but assuming more importance after the destruction of Shiloh (Jer 7:14; Ps 78:60). Just exactly what about Gilgal aroused the ire of the prophets is not specifically stated; some think they harbored animosity toward the kingship. More likely the object of their ire was the development of a ritual without ethical content, which was a turning-away from the law of YHWH.

THE INFLUENCE OF THE MONARCHY

The establishment of the Davidic dynasty (2 Sam 7), ideally, should have ended the days of apostasy and ushered in the everlasting kingdom (7:13). With the inauguration of a new phase of the prophetic office to give YHWH's word to the king, and with the power of two mighty kings—David and Solomon—in succession, how could it be otherwise? But the story quickly shows the fallacy of thinking that the solution is found in the national leader. Solomon, after an auspicious beginning, degenerated into an apostate

(1 Kgs 11:4–11). The division of the kingdom into two parts (11:13; 12:20) was the beginning of the end. The erection of cult centers at Bethel and Dan by Jeroboam (12:28–30), with a golden calf at each shrine, was specifically intended to replace Jerusalem, and the calves were not (as sometimes suggested)[13] visible supports of the invisible YHWH, but of the "gods" who had brought them out of Egypt (12:28).

But YHWH is patient, and he gave his people the opportunity to repent. He also attempted various means of persuasion: war, drought, famine, and pestilence (see Amos 4:6–11). There were good kings who followed in the way of David and who destroyed the "high places," or centers of apostate cults. And there were bad kings who did not walk in the way of David, who built altars and high places. When Jezebel attempted to wipe the worship of YHWH from the land and install the prophets of Baal and Asherah, YHWH sent the prophet Elijah to confront these prophets (1 Kgs 18:17–40). When the army of Benhadad besieged Samaria, the prophet Elisha was empowered to bring about the flight of the Syrians (2 Kgs 6:24; 7:20). One of the sons of the prophets, a disciple in a training school led by Elisha, anointed Jehu as king to destroy the house of Ahab (9:1–11). And there were other events that demonstrated YHWH's desire that his people should return to him.

On occasion, there was an event that could lead us to incorrect conclusions. Joash was a "good" king (12:2); therefore, we might assume that everything he did was in accordance with YHWH's will. When Hazael, king of Syria, took Gath and then turned toward Jerusalem, Joash took the votive gifts and the gold of the treasuries of the temple and palace and, with these treasures, bought off Hazael (12:17–18). The account contains no remonstration, but we know from similar situations that this act demonstrated a lack of faith in YHWH. Later prophets would consider such actions a perverse kind of harlotry, in which the harlot pays her lovers for their favors (see Ezek 16:33–34).

At the beginning of the eighth century B.C., Jeroboam II succeeded his father Jehoash, first as coregent and then as king of Israel. At the same time, Amaziah was king of Judah, and Azariah (Uzziah) became his coregent. For the next forty years, both the Northern and Southern Kingdoms enjoyed splendid, prosperous days. It was as though YHWH were giving them one last chance. From Amos, we know what happened, particularly in Jeroboam's kingdom. Luxury, oppression, and disobedience to YHWH's law pervaded Israel, and even extended to Judah (Amos 2:4–8). The mention of Beersheba as one of the cult centers of Israel, along with Gilgal and Bethel (5:5), suggests that northerners were making pilgrimages to the southernmost part of Judah.[14] "The way *(derek)* of Beersheba" (8:14) may refer to either the pilgrim route or the ritual performed there.[15]

Jeroboam II was succeeded by five kings in the next twenty years—a time of great turmoil (2 Kgs 15:8–31), and then Hoshea reigned for nine years as the last king of Israel. The Assyrian king, Tiglath-pileser, claimed he made Hoshea king,[16] but this is not suggested by the biblical account. Tiglath-pileser had already taken much of the Northern Kingdom and probably exacted tribute from Hoshea, as did his successor Shalmaneser (17:1–3). Hoshea is described as one "who did what was evil in the sight of YHWH, yet not as the kings of Israel who were before him" (17:2). Finally, when Hoshea turned to Egypt for aid, the Assyrian king laid Samaria under siege (17:4–5). In 722 B.C. Samaria fell, and the Northern Kingdom was no more. Amos' prophecy to Amaziah, the priest of Bethel, had been fulfilled (see Amos 7:16–17).

THE KINGDOM OF JUDAH

It is important to note that YHWH did not destroy Judah at the same time. However, the prophecy of Amos seems to include Judah with Israel in the coming judgment (2:4–5; 9:11). Likewise the northern prophet Hosea includes Judah in his prophecy of judgment (Hos 12:2). And it is true that Judah must undergo judgment. But there was a period of more than a century during which YHWH's prophets attempted to turn Judah back to his law. These prophets were Isaiah, Zephaniah, Jeremiah, and probably Habakkuk, Obadiah, and Joel.

The sins of Judah were deep-rooted, going back to Solomon. Not only was his apostasy a sin, but his trust in material power was contrary to the will of YHWH (Pss 20:7; 33:17; 2 Chr 32:8; Jer 17:5). Moreover, because of the heavy burden of taxation he imposed on the people, and because his son and successor, Rehoboam, refused to alter this policy, the northern tribes revolted (1 Kgs 12:12–16). Under Rehoboam, there was a considerable turning to false gods. In addition, he paid tribute to Egypt (14:22–26).

Jehoshaphat is generally regarded as one of the "good" kings of Judah; he not only "did what was right in the sight of YHWH" but also entered into a peace treaty with the Northern Kingdom (22:43–44). It is ironic that (possibly as a part of this treaty) his son and successor should be closely tied with Ahab's children: Jezebel's daughter, Athaliah, became his daughter-in-law (2 Kgs 8:16–18), and Ahaziah, Ahab's grandson (as well as his own) succeeded Jehoram as king of Judah (8:25–26).[17] Even more ironic is the fact that Ahaziah died within the year and was succeeded by his wife, Athalia, who attempted to destroy all the royal family (11:1–3). "That wicked woman" certainly attempted to replace all remaining worship of YHWH with Baalism (2 Chr 24:7). When Jehoiada the priest led a revolt against her and set Joash on the throne (2 Kgs 11:12), it was necessary to destroy the house of Baal and slay the priest of Baal in order to restore the covenant with YHWH (11:18).

Again we see how shallow attempts at reformation were. Joash, who had been saved from Athalia's plot by Jehoiada's wife, placed on the throne by Jehoiada, and instructed by him in the way of YHWH, seems to have lost confidence in Jehoiada (11:2, 7, 12). After the death of Jehoiada, Joash turned to the princes of Judah for counsel, and once more there was worship of the Asherim and the idols. Finally, Joash was slain in a palace coup; according to the Chronicler he was slain because he was responsible for the death of Jehoiada's son (2 Chr 24:17–18, 22, 25).

This brings us to the eighth century B.C., the hour of doom for the Northern Kingdom. In this century, the kings of the Southern Kingdom were Uzziah, Jotham, Ahaz, and Hezekiah. Uzziah was a "good" king (2 Kgs 15:3), but he became proud, undertook to perform a priestly prerogative, and was smitten with leprosy (2 Chr 26:16–19). According to Josephus, the earthquake (see also Amos 1:1; Zech 14:5) occurred while Uzziah was defending this action.[18] Isaiah was probably a member of his court, and it was in the year Uzziah died that Isaiah "saw YHWH" and was called to prophesy (Isa 6:1, 9).

Jotham became coregent (ca. 751 B.C.) when Uzziah's leprosy barred Uzziah from public life (see 1 Kgs 15:5). Jotham was a "good" king, but his people were corrupt (2 Chr 27:2). Ahaz became coregent in 735 B.C., and the following year, Tiglath-pileser III led an expedition into Philistine territory. Rezin of Syria, Pekah of the Northern Kingdom, and a number of smaller states formed the Syro–Ephraimite coalition to oppose the Assyrians, and they attempted to get Ahaz to join them. When he refused, they launched an attack on Judah (2 Kgs 15:37; 16:5). Ahaz was terrified, but Isaiah counseled him to put his trust in YHWH (Isa 7:1–9), predicting that within a very short time the "two smoldering stumps of firebrands" (7:4), Rezin and Pekah, would no longer be a threat.

Ahaz, nevertheless, rejected YHWH's word, turned instead to the king of Assyria for aid (2 Kgs 16:7–9), and became his vassal. The apostasy of Ahaz is marked by a number of wicked deeds, including making molten images for the Baals, burning incense in the valley of Hinnom, sacrificing on high places, burning his own son after the fashion of the pagan nations (2 Kgs 16:3–4; 2 Chr 28:2–4), and copying an altar at Damascus and erecting it in the temple and offering sacrifices on it (2 Kgs 16:10–16; compare 2 Chr 28:22–27). Tiglath-pileser struck at the Syro-Ephraimite alliance, overthrowing Pekah, establishing Hoshea on the throne of Samaria, and carrying away many captives.[19] YHWH was giving Judah a strong warning.

TWO LAST RAYS OF HOPE

Hezekiah became regent shortly after the coup that put Hoshea on the throne of the Northern Kingdom.[20] His reign began like a fresh wind from the Hermon. He opened the doors of the house of YHWH, which had been closed by the apostasy of Ahaz (2 Chr 29:3). He celebrated the Passover—a month late because of the time required to sanctify the temple (29:17–19; 30:3, 15). In an effort to demonstrate the unity of YHWH's people, Hezekiah even invited Israelites from the Northern Kingdom, but except for a small number, they ridiculed his suggestion (30:6–12). He put a new spirit in the priesthood and cleansed the land of much of its idolatry (chap. 31). In Hezekiah's reign, the relationship of the prophet (Isaiah) as advisor to the king assumed normalcy (Isa 37:1–7, 21).

When Sennacherib of Assyria invaded Judah, Hezekiah bought him off by paying tribute (2 Kgs 18:14). But when the Assyrians besieged Jerusalem,

Hezekiah acted with faith, accepting the counsel of Isaiah. YHWH rewarded his faith by delivering him from the Assyrian king (2 Chr 32:1–23). Hezekiah became gravely ill, but YHWH gave him the promise of fifteen additional years of life (2 Kgs 20:1–11; Isa 38:1–8). His illness brought a visit from envoys of Merodach-baladan, king of Babylon, who had staged a successful revolt against Assyria, only to be subjugated again. It is quite likely that the Babylonian was seeking an ally in the west against his Assyrian overlord.[21] Hezekiah opened up his treasure house — an act which brought strong condemnation from Isaiah, including the prophecy that Babylon would carry away everything that was in the king's house (2 Kgs 20:12–19; Isa 39:1–8).

After Hezekiah, things deteriorated rapidly in Judah. Manasseh apparently became regent in 696 B.C., at the age of twelve (2 Kgs 21:1); his gaining the regency was probably due to Hezekiah's illness, and he acceded to the throne on his father's death in 687 B.C. The fifteen years which had been added to Hezekiah's life, therefore, date from 701 B.C., the year of Sennacherib's invasion. The record of Manasseh's life can be briefly stated: he is likened to Ahab of Israel (21:3). He undid all the reforms made by his father Hezekiah. It must be recognized that his entire reign was spent under the suzerainty of Assyria, having been summoned by Esarhaddon[22] and forced to pay tribute by Ashurbanipal.[23] The latter event is probably what is referred to in 2 Chr. 33:13, and the repentance recorded there could hardly have been more than surface-deep. On the king who had the longest reign in Judah, and whose apostasies exceeded all others, YHWH laid the responsibility for the coming judgment (2 Kgs 21:10–16). In an ultimate sense, Manasseh's reign was the point of no return for Judah (2 Kgs 23:26; 24:3; Jer 15:4).

The reign of Josiah, grandson of Manasseh, was a final ray of hope. He was a "good" king (2 Kgs 22:1–2) and was placed on the throne by the people (21:24). In his days, when the temple was undergoing a thorough housecleaning, the "book of the law" was found (22:8). Whether this was the Pentateuch or simply a part or all of the Book of Deuteronomy is debatable.[24] At any rate, the reading of it led to repentance and revival (23:1–25).

The reign of Josiah coincided with the opening part of Jeremiah's prophetic ministry. The chronology of this prophetic work is very difficult to ascertain. About half of the first sixteen chapters of the Book of Jeremiah, as well as chapters 30–31, belong to this period;[25] YHWH's judgment of Judah's sin takes up a large part of chapters 2–6 and 8–9; the folly of depending on other gods is the theme of chapter 13; the command of YHWH to Jeremiah not to marry in view of impending judgment is found in 16:1–9. Assyria collapsed and was replaced by Babylonia. Egypt was too weak to be of much help. A boiling pot in the north was about to overwhelm Judah and Jerusalem (Jer 1:13–19). Josiah's reforms would strengthen the remnant of the faithful in Judah, but nothing could turn away the final doom.

Following Josiah, who was slain at Megiddo by Pharaoh Neco (2 Kgs 23:29), Jehoahaz (Shallum) reigned for three months, then was taken in bonds by Neco, who levied a heavy tribute and put Eliakim (Jehoiakim) on the throne (2 Kgs 23:31–34; Jer 22:11–19). Jehoiakim was Neco's tributary; later he became Nebuchadnezzar's vassal for three years but then revolted.[26] The only thing that saved him from the immediate wrath of Nebuchadnezzar was the fact that the Babylonian king was busy rebuilding his army.[27] When Nebuchadnezzar was ready to invade the region, Jehoiakim was dead and Jehoiachin reigned in his stead. When Nebuchadnezzar besieged Jerusalem, Jehoiachin surrendered and was taken to Babylon, and Zedekiah (Mattaniah), Jehoiachin's uncle and the son of Josiah, was placed on the throne (2 Kgs 24:10–17). When Zedekiah revolted nine years later, Nebuchadnezzar returned, besieged Jerusalem, and finally destroyed it in 586 B.C. (25:1–12).[28]

CONCLUSION

The Book of Judges lists a series of events that may be roughly outlined as follows: (a) the Israelites turn from YHWH to false gods; (b) YHWH sends an oppressor; (c) after a time, the people cry out for salvation; (d) YHWH sends a savior or "judge" (šōpēṭ) who delivers them; (e) the land has rest. This outline is quite clear in Judg. 3:7–11, and a similar pattern can be discovered in the situations under other judges in the same book.

It should have become clear to the Israelites that YHWH was indeed a "jealous" God who insisted on their absolute covenantal loyalty to him and at the same time a patient God who desired their repentance and return to him. This, in a few words, is the message of the Hebrew Bible, and in particular the message of the prophets of Israel.

However, the apostasy of kings and people in the monarchic period caused the cycle of apostasy, judgment, repentance, and salvation to be suspended by the exile. The gradual gravity built into YHWH's judgments went unheeded until a point of no return was reached. In the end there was no savior, no rest. Both king and people had strayed irrevocably from the covenant, failing to accept YHWH's warning voice through his prophets. As YHWH's messengers in a period of decline for Israel, the prophets were in a very real sense markers of the decline itself.

NOTES

1. See J. P. Hyatt, *Prophetic Religion* (New York and Nashville: Abingdon–Cokesbury, 1947), 17–18, 136–37.
2. See Acts 3:24; 13:20.
3. For a discussion, see H. H. Rowley, *The Servant of the Lord and Other Essays on the Old Testament*, 2d ed. (Oxford: Basil Blackwell, 1965), 105–8.
4. Baba Bathra 47b.
5. For a fuller discussion, see W. S. LaSor, D. A. Hubbard, and F. W. Bush, *Old Testament*

Survey (Grand Rapids, Mich.: Wm. Eerdmans, 1982), 190–96, 298–306. Obviously, if Jeremiah had been writing only for the king, there would be no reason to rewrite his prophecy after Jehoiakim destroyed the first copy (Jer 36:23–28).

6. Some would date Joel earlier than Amos (see J. Robertson, "Joel," *ISBE* [1929]: 3:1690).

7. The twentieth-century attempt to explain Israel by comparing its situation with modern socio–economic problems is likewise doomed to failure (see N. K. Gottwald, *The Tribes of Yahweh, A Sociology of the Religion of Liberated Israel, 1250–1050 B.C.* [Maryknoll, N.Y.: Orbis Books, 1979]). There were, of course, such problems, just as there were international problems. Israel did not exist in a vacuum. But the prophetic (and biblical) view sees God's hand at work in a specific and peculiar way with reference to Israel.

8. Ezra's efforts to secure a pureblood Israel were well intentioned and, for the contemporary situation, necessary. But we cannot help but wonder what he would have done with the gentile sojourners and the children of marriages with Gentiles that had occurred in Israel prior to the exile. And we must ask ourselves, how many of the Jews of the Second Commonwealth were descended from the priests, Levites, and Israelites who had married foreign women during the exile (see Ezra 10:18–44; verse 44, incidentally, contains a serious textual problem; see the commentaries).

9. According to the Liddell & Scott *Greek-English Lexicon* (1:509), *ekklēsia* is "an assembly duly summoned," and *ekklētos* is one "selected to judge." The basic idea is election or selection, not separation (for a fuller discussion, see *TDNT*, 3:494–96, 502–36). *Ekklēsia* occurs about 100 times in LXX, usually translating Hebr. *qāhāl*, "assembly, congregation."

10. "The people had broken loose" (RSV); "the people were running wild" (NIV); "The people were out of control" (NASB); "the people were naked" (KJV). The Hebrew verb *pāra‛* sometimes means "uncover," which may support KJV. LXX, however, translates "were scattered, dispersed."

11. The generation that came out of Egypt was denied entrance into Cannaan because of their unbelief (Num 14:23; 26:63–65; 32:11–14; Josh 5:6). However, it is inconceivable that there was no overlap of generations. Many of the children born in the wilderness were witnesses of the events recorded in the exodus narratives or had heard the stories that were told by their elders, and they were the ones who made the final journey to the land of Canaan (Josh 5:7).

12. There is a possibility that the ark was moved first to Bochim (Bethel) (see Judg 2:1; 20:18–28; for discussion, compare *ISBE* 1 [1979]: 292).

13. K. Th. Obbink, cited by W. F. Albright, *From the Stone Age to Christianity* (Baltimore: Johns Hopkins Press, 1940), 229.

14. Josephus mentions a Beersheba in Galilee (*Wars* 2.20.6 §573), but there is neither biblical nor archaeological reason to suppose that Amos referred to this place. Archaeological discoveries prove that Beersheba in Judah was a cult center in the ninth and eight centuries (see A. F. Rainey, "Beer-sheba," *ISBE* 1 [1979]: 450).

15. LXX reads "thy God, O Beersheba," influencing the emendation of *derek* to *dôdkâ* in BHS. However, I do not find *dôd* used with this meaning in the Hebrew Bible. It is used allegorically of YHWH in *Canticles Rabbah* to 1:4, hardly sufficient to support the emendation.

16. *ARAB* 1 §816; *ANET*, 283–84.

17. The similarity of names in the ruling families of Israel and Judah at this time is a source of confusion to the student who is not careful when referring to them. But even more, it is a proof that Judah was closely linked to Israel in this period. It is possible that Jehoshaphat, king of Judah (873–848 B.C.), was a vassal of Ahab, king of Israel (874–853 B.C.) (see 1 Kgs 22:1–4; 2 Chr 18:1–3). Note that Jehoshaphat was with Ahab in the Israelite capital of Samaria, when Ahab made the decision to go to war against Hazael and that Jehoshaphat bowed to it (1 Kgs 22:4). Ahaziah, king of Israel (853–852 B.C.), was the son of Ahab and Jezebel, whereas Ahaziah, king of Judah (841 B.C.), was the grandson of Ahab and Jezebel. Jehoram, king of Judah (853–851 B.C.), the son of Jehoshaphat, was the son-in-law of Ahab and the brother-in-law of Jehoram, king of Israel (852–841 B.C.), a son of Ahab (2 Kgs 8:16); for Ahaziah had no son (1:17).

18. Josephus *Antiquities* 9.10.4 §224–25.
19. *ARAB* 1 §816; *ANET*, 284.
20. If we accept the theory that Hezekiah became coregent in 728 B.C., the problems raised by scholars relative to the existence of Israel and the invitation to the north to attend the Passover disappear. Hezekiah became king on the death of his father in 716 B.C. The chronology of 2 Kgs. 18:9 is thus in agreement with dates for Israel, Judah, and Assyria.
21. Josephus *Antiquities* 10.2.2 §30–34.
22. *ANET*, 291; this portion is omitted in *ARAB*.
23. *ARAB* 2 §876; *ANET*, 294. It is possible that Manasseh had supported the revolt of Shamash-shum-ukin (see *NBD*, 779). But this was connected with Ashurbanipal's sixth campaign, and the reference to Manasseh is in the account of his first campaign.
24. The theory that Deuteronomy was composed at the time, hidden in the temple, and then "found" is discredited and should be abandoned by every serious scholar. There is far too much evidence in the prophets of the eighth century that the law of YHWH was already not only known but expressly disregarded (see R. E. Clements, *Prophecy and Covenant* [London: S.C.M. Press, 1965], esp. 69–85).
25. For one reconstruction, see LaSor et al., *Old Testament Survey*, 428–30. For a slightly different scheme, see C. Lattey in *A Catholic Commentary on Holy Scripture* (New York: Thomas Nelson & Sons, 1953), 574, §452b.
26. Josephus *Antiquities* 10.6.1 §87; 2 Kgs. 24:1. Jeremiah 25 belongs to this period.
27. See D. J. Wiseman, *Chronicles of Chaldaean Kings* (London: British Museum, 1956), 28–32, 70–73.
28. For a detailed chronology of this period, with full documentation, see W. S. LaSor, "Jerusalem," *ISBE* 2 (1982): 1016.

6

The Priestly Era in the Light of Prophetic Thought

C. Hassell Bullock

The fall of Jerusalem in 586 B.C. meant the loss of the three major mainstays of Israelite life: temple, monarchy, and land. The devastating effect of this crisis is difficult to assess from a vantage point twenty-six centuries after its occurrence. Many of the emotional components of that horrible tragedy—the pain, tears, and trauma—are beyond the retrieval of scholarship. What remains in the prophetic books and Lamentations is only a minimal residue from that age. Likewise, the loss of the three mainstays of preexilic society has resulted in only minimal evidence of its impact on the literature of the postexilic period.

The restoration that followed the Decree of Cyrus, in 538 B.C., resulted in the Jews' recovery of temple and land. The exiles were permitted to return to the land they had forfeited by sin. The prime thrust of that royal decree, however, was the rebuilding of the temple. The Book of Chronicles concludes with the proclamation of Cyrus; the Book of Ezra opens with the same proclamation (2 Chr 36:23/Ezra 1:2–4). Cyrus understood that the rebuilding of the temple was to be his divinely appointed destiny: "YHWH, the God of heaven, has given me all the kingdoms of the earth, and *he has charged me to build him a house at Jerusalem, which is in Judah*" (emphasis added). Understandably, the monarchy was not part of the program of Cyrus. So the question surfaces: How did the absence of the monarchy in postexilic life affect the community? What compensation was made for the kingship, once Israelite life began to assume its new shape?

We will discuss this question within the boundaries of the literature produced in the postexilic age. We have already admitted that the evidence is sparse, and it addresses the question indirectly rather than directly. The principal prophetic books describing the postexilic community are Haggai, Zechariah, and Malachi. Also, windows into that period are built into the Book of Chronicles, not in the sense that it deals with the events of those times, but rather that it is written from a postexilic perspective. Although Chronicles is not canonically included among the prophetic books, in its spirit and outlook it is prophetic in the same sense as the Book of Kings, which finds its place in the Former Prophets of the Hebrew canon.[1]

EZEKIEL'S PARADIGM

The continuity of the postexilic community in Palestine with preexilic life hardly needs to be emphasized. The restoration was just that—it represented, in many ways, a picking up of the pieces of a culture that had been tragically interrupted for many Judeans and which had been ended for numerous others. Even those whom the Babylonians left in Judah found life to be very different from that which they had known. And for those whose destiny led them to Babylonia, readjustment was filled with anxiety (Jer 28–29).

The efforts of Jeremiah and Ezekiel to stabilize the Hebrew community in Babylonia in those early years of captivity, judging from their writings, made a considerable impact. Jeremiah recommended settling into a normal routine and cycle of life, because the exile would surely endure the seventy weary years he had predicted. Ezekiel, himself among the early captives of 597 B.C., shared the life of the alien community in Babylonia and offered counsel and hope. His model of the restored community (Ezek 40–48) put the temple at the geographical and theological center of the new society (Ezek 45).

While Ezekiel's blueprint was novel in prophetic literature, the centrality of the temple in the new age had its precedent in the thinking of the prophets. Micah had spoken of its destruction and restoration, with Zion becoming the highest of the mountains (Mic 3:12; 4:1–4). Isaiah joined him in that expectation (Isa 2:2–4). If these two prophets quoted a common source for their duplicate oracles, we may surmise that the elevation of Zion was a general concept of that time.

The dawn of the messianic age was conditioned on the restoration of the temple.[2] It is thus not mere coincidence that Ezekiel was transported in vision to the temple mount, which he described as "a very high mountain" (Ezek 40:2). Nor is it surprising, in view of prophetic precedent, that Ezekiel's description of the restoration took the form of a rebuilt temple. It was the symbol of YHWH's presence with Israel forever, and an assurance that Israel would never again profane his name (Ezek 43:7–9).

In addition to the theological premise that the temple should be at the center of the eschatological community, Ezekiel's term for Israel's leader in the new age was that of *prince*, rather than *king*. In his account of the revitalization of the valley of dry bones, he predicted that David would be *king* over restored Israel (37:24), but he applied the term *prince* to him in the next verse and associated his rule with the reestablishment of the sanctuary (37:25–27). In his description of the new temple (chaps. 40–48), all references to the leader of the community employ the word *prince* (45:9, 17; 46:2–8, 10, 12; 48:21). If Ezekiel saw any future role for Davidic kingship, it was inferior to the role it had enjoyed before the fall of Jerusalem.

W. J. Dumbrell has pointed out that in Ezekiel 40–48 this abridged role of the monarch is consistent with the diminished role assigned to David in the earlier chapters of the book.[3] It could be, of course, that at the late date of Ezekiel (572/571 B.C.) the use of the royal term *king* was not in good political taste. Such a sovereign title would have raised the eyebrows of the Babylonian authorities. Whatever Ezekiel's reason for selecting the term, the prince's position in this account is certainly auxiliary to that of the priest so far as the temple was concerned. The prince was not in control of it. Whether Ezekiel consciously thought in terms of a temple-dominated society with a less-than-sovereign leader is not entirely clear. But when seeking a model that fit the realities of their situation, the postexilic community likely found it in this prophet's thought.

Further, when the temple was rebuilt, YHWH would be restored to his rightful place of honor among the nations of the world. This would commence a new era: "I will bless them and multiply them, and will set my sanctuary in the midst of them forevermore. My dwelling place shall be with them; and I will be their God, and they shall be my people. *Then the nations will know that I YHWH sanctify Israel, when my sanctuary is in the midst of them forevermore*" (Ezek 37:26c–28; emphasis added).

In point of fact, a passionate anticipation of the Day of YHWH sets apart the literary structure of Ezekiel. The roots of this anticipation were deeply anchored in prophetic theology. Amos had announced that day as one of judgment upon Israel—at a time when the popular view insisted that it would be a day of blessing (Amos 5:18–20). Both Zephaniah and Jeremiah predicted its imminence in no uncertain terms.

Subsequently, upon the fall of Jerusalem, the author of Lamentations and the prophet Obadiah announced that the Day of YHWH, constituted by that tragedy, had come for Judah. The dark hues of that tragic day, in compliance with Amos' prophecy, were observed and announced as accomplished by Ezekiel. But then Ezekiel's attention turned to that day's counterpart for the nations:

> Wail, "Alas for the day!"
> For the day is near,
>   for the day of YHWH is near;
> it will be a day of clouds,
>   a time of doom for the nations. (Ezek 30:3)

The day of judgment for Israel's enemies constituted the other side of the coin. The sequence that emerges in prophetic eschatology is that first, judgment would fall on Israel—the primary phase of the Day of YHWH—and second, a similar catastrophe for Israel's enemies would follow; then (whether conceived as being simultaneous to the second phase or a sequel to it is not always clear), Israel's restoration would take place. The arrangement of the Book of Ezekiel reinforces his eschatological outline. The first section focuses on Judah's day of doom (chaps. 1–24); the second section focuses on the Day of YHWH for the nations (chaps. 25–32); while the last section presents the third phase, the restoration of Israel (chaps. 33–48).

In summary, Ezekiel's paradigm for the restored community put the rebuilt temple at the center of the new community. In the renovated order, as described in chapters 40–48, the prince's position was an auxiliary to the temple. The monarchy, though figuring in Ezekiel's restoration plans, took second place to the temple. Moreover, temple restoration would vindicate YHWH before the eyes of the nations. The exile of Israel to Babylon, contrary to appearances, was not an expression of YHWH's impotence. The restoration would prove this, and the new temple would be to the nations the symbol of his sovereign rule.

POSTEXILIC ADAPTATION

Now our discussion must move to the postexilic prophets and their view of the restoration. The Decree of Cyrus in 538 B.C. set in motion the wheels of the return and restoration. First, an attempt to rebuild the temple was led by Sheshbazzar, perhaps as early as 537/536 B.C., but for reasons not entirely clear, the effort failed. In the reign of Darius II, a second attempt was made — led by Zerubbabel, a Davidic descendant and Persian-appointed governor. Zerubbabel was joined by the high priest Joshua and encouraged by the prophets Haggai and Zechariah. The building was begun in 520 and completed in 516 B.C.

The books of Haggai and Zechariah (chaps. 1–8) present the reconstruction of the temple as a three-pronged venture. Probably at no time in Israel's history since David had such a major cooperative effort been executed successfully. Haggai was a single-minded prophet whose driving passion was the reconstruction of the temple. He found the community devastated by drought and poverty (Hag 1:6) and explained that YHWH was using these means to arouse their concern for his house (Hag 1:7–11).

P. R. Ackroyd observes that one group of Haggai's oracles deals with the predicament of his people and the predicament's causes (1:2, 4–8, 9–11; 2:11–14, 15–19), while another group of oracles offers the assurance of YHWH's presence and intervention (2:4–5, 6–9, 21–23); the temple is the link between the two groups.[4] Speaking to all three constituents of the community (royalty, priesthood, and people — 2:4), Haggai dealt with the second major crisis of his ministry: the second temple would not equal Solomon's in beauty (2:1–9). Yet he assured the Hebrew community that YHWH was still with his people as he had been when they came out of Egypt and that he would reveal himself to them as he had done at Sinai. For this prophet, the temple was the symbol of YHWH's presence; when it stood on Mount Zion again, the nations would give homage to Israel's God.

Haggai places no special emphasis on the role of Zerubbabel in temple reconstruction. The Davidic descendant stands in conjunction with the high priest and the people to accomplish the job. However, with Zechariah there can be no mistake about Zerubbabel's role in temple rebuilding. Zechariah's vision of the two olive trees (which supply oil to the golden lampstand between them) illustrates the coordinate roles of the priesthood and dynastic representative. But the responsibility of temple construction lay squarely, as it did in David and Solomon's day, with the royal house: "The hands of Zerubbabel have laid the foundation of this house and his hands shall also complete it" (Zech 4:9; 6:12–13). Both offices collaborated in the reconstruction project, although Zerubbabel's primary role in completing the temple is emphasized. Beyond that, however, his powers and responsibilities are difficult to determine.

At the end of the book, however, Haggai does raise the issue of Zerubbabel and thus of David's place in the new era. It seems significant that the shaking of the heavens and the earth connects Message II (2:1–9 — dealing with temple reconstruction) and Message IV (2:20–23 — dealing with the revival of the Davidic dynasty), thus suggesting the monumental importance of both of them. Yet the placement of the verse dealing with Zerubbabel's elevation as YHWH's "signet ring" relegates that event to the eschatological future in the same way the filling of the second temple with YHWH's splendor is assigned to the future. The difference is that the second temple was a reality in Haggai's time — only its splendor was delayed. The elevation of the Davidic dynasty, however, was postponed.

The idea of postponement also finds expression in Zechariah's prophecy of "the Branch," a royal descendant of David (Zech 3:8).[5] While Joshua is properly arrayed for the office of high priest (3:1–5) and charged with the oversight of the temple (3:6–7), "the Branch," or the Davidic representative, is designated as the agent who will usher in the eschatological age (3:8).

In Zech. 6:9–15, two crowns are placed on Joshua's head, but the accompanying oracle concerns Zerubbabel as the builder of the temple (v 13). Some commentators insist that the name Zerubbabel — instead of Joshua — was originally in verse eleven. However, in the absence of textual warrant for this change, it is better to allow the text to stand as it is. The future orientation, and thus the postponement of Zerubbabel's rule, seems a foregone conclusion in the face of the political reality of the Persian period. Only the high priest could be crowned without political risk; so he embodied both aspirants.

That the crowns are deposited in the temple as a memorial (6:14) reaffirms the postponement of the Branch's rule. The ground for combining the two offices in this interim period was already prepared in an earlier era (1 Sam 2:35; Jer 33:20–22; Ezek 40–48).[6] And the leading role of the high priest has its model in Ezekiel 40–48. As K. Koch observes, this text does not involve a refutation of dynastic hope but an adaptation.[7] The priesthood did not become a substitute for the monarchy, but the cult — the priesthood's sphere of operation — carried a minimum of political implications. The monarchy, however (represented by the subordinate office of governor), had serious limitations because of its political nature. The close association of these two offices in this period was a virtual necessity. In fact, as history testifies, the high priesthood eventually became the dominant of the two offices in developing Judaism.

The final chapters of Zechariah (chaps. 9–14) do not address this topic with any precision. The prophet is far less concerned with the offices of king and high priest than he is with the coming kingdom of God. Yet the postponement of an active and viable monarchy no longer describes the situation, for the eschatological era anticipated in chapters 1–8 is the very subject of this material. In Zech. 9:9–10, the term *king* is applied to a humble monarch making his royal entry on a donkey; YHWH will take the task of conquest into his own hands and deliver the captives (9:11–15). The king's role would be that of a shepherd (11:4–7), an image detailed by Ezekiel (Ezek 34:23–31; 37:24). That Zechariah's shepherd is a royal figure is substantiated by the occurrence of the two words in parallel lines in Zech. 11:5–6, and in 13:7 YHWH calls him "the man who is my fellow" (*geber ʿămîtî*). Of special interest is the description of YHWH's kingdom, in which the holiness that characterizes the temple precincts and sacred vessels will be disseminated so broadly in the land that common cooking vessels may be used for sacrificial purposes (14:20–21). The centrality of the temple, dominating the first eight chapters of Zechariah, thus becomes symbolic of the degree to which the whole land is to be purified.

The prophetic support of this diarchical system—implicit in Haggai and clearly formulated in Zechariah—may be seen in the fact that they emphasize the centrality of the temple and the leading role of the priesthood. It hardly needs to be said that our interpretation of the period's literature does not allow for the struggle between the ruling priesthood and the prophetic group, as P. D. Hanson has proposed.[8] E. M. Meyers makes a convincing case for a "proto-rabbinic" interpretation of the word *torah* in Hag. 2:11 and Mal. 2:7, designating it not a *word of God*, but a *ruling* on some cultic or ritual matter. The phrase "to seek a *torah*" from the priest shows, in his view, how close prophecy drew to the priesthood.[9] Prophecy was by no means swallowed up by the cult, but with the passing of time transferred its function in part to the priest and in part to the wise man. We can agree that this view of the peaceful transition from prophet to priest and sage corresponds well with later rabbinic opinion.[10]

By the time of Malachi (ca. 475–457 B.C.), the predominance of the priesthood had become accepted, attested by the fact that Malachi carried on his disputation with the priests. So strategic was their role that the prophet attributed Israel's ills to the unlawful behavior of the priesthood. YHWH's covenant with Levi had been the determinative factor in history (Mal 2:4–7), and the priestly violation of the covenant was the direct cause of present woes. In contrast, the governor (whether Davidic or not we cannot be sure) assumed a minor position in Malachi's oracles. He was sure only that the governor would not be delighted with the inferior sacrifice and service the priests were offering YHWH (Mal 1:8).

In the Book of Malachi, however, the prophet/priest coalition is obvious, for the role of YHWH's messenger is to prepare the way among his people, before YHWH himself appears suddenly in the temple (3:1). The prophecy concludes with the model prophet Elijah, who is to appear before the Day of YHWH to continue what the prophets had always sought to do—to bring unity through covenantal allegiance lest YHWH should come, not to save but to smite the land with a curse (4:5–6). The prophetic voice again joins the voice that has spoken the law of Moses—the priesthood—to divert the threatened curse in the coming day of judgment (4:4–6).

The Book of Chronicles, of special interest to our thesis, portrays David in a pivotal position as organizer of temple personnel and services and as prime mover of the first temple's construction. The Chronicler, who wrote at a time when the temple was central and considered determinative of Israel's destiny, oriented his history of Israel toward the temple and its welfare. After David and Solomon, whose reigns were preoccupied with the temple, the kings of Judah are judged on the basis of their patronization of the cult. During the divided kingdom, the Chronicler gives five kings favorable marks for their interest in the cult, with eleven of them receiving unfavorable reviews. Asa, Joash, Uzziah, and Manasseh receive a combination of favorable and unfavorable reviews.[11] The prophets were seen as collaborators in this program. As early as Asa, the prophet Azariah announces that political success was contingent on seeking YHWH, possessing the Law, and having a teaching priest (2 Chr 15:2–3). The book ends with the Decree of Cyrus, which outlines his divinely assigned task of building a house for YHWH (2 Chr 36:22–23).

It cannot be maintained that the Chronicler had no interest in the continuance of the Davidic monarchy beyond the exile. H. G. M. Williamson proposes that the Chronicler believed the king was necessary for the maintenance of the temple cult. Williamson's view is that the king would maintain a balance of power with the priests—in contradistinction to an insistence that the high priests were the legitimate successors of the kings.[12] Certainly by the Chronicler's time (possibly late fifth century B.C.), the hope of dynastic revival was growing thin. However, the question arises: if a balance of power was the Chronicler's purpose, he accomplished it, for he looks at the kings through the temple and ritual. Nevertheless, it may well be true that he sought to keep alive the hope of monarchical restoration by alerting the community to the need and benefits of cultic loyalty.[13] The hope of dynastic renewal was not abandoned, but the Chronicler was aware of its postponement and sought to keep it alive.

CONCLUSION

To summarize our thesis, in the postexilic era the temple was the central focus of the prophets, who encouraged temple restoration and the resumption of priestly functions. The diarchical role of the high priest and Davidic dynasty is explicated by Zechariah: the priesthood plays the dominant role, although the royal representative carries the weight of responsibility for the reconstruction of the temple.

Yet the resumption of the monarchial system was not an idea that had been laid aside—only postponed until the eschatological era. The precedent for the coordinate function of priesthood and dynastic representative was set forth in Ezekiel's model of the new age, with allowance for priestly dominance. The prophetic role was one of support and encouragement, forming a three-pronged system of priest–dynasty–prophet. While complete harmony among these three offices may not be pressed too far, a cooperative spirit held sway and brought the restoration to a successful conclusion.

The continuance of the predominant role of the temple and cult is confirmed by Malachi and the author of Chronicles. By their time, Judah's history and destiny had come to be understood largely in terms of the temple and the ritual system. Compensation for the loss of the monarchy was to be found in the temple and priesthood, but an assumption of dynastic responsibilities by the high priest was to last only until the eschatological era.

NOTES

1. See, for example, the discussion of prophecy in Chronicles by Adam C. Welch, *The Work of the Chronicler: Its Purpose and Its Date* (London: British Academy, 1939), 42–54.
2. Joyce G. Baldwin, *Haggai, Zechariah, Malachi*, Tyndale Old Testament Commentaries (Downers Grove, Ill.: Inter-Varsity Press, 1972), 85–86.
3. W. J. Dumbrell, "Kingship and Temple in the Post-Exilic Period," *Reformed Theological Review* 37 (1978): 36–37.
4. Peter R. Ackroyd, "Studies in the Book of Haggai," *JJS* 3 (1952): 12.
5. This term occurs earlier in Isaiah (4:2) and Jeremiah (23:5; 33:15). In the latter prophet, the Davidic descent of this person is unmistakable.
6. Klaus Koch, *The Prophets: The Babylonian and Persian Periods*, trans. Margaret Kohl (London: S.C.M. Press, 1982), 163–64.
7. Ibid., 166.
8. Paul D. Hanson, "Jewish Apocalyptic against Its Near Eastern Environment," *RB* 77 (1971): 31–58.
9. Eric M. Meyers, "The Use of *Tora* in Haggai 2:11 and the Role of the Prophet in the Restoration Community," in *The Word of the Lord Shall Go Forth*, ed. Carol L. Meyers and M. O'Connor (Winona Lake, Ind.: Eisenbrauns, 1983), 71.
10. Ibid., 74; see Aboth 1:1.
11. H. G. M. Williamson, "1 and 2 Chronicles," New Century Bible Commentary (Grand Rapids, Mich.: Wm. Eerdmans, 1982), 29.
12. Ibid.
13. See also the essays by John M. Lundquist, "Temple, Covenant, and Law in the Ancient Near East and in the Hebrew Bible," and Wayne O. McCready, "The 'Day of Small Things' vs. the Latter Days: Historical Fulfillment or Eschatological Hope?" in this volume.

7

Egypt As an Arm of Flesh:
A Prophetic Response

James K. Hoffmeier

Since the beginnings of Assyriology, the study of cuneiform texts has gone hand-in-hand with the study of the Hebrew Bible. However, Egypt, Israel's neighbor to the south, also played a critical role in Israel's history. This is most evident in the fact that after Israel, Egypt is the most frequently mentioned nation in the Hebrew Bible. Scholars have by and large been slow to recognize the Egyptian influence on Hebrew writers. However, this situation is changing, especially in the field of Wisdom literature.

In the following pages I will examine the history of Egyptian–Israelite relations. Egypt at times is a feared foe, at other times an ally. My primary question is, How did the Hebrew prophets assess this relationship?

THE UNITED MONARCHY

In the years after the exodus from Egypt, before the time of Solomon, direct contact between Israel and Egypt was very limited. G. Rendsburg has recently reminded us of the linguistic reasons for correlating the toponym ma'yan mê neptôaḥ ("the spring of Me[r]neptah") in Josh. 15:9 and 18:15 with Merneptah, the 19th Dynasty monarch (1213–1204 B.C.).[1] That these allusions were added to the Egyptian epigraphic material for Merneptah's campaign in Palestine (that is, the "Israel Stela," the Karnak inscription, and the Amada inscription) is ample evidence for military contact between Egypt and some Israelites.[2]

This interpretation is strengthened by F. Yurko's identifying an inscription and scene of Merneptah at Karnak. The inscription seems to contain another version of the "Israel Stela"; in this case it depicts scenes illustrating the nine cities of the "Nine Bows" mentioned in the stela. Included as one of the conquered nations is a group of people whose name has unfortunately been obliterated; Yurko suggests this nation is Israel.[3]

It is now quite clear that some Egyptian military action was directed against Palestine, which included Israel, in the late thirteenth century B.C. That there is no direct mention of this incursion in Joshua or Judges is surprising indeed, especially since Judges records many of the assaults on Israel by her enemies from the time of Cushan-rishathaim of Aram-Naharaim (Judg 3:8–10), when Othniel was judge, until the new menace, the Philistines, appeared just after 1200 B.C.

Evidence of contact between Egypt and Israel during the early days of the monarchy is also virtually nonexistent. However, D. B. Redford[4] and A. R. Green[5] believe that Psusennes I, a contemporary of David, may have carried out Egyptian activity in Philistia. But, if Psusennes had been engaged in some policing action in the Levant, there appears to have been no military clash with David.

In the record of David's mighty men, Benaiah is credited with killing an Egyptian (2 Sam 23:21), who is described as being "a giant of a man" (1 Chr 11:23), not a "handsome man" (RSV of 2 Sam 23:21). Benaiah, armed only with his staff or club, attacks the Egyptian, who is armed with a spear (ḥănît), and kills him with his own spear.[6]

Important questions, such as where did this confrontation take place, under what circumstance, and why was the Egyptian in the region, are not answered. Perhaps the Egyptian was a soldier in Psusennes I's policing action and had strayed into Israelite territory and onto Benaiah. One hesitates to speculate too much about this reference. However, it may be an allusion to an Egyptian military presence in Philistia at the time of David, as posited by Redford[7] and Green.[8] This same military action by Egypt in Philistia may have made David's campaigns against the Philistines an easier task. David routed the Philistines from Israelite territory "as far as Gezer" (2 Sam 5:25). This expulsion appears to have taken place just after David consolidated his united kingdom (year 7 or slightly later; 1 Sam 5:1–25).[9]

Redford has convincingly shown that during the 21st Dynasty Egypt would have looked positively on David's consolidation of Israel.[10] Given Egypt's paranoia of invasion from the Levant, such an attitude is at first surprising. But Redford argues that Egypt was traditionally more concerned with the Shasu bedouin, nomadic and seminomadic Asiatics, infiltrating the Delta[11] than with an attack from one of the city–states or kingdoms of Palestine. And even before David was proclaimed king of Judah in Hebron (2 Sam 5:1–5), he had been fighting the bedouin population of the Negev and northern Sinai (1 Sam 27:8–12). Thus David and the Egyptians had a mutual enemy.

They also had a mutual enemy in the Philistines. Less than two centuries had passed since the Sea Peoples, which included the Philistines, had attacked Egypt. Therefore, the Egyptians may have been concerned lest there be another attempted invasion. For Israel's part, the Philistines had been archenemies since the end of the Judges period (Judg 15–16), during Samuel and Saul's time (1 Sam 4–7; 13–14; 17; 28–31), and up until David's mastery of them (2 Sam 5:17–25). If David could exercise control over Philistia, it would be to Egypt's political and economic advantage,[12] whereas if Philistia were not properly controlled, she could disrupt the sea trade between Egypt and Phoenicia. The Egyptian tale of Wen-Amun,[13] which has been dated to the beginning of the 21st Dynasty, reflects the sort of piracy and disruption of the sea lanes the Egyptians feared.

Egypt and Israel had a mutual ally and trading partner in the Phoenicians.[14] A trade accord between Egypt, Israel, and Phoenicia would have been beneficial to all three powers.[15] The significance of a favorable climate between David and Psusennes I and Amenemope (1039–984 B.C.) is that these relations would have established a foreign policy for Israel that Solomon could have continued.

Two recent studies provide another sort of evidence for favorable relations between Egypt and Israel during David's time. E. Ball[16] has suggested that the coregency of David and Solomon most closely resembles the Egyptian model that was used considerably during the Middle Kingdom, occasionally in the Empire Period, and also during the Third Intermediate Period.[17] L. G. Perdue has made the ingenious suggestion that the testament of David (1 Kgs 2:1–112) was modeled after the royal instruction genre of Egypt. A royal instruction made by an aged king (for example, Meryibre for Merikare) or a (now) dead king (for example, Amenemhet I for Senusret I) provided his successor with counsel. The purpose of such a testament, argues Perdue, was to help legitimize the new king and his policies in case of political opposition or of succession problems.[18] That Amenemhet made Senusret his coregent, and that a posthumous instruction ("The Instruction of Amenemhet") was written for Senusret is noteworthy.[19]

Under Solomon, the relationship between Egypt and Israel reached an apex with the marriage alliance between the two nations (1 Kgs 3:1). Since the name of the pharaoh and the circumstances surrounding the alliance are not preserved, this episode has been discussed at great length over the past decades.[20] Recent studies in Egyptian chronology have enabled biblical scholars to investigate the synchronism with greater precision.[21] This has led many scholars to confidently identify Siamun (979/978–960/959 B.C.) as the unnamed pharaoh of 1 Kgs. 3:1.[22] Others are more cautious, suggesting Psusennes II (depending on the length of Sheshonk's reign: twenty-one years according to Manetho, or thirty-five as preserved by Eusebius) or Siamun could have been the king.[23]

The biblical tradition of 1 Kgs. 3:1 suggests that the alliance took place early in Solomon's reign, and this is the consensus of a number of scholars.[24] It certainly took place prior to the completion of Solomon's palace, which took thirteen years to build (7:1), because 1 Kgs. 3:1 informs us that the Egyptian princess lived in David's palace until the completion of Solomon's replacement. But before the completion of the new palace, Solomon had a change in plans and built the princess her own house (1 Kgs 7:8; 2 Chr 8:11).

K. A. Kitchen, and more recently Green, has pointed out that the conquest of Gezer and the marriage alliance (when Gezer was given to Solomon as a part of the dowry; 1 Kgs 9:16) most likely occurred before Solomon's fourth regnal year, when work on the temple began (6:1). They reason that since the timber for the temple came from Tyre via Joppa (2 Chr 2:16), it almost certainly had to pass through Gezer on its way to Jerusalem. Therefore, Gezer must already have been under Solomon's control.[25]

If the tradition preserved in Kings concerning the marriage is correct—and there is no reason for it to be questioned—it is a unique occurrence in the history of Egyptian diplomatic marriages.[26] A. R. Schulman has gathered evidence for such marriages in ancient Egypt and, with the exception of 1 Kgs. 3:1, foreign princesses always went to Egypt.[27] Schulman calls Egypt's policy one-sided;[28] clearly the Egyptians regarded themselves in the superior position in such relationships. The Hittite marriages with Ramses II[29] sealed a "parity treaty," but there is nothing in either Hittite or Egyptian records to suggest that an Egyptian princess was married to Ḫattušiliš III. This reflects more on Egypt's ethnocentric attitude than the nature of the treaty. Egypt during Solomon's time was simply not the Egypt of the Empire Period, a fact which likely accounts for the shift in policy. That there is no record of a daughter of Solomon being sent to Egypt suggests that he was the superior partner in the treaty.[30]

What sparked the Egyptian army to invade Palestine and conquer Gezer? A number of scholars[31] follow A. Malamat's suggestion[32] that Egypt was attempting to conquer Palestine and exercise sovereignty over that area just as it had during the Empire Period. According to this theory, the Egyptians invaded at the accession of Solomon, thinking he would be preoccupied with internal matters. When the Egyptians found they had underestimated Solomon's military prowess, they decided to make an alliance and hand over Gezer as a gesture of goodwill.

Kitchen finds this scenario to be "theoretically possible, but . . . entirely unsupported and needless."[33] Redford, as mentioned before, feels that relations between Egypt and David were cordial,[34] and this view has been endorsed by J. A. Soggin and by Green.[35] Green goes so far as to suggest that an alliance existed between David and Psusennes I. While this suggestion is intriguing, there is simply no evidence to support it.

If Egypt and Israel were on friendly terms, and perhaps even allies, why would the Egyptian king invade Palestine? Kitchen maintains that the reasons were more commercial than political, the aim being to "crush Philistine commercial rivalry"[36] or, as previously suggested, to control Philistia so that she could not disrupt Egypt's sea trade with Phoenicia. I agree with Malamat that the biblical record does not claim that David actually conquered Philistia. He merely pushed the Philistines out of his territory as far as Gezer (2 Sam 5:25). Without conquering, David was still able to maintain nominal control over Philistia.[37]

It might be suggested that at the death of David, or even just before, when the jockeying for his successor was taking place, Siamun (?) invaded Philistia to ensure that she would not upset the accord Israel and Egypt had enjoyed after David's campaigns. It is noteworthy that the Egyptian king's campaign did not penetrate Palestine beyond Gezer, which had remained a

Canaanite enclave under Philistine control (Judg 1:29; 1 Kgs 3:1), to go into Israelite territory. In other words, David's earlier military action had been a boon for Egypt, and now Egypt could return the favor at a time when Israel was undergoing some internal dynastic problems.

The marriage alliance seems to have taken place because of the accession of a new king in Israel and the opportunity this afforded to forge an alliance. Schulman observes that Egypt usually "negotiated a fresh marriage each time a new foreign ruler ascended to the throne in a neighboring state."[38] With Solomon on the throne, it seemed expedient for the Egyptians to formalize relationships which had previously been cordial, but not officially consummated. This seems a more likely view than that the two nations came to an understanding after a near confrontation that Egypt recognized she could not win.

The good relations between Israel and Egypt led to a period of unprecedented prosperity and peace for Israel. Solomon was able to undertake massive building projects, which included the temple and his palace (1 Kgs 6–7), as well as the defense systems at Jerusalem, Hazor, Megiddo, and Gezer (9:15). Cities with defense systems were also built at Lower Beth Horon, Baalath, and Tamar (9:17–18).

Because of the alliance with Egypt, Solomon could look to Egypt for horses and chariots to outfit his army and in addition could serve as middleman in the movement of the same to points north (10:26–29). Y. Ikeda[39] has finally laid to rest the notion that Anatolia, not Egypt, was the place where, along with Kue, horses and chariots were obtained (10:28).[40] Egyptian records found in the tomb biography of Ahmose Si Abena[41] date the horse and chariot from the time of King Ahmose (ca. 1570 B.C.). Chariot workshops are depicted in the tombs of Menkheperrasonb[42] and Puyemre,[43] from Thutmose III's reign, and in the tomb of Hepu,[44] who served Thutmose IV. Clearly by the time of Thutmose III chariots were being made in Egypt and chariot horses were being bred.[45] I have observed elsewhere[46] that during Thutmose III's reign there was a period of experimentation with chariots in Egypt; the wheelwrights and craftsmen were trying to produce a vehicle which would be best suited for the battlefield. By Solomon's time there was a well-established tradition of horsemanship and chariotry in Egypt, so Solomon naturally looked to his ally and benefited from the association.

Under Solomon's reign Israel's chariotry grew to a size of 1400 (1 Kgs 10:26). This figure is not exaggerated, according to J. Gray and Kitchen.[47] The Black Obelisk of Shalmaneser III records that Ahab had 2000 chariots involved in the battle of Qarqar, while Hadadezer had 1200.[48] Solomon did indeed build up Israel's chariotry considerably—chariots were just beginning to make an appearance in Israel at the beginning of the monarchy, and only in limited numbers (2 Sam 8:4).[49]

Let us consider the prophetic response to this development. Deut. 17:14–20 contains the kingship laws, which many commentators of Deuteronomy regard as a "deuteronomic polemic" against Solomon.[50] Verse 16 is critical to this study:

> Only he [the king] must not multiply horses for himself,
>   or cause the people to return to Egypt in order to multiply horses,
> since YHWH has said to you,
>   "You shall never return that way again."

Many scholars interpret this verse to mean that Israel was exchanging Israelite slaves or mercenaries for horses and chariots.[51] Since there is no evidence from 1 Kings to suggest that this ever occurred, this interpretation is questionable. In fact, 1 Kgs. 10:26 indicates that Solomon paid 600 shekels of silver for a chariot and 150 for a horse. Ikeda undoubtedly is correct in thinking that 600 shekels represents the highest price paid for an Egyptian chariot, while 150 shekels was the price of a high quality steed, not an ordinary horse.[52]

If Deut. 17:14–20 was a "deuteronomic polemic," it is surprising that the deuteronomic historian, when writing about Solomon's activities in 1 Kgs. 10:26–29, did not condemn the practice of going to Egypt for horses and chariots. In 1 Kgs. 3:3, Solomon's worship at the high place at Gibeon is denounced. So, clearly, there was no hesitation to criticize him.

Exod. 23:32; 34:13–15; and Deut. 7:2 make it clear that YHWH did not want Israel to make covenants *(kārat běrît)* with the inhabitants of Canaan. If Israel remained faithful to her covenant with YHWH, YHWH himself would give Israel victory (Deut 11:22–23). Rather, alliances with foreigners would be harmful to Israel's well-being. To make a covenant with another nation would be to bring them into the covenant community.[53] This was unthinkable.

But Deut. 17:16 makes no mention of a covenant with Egypt. Something else must be envisioned instead. For Israel to "return" to Egypt for horses is tantamount to "a divine liquidation of the whole history of salvation brought by Yahweh," says G. von Rad.[54]

Perhaps the passage recalls the events of Exod. 14:5–31. A division of 600 Egyptian chariots (compare 14:7) was wiped out by YHWH's victorious arm.[55] The "Song of the Sea" bears this out rather graphically:

> Pharaoh's chariots and his host he cast into the sea;
>   and his picked officers are sunk in the Red Sea.
> The floods cover them;
>   they went down into the depths like a stone.
> Thy right hand, O YHWH, glorious in power,
>   thy right hand, O YHWH, shatters the enemy.
>   (Exod 15:4–6)

Egyptian chariots proved to be ineffective against Israel when YHWH flexed his arm, so why should any king think that he could achieve victory with Egyptian chariots? Perhaps Deut. 17:16 uses a touch of irony to make the point.

In 1 Kgs. 11:1–13, the writer condemns the results of marriage alliances with foreign kings, because Solomon's pagan wives had turned his heart away from YHWH. But there is no disapproval of the alliances themselves, and, as already mentioned, the deuteronomic historian does not reprove Solomon for the horse and chariot trade with Egypt. This stands in sharp contrast to later

prophets, who consistently censure any military aid from or association with
Egypt. Isa. 31:1 states:

> Woe to those who go down to Egypt for help
>   and rely on horses,
> who trust in chariots because they are many,
>   and in horsemen because they are very strong,
> but do not look to the Holy One of Israel
>   or consult YHWH!

An obvious question emerges: why is the prophetic response to
Israelite–Egyptian relations radically different after the time of Solomon? Two
suggestions come to mind. First, what angered the prophets was dependence
on Egypt, which caused Israel and Judah to turn away from reliance on
YHWH. This seems to be the point of Isa. 31:1. During Solomon's day, Israel
was not dependent on Egypt. They enjoyed good relations which benefited
both nations. Clearly, Israel was the stronger of the two.

Second, with the passing of Psusennes II, the last king of the 21st Dynasty,
Egypt came under control of the Libyan chieftain Sheshonk (Shishak). This, of
course, meant that the alliance with Solomon was off. A hostile attitude toward
Israel appeared even before the death of Solomon when Jereboam ben Nebat
escaped from Solomon's wrath to Egypt and found sanctuary with Sheshonk
(1 Kgs 11:40). Then, in Rehoboam's fifth year (926/925 B.C.),[56] Sheshonk
invaded Canaan, destroying many cities and exacting tribute from Rehoboam
(1 Kgs 14:25–26; 2 Chr 12:2–9).[57] This event illustrates that Egypt was no
longer a reliable partner or vassal and could not be trusted.

The schism between Israel and Judah five years earlier so severely weakened the two that from that point on Egypt was the more powerful kingdom.
Israel and Judah found themselves in squabbles with the Aramaeans, Assyrians, and Babylonians, and military dependence on Egypt became attractive.
The Canaanites for years had done the same thing. The Amarna letters[58] are
filled with requests to pharaoh to send troops and chariots. Thus the tendency
to look to Egypt for help was established prior to the Israelite monarchy. The
kings of Israel and Judah, it appears, were simply doing what their Canaanite
predecessors had done centuries earlier. It is precisely this dependence on
Egypt for armaments or troops that subsequent prophets deplored. The historical events that follow illustrate this well.

THE NINTH CENTURY B.C.

Less than thirty years after Sheshonk's invasion, during the reign of Asa
(2 Chr 14:9), the Egyptian presence was felt again in Israel. The leader of the
incursion this time was Zerah *(zrḥ)* the Cushite. Trying to determine the identity of this commander and his army has given rise to a great deal of speculation. Chronologically, the reign of Asa (911–870 B.C.) does not synchronize
with the Cushite 25th Dynasty (730–656 B.C.). Etymologically, *zrḥ* cannot be

equated with Osorkon I (the reigning pharaoh),[59] and the text states nowhere that Zerah was a king.

J. Bright follows W. F. Albright in thinking that when Sheshonk withdrew from Palestine after his raid in Rehoboam's fifth year (925 B.C.) he left a garrison of troops "on the frontier around Gerar."[60] Zerah, then, would likely have been the garrison commander or a mercenary leader. Kitchen points out that by the year 897 B.C., when the invasion would have taken place (that is, in Asa's fourteen–fifteenth year), Osorkon I would have been an old man and hence would have sent his military commander.[61]

If Zerah represented Egypt (as Kitchen, Bright, and others believe), the text nowhere specifies this. Zerah's force is said to be made up of Cushites and Libyans (2 Chr 16:8). The reference to Libyans might be expected because Sheshonk's dynasty was of Libyan extraction and there was a significant Libyan presence in the western Delta at this time.[62] S. Hidal theorizes that Zerah was a bedouin chieftain, that Cush ought to be identified with Cushan (as in Hab 3:7), and that it probably was located around Midian.[63] However, the Libyan and Nubian ethnic makeup of the force, along with the mention of the presence of 300 chariots, does not fit the description of bedouin tribes from northwestern Arabia.

Another matter which has lent some doubt to the authenticity of Zerah's invasion is the size of his army: 2 Chr. 14:9 indicates that there were 300 chariots (a modest number when compared with the chariot corps mentioned above) and a force of 1,000,000 (*)elep)ălāpîm*). This latter figure has been seen as an exaggeration, although the event is historical.[64] Alternatively, *)ălāpîm* could mean "units," hence a force of 1000 units. G. E. Mendenhall suggests that if pointed as *)allŭp*, it would mean "fully-armed soldier."[65] This would indicate a total of 1000 armed men, which might be considered a token force or garrison. This second suggestion, while possible, does not match the prophet Hanani's statement in 2 Chr. 16:8, in which the invading army is described as being very large. Then, too, Asa's prayer (14:11) suggests that a large number was involved. Under no circumstances, even during the height of her empire, could Egypt have mustered a force of 1,000,000 men. Another interpretation of this figure comes to mind. In military contexts, excessively large numbers were used to indicate a countless force, a myriad. On Tutankhmun's famous painted box,[66] which shows the chariot-riding king militarily engaged against Asiatics, the inscription reads that he "trampled hundreds of thousands" *(ptpt ḫfnw)*. Thutmose III, in his Poetical Stela, says, "I bound tens of thousands Nubian Bowmen and hundreds of thousands *[ḫfnw]* Northerns as prisoners of war."[67] While the word *ḫfnw* means one hundred thousand it also has the abstract meaning "great quantity."[68] Similarly, the "Legend of King Keret" mentions that his army *(ṣbu)* consisted of *tlt-m'at-rbt*, which G. R. Driver rendered as "three hundred times ten thousand."[69] H. L. Ginsberg renders this line "three hundred myriads,"[70] which brings out the idiomatic sense. This sense of a "myriad" or "countless host," it might be suggested, is the intended meaning of Zerah's *)elep)ălāpîm*.

Therefore we can confidently conclude that Asa experienced a real invasion from the south, most likely from Egypt, by a huge army. Because of his reliance on YHWH, Asa was victorious. On his return from defeating Zerah, Asa was met by Azariah the prophet, who encouraged him by saying that when the king trusts YHWH victory will be Israel's, even when she is outnumbered on the battlefield (2 Chr 15:1–7). This theme will be repeated to Asa years later by Hanani the seer in (16:7–8).

THE EIGHTH CENTURY B.C.
THE ASSYRIAN PERIOD

The first documented occurrence of Israel's seeking military assistance from Egypt is King Hoshea of Samaria's attempt (ca. 726/725 B.C.) to remove the yoke of Assyria's bondage:

> But the king of Assyria found treachery in Hoshea; for he had sent messengers to So, king of Egypt, and offered no tribute to the king of Assyria.
>
> (2 Kgs 17:4)

This act of rebellion led to the three-year siege of Samaria (17:5), her fall in 722/721 B.C., and the subsequent deportation by Sargon II (17:6).[71] There is no evidence from biblical, Egyptian, or Assyrian sources that help came.

The problem with 2 Kgs. 17:4 has been the identity of So, a complex problem which cannot be discussed at length here.[72] Kitchen thinks that *So* is an abbreviation for O(so)rkon IV (730–715 B.C.) of the 22nd Dynasty, whose capital was Tanis (biblical Zoan).[73] Most recently, Redford has built on H. Goedicke's ingenious suggestion that the name *So* is related to Sais (for example, *sʾw*), the Egyptian town in the western Delta. While Goedicke thinks Hoshea "sent messengers to So (that is, Sais) [to] the King of Egypt" (17:4),[74] Redford postulates that *So* may be related to Manetho's (the third century B.C. historian–priest's) epithet *pso*, attached to Neco's name. He observes that *pso* is derived from the Egyptian *pʾ sʾw(w)*, "the Saite."[75] The So of 2 Kgs. 17:4 may be derived from this expression, making the pharaoh in question "a Saite." While this interpretation has merit, it does not deal with the question of the proximity of Sais to Israel as compared with Tanis, located about sixty miles closer. Is it likely that Hoshea would have bypassed the closer Tanite king, Osorkon IV, for Tefnakht, the 24th Dynasty ruler from Sais? Kitchen points out that there may have been some commercial ties between Samaria and Tanis as early as the days of Ahab. Therefore Hoshea would naturally look to the house of Tanis, an old friend, and the closest Egyptian seat of power to him.[76]

The appeal to Egypt did not go unnoticed by Israel's prophets. Isaiah 19 appears to contain several oracles, which may be of separate origin,[77] that deal with Egypt. Verses 11–15 speak derogatorily of the princes of Tanis, calling them "fools" *(ʾĕwilîm)* and their advisors "stupid" *(nibʿārâ)*.

There is disagreement among commentators on Isaiah as to the historical context of this material. O. Kaiser thinks that chapter 19 is non-Isaianic and that the historical context being described dates "between the revolt of Amytaios, 404 B.C., and the final reconquest of Egypt by Artaxerxes III Ochos, 343 B.C."[78] A. S. Herbert and E. J. Young think it might fit into the beginning of the 25th Dynasty (ca. 730 B.C.).[79] Kitchen dates it to the events surrounding the fall of Samaria, specifically in response to Hoshea's appeal to Egypt to help overthrow Assyrian control.[80] This position makes good sense if So of 2 Kgs. 17:4 is indeed Osorkon IV from Tanis. It would explain why Tanis is singled out for the prophet's wrath in Isa. 19:11–15. Egypt could not help Israel because Egypt, too, was going to submit to a "hard master" (19:4)— as the entire Levant had periodically done.

Isa. 30:1–7 may also fit into this setting.[81] Israel is rebuked for taking "refuge in the protection of pharaoh" (30:2). Again Tanis is mentioned (30:4), a fact that could tie this oracle to the period under study. The prophet concludes by saying, "For Egypt's help is worthless and empty; therefore I have called her 'Rahab who sits still' " (30:7).

Like Rahab, the powerful sea monster that symbolized primeval chaos,[82] Egypt had a reputation for being powerful when she was actually powerless. YHWH demonstrated his mastery over the powers of disorder in creation, and over Egypt in the Exodus.[83]

Hos. 11:5 seems to echo the concern of Isaiah about Israel's reliance on Egypt for help. J. L. Mayes and H. W. Wolff each think that this passage could point to King Hoshea's appeal to Egypt.[84] But F. I. Anderson and D. N. Freedman believe that reference is being made here to fleeing to Egypt for refuge from the coming judgment.[85] The implication behind either interpretation is the same: "My people are bent on turning away from me" (11:7). Egypt should not be regarded as a source of aid or a place of refuge for Israel.

The next occasion when Egypt involved herself in Levantine affairs was in 701 B.C. during Sennacherib's invasion. The biblical witness to this event is woefully brief and leaves a number of questions unanswered. Both 2 Kgs. 19:9 and Isa. 37:9 report that Tirhaka, the Cushite king, was approaching, without stating either what induced the Cushite/Egyptian presence or what happened to that force. Sennacherib's Annals tell us that the Egyptians were repulsed by Eltekeh.[86]

In this paper I cannot delve into the problems surrounding Sennacherib's campaign(s), the date(s), or the age of Tirhaka. Studies of these critical issues over the past decade have by and large clarified the problems.[87] Kitchen concludes that Tirhaka was acting on behalf of Shebitku, his elder brother (and king), in 701 B.C., when Tirhaka would have been at least twenty years old.[88]

Isaiah, of course, was the central prophetic figure who worked alongside Hezekiah during the trying days of Sennacherib's invasion of Judah. Both Isa. 30:1–7 and 31:1–3 are most often regarded as a prophetic response to Judah's looking toward Egypt for help during the Assyrian crisis.[89] However, there is nothing specific in these statements that requires their assignment to the events of 701 B.C. Furthermore, nothing in 2 Kings 18–19 or Isaiah 36–37 suggests that Hezekiah had sent to Shebitku for assistance.

The Rabshakeh, speaking for Sennacherib who was besieging Lachish, in 2 Kgs. 18:19–21 and Isa. 36:4–6, asks Hezekiah a series of questions: "On what do you rest this confidence of yours? Do you think that mere words are strategy and power for war? On whom are you relying, that you have rebelled against me?" Most translations and commentators treat Isa. 36:6 and 2 Kgs. 18:21 as being statements of accusation: "Behold, you are relying on Egypt." NEB, however, regards the question as continuing: "on Egypt?" The combination of ʿattâ hinnēh in 2 Kgs. 18:21, which has apparently dropped out of Isa. 36:6, seems to mark the beginning of a strong statement. Thus the Rabshakeh seems to be accusing Hezekiah of relying on Egypt. Sennacherib's Annals indicate that Hezekiah, in fear, called on Egypt for help.[90]

It is intriguing that there is no direct condemnation of Hezekiah for calling on Egypt, either in Isaiah 36–37 or in 2 Kings 18–19. The only biblical evidence that has been cited to show that Hezekiah was relying on Egypt is Isa. 30:1–5 and 31:1–3.[91] But neither of these passages implicates Hezekiah, nor can either be securely tied to the events of 701 B.C. It is plausible, as suggested before, that these are denunciations for the reliance on Egypt that originated with Hoshea's appeal to Egypt in 2 Kgs. 17:4. These same words would surely serve as a warning to Hezekiah against such folly.

The silence of Isaiah and the deuteronomic historian concerning any wrongdoing on Hezekiah's part strongly suggests that he may not have appealed to Egypt for help. Hezekiah's demonstration of faith in YHWH in Isa. 37:14–20 and the oracle which followed (37:21–29) indicates that YHWH was going to rescue Jerusalem because of this faith. This hardly would have been true had Hezekiah sought help from Egypt.

The Chronicler portrays Hezekiah's faith even more positively (2 Chr 32:7–8). The king's words in verse 8 underscore his faith in YHWH and his recognition that Assyria simply would not be able to destroy Judah:

> With him [the king of Assyria] is the arm of flesh; but with us is YHWH our God, to help us and to fight our battles.

The exodus from Egypt saw YHWH's arm *(zĕrôaʿ)* triumph over pharaoh's.[92] Israel, when relying on YHWH, was assured that YHWH would be with her in battle, making all opposing powers "arms of flesh" *(zĕrôaʿ bāśār)*.

During this period of Egyptian history, Egypt was not the power she had been, a point recognized by the Assyrians:

> Behold you are relying on Egypt, that broken reed of a staff, which will pierce the hand of any man who leans on it. Such is Pharaoh king of Egypt to all who rely on him.
>
> (2 Kgs 18:21)

The choice of the term *reed (haqqānēh)* has been recognized as a fitting metaphor to describe Egypt, since it was known for its reed-filled marshes.[93] An even more likely reason for using *haqqānēh* is that the Egyptian word for king *(nsw)* means "he who is of the reed or sedge."[94] Clearly, pharaoh could offer no real help, and Tirhaka's efforts proved fruitless.[95]

Could it be that the Cushites acted independently against Assyria as a preventative measure to keep Assyria from invading Egypt, which was their ultimate goal?[96] Or had one of the other Palestinian cities such as Ekron, which had rebelled against Assyria, made the call?[97] Isaiah's admonition in Isa. 31:1–3 is directed to "those who go down to Egypt," not specifically at Judah or Hezekiah. The point of the prophet's denouncement is that Egyptian assistance was worthless because the Egyptians were human *('ādām)*, not divine *('ēl)* (31:3). (I have already mentioned the significance of the reference to Egyptian horses and chariots.)

THE LAST DAYS OF THE KINGDOM OF JUDAH

In the closing two decades of Judean history, the Egyptians, under the 26th Dynasty Saite kings, once again were involved in Palestine, and again the prophets stood opposed to Egyptian help.

Neco II (610–595 B.C.), the ambitious pharaoh who sought to reestablish Egypt's influence in Syria–Palestine, killed Josiah in 609 B.C. (2 Kgs 23:29; 2 Chr 35:20) when Josiah tried to block Neco's efforts to aid Assyria.[98] Three months later, Neco returned to Judah, where he removed Jehoahaz II from power and replaced him with Jehoiakim (2 Kgs 23:33–34). Egyptian influence in the region was short-lived, however, for in 606/605, Nebuchadnezzar, the Babylonian crown prince, beat the Egyptians at Carchemish, according to the Babylonian Chronicle.[99] This event is mentioned in 2 Kgs. 24:7:

> And the king of Egypt did not come again out of his land, for the king of Babylon had taken all that belonged to the king of Egypt from the brook of Egypt to the river Euphrates.

Egypt had not learned her lesson about meddling in territory that Babylon considered to be hers, and Neco's two successors ventured into Palestine. Herodotus informs us that Psammetichus II launched an invasion into Nubia,[100] which, according to Papyrus Rylands IX, was followed by an expedition to Palestine.[101] The purpose of the march to Palestine was not to conquer so much as to convince the petty kingdoms of the area that Egypt had regrouped after Neco's humiliating loss at Carchemish.[102] Zedekiah, the Judean king (597–586 B.C.), was apparently impressed with what he saw and decided to rebel against Nebuchadnezzar in 591 B.C., believing that Egypt could make the difference.[103]

The Babylonians returned to Palestine in 588 B.C. for what would become the termination of the state of Judah (2 Kgs 25:1). The call to Egypt went out by the envoy Coniah, son of Elnathan, according to Lachish Letter III.[104] Coniah may have been the son of Elnathan, son of Achbor (Jer 26:22–23), who had been an ambassador to Egypt early in the reign of Jehoiakim. The pharaoh who responded to the call for help was Hophra/Apries, who reigned from

589/588–570 B.C. Jeremiah, a resident in Jerusalem at that time, states that the Egyptian army reached Jerusalem during the siege, thus forcing the Chaldeans to withdraw temporarily and fight the Egyptians (Jer 37:5).[105] Since Jerusalem was besieged again a short while later (39), it appears that Jeremiah was correct in saying that the Egyptians would soon return to their own land (37:7).

Jeremiah 46 contains at least two oracles concerning Egypt. One, 46:1–12, is directed at Neco and reflects the events of 609–605 B.C.; but the other, 46:13–24, I have argued, belongs to the period of Apries' reign.[106] Egypt is informed that she will be defeated and her king is called a fool, apparently for trying to assist Israel. Earlier in his career, Jeremiah had warned against alliances with Assyria or Egypt. Jer. 2:18 accuses Judah of drinking from the waters of the Nile and "the River" (that is, the Euphrates). In Egyptian thought, to be "on the water" of another is to be loyal to someone[107]—an ally.

Such alliances led to a sentence being passed on Hophra, namely that he would be given "into the hand of his enemies . . . as I gave Zedekiah king of Judah into the hand of Nebuchadnezzar" (44:30). In this case both the king who had called for help and the Egyptian ally were personally judged. Zedekiah was captured, blinded, and taken to Babylon (39:5–7); his city was destroyed and his people were deported (2 Kgs 25:8–12). Hophra faced a civil war against one of his generals, Amasis, who eventually usurped the throne. Herodotus and Diodorus claim that Amasis captured Apries and turned him over to a mob, which strangled him.[108] Then in 568 B.C., Nebuchadnezzar invaded Egypt.[109] So indeed, both monarchs and their nations suffered similar fates.

A contemporary of Jeremiah was Ezekiel, who pronounced oracles against Egypt (Ezek 29–30); these are dated to the tenth through twelfth years of the exile (587–586 B.C.).[110] Ezekiel's description of Egypt is very similar to Isaiah's. Isaiah refers to Egypt as *Rahab*, who was powerless (Isa 30:7), while Ezekiel calls pharaoh a "great monster" *(hattannîm haggādôl)* (Ezek 29:3)[111] that will be caught by YHWH and placed in the wilderness. Ezekiel points out, as does Isaiah (Isa 36:6), that Egypt had been a reed *(qāneh)*, a support, to Israel (Ezek 29:6), and so would be judged.

Ezek. 30:21–22 contains an oracle which deals a blow to Egypt's arm of flesh:

> Son of man, I have broken the arm *[zĕrôa']* of pharaoh king of Egypt; lo, it has not been bound up, to heal it by binding it with a bandage, so that it may become strong to wield the sword. Therefore thus says the Lord YHWH: "Behold, I am against pharaoh king of Egypt, and will break his arms, both the strong arm and the one that was broken; and I will make the sword fall from his hand."

Some have observed that this statement about pharaoh might be connected with the defeat of Apries when he came to the aid of Jerusalem.[112] The symbolism of the "arm" and "sword" appears to tie this denunciation directly to Apries,[113] for he bore the Golden Horus and Two Ladies names of *nb ḫpš*, which means "possessor of a powerful arm."[114] Then too, there may be a play on the Egyptian word for *sword*, which was also *ḫpš*.[115]

Ezekiel's oracle stands at the end of a long prophetic tradition which saw Egypt as an enemy that had been convincingly defeated by YHWH's arm at the Exodus.[116] Therefore, it was futile for Israel to trust in Egypt for support against Assyria or Babylon. Hezekiah realized that YHWH would help Israel, that Israel's enemies were an arm of flesh (2 Chr 32:8). Sadly, not many of Israel's or Judah's kings had the faith to believe YHWH's prophets. To their own detriment, their tendency was to seek help from Egypt.

NOTES

1. Gary Rendsburg, "Merneptah in Canaan," *Journal of the Society for the Study of Egyptian Antiquities* 11 (1981): 171–72.
2. For the Israel Stela, see K. A. Kitchen, *Ramesside Inscriptions* (Oxford: Blackwell, 1975), 4:12–19; the Karnak inscription, F. Yurko, "Merneptah's Palestinian Campaign," *Journal of the Society for the Study of Egyptian Antiquities* 8 (1978): 70; see also, F. Yurko, "Merneptah's Canaanite Campaign," *JARCE* 23 (1987); see also G. W. Ahlström and D. Edelman, "Merneptah's Israel," *JNES* 44 (1985): 59–61.
3. Yurko, "Merneptah's Palestinian Campaign," 70.
4. D. B. Redford, "Studies in Relations during the First Millennium B.C. (II), The Twenty-Second Dynasty," *JAOS* 93 (1973): 3–17.
5. A. R. Green, "Solomon & Siamun: A Synchronism between Early Dynastic Israel and the Twenty-First Dynasty Egypt," *JBL* 97 (1978): 362, n. 48.
6. J. Mauchline, *1 and 2 Samuel*, New Century Bible (Grand Rapids, Mich.: Wm Eerdmans, 1971), 319.
7. Redford, "Twenty-Second Dynasty," 4.
8. Green, "Solomon & Siamun," 362.
9. A. Malamat, "A Political Look at the Kingdom of David and Solomon and Its Relations with Egypt," in T. Ishida, ed., *Studies in the Period of David and Solomon and Other Essays* (Winona Lake, Ind.: Eisenbrauns, 1982), 189–204.
10. Redford, "Twenty-Second Dynasty," 3–5.
11. D. B. Redford, "The Acquisition of Foreign Goods and Services in the Old Kingdom," *Scripta Mediterranea* 2 (1981): 5–6.
12. Redford, "Twenty-Second Dynasty," 4–5.
13. A. H. Gardiner, *Late Egyptian Stories*, Bibliotheca Aegyptiaca 1 (1932): 61–76; *ANET*, 25–29; M. Lichtheim, *Ancient Egyptian Literature* (Berkeley: University of California Press, 1976), 2:224–29.
14. Redford, "Twenty-Second Dynasty," 5.
15. For a recent discussion of the relations between Israel and Phoenicia during this period, see H. Donner, "The Interdependence of Internal Affairs and Foreign Policy during the Davidic–Solomic Period (with Special Regard to the Phoenician Coast)," in Ishida, ed., *Studies in the Period of David and Solomon*, 205–14.
16. E. Ball, "The Co-Regency of David and Solomon (1 Kings 1)," *VT* 27 (1977): 268–69.
17. W. J. Murnane, *Ancient Egyptian Co-Regencies*, in *Studies in Ancient Oriental Civilization*, vol. 40 (Chicago: Oriental Institute, 1977).
18. L. G. Perdue, "The Testament of David and Egyptian Royal Instructions," in *Scripture in Context*, ed. W. Hallo et al. (Winona Lake, Ind.: Eisenbrauns, 1983), 2:279–96.

19. W. K. Simpson, "The Single-Dated Monuments of Sesotris I: An Aspect of the Institution of Co-Regency in the Twelfth Dynasty," *JNES* 15 (1956): 214–19. Murnane, *Ancient Egyptian Co-Regencies*, 40:2–5.

20. P. Montet, *Egypt and the Bible* (Philadelphia: Fortress Press, 1959), 36–40; A. Malamat, "Aspects of the Foreign Policies of David and Solomon," *JNES* 22 (1963): 1–17, updated as "A Political Look at the Kingdom of David and Solomon," in Ishida, ed., *Studies in the Period of David and Solomon*, 189–204; S. H. Horn, "Who Was Solomon's Egyptian Father-in-Law?," *BR* 12 (1967): 3–17; H. D. Lance, "Solomon, Siamun and the Double Ax," in *Magnalia Dei: The Mighty Acts of God*, ed. Frank Moore Cross, Jr., et al. (Garden City, N.Y.: Doubleday, 1976), 209–23; Green, "Solomon & Siamun," 353–67.

21. K. A. Kitchen, *The Third Intermediate Period in Egypt (1110–650)* (Warminster, England: Aris & Phillips, 1973); K. A. Kitchen, "Further Thoughts of Egyptian Chronology in the Third Intermediate Period," *REg* 34 (1982–83): 59–69; K. Baer, "The Libyan and Nubian Kings of Egypt: Notes on the Chronology of Dynasties XXII–XXVI," *JNES* 32 (1973): 4–25; E. Wente, "On the Chronology of the Twenty-First Dynasty," *JNES* 26 (1967): 155–76; M. Bierbrier, *The Late New Kingdom in Egypt (1300–664)* (Warminster, England: Aris & Phillips, 1975); W. Barta, "Die Mondfinsternis im 15. Regierungsjahr Takelots II," *REg* 32 (1980–81): 3–17; A. Niwiński, "Problems in the Chronology and Geneology of the XXIst Dynasty: New Proposals and Their Interpretation," *Journal of the American Research Center in Egypt* 16 (1979): 49–68.

22. Kitchen, "Egyptian Chronology," 68; Kitchen, *Third Intermediate Period*, 280; Horn, "Who Was Solomon's Egyptian Father-in-Law?"

23. Redford, "Twenty-Second Dynasty," 7; Lance, "Solomon, Siamun and the Double Ax," 209; A. R. Schulman, "Diplomatic Marriage in the New Kingdom," *JNES* 38 (1979): 193.

24. Horn, "Who Was Solomon's Egyptian Father-in-Law?," 8–11; J. Gray, *I & II Kings*, OTL (Philadelphia: Westminster Press, 1970), 117–18; J. Robison, *The First Book of Kings*, Cambridge Bible Commentary (Cambridge: Cambridge University Press, 1972), 47–49; Lance, "Solomon, Siamun and the Double Ax," 210–11; Kitchen, *Third Intermediate Period*, 280; Green, "Solomon & Siamun," 359–60.

25. Kitchen, *Third Intermediate Period*, 280; Green, "Solomon & Siamun," 360.

26. One notable marriage between the royal house of Egypt and a foreign prince is that of Hadad the Edomite with the sister of Tahpenes early in Solomon's reign (1 Kgs 11:14–22). But this marriage, at least initially, was made with a foreign prince who was living in Egypt. So it was not a case of an Egyptian princess being sent to a foreign land. For a discussion of this, see J. R. Bartlett, "An Adversary against Solomon, Hadad the Edomite," *JBL* 88 (1976): 205–26.

27. Schulman, "Diplomatic Marriage in the New Kingdom," 177–93.

28. Ibid., 179.

29. Ibid., 186–87.

30. Malamat, "Foreign Policies of David and Solomon," 10.

31. J. Bright, *History of Israel*, 3d ed. (Philadelphia: Westminster Press, 1981), 212; S. Herrmann, *A History of Israel in Old Testament Times*, trans. J. Bowden (Philadelphia: Fortress Press, 1981), 175.

32. Malamat, "Foreign Policies of David and Solomon," 16–17; compare Malamat, "A Political Look at the Kingdom of David and Solomon," 198–99.

33. Kitchen, *Third Intermediate Period*, 281, n. 227.

34. Redford, "Twenty-Second Dynasty," 3–5.

35. J. A. Soggin, "The Davidic–Solomonic Kingdom," in *Israelite and Judaean History*, ed. J. Hayes and J. M. Miller, OTL (Philadelphia: Westminster Press, 1977), 375; Green, "Solomon & Siamun," 362, n. 48.

36. Kitchen, *Third Intermediate Period*, 281.

37. Malamat, "Foreign Policies of David and Solomon," 14–16; compare Malamat, "A Political Look at the Kingdom of David and Solomon," 194.

38. Schulman, "Diplomatic Marriage in the New Kingdom," 192.

39. Y. Ikeda, "Solomon's Trade in Horses and Chariots in Its International Setting," in Ishida, ed., *Studies in the Period of David and Solomon*, 215–31.

40. Many have felt that the reading *miṣrāyim* ought to be emended to *muṣri* (for discussion, see Gray, *I & II Kings*, 268–69). If *muṣri* is regarded as a major source for horses, it is strange that this Neo-Hittite kingdom of southern Asia Minor sent only 100 soldiers and apparently no chariotry or cavalry to the battle of Qarqar (see *ANET*, 279). The implication would be that Solomon was the middle man in the trade between the Syrian/Neo-Hittite states and *miṣrāyim* (see 1 Kgs 10:28–29). However, it makes little sense for two nations adjacent to each other to have a middle man some distance to the south. On the other hand, if Egypt were the source and Syria/Anatolia the recipient, Solomon was ideally situated to control the trade.

41. *Urkunden der 18. Dynastie* 3.6. The term *ḥtry* occurs in the Kamose Stela (L. Habachi, *The Second Stela of Kamose and His Struggle against the Hyksos Ruler and His Capital* [Glouckstadt, West Germany: J. J. Augustic, 1972], 36), and Wilson renders this as "chariotry" (*ANET*, 554). Alan R. Schulman ("Chariots, Chariotry, and the Hyksos," *Journal of the Society for the Study of Egyptian Antiquities* 10 [1980]: 112–13) points out that since the chariot determinative is not written, it probably means a "span" or "yoke of oxen" (see *Concise Dictionary of Middle Egyptian*, 180). I had made the same point earlier in a paper presented at the Annual Meeting of the Society for Mediterranean Studies in Toronto (13 March 1980). So the first clear reference to chariots in Egypt is from the tomb of Ahmose si Abena.

42. N. De Garis Davies, *The Tombs of Menkheperrasonb, Amenmose, and Another* (London: Egypt Exploration Society, 1933), pls. 11–12.

43. N. De Garis Davies, *The Tomb of Puyemre at Thebes* (New York: Egyptian Expedition, 1922–23), pl. 23.

44. N. De Garis Davies, *Private Tombs of Thebes IV* (Oxford: Oxford University Press, 1963), pl. 8.

45. Ikeda, "Solomon's Trade in Horses and Chariots," 227–31.

46. J. Hoffmeier, "The Evolving Chariot Wheel in the Eighteenth Dynasty," *Journal of the American Research Center in Egypt* 13 (1976): 44.

47. Gray, *I & II Kings*, 268; K. A. Kitchen, *The Bible in Its World* (Downers Grove, Ill.: Inter-Varsity Press, 1977), 102.

48. *ANET*, 278–79.

49. Y. Yadin, *The Art of Warfare in Biblical Lands*, trans. M. Pearlman (New York: McGraw–Hill, 1963), 2:284–85.

50. A. Phillips, *Deuteronomy*, Cambridge Bible Commentary (Cambridge: Cambridge University Press, 1973), 121.

51. G. von Rad, *Deuteronomy*, OTL, trans. D. Barton (Philadelphia: Westminster Press, 1966), 119; A. D. H. Mayes, *Deuteronomy*, New Century Bible Commentary (London: Marshall, Morgan and Scott, 1979), 272; Phillips, *Deuteronomy*, 121; P. C. Craigie, *The Book of Deuteronomy*, New International Commentary of the Old Testament (Grand Rapids, Mich: Wm. Eerdmans, 1976), 255–56.

52. Ikeda, "Solomon's Trade in Horses and Chariots," 225, 231.

53. Phillips, *Deuteronomy*, 60.

54. von Rad, *Deuteronomy*, 76.

55. For a discussion of the motif of YHWH's victorious right arm and possible connections with the Egyptian king's *ḫpš*, see J. Hoffmeier, "Egyptian Motifs Related to Warfare and Enemies and Their Old Testament Counterparts," in *Egyptological Miscellanies (Ancient World 4)*, 66–67. On the origins of this motif, see J. Hoffmeier, "The Arm of God Versus the Arm of Pharaoh in the Exodus Narratives," 67 *Bib* (1986): 3:378–87.

56. Kitchen, *Third Intermediate Period*, 72–75.

57. B. Mazar, "The Campaign of Pharaoh Shishak to Palestine," VTSup 4 (1957): 57–66; Kitchen, *Third Intermediate Period*, 432–47.
58. *ANET*, 483–90.
59. W. F. Albright, *JPOS* 4 (1924): 147; Kitchen, *Third Intermediate Period*, 309.
60. Albright, *JPOS* 4:146–47; Bright, *History of Israel*, 234–35.
61. Kitchen, *Third Intermediate Period*, 309.
62. Ibid., 291.
63. S. Hidal, "The Land of Cush in the Old Testament," in *Svensk Exegetisk Årsbok*, 41–42 (N.p., 1976–77): 100–1.
64. Bright, *A History of Israel*, 235, n. 20.
65. G. E. Mendenhall, "The Census List of Numbers 1 & 26," *JBL* 77 (1958): 52–66.
66. N. De Garis Davies, *Tutankhamun's Painted Box* (Oxford: Oxford University Press, 1962), pl. 1.
67. *Urkunden der 18. Dynastie* 612.15–16. This couplet may be a parallel to the Hebrew expression "thousand and ten thousand," as in 1 Sam. 18:7 and Mic. 6:7.
68. *Concise Dictionary of Middle Egyptian*, 168; Adolph Erman and H. Grapow, eds., *Wörterbuch der Aegyptischen* (Leipzig, East Germany: J. C. Hinrich, 1929), 3:74.
69. G. R. Driver, *Canaanite Myths and Legends* (Edinburgh: T & T Clark, 1956), 30 (Text I ii, 36), trans., 31.
70. H. L. Ginsberg, *ANET*, 143. The Assyrians used to describe the armies of their enemies similarly. Sennacherib refers to Tirhaka's army as "beyond counting" (*ANET*, 287).
71. *ANET*, 284–85.
72. For the most recent discussion of the problem, see my forthcoming article "So," in *International Standard Bible Encyclopedia*, vol. 4. Kitchen's review of the problem in *Third Intermediate Period*, 372–76, is most thorough for the literature up to 1972.
73. Kitchen, *Third Intermediate Period*, 272–73.
74. Hans Goedicke, "The End of 'So, King of Egypt,'" *BASOR* 171 (1963): 64–66.
75. D. B. Redford, "A Note on II Kings 17:4," *Journal of the Society for the Study of Egyptian Antiquities* 11 (1981): 75–76.
76. Kitchen, *Third Intermediate Period*, 324.
77. A. S. Herbert, *Isaiah 1–39*, Cambridge Bible Commentary (Cambridge: Cambridge University, 1973), 121; O. Kaiser, *Isaiah 13– 39*, OTL (Philadelphia: Westminster Press, 1973), 99.
78. Kaiser, *Isaiah 13–39*, 99. However, a date in the Persian period is most unlikely. First, although Isa. 19:11 refers to pharaoh, during the Persian occupation, the Persian emperor bore the title "pharaoh." In the absence of the emperor, a satrap was the actual ruling figure. Second, Noph (Memphis) was the seat of the satrapy mentioned in 19:13. But Zoan (Tanis) occurs twice in this passage and appears to be the focus of the prophet's wrath. During the Persian period, Zoan played no significant political role in Egypt to warrant the condemnation received in the text. At the end of eighth century B.C. in Egypt, when Hoshea would have made his call for help, there were several concurrent dynasts. Piankhy was establishing Cushite control, and Memphis was the Cushite capital. Sais was the seat of power of the 24th Dynasty kings, while Tanis was the capital of the 22nd Dynasty. Isa. 19:2 mentions the Egyptians being against the Egyptians, and verses 11 and 13 refer to princes (*śārîm*) of Tanis and Memphis. This precisely portrays the political turmoil that existed in Egypt between 750–730 B.C., but not in the Persian period. (I should like to thank Professor Kitchen for corresponding with me on the matter, as well as Kenneth Hoglund, who wrote his doctoral dissertation [Duke University] on the Persian period, with special interest in Egypt. Their letters support the conclusions I had already reached on the question.)
79. Herbert, *Isaiah 1–39*, 121; E. J. Young, *Isaiah I* (Grand Rapids, Mich.: Wm. Eerdmans, 1969), 15.
80. Kitchen, *Third Intermediate Period*, 373–74.
81. Kaiser, *Isaiah 13–39*, 283; Herbert, *Isaiah 1–39*, 172; B. S. Childs, *Isaiah and the Assyrian*

Crisis (London: S.C.M. Press, 1967), 32–33. Young, *Isaiah I*, 335, ties this material to Hezekiah's time, which is certainly possible.

82. T. H. Gaster, "Rahab," in *IDB*, 4:6.

83. Hoffmeier, "Arm of God."

84. J. L. Mayes, *Hosea*, OTL (Philadelphia: Westminster Press, 1969), 155; H. W. Wolff, *Hosea* (Philadelphia: Fortress Press, 1974), 200.

85. F. I. Anderson and D. N. Freedman, *Hosea*, Anchor Bible (Garden City, N.Y.: Doubleday, 1980).

86. *ANET*, 287.

87. For references to Egyptologists who disagree with the views of many Old Testament scholars, see Kitchen, *Third Intermediate Period*, 158–72, esp. 164, n. 340; see also his "Late-Egyptian Chronology and the Hebrew Monarchy," *JANESCU* 5 (1973): 225–31. One who no longer sees a problem with Tirhaka's being in Palestine in 701 B.C. is Gray, *I & II Kings*, 660–61.

88. Kitchen, *Third Intermediate Period*, 176–77.

89. Childs, *Isaiah and the Assyrian Crisis*, 32–35; Kaiser, *Isaiah 13–39*, 283–84, 311; K. Koch, *The Prophets I: The Assyrian Period*, trans. M. Kohl (Philadelphia: Fortress Press, 1978), 128–29; Herbert, *Isaiah 1–39*, 180.

90. *ANET*, 287.

91. Childs, *Isaiah and the Assyrian Crisis*, 32–35; Koch, *Prophets I*, 127; Kaiser, *Isaiah 13–39*, 283–84, 312; Herbert, *Isaiah 1–39*, 172.

92. Hoffmeier, "Arm of God."

93. E. J. Young, *Isaiah II* (Grand Rapids, Mich.: Wm. Eerdmans, 1969), 461; C. F. Keil and F. Delitzsh, *Isaiah*, vols. 19 and 20, Commentary on the Old Testament, trans. James Martin et al. (Grand Rapids, Mich.: Wm. Eerdmans, 1949–50), 87.

94. A. H. Gardiner, *Egyptian Grammar*, 3d ed. (London: Oxford University Press, 1957), 73.

95. *ANET*, 287–88; K. A. Kitchen, "Egypt, Levant and Assyria in 701 B.C.," in *Ägypten und Altes Testament 5, Fontes Anque Pontes*, Eine Festgave Für Hellmut Brunner (Wiesbaden, West Germany: In Kommision Bei O, 1983), 247–51. On Egypt's military machine during the Cushite period, see A. Spalinger, "Notes on the Military in Egypt during the XXVth Dynasty," *Journal of the Society for the Study of Egyptian Antiquities* 11 (1981): 37–58.

96. A. K. Grayson, "Assyria's Foreign Policy in Relation to Egypt in the Eighth and Seventh Centuries B.C.," *Journal of the Society for the Study of Egyptian Antiquities* 11 (1981): 85–88; see 85, n. 1, for other bibliographic information.

97. Kitchen, "Egypt, Levant and Assyria in 701 B.C.," 246.

98. Among those who think that Neco was aiding Assyria, see Herrmann, *History of Israel*, 271–72; B. Oded, in *Israelite and Judaean History*, ed. J. H. Hayes and J. M. Miller (Philadelphia: Westminster Press, 1977), 468; Bright, *History of Israel*, 324–25; Kitchen, *Third Intermediate Period*, 407.

99. D. W. Thomas, ed., *Documents from Old Testament Times* (Edinburgh: Thomas Nelson and Sons, 1958), 78–79.

100. Herodotus 1:161.

101. F. L. Griffiths, *Catalogue of the Demotic Papyri in the John Rylands Library*, Manchester, 3 vols. (1909), 2:64–65. For discussion of these events, see J. Hoffmeier, "A New Insight on Pharaoh Apries from Herodotus, Diodorus and Jeremiah 46:17," *Journal of the Society for the Study of Egyptian Antiquities* 11 (1981): 165–70.

102. Ibid.; see also D. B. Redford and F. S. Freedy, "The Dates in Ezekiel in Relation to Biblical, Babylonian and Egyptian Sources," *JAOS* 90 (1970): 462–87; A. Spalinger, "The Concept of the Monarchy during the Saite Epoch—An Essay of Syntheses," *Or* 47 (1977): 12–36.

103. Hoffmeier, "New Insight on Pharaoh Apries," 166.

104. *ANET*, 337.

105. Josephus *Antiquities* 10.108–10 reports on this event and apparently relies on Jeremiah 37 as his source.

106. Hoffmeier, "New Insight on Pharaoh Apries," 167.

107. *Concise Dictionary of Middle Egyptian*, 105.
108. Herodotus 2:169; Diodorus 68:4–5.
109. D. J. Wiseman, *Chronicles of Chaldean Kings (626–556 B.C.) in the British Museum* (London: Trustees of British Museum, 1961), 94; *ANET*, 308.
110. Redford and Freedy, "Dates in Ezekiel," 484.
111. Some versions read *jackals*, but *tannîm*/"sea-monster" fits the picture better. This latter reading also suits LXX, where *drākonta* is used. For this reason most commentators believe *tannîm* to be correct; compare J. W. Wevers, *Ezekiel*, New Century Bible Commentary (London: Marshall, Morgan and Scott, 1982), 160–61; J. B. Taylor, *Ezekiel*, Tyndale Old Testament Commentaries (Downers Grove, Ill.: Inter-Varsity Press, 1969), 199–200; K. W. Carley, *The Book of the Prophet Ezekiel*, Cambridge Bible Commentary (Cambridge: Cambridge University, 1974), 197, n. 3.
112. Redford and Freedy, "Dates in Ezekiel," 482–83.
113. Ibid.; Hoffmeier, "New Insight on Pharaoh Apries," 168.
114. H. Gauthier, *Le Livre des rois d'Égypte* (Le Caire: Impr. de l'Institut francais d'archéologie Orientale, 1914), 4:111. For the meaning, see Erman and Grapow, eds., *Wörterbuch der Aegyptischen*, 3:269.
115. See Redford and Freedy, "Dates in Ezekiel," 482–83. For *ḫpš* meaning "sword," see Erman and Grapow, eds., *Wörterbuch der Aegyptischen*, 3:270.
116. Hoffmeier, "Arm of God."

8

Israel's Apostasy: Catalyst of Assyrian World Conquest

Paul R. Gilchrist

The rise and fall of Israel as a nation is a well-chronicled history, though it has many gaps and unanswered questions. Some studies have been done on Israel vis-à-vis the nations.[1] This essay attempts to show that as long as Israel remained loyal to her covenant Lord, and thus loyal to her mission, God would keep his word not to allow another power such as Assyria to gain ascendancy to world domination. I will (1) review the biblical data dealing with Israel's destiny as "the head of the nations" (Deut 28:1); (2) examine explicit prophetic evaluations of Israel's final years (largely Isa 7–10) to determine what principles were used; and (3) correlate the fluctuating rise of Assyria to world domination with Israel's successive stages of apostasy by applying the prophetic principles to show that Israel's apostasy did serve as a catalyst for Assyrian world conquest.

ISRAEL'S DESTINY: THE HEAD OF THE NATIONS

Israel's destiny as a nation is best seen in the light of the covenant.[2] A brief survey of passages will suffice. One of the earliest intimations of Israel's destiny is found in the covenant promises made to Abram: "And I will make you a great nation . . . and in you all the families of the earth shall be blessed" (Gen 12:2–3). This is further amplified in Gen. 17:4–5 when Abram's name is changed to Abraham: "For I have made you a father of many nations [gôyîm]."[3] These promises are couched in the language of blessing, which immediately suggests the blessing and curse formula of the covenants. The most complete proclamation of blessings and curses is found in Deuteronomy 28, a passage that expands on the conditional clause of Exod. 19:5–6: "If you will indeed obey my voice and keep my covenant, then you shall be a special treasure to me above all people; for all the earth is mine. And you shall be to me a kingdom of priests and a holy nation."

It is important to note the phrase "for all the earth is mine." YHWH revealed himself as the owner of the world, by virtue of his creation and providence. But Israel as a holy nation belonged to the Almighty not only by virtue of creation and providence, but more significantly by virtue of redemption. These are the words of the sovereign Lord (YHWH) of the universe, not just a god of a small nation (see Deut 7:7).

The condition, "If you will indeed obey my voice and keep my covenant," was an appropriate responsibility placed upon the people of the nation, individually and collectively, as a recognition of their free agency. They were not coerced into unwilling submission. Clearly, YHWH, as Israel's great king, took an oath to keep his part of the covenant (compare Gen 15:8–17).[4] Thus Deut. 7:8–9 uses this notion of a god who is faithful to keep his covenant as an encouragement to his covenantal people to do the same. Will Israel follow the pattern set by the great king? The alternatives are clearly set forth in 7:9–10, the blessing of covenant-love to those who love him and maintain their loyalty to him[5] and the curse of covenant-retribution to those who hate him and break the covenant relation. This retribution is precisely what was operative in the program of conquest over the Canaanites.[6]

Deuteronomy 28 makes three references to YHWH's placing Israel over the nations in the context of covenant blessings. On condition of faithfulness to him, "YHWH your God will set you high above all nations of the earth" (v 1; compare 26:19); "YHWH will cause your enemies who rise against you to be defeated before your face" (v 7); and "YHWH will make you the head and not the tail; you shall be above only, and not beneath" (v 13). Centuries later, Isaiah developed this theme in an eschatological message: "The mountain of YHWH's house shall be established as the chief of the mountains . . . and all the nations shall flow to it" (Isa 2:2).

Thus, so long as Israel remained loyal to her covenant Lord, her mission of universal leadership would be assured. However, disloyalty to the great king could only result in a series of curses (Deut 28:15–68) of increasing intensity, designed primarily to confront Israel with her rebellion in order to restore the nation. Instead of blessing, the curses would have a converse effect on Israel.

The warnings and threats of the curses were clear and forthright. Rather than Israel defeating the nations, "YHWH will cause you to be defeated before your enemies" (Deut 28:25). Instead of being high and exalted, "the alien who is among you shall rise higher and higher above you, and you shall come down lower and lower" (v 43). And instead of being the head, the alien "shall be head, and you (Israel) shall be the tail" (v 44). The tragedy of invasion by a foreign power with all its attendant horrors was further threatened in verses 49 to 57. Even the awful specter of being "scattered among all peoples, from one end of the earth to the other," was raised as a final form of discipline. Ultimately, restoration was prophesied in Deut. 30:1–8 and reiterated by the prophets (for example, Isa 27:13; 59:20–21).[7]

It seems, then, that the revealed will of YHWH for Israel as head of the nations suggests that world domination by any other nation would take place only if Israel deliberately rebelled against her covenant Lord, denying YHWH as the true mediator and redeemer of the world.

The contrasting alternatives are recorded in the books of Joshua and Judges. In Joshua, the blessings were manifested in the conquest of the Canaanite nations; while in Judges, the curses were exhibited in the hopeless disarray of Israel's doing "what was right in their own eyes" (Judg 21:25) and being over-run by one or another of the surrounding nations. The historical–literary motif of sin, judgment, repentance, and restoration exhibited the apostate tendency in Israel and should have been an early warning to Israel that YHWH, the great king of the covenant, meant to stand by the sanctions of blessings and curses. It was not until the Davidic and Solomonic period of the united monarchy that Israel experienced a high point of her mission. Israel had conquered her enemies, made them vassals, and enjoyed a reputation of grandeur, power, wealth, and wisdom.

It is here that we begin to see the identification of the nations with Israel. The expansion of the kingdom of Israel reached its apogee when "Solomon reigned over all the kingdoms from the River (Euphrates) to the land of the Philistines, as far as the border of Egypt" (1 Kgs 4:21; compare 4:24; 8:65).[8] This expansion took place in accord with the promise of Exod. 23:29–31 that it would not take place in a year, but "little by little I will drive them out before you, until you have increased, and you inherit the land." In Israel's experience, especially under Joshua, David, and Solomon, whenever Israel was true to her mission YHWH enlarged her borders and gave her dominion over the nations, either by expropriating their land or by making them vassals to Israel.

A. Gileadi makes a further observation concerning the eschatological iden-tification of the nations with Israel. He points out that this will be effected politically, "because Israel has since mingled and become identified with the nations," and theologically, "because covenant curses in the Book of Isaiah extend as much to the nations as they do to Israel (see esp. 24:5), and because all are accepted into the covenant who prove loyal to Israel's God (see 56:1–8; 66:18–21)."[9] Indeed, this theological element is supported by the Davidic cov-enant (2 Sam 7:10–11). It is supported eschatologically by the royal messianic Psalm (2:6–8) that points to the formal installation of the "son" as king and promises, "Ask of me, and I will give you the nations for your inheritance, and the ends of the earth for your possession." One cannot help but wonder what might have happened if Solomon and his descendants had remained loyal to their covenant Lord.

In summary, the scriptures reveal that YHWH's great covenantal design for his chosen people was that Israel become a great nation. More than that, she was to be the "head of the nations," "the chief of the mountains," and all nations would flow to her. Further, eschatologically, the nations were to be her inheritance and the ends of the earth her possession. However, the condition of that covenantal relation was that Israel be faithful and loyal to YHWH, the great king of the covenant. Breaking the covenant by going after other gods, that is, by substituting suzerains, would be tantamount to the most heinous kind of rebellion against the divine Suzerain.

DETERMINING PRINCIPLES
FOR PROPHETIC EVALUATION

Let us examine a prophetic evaluation of Israel's final years. We will seek to determine what principles were used in such assessment. We will look at Isaiah 7-10, one of the most explicit dialogues on the subject of Israel and Assyria. At the outset, however, we may do well to remember that the prophets were messengers of YHWH to Israel, his people. J. Lindblom correctly claims: "The prophets were conscious of the fact that they were called and sent to proclaim a divine message. Their task was to utter oracles and to bring to their people an urgent communication from God about sin and repentance, judgment and salvation."[10] E. J. Young is more pointed in his reference to the prophetic institution as guardian of the theocracy: "The prophets were to build upon the foundation of the Mosaic Law, and to expound that law unto the nation. They would thus be the preservers and defenders of the principles upon which the theocracy had been founded by God."[11]

It is our task to cull from the pages of the prophets the divine assessment of the rise of Assyria to world power. We will look primarily to Isaiah, who made some of the clearest prophetic pronouncements on the subject, then to other prophets who addressed the Assyrian problem, distilling principles we may then apply to some of the earlier historical situations.

Many of the eighth-century B.C. prophets intimated that Israel would be taken captive into Assyria.[12] During the closing years of Pekah's reign in Israel, Isaiah very explicitly stated, "Inasmuch as these people refuse the waters of Shiloah that flow softly, and rejoice in Rezin and in Remaliah's son; now therefore, behold, YHWH brings up over them the waters of the River, strong and mighty—the king of Assyria and all his glory; he will go up over all his channels and go over all his banks. He will pass through Judah, he will overflow and pass over, he will reach up to the neck; and the stretching out of his wings will fill the breadth of your land, O Immanuel" (Isa 8:6–8; compare 7:7–9; 16–20).

Several observations are in order. First, we must note that the speaker is YHWH, the great king of the covenant (8:5),[13] revealing that the mighty acts about to take place in history are to be the acts of the sovereign Lord (8:7). He is about to bring on his people "the waters of the Euphrates, even the king of Assyria." Indeed, judgment is pronounced and will inexorably come upon those who refuse to acknowledge YHWH as the great king, the lord of lords and king of kings. YHWH himself is zealous to maintain his distinctive status among all the nations of the world. And it is his word that controls the course of history. As O. P. Robertson has so ably demonstrated, "The entire history of the monarchy in Israel hinges on the word of the Lord. Having established the basis of his covenant relationship with David, God faithfully demonstrates the veracity of his word. From the first chastisement against Solomon to the ultimate deportation of the nation, God's word of the covenant controls history."[14]

That the sovereign God of history, the Lord of the covenant, is in control of Assyria is further supported when the threat of judgment is pronounced using "Assyria, the rod of my anger" (10:5). It is YHWH who claims, "I will send him against an ungodly nation, and against the people of my wrath I will give him charge . . . yet he does not mean so, nor does his heart think so" (10:6–7). But YHWH's control does not stop there, for in a concluding section, Isaiah foresees the destruction of Assyria by the self-same covenant Lord: "So it will be that when YHWH has completed all his work on Mount Zion and on Jerusalem, he will say, I will punish the fruit of the arrogant heart of the king of Assyria and the pomp of his haughtiness" (10:12). Later he adds, "YHWH of Hosts will arouse a scourge against him" (10:26). These passages are clear in expressing the divine concurrence and governance in the affairs of the nations in general,[15] and of Assyria in particular.

In the second place, we must take note of the reason given by Isaiah (8:6–7) for the judgment to come on Israel and Judah. There is a negative and a positive aspect: the rejection of the gently flowing waters of Shiloah and the rejoicing in Rezin and Pekah. The reference may be to the stream connecting *En sitti Miryam* and *En Silwan*, because it flowed from under the temple area in Jerusalem.[16] Or perhaps the reference to the waters of Shiloah is better understood by its identification with Gihon, the place where Davidic kings were anointed. Thus it would be a symbol of the enduring Davidic dynasty.[17] Hence the rejection is of YHWH, the great king, whose presence has filled the temple (1 Kgs 8:10–11; compare Isa 6:1) and who is closely identified with his vassal king. The people's "rejoicing" in Rezin and Pekah belies their dependence on a fragile treaty between Samaria and Damascus, believing that a three-way alliance will hold back the growing menace of Assyrian world domination.

Clearly, Isaiah's message is that Israel and Judah have rebelled against their suzerain, YHWH, the great king, and have found a substitute in a tripartite alliance of weak nations. In keeping with their rejection of "the softly flowing waters of Shiloah," YHWH will send instead the torrential flood of the Euphrates, namely, the king of Assyria. Ironically, Ahaz, the pro-Assyria king of Judah, has been rebuked for secretly making an alliance with Assyria to ward off the Syro–Ephraimite conspiracy against his administration in Judah. But in so doing, Ahaz has deliberately rejected YHWH as his suzerain and substituted Tiglath-pileser of Assyria. This rejection of YHWH as the covenant King results in the pointed judgment pronounced by Isaiah (7:17–25). The judgment on Israel is fulfilled by the destruction of Samaria in 723 B.C. and the languishing desolation of Judah in the days of Manasseh and Amon. The only reprieve from judgment comes under the Judean kings Hezekiah and Josiah, a reprieve that reflects amazingly Isaiah's vision of the overflowing Euphrates — "It will reach up to the neck" (8:8).

We should take note of another passage in this context, Isa. 9:8–10:4. When Isaiah confronts Ahaz at the time of the Syro–Ephraimite conspiracy, he seeks to persuade Ahaz to put his trust in YHWH, his covenant Lord, not in the Assyrian suzerain. Even though Isaiah has declared that YHWH will send Assyria not as friend but as foe, he seeks to make clear that YHWH is very much concerned for his land and his people. This is expressed in Isaiah's urging them to repent, to renew the covenant, and to trust in YHWH. Ultimately, YHWH will be vindicated by the coming of the Prince of Peace, who will sit on the throne of David and rule over his kingdom (9:2–7). But throughout the period of Israel's apostasy, YHWH has engaged in actions that seek the restoration of covenantal relations.

In this four-stanza message to Israel, Isaiah warns and implores Israel to return to her covenant Lord. The warning is accompanied by recounting some recent events YHWH has used to try to bring Israel to her senses. The earlier invasions of Tiglath-pileser that destroyed the "houses of well-hewn stone" (Amos 5:11) provoke a response of entrenched arrogance instead of repentance (Isa 9:9–10). Even the attacks of Syria and the Philistines cannot prick Israel's conscience (9:12). The clear evidence of a corrupt leadership and bankrupt society arouses only apathy (9:14–17). The fury of YHWH's anger, rather than awakening a faint call for help, turns into the chaos of civil war (9:18–21). Each stanza closes with the ominous refrain, "For all this his anger does not turn away and his hand is stretched out still." There is a melancholy note in this refrain, for the prophet is assuring the long-suffering patience of YHWH, while calling his people to turn from their apostate ways. Here, Isaiah is only reiterating the same kind of message Amos gave some thirty years before, in which a review of YHWH's providence through famine, drought, locust plague, war, and earthquakes constituted a call to repentance (Amos 4:6–13). Amos' message was punctuated by the recurring phrase, "Yet you have not returned to me, declares YHWH."

These messages by Amos and Isaiah are a faithful exposition of the covenantal curse sanctions (Lev 26:14–45; Deut 28:15–68) and the intercessory prayer of Solomon at the dedication of the temple (1 Kgs 8:31–53). Speaking of Solomon, we would do well to recall that even the disruption of the kingdom after Solomon's death was a severe measure taken to correct any further influence of Solomon's apostasy. After being warned twice about worshiping the Canaanite gods, Solomon had refused to turn back to YHWH (1 Kgs 11:9). It needs to be emphasized that the disruption of the kingdom came about because of Solomon's religious sins, not because of social or political injustices (1 Kgs 11:11, 33), nor for his polygamy. The point that needs to be stressed is that YHWH, the great king of the covenant, would providentially bring calamity and disaster with increasing severity for the expressed purpose of calling his people to repentance and faith.[18]

In sum, three important principles underlie the prophetic view of the history of Israel. First, it was based on the covenantal word of YHWH, whereby the course of history involved the covenant sanctions for good or evil, for blessing or curse. Second, the reason for such judgment on his people was that they had rebelled against the covenant by rejecting YHWH as their great king; they had deliberately committed themselves to idolatrous deities and cultic practices. And third, YHWH, who is faithful to his covenant, had to implement the sanctions by sending one calamity after another with increasing severity, ever seeking to bring Israel to repentance through renewal of the covenant and wholehearted commitment to him. With these principles in mind, I will trace the history of Israel vis-à-vis Assyria.

THE CORRELATION OF ASSYRIA'S RISE TO POWER AND ISRAEL'S APOSTASY

I will now correlate the fluctuating rise of Assyria to world domination with Israel's successive stages of apostasy. By applying the prophetic principles of evaluation, I will seek to show that Israel's apostasy served as a catalyst for Assyria's rise to world conquest.

During the Middle Assyrian Period (1300–900 B.C.) the Assyrians were emerging from the dark ages imposed on them by the Mitanni and Hittite empires. Except for a couple of forays to the west,[19] Assyrian power was eclipsed until Tukulti-ninurta II (890–884 B.C.). The first major expansion, however, was under Ashurnasirpal II (884–860 B.C.) and his son Shalmaneser III (859–824 B.C.). A. L. Oppenheim, from a strictly historical perspective, states that from the time of Shalmaneser III to Sargon II (722–705 B.C.) "Assyria posed an immediate threat to the two kingdoms of Judah and Israel (that is, in the period from Omri [876–869 B.C.] to Manasseh [687–642 B.C.]) but, in fact, *all the fluctuations of Assyrian military might*, beginning with Tiglath-pileser II (966–935 B.C.; a contemporary of Solomon), *had their reflections in the political stability of Syria and Palestine.*"[20]

Beginning with Ashurnasirpal II and Shalmaneser III, the royal inscriptions give evidence of a new attitude of aggression and cruelty as these leaders pushed toward the Mediterranean and into Syria, even in the face of strong resistance by the Aramaeans. This western expansion began in the period of the Omride dynasty (885–841 B.C.) and Jehu (841–814 B.C.) in Israel, coinciding in Judah with the period from Asa to Joash. Omri was proclaimed king of Israel while leading a part of the army in a border clash with the Philistines at Gibbethon. Israel had been sufficiently weakened by wars with Asa of Judah and Ben-Hadad I of Syria. Furthermore, the political conspiracies resulting in the assassinations of Elah and Zimri within a week of each other resulted in the civil war in which Omri challenged the claim of Tibni ben Ginath to be king (1 Kgs 16:8–28).

Upon Tibni's death in 880 B.C., Omri became sole ruler of Israel. He strengthened the nation militarily, politically, and economically. His moving the capital from Tirza to Samaria was designed defensively to preclude attacks from Syria and economically to get involved in the lucrative international trade. In his short six-year reign as sole ruler of Israel, he established a reputation for himself and his successors.[21] His son Ahab (874–853 B.C.) carried his father's tradition further by making commercial and military alliances with Sidon and Judah.

The prophetic concern, however, focused on the religious implications of these alliances. Of Omri it is said that for the first time since Jeroboam he acted "more wickedly than all who ruled before him" (1 Kgs 16:25). But Ahab was worse yet. Having established a treaty with Ethbaal of Sidon, he sealed it by marrying Ethbaal's daughter Jezebel. Beyond that, he "went to serve Baal and worshiped him" (1 Kgs 16:31). He even did the unthinkable: he erected an altar to Baal in Samaria, and made the Ashera, doing "more to provoke YHWH, God of Israel, than all the kings before him" (1 Kgs 16:31–33). The confrontations by Elijah, Micaiah, and other unnamed prophets show that a significant turn of events had taken place in Israel. The situation for Judah was not much better, as the usurpation of the throne by Athaliah reveals (841–835 B.C.).

Meanwhile, during this whole period, Assyrian resurgence was taking place. Tukulti-ninurta II had taken strong military action that led to the reestablishment of the Assyrian Empire. Ashurnasirpal II marched against Bit-Adini (the Beth-Eden mentioned in Amos 1:5), preparing the way for a major incursion in 877 B.C. into Syria, Tyre, Sidon, Byblos, and back up to the Amanus Mountains before returning home. He received tribute from Tyre, Sidon, and Byblos. That expedition might well have served as an ominous warning to Omri and Ahab. But rather than turn to YHWH, the response was to trust in the well-defended capital of Samaria and strong military alliances. These alliances, unfortunately, were accompanied by commitment to idolatrous gods and religious practices.

When Shalmaneser III succeeded to the throne, he spent his first three years in campaigns to the west, capturing Carchemish in 857 B.C. and annexing Bit-Adini in 856 B.C. The Arameans saw the meaning of all this and determined to oppose it by a coalition of "twelve kings of the sea coast," including Ahab, who supplied ten thousand infantry and two thousand chariots.[22] The battle, fought at Qarqar on the Orontes in 853 B.C., seems to have been won by the defenders, even though Shalmaneser claimed victory. In any case, the Assyrians did not return for several years. It has often been pointed out that Ahab's chariots were more than half the chariots of the twelve-nation coalition, an indication of Israel's formidable military strength in that period.

Shalmaneser regrouped his forces, assembling an army of 125,000 by 845 B.C. When Hadadezer of Syria was assassinated in 842 B.C., Shalmaneser marched against the usurper Hazael and routed his army at Mount Senir (Hermon) but failed to capture Damascus. Nevertheless, the Assyrians ravaged the Hauran plain and marched across to Mount Carmel *(Ba⟨li ra⟩si)*, where he received tribute from Jehu *(Yaua mār Ḫumri)*, as well as from Tyre and Sidon. The last attempt of Shalmaneser to take Damascus was in 838 B.C., but he failed, making no further campaigns to the west. The rest of his reign was marked by domestic revolutions.

The people of YHWH in Israel, and to some extent in Judah, should have realized the implications of the resurgence of Assyria to world dominance during these five decades. After all, the major world powers in the course of history had been the Mesopotamian countries of Assyria and Babylon, as well as Hatti and Egypt. Perhaps the more immediate threat of Damascus and the other Aramaean states took their minds off the greater problems. However, the real threat was not the external geo-political situation, but the internal religious and moral decay of Canaanite religion, imported and promoted by Jezebel. The marriage alliance that Ahab had concluded with Ethbaal, king of the Sidonians, may have been a boon to commerce and defense, but it was a disaster for Israel's covenant relationship with YHWH. The treaty with the Phoenicians was effected by compromising and prostituting the covenant; Israel's apostasy took a turn for the worse.

YHWH's warnings through dramatic encounters with Elijah on Mount Carmel and with Micaiah were deliberately rejected. The prophetic revelation from YHWH, supported by miraculous events and by fulfillment of prophecies, simply went unheeded. If they would not listen to Moses and the prophets, why should they respond to the ominous providence of a God who brought the Assyrians on the horizon? This seems to be but another mighty act of YHWH as great king, fulfilling the early warnings of the covenant sanctions, calling his people back to covenantal renewal.

The next incursion of Assyria that brought her face to face with Israel occurred in the days of Adad-nirari III (810–783 B.C.). Although in some ways it was minor, it has some significance. Assyria had been weakened by internal resistance to the central authority of the king. As a matter of fact, this weakness was to continue until Tiglath-pileser III came to the throne in 745 B.C. Nevertheless, the young king Adad-nirari II, having taken full regal powers in 806 B.C., mounted an expedition to northern Syria, and within the next two years he broke the power of the Aramaeans, receiving tribute from those states which had been vassals of Aram-Damascus: Philistia, Edom, and Israel (still known as *bît Ḥumri*, "house of Omri"; compare 2 Kgs 13:3).

Ironically, this exchange of vassal tribute from Syria to Assyria was a welcome respite for Israel, for 2 Kgs. 13:4–5 says: "Jehoahaz pleaded with YHWH, and YHWH listened to him; for he saw the oppression of Israel, because the king of Syria oppressed them. Then YHWH gave Israel a deliverer, so they escaped from under the hand of the Syrians." It is no coincidence that the term *deliverer* (*môšia⁽*) was the same term used of the heroic men who saved the nation during the Period of the Judges (compare Judg 2:16; 3:9, 15; 8:22; 12:3; Ps 18:42; see also Deut 28:29, 31). A summary in 2 Kgs. 13:22–23 mentions that Hazael, king of Syria (841–801 B.C.), oppressed Israel all the days of Jehoahaz (814–798 B.C.) (compare Amos 1:3); "but YHWH was gracious to them and had compassion on them and turned to them because of his covenant with Abraham, Isaac, and Jacob." An inscription of Adad-nirari refers to tribute being received from *Ya⁾asu māt Samerinā*, Jehoash of Samaria (798–782 B.C.). It is likely that through this tribute Jehoash was allowed to strengthen trade relations and to recover lost territory, as mentioned in 2 Kgs. 13:25.

The significance of these events should not have been lost on Israel. These were the late years of that benevolent and faithful prophet Elisha, whose last prophecy to Jehoash of Israel was about "YHWH's arrow of victory . . . over Syria" (2 Kgs 13:17). There can be no question that YHWH, Israel's great king, was in control. He had spoken, and his covenant word had set the course of history. Even when he used the scourge of the Aramaean forces, he was still in control of Assyria, sending Adad-nirari as a deliverer from the oppression of the Syrians. Thanks to Adad-nirari, the Syrians never posed a real threat to Israel again. All this revealed once again the faithfulness of the great king to his covenant, as well as his gracious and compassionate nature.

Before we leave Adad-nirari and move on to Tiglath-pileser, Shalmaneser, Sargon, and the fall of Samaria in 723 B.C., we would do well to look at one more major evidence of the covenant love and faithfulness of YHWH. Very likely during the coregency of Jehoash and Jeroboam II (793–782 B.C.), Jonah ben Amittai prophesied that Jeroboam would restore the borders of Israel from Hamath to the Arabah (2 Kgs 14:25–27). The reason given for this encouraging prophecy was that "YHWH saw that the affliction of Israel was very bitter; . . . and YHWH had not said he would blot out the name of Israel from under heaven." The history of Jeroboam's solo tenure (782–753 B.C.) proved the prophecy to be true. Assyrian records show that Adad-nirari was engaged in wars with Urartu and that Assyria was weakened until Tiglath-pileser III rose to power. In spite of this clear evidence of YHWH's covenantal grace, Israel had lost her sense of mission to the nations. Materialism, hedonism, and provincialism were the order of the day.

Toward the end of this period of prosperity, Jonah ben Amittai was assigned to prophesy in Nineveh. Much to the chagrin of the prophet, his message was received with faith and repentance, revealing YHWH's universal covenant love and compassion (Jon 4:2). Having returned from his mission, Jonah admits in a most heart-searching way that YHWH's covenant must not be interpreted in a narrow, nationalistic way (4:11).

One cannot help but consider what might have been, had Israel taken her mission to the nations seriously. But that message was lost on Israel. Amos and Hosea underscore the covenantal concern of YHWH, the great king. But the nation, king and people alike, rejected those overtures of YHWH's grace and, in effect, brought the covenant curses on themselves. That recalcitrance, I suggest, was the catalyst that brought Assyria to world power once again. YHWH's use of Adad-nirari as deliverer would be reversed in Tiglath-pileser and his successors who served as a rod of YHWH's anger. Yet the Assyrians did not understand their part in YHWH's plans (Isa 10:5–7).

The most significant expansion of Assyria toward Israel began with Tiglath-pileser III (745–727 B.C.). He is credited with consolidating his power by completely annexing conquered territories instead of keeping independent, tribute-paying rulers at the frontiers of his empire. His policy of systematic transplantation of conquered peoples became the basis for the Assyrian Empire under the Sargonides, as his family and successors were known. Within his first three years he subdued incursions from Urartu to the north and the upper

Euphrates region. Then he began systematic expansion into northern Syria, moving briskly further south, receiving tribute from Tyre and Damascus. He quelled a revolt led by Azriyau of Yaudi (probably to be identified with Azariah, otherwise known as Uzziah, who died 740/739 B.C.). Furthermore, Menahem, king of Israel (752–742 B.C.), paid heavy tribute to strengthen his position against Pekah in the ongoing civil wars (compare 2 Kgs 15:19).[23] These were the ominous early years of Tiglath-pileser. Hamath was annexed as a province of Assyria, and massive deportations took place.

Tiglath-pileser's next territorial expansion was that discussed earlier when Isaiah confronted Ahaz (ca. 734 B.C.). Ahaz had secretly made an alliance with Tiglath-pileser (biblical "Pul") by urging him to attack Damascus and Samaria. The results were devastating for Rezin of Damascus, for by 732 B.C. Syria was conquered and annexed as an Assyrian province. Gilead and the northern territory of Israel were also overrun and incorporated (2 Kgs 15:29). Ammon, Moab, and Edom were forced to pay tribute. Ahaz's plan backfired when he, too, had to pay heavy tribute, even though he had accepted vassal status (compare 2 Kgs 16:7). I have already noted the prophetic assessment of these events.

It was under Shalmaneser V (727–722 B.C.), however, that the beleaguered Northern Kingdom suffered its final days. Hoshea, the vassal king since 732 B.C., failed or refused to pay tribute, and tried to form a conspiracy with Egypt, but Shalmaneser devoted three years (725–723 B.C.) to the conquest of Israel (2 Kgs 17:4–5). Samaria finally fell,[24] and Hoshea was captured. Again, the policy of mass deportation was implemented (2 Kgs 17:6). With this deportation and exile, the very strong words of warning found in the covenant sanctions in Leviticus 26 and Deuteronomy 28 reached their disastrous fulfillment. Micah and Isaiah had joined the chorus of prophets crying out to stem the tide of apostasy, but to no avail.

In 2 Kgs. 17:7–23 appears the historian's prophetic summary of the reasons for the collapse of Samaria and the Northern Kingdom of Israel. This deuteronomistic message agrees completely with the prophetic assessment. At heart, Israel had rejected the covenant, as well as YHWH, who had redeemed her from Egyptian bondage (esp. vv 7, 14–17). Israel had adopted the religious culture of the nations she had conquered, serving their gods, etc. (vv 8–12, 21–22). Furthermore, YHWH, the great king, had sent his servants the prophets as messengers of the covenant to warn Israel of impending disaster, namely, the visitation of the covenant sanctions (vv 13, 23). Finally, the anger of the divine Suzerain fell on Israel, and he removed her from his sight. Judah, meanwhile, escaped conquest and deportation, even though she was following in Israel's path of rebellion (vv 18–20).

Israel's fall should have been a lesson to Judah, as the prophets made very clear (compare Jer 3:6–11; 16:51; Ezek 23). Hosea, along with Micah and Isaiah, in the meantime had identified himself with Judah. Their message was the same for the Southern Kingdom. As for the Assyrians, Sargon II (722–705 B.C.) continued the policy of annexation. Judah, though remaining independent, was nevertheless a vassal. Hezekiah was tempted to trust in alliances with Egypt, Babylon, and others (ca. 711 B.C.), but he backed off reluctantly on the advice of Isaiah, his counsellor (Isa 30–31; 39). In Isaiah 39, the prophet records that Hezekiah received an envoy with gifts from Merodach-baladan, king of Babylon. Hezekiah foolishly entered into an alliance with them, displaying all his possessions, including the treasures in the temple. It was in this connection that Isaiah prophesied that Judah would suffer the same calamity as Israel, not under Assyria, but under the Babylonians.

The Assyrian thrust continued under Sennacherib (705–681 B.C.), especially in the crucial year 701 B.C. He boasted that "as to Hezekiah, the Jew, he did not submit to my yoke. I laid siege to forty-six of his strong cities . . . and conquered. . . . Himself I made a prisoner in Jerusalem, his royal residence, like a bird in a cage."[25] Sennacherib also claimed to have captured 200,150 people, as well as receiving tribute from Hezekiah (compare 2 Kgs 18:13–16; Isa 36:1). Though isolated, Hezekiah was spared, for Sennacherib had to raise the siege of Jerusalem through the intervention of the angel of YHWH (2 Kgs 19:33–35).[26] There may well have been uprisings in Babylon, perhaps also a factor that precipitated the withdrawal (compare 2 Kgs 19:7). Nevertheless, Hezekiah remained independent at a time when all the surrounding nations had been annexed as Assyrian provinces.

We do well to reflect on Hezekiah's reign in light of the Assyrian crisis. Sargon II and Sennacherib represented the greatest threat to Judah's national existence since the days of Solomon. Hezekiah's religious reforms were evidence of his taking his covenantal responsibilities seriously. He was commended by the prophets, who wrote, "He did right in the sight of YHWH, according to all that his father David had done. . . . He trusted in YHWH, the God of Israel . . . he clung to YHWH . . . kept his commandments . . . and YHWH was with him; wherever he went he prospered" (2 Kgs 18:3–7).

One cannot help but recognize that reprieve from Assyrian domination, that is, a reversal of complete Assyrian military ascendancy in Judah, was exactly in accord with the purpose of divinely sent disaster, which was to bring YHWH's people back to repentance and to renewal of the covenant. Then the blessings of the covenant would again be exhibited. The same could be said for Josiah (640–609 B.C.), whose reforms and renewal of the covenant reversed the trend of territorial loss. It would be fair to say that the expansion of his territory to include much of the northern area around Jezreel and Galilee (compare 2 Chr 34:6) must be understood as an expression of the blessings of the covenant.

The respite for Judah from Assyrian world domination under Hezekiah and Josiah was in complete contrast to the low ebb during Manasseh's reign (695/686–642 B.C.). This period saw the farthest expansion of Assyrian domination under Esarhaddon (681–669 B.C.) and Ashurbanipal (669–633 B.C.). Egypt was invaded in 671 B.C., with Thebes falling in 663 B.C. Manasseh had been one of many vassal-rulers present in public ceremonies in 672 B.C. when Esarhaddon appointed Ashurbanipal as crown prince of Assyria. At these ceremonies the vassals were given oral and written treaties, listing conditions of the arrangements, including curse sanctions for default and rebellion. It may have been after this that Manasseh was sent to Babylon with hooks and bronze chains (2 Chr 33:11). Even though he repented and returned to Judah, his reign was characterized by the prophetic historian as one of the most wicked in Judah (2 Chr 33:1–9).

In summary, there were two major incursions of the Assyrians, each occurring simultaneous with evidence of major religious apostasy on the part of Israel. The first took place during Israel's Omride dynasty down to the time of Jehu. This period of time saw the rise of a cluster of prophets, Elijah and Elisha being the most prominent, who called king and people alike back to covenantal renewal. A second great Assyrian advance occurred under Tiglath-pileser. This took place within a quarter of a century after Jeroboam II's great reign of prosperity. But unfortunately, that prosperity was associated with great spiritual decline, accompanied by moral, social, and political chaos. Again, YHWH sent a cluster of prophets, among them Jonah, Amos, Hosea, Micah, and Isaiah, who warned of the calamity that awaited Israel, who called for repentance and a return to her covenant Lord. In between these two major incursions, another took place, used by YHWH to deliver the Israelites from their longtime enemies, the Aramaeans. This evidence of the covenantal goodness of YHWH was not taken to heart. Thus, the doom of Israel was sealed.

Judah as a nation was also doomed to destruction, not by Assyria, but by Babylon. The prophets clearly had seen YHWH effectively stay the Assyrian power on account of Hezekiah. In spite of Josiah's valiant attempts, the nation was neither ready nor truly willing to reform her ways. Thus, if Babylon was to repeat the scenario, it was because a recidivist people had not learned the lesson. The same prophetic and theological principles would apply.

SUMMARY AND CONCLUSION

We have examined various texts that clearly express the mission of Israel as a nation and as a people of YHWH. Because of her covenantal relationship with him, she was to be the head of the nations and a blessing to them. The one condition was that she remain loyal and faithful to YHWH, the great king of the covenant. Failure to keep the covenant would result in the invocation of curse sanctions on the nation, with disastrous consequences. The prophets of Israel spoke against the tendency of the people of Israel to apostatize. We have examined pertinent passages to determine what principles were at the heart of their message. They started with the covenant relationship, suggesting that the covenantal word of YHWH set the course of history. This included the sanctions of blessings and curses. We have noted that the reason given for judgment on Israel was that she had rebelled against the covenant by rejecting YHWH, the great king, and had committed herself to idolatrous deities and heinous religious practices. YHWH, faithful to his covenant, had to implement the curse sanctions with increasing severity, yet always with the repentance of Israel in view.

Finally, by correlating the histories of Assyria and Israel, we have seen that the fluctuating rise of Assyria to a great degree reflected conversely the political stability of Syria and Palestine. Israel surely played a major role in maintaining the stability of that area. More specifically, Israel's political and military power were dependent on her faithfulness to the covenant. Thus, the prophetic assessment identified the heart of the problem as being Israel's apostasy from her covenant Lord, not political, economic, social, or moral depravity. These last can properly be seen as consequences of religious degradation. It may thus be said fairly that Israel's apostasy served as a catalyst for Assyrian expansion and ascendancy.

NOTES

1. Merrill F. Unger, *Israel and the Aramaeans of Damascus* (London: James Clarke Co., 1957); Frederick F. Bruce, *Israel and the Nations* (Grand Rapids, Mich.: Wm. Eerdmans, 1963); D. J. Wiseman, ed., *Peoples of Old Testament Times* (Oxford: Clarendon Press, 1973); David F. Payne, *Kingdoms of the Lord* (Grand Rapids, Mich.: Wm. Eerdmans, 1981).
2. Ever since George E. Mendenhall's *Law and Covenant in Israel and the Ancient Near East* (Pittsburgh: Biblical Colloquium, 1955), a spate of learned articles and books have been published, including Meredith G. Kline, *Treaty of the Great King* (Grand Rapids, Mich.: Wm. Eerdmans, 1963); D. J. McCarthy, *Treaty and Covenant: A Study in Form in the Ancient Oriental Documents and in the Old Testament* (Rome: Biblical Institute Press, 1963); and J. A. Thompson, *The Ancient Near Eastern Treaties and the Old Testament* (Grand Rapids, Mich.: Wm. Eerdmans, 1964).
3. Compare also Gen. 18:18 and the interpretation in Acts 3:25 and Gal. 3:8.
4. Compare the insight of Heb. 6:13–18.
5. See Norman H. Snaith, *The Distinctive Ideas of the Old Testament* (Philadelphia: Westminster Press, 1946), 94–130.
6. See Kline, *Treaty of the Great King*, 32, 67–70. Increasing evidence supports the fourteenth/thirteenth century B.C. dating of Deuteronomy, which is the assumption made here (see K. A. Kitchen, *The Bible in Its World* [Downers Grove, Ill.: Inter-Varsity Press, 1977], 79–85; Meredith G. Kline, *The Structure of Biblical Authority* [Grand Rapids, Mich.: Wm. Eerdmans, 1972], 45–75; and G. T. Manley, *The Book of the Law, Studies in the Date of Deuteronomy* [Grand Rapids, Mich.: Wm. Eerdmans, 1957]).
7. Supported also in Rom. 11:26–27.
8. See G. Ernest Wright, "The Nations in Hebrew Prophecy," *Enc* 26 (1965): 225–37; and John Mauchline, "Implicit Signs of a Persistent Belief in the Davidic Empire," *VT* 20 (1970): 287–303.
9. Avraham Gileadi, *The Apocalyptic Book of Isaiah* (Provo, Utah: Hebraeus Press, 1982), 178.
10. J. Lindblom, *Prophecy in Ancient Israel* (Philadelphia: Fortress Press, 1962), 148.
11. Edward J. Young, *My Servants the Prophets* (Grand Rapids, Mich.: Wm. Eerdmans, 1952), 82.
12. For example, Hos. 8:8–9; 9:3; 10:6; 11:5; Amos 5:27; 6:1–7; 7:17.
13. See bibliography in note 2 above.
14. O. Palmer Robertson, *The Christ of the Covenants* (Grand Rapids, Mich.: Baker Book House, 1980), 266.

15. Compare Gen. 45:5; Josh. 11:6; Job 12:23; Pss. 22:28; 66:7; Prov. 21:1; Acts 17:26.
16. Edward J. Young, *The Book of Isaiah* (Grand Rapids, Mich.: Wm. Eerdmans, 1965), 1:305, n. 11. Isa. 7:3 could well be the point of the allusion.
17. I am indebted to Avraham Gileadi for alerting me to this interpretation.
18. Compare Lev. 26:18, 23, 27, 40–42; 1 Kgs. 8:33, 35, 38, 44, 48. One is reminded of the increasing severity of the plagues against pharaoh in the Book of Exodus.
19. There were expansions to the west by Ashur-uballit I (1365–1330 B.C.) and later by Tukulti-ninurta I (1244–1208 B.C.), but they were of no major consequence. Tiglath-pileser II (966–935 B.C.), a contemporary of Solomon, was fairly weak.
20. *IDB*, 1:272; emphasis added.
21. For example, years later, Jehu was identified in the Black Obelisk of Shalmaneser III as *mār Ḫumri*, "son of Omri"; indeed from the ninth through the eighth centuries, northern Israel was designated *bît Ḫumri*, "house of Omri," in the Assyrian inscriptions.
22. See *ANET*, 278–79.
23. Compare the Assyrian inscription, *ANET*, 283.
24. The biblical text does not identify which Assyrian king finally captured Samaria. The problem arises because Sargon II (722–705 B.C.) makes the boastful claim that he conquered the city, but this claim is in an inscription written about fifteen years after the event. No inscriptional information is left for us from Shalmaneser V. Edward R. Thiele in *The Mysterious Numbers of the Hebrew Kings* (Chicago: University of Chicago Press, 1951), 141–47, marshals the evidence, giving convincing arguments that Sargon was doctoring history and that in actuality Samaria fell to Shalmaneser in 723 B.C. before Sargon became king. To be sure, Sargon did have to quell revolts in 720 B.C. in Samaria, but that does not mean he conquered Samaria.
25. *ANET*, 288.
26. Compare Herodotus 2.141, who mentions a plague of mice devouring the Assyrian bowstrings and shield-straps.

9

Babylonian Idolatry
in the Prophets
As a False Socio-Economic System

John D. W. Watts

"The Bible is utterly unaware of the nature and meaning of pagan religion," asserts Y. Kaufmann.[1] By this he means that the biblical writers treat idolatry as the worship of things (fetishism), with no apparent awareness that pagans thought of their worship very differently. He suggests that these writers show no real understanding of the rich mythology that lay behind the cults of idols; they evidenced not even a basic awareness of the great nonmaterial realities that pagans conceived to be symbolized by the images, temples, and cults they sponsored and revered. Kaufmann then goes on to describe pagan religion in some detail.

IDOLS AS SYMBOLS

Kaufmann's observation raises the question, What did the biblical writers perceive idolatry to be and to represent? Did they really think idolatry only a worship of things? While the biblical writers show little interest in mythologies and cults, as Kaufmann has noted, they are nonetheless very concerned about the idea of idols as symbols for value systems. Idols, which human beings try to manipulate to accomplish their own goals, are contrasted with YHWH, who controls human destiny to accomplish his goals in society. In the Hebrew Bible, idols are seen as symbols of these value systems. Systems which have no value or power other than that which worshipers place in them are contrasted with the system YHWH has established, and which he himself empowers and directs.

Israel was vulnerable to the popular paganism of her environments, whether Canaanite, Babylonian, or Egyptian. Thus one battle against idols concerned the symbols of the superstitious and self-indulgent religions to which those nations fell prey. The battle against idols was equally a resistance to cultural absorption.[2] Israel was plagued by the assumptions of the great cult religions, with their idols and mythologies, and by the ideas of evil and fate that found expression in them. Part of the Bible's battle for monotheism deals with overcoming these philosophies.

But Israel also had to deal with those idols which represented certain socio-economic-political systems that were prevalent. Having a king "like that of the nations" (1 Sam 8:5) entailed such a challenge. The challenges of Assyria, Babylon, and Egypt in the eighth and seventh centuries B.C. (and later the Hellenistic powers) were in coming to grips with these socio-economic-political systems.

WORSHIP OF HUMAN INSTITUTIONS

With the myths and cults that support them, idols are symbols representing particular social, economic, mytho-political, and religious views. When the prophets criticized idols as simply being wood and stone, they also challenged the integrity and validity of the things that idols represent. Idols in the ancient world represented certain value systems. As the swastika represented the Nationalist Socialist party, or the hammer and sickle represent Marxist Communism, so specific idols represented ways of life for their adherents. The symbol was explained and given meaning by certain rituals, sometimes at temples with regular priesthoods and retainers, but also in seasonal festivals with or without professional priests. Idols were further explained by myths that told their stories and explained their relevance, as well as their mode of operation.

But the substance of what idols stood for lay in much more mundane things. The little household idols (Gen 31:32) represented the patrimony, the rights of inheritance. When Rachel took them, it was like stealing a lockbox full of land deeds. The little figurines of sex goddesses were prayers and dreams of fecundity, prosperity, and hedonistic pleasure. Baal statues of bulls represented agricultural powers that made fields and animals bear. Other idols, and the rituals and myths associated with them, supported the political structures of monarchies and city-states of the ancient Near East. These had political, social, and economic implications for each of their societies. Israel was called to see in YHWH's covenant and the torah the symbols of a way of life that contrasted sharply with the paganism of Canaan's idols. The problem was not so much idols; the problem lay in the high places and other symbols of Baalism and related cults. The temptation to Israel to follow these pagan value systems was as pernicious for the ancient Israelites as it is for us today.

To worship the "gods of Amorites" meant, in part, acceptance of Canaanite ideas of land-tenure and usage that contrasted with Israel's laws cited in Numbers and Joshua. Such worship implied acceptance of Baalist views of the basis for fertility. These views contradicted and undermined Israel's faith in YHWH as caretaker of the land (Deut 11:12).

The erection of a sun disk in the temple was different (2 Kgs 23:11). The sun disk was primarily a political symbol of vassalage, a recognition of Assyrian sovereignty over Judah and an acceptance of the Assyrian Empire's system of political and economic values. To place this symbol in Jerusalem's temple was to acknowledge Assyria's political ascendancy, to submit, as a vassal, to Assyria's king and to recognize Ashur's reign in the pantheon. Worship of the Queen of Heaven appears to have been a popular acceptance of similar values.

All these symbols are condemned in various ways in the Hebrew Bible. The attack on Canaan's value system is endemic to YHWH's torah, and it continues in the fight against pagan values in Canaanite Palestine in each succeeding era down through the Hellenistic period. Elijah's campaign against Baal–Melqart had a particular focus in the ninth century B.C.[3] Later the Deuteronomist condemns the incursions of Assyrian symbols in the reigns of Ahaz and Manasseh.

Israel had her own values, and her own symbols for those values. She was called on to abandon the teraphim (Josh 24:14, 23) in order to take her place as a people owing land rights to YHWH alone. The land was hers as YHWH's free gift, rather than by any rights of patrimony; that is, the land was hers on Abraham's terms rather than those which Rachel tried to protect by stealing her father's teraphim (Gen 31:14–34).

THE GODS OF BABYLON

All-out attacks on idols as such appear only in Isaiah 41–44; attacks on specific idols also appear in Isaiah 45–47, Jeremiah 50–51, and Daniel 3. Why is this true, and what does it mean? What does it mean for both kinds of attacks on idols to be set against Babylon in the sixth century B.C.?

As no other city in the pre-Roman world, Babylon was looked upon as the city of destiny. Perhaps this came from her reputation for antiquity and mystique. Her history is remarkable. Babylon is mentioned in tablets dated to 2,500 B.C. She was recognized as a provincial capital in the Third Dynasty of Ur. By the following period she had apparently become the capital of a small independent kingdom. This kingdom grew, under Hammurabi, to control most of southern Mesopotamia. The rulers changed many times during the following millennium, but the religious mystique, symbolized by her gods and temples, represented power and rule. Babylon was known as the old, original empire.

Bel (also known as Marduk) and Nebo were this city's symbols. They represented the political, social, military, and economic system that produced successful empires from the days of Hammurabi on. They were symbols of imperial privilege, power, and wealth gained by violent seizure. They were also symbols of arrogance, pride, and unbridled ambition. Thus, the Assyrians represented themselves as heirs to Babylon's place in the service of Marduk. Cyrus and succeeding Persians did the same. The cult of Bel/Marduk, in sixth-century Babylon, represented a claim to the right of empire. It represented a social system of oppression and exploitation, a theory of the exercise of raw power that was incompatible with the worship of YHWH on any level.

Of course such a system was pagan, dependent on cult-magic, divination, and the other devices of paganism. And, of course, it had its own mythologies (Marduk had taken the seat of Bel) to support its claims and practices. But the heart of the matter was the socio-economic system it symbolized. Presented in this sense, Babylon, in Genesis 11, is the symbol of self-exaltation and revolt against God. Babylon's ambition was to become as great as God, to be independent of his rule. No idol is mentioned; the city is her own symbol. Similarly, in all the other accounts, the city is a greater symbol than her idols (see esp. Isa 47).

From the eighth to the fifth centuries B.C., the city had a history of rebellion. Merodach-baladan captured the city in 722 B.C., held her against the Assyrians until 710 B.C., and retook her briefly in 705 B.C. Other rebellions occurred again in 689 and in 648 B.C. By the end of the century, Babylon ruled the empire. The Persians did not take control of the city until 539 B.C. But Persia, too, experienced a series of revolts from the city (in 522, 486, and 482 B.C.). The Persians met the problem by attacking the cult that supported the city's mystique. Xerxes destroyed the ziggurat and removed the statue of Marduk. He also decreed that Ahuramazda, a Persian god, be worshiped, but this decree was apparently largely ignored. Artaxerxes II (404–359 B.C.) introduced the cults and statues of Aphrodite, also called Anahita.

PROPHETIC INTERPRETATIONS

It is against this background that the treatment of Babylon's idols will be undertaken. I will attempt to define the way literary prophecy in Jeremiah 50–51, Isaiah 41–47, and Daniel 3 portrays Babylonian idolatry and then relate that to understanding the nature of Babylon's social and economic system.[4] The attitude of the vision of Isaiah on Babylon is radically different from that expressed toward either Assyria or Persia. Both of the latter are thought of, in some sense, as agents of YHWH (Isa 10:5–12; 44:28–45:6). Babylon, which actually accomplished the final judgment on Jerusalem in 587 B.C., is not.

Jeremiah 50–51 is a collection of strong oracles directed against Babylon in the spirit of other prophecies by Jeremiah against foreign powers. It shows no similarity to Jeremiah's messages to Judah, which picture the events of that time in terms of YHWH's judgment on his people. On the contrary, Jeremiah 50–51 claims that YHWH has not abandoned his people or his city but will bring vengeance and retribution on Babylon for all her acts of violence against them. With regard to Babylon there is no hint of ambivalence in YHWH's control of history as there was when he had to bring judgment on his people.

In these chapters the gods of Babylon are Bel and Marduk (Jer 50:2). Babylon's defeat will bring shame and terror to their images—and presumably to their worshipers. YHWH's judgment against Babylon and all she stands for

(51:41–43) is paralleled by the punishment of Bel in Babylon (51:44). Babylon will be made to vomit out all that she had swallowed. When the nations no longer "stream to Bel," Babylon's influence and power will have vanished. Parallel lines tell us that when God "punishes the idols of Babylon" the land will be disgraced because of her "slain" (51:47). The idols will be punished even if Babylon "reaches for the sky" or multiplies her fortifications (51:53). Human efforts cannot prevent the collapse of a false system, no matter how great.

Notwithstanding Babylon represented the very spirit of imperial right and power (in the names of its gods, emperors from Hammurabi to Nebuchadnezzar had conquered nations and demanded the allegiance of many peoples) Babylon served YHWH's purpose well as a weapon to punish his people's sins. But otherwise there was no hope of "healing" or reforming Babylon's ruthless and tyrannical ways. Her idols—symbols of human greed, arrogance, and pride—contained no element capable of redemption or reformation. The system failed when challenged; justice for the people had no place in it. The idols were useless for anyone except a successful warrior, and then only when he won. Such systems only have place for a winner.

YHWH's action against Babylon and her king in the Book of Jeremiah is like that in Isaiah 13–14, although it refers to a very different era in history. Isaiah 13–14, 21, and 39 ostensibly portray eighth-century Babylon, under Merodach-baladan. Of course, this king is a usurper. But he acts in the traditional role of the city by rebelling against constituted authority and setting himself up—presumably with the support of Babylon's gods—to defy the world. In the Book of Isaiah this is understood as defying YHWH himself, who had ordained that Assyria should rule the East. Thus the attributes of arrogance and pride fit the pattern of humanity's major sins (compare Isa 2:12–22) and qualify Babylon for YHWH's wrath.

The Isaiah chapters of primary interest to this paper (Isa 41–47) devote a major section (chap. 47) to a description of Babylon's fall as mistress or queen of the nations. The tone is very different from Isaiah 13–14. There is no mention of either her king or her gods. Babylon's humiliation and shame lie in the exposure that her claims and self-estimation were without basis. She had thought that her status and privilege were eternal (47:7). She thought of herself as autonomous and invulnerable: "I am, and there is none beside me. I will never be a widow or suffer the loss of children" (47:8). She presumed that "no one sees me" (47:10a); she had no sense of accountability to God or mankind. She depended on the pagan powers of sorcery, necromancy, and astrology. These were her "science," and "understanding." She had to come to the bitter recognition that these had no power at all, no power to preserve or to save her (47:9–15). Isa. 46:1–2 pictures her collapse in terms of her idols, Bel and Nebo, being toppled and carried off, helpless to prevent the change.

These descriptions of the relationship of idolatry to paganism, and of the dethronement of Babylon's idols, accord well with the attested policies of the Persian government in the fifth and fourth centuries B.C. But the treatment of idolatry in Isaiah 41–47 is not primarily intended to give a historical presentation. Nor does it repudiate the theoretical worship of fetishes, as Kaufmann ingenuity and strength. Israel is tempted to commit herself to something of pure human fabrication rather than to what is of YHWH. This point is clearly made in 40:18–20; 42:8, 17; 43:10; 44:8–20; 45:20; 46:5–7. Jer. 51:17–18 makes the same point: YHWH's control of creation and human history, his knowledge and understanding of world events, and his continuing acts relating himself to Israel are contrasted with the man-made wood and metal of idols. One can hardly believe that Israel was tempted to substitute a fascination for the carvings themselves for the worship of the living God. There is certainly something more at stake here. The temptation for Israel was something much more mundane and real than that.

Jer. 51:6–53 can be a start to understanding. The chapter is a call for Israel to flee Babylon so that YHWH's people will not be destroyed because of Babylon's sins (51:6; compare Isa 48:20). This hints at the danger that Israel would identify herself and her future with the great world power that had taken her captive. How easy it would be to assume the validity of Babylon's values, her way of doing things, when Babylon was apparently so successful. Nebuchadnezzar had built his New Babylonian Empire on the concepts, values, and religious symbols of the fabled Old Babylonian Empire—the myths and rituals of Marduk, Bel, and Nebo. His success in asserting himself as heir to the Assyrian Empire could easily be understood as proof of the validity of his (and Babylon's) doctrines of naked power, ruthless aggression, and arrogant pride, all of which had made and would make Babylon a city and people as high as heaven itself (Gen 11).

Daniel 3 illustrates Nebuchadnezzar's compelling power toward Shadrach, Meshach, and Abednego—Jewish exiles who had been trained for government service and had advanced to high office in Nebuchadnezzar's government. The great golden statue they were asked to worship is not named. It could have been one of Marduk, Bel, or Nebo. Whatever its name, it represented Babylon and her king. To worship it meant total and absolute commitment to the imperial government and to the system it represented.

Shadrach, Meshach, and Abednego refused worship of the idol and were rescued from the fiery furnace in vindication of the same principle preached in Isaiah 41–47: worship of the image emphasized the human and temporal nature of what it stood for. Nebuchadnezzar's motivation for setting up the idol was clearly political. The men were accused of serving neither Nebuchadnezzar's gods nor bowing to the image (Dan 3:12). Thus the implication was that they were politically unreliable. Nebuchadnezzar assumed that his power was greater than that of any god: "Then what god will rescue you from my hand?" He did not expect his gods to punish: they were simply representatives of his own authority and power.

This is the issue in the Book of Isaiah as well. Israel is called to be the servant of YHWH, even when her people live and work in Babylon. The social, economic, and religious values imbedded in the Babylonian system are portrayed as pure human fabrications, temporal, partial, and subject to change and judgment. Israel is called to maintain her commitment to YHWH, to adhere to his values, and to accept that his plans and directions provide the only valid hope for life and stability in the future.

The point of chapters 41–47 is that the entire structure and system of the Babylonian Empire (represented by her idols) was developed by humans; Babylon had no lasting divine sanction. Just as an idol is of human fabrication, with no autonomous power or usefulness of its own, so the entire Babylonian system of society, economics, and politics was a human fabrication which in time would collapse. Israel, then, must reserve her worship, her ultimate commitment, for YHWH. This commitment must stand above all other systems and values. YHWH may grant these systems (including Assyria, Persia) temporary sanction to do his will, but he also reserves the right to repudiate and destroy them. Only YHWH deserves worship.

Babylon's political structure will be replaced by other forms. Her great leaders will give way to others of different nationality and method. Her mores, social structures, cultural treasures, economic policies, laws, and ideals — symbolized by her temples, gods, and religion — will pass away. They all belong to the passing parade of mere human achievements. The ultimate sin is to assume that these man-made institutions are in themselves of divine quality, that they will last forever, that they are indeed autonomous. Babylon is not God, nor do her ways partake of the qualities of God's law.

In these chapters Isaiah calls upon Israel, now living in a secular environment (that is, one not structured by YHWH's law or consciously subject to it), to differentiate clearly between her loyalties to human structures, authorities, and economies, and that commitment which she owed to YHWH, her God, her Savior, and her Lord. She was to be consciously his "servant." Yet these chapters equally imply that such committed service to YHWH was and would be possible in a pagan environment, that is, in Babylon. It was not necessary to create a perfect environment, such as a state in Canaan run by priests, dictated by the torah, to be YHWH's servant. On the contrary, Israel is called to assume the role of YHWH's servant in the diaspora in which she now finds herself. The stories in Daniel 1–6 are examples showing that such subservience to YHWH in Babylon can not only successfully be maintained but can also bring immense spiritual rewards.

NOTES

1. *The Religion of Israel*, trans. and abr. Moshe Greenberg (London: Green, Allen & Unwin, 1961), 7.

2. We have long been aware that idolatry involved much more than bowing down to images. Sir Francis Bacon understood idolatry to consist of false tendencies of the mind that hinder clear thought. Giordana Bruno wrote in *Novum Organum* (1620) of four kinds of idols: idols of the tribe, which foster enmity against the human race; idols of the cave, which are

peculiar to individuals; idols of the market place, which are encouraged by one's social group or mother tongue; and idols of the theater, which are taught and encouraged by various schools of thought (*Ency. Brit.*, 6:242). A little reflection on these categories suggests that some idols are supported by more than one of these forms.

3. See James R. Battenfield, "YHWH's Refutation of the Baal Myth through the Actions of Elijah and Elisha," in this volume.

4. Modern concern with ideological symbols has also been applied to the Hebrew Bible (see N. K. Gottwald, *The Hebrew Bible: A Socio-Literary Introduction* [Philadelphia: Fortress Press, 1985], 256–60 passim).

10

The Phenomenon of Conditionality within Unconditional Covenants

Bruce K. Waltke

E. Kutsch made an important contribution to biblical studies by defining Hebrew *běrît* (traditionally, and misleadingly, rendered in English "covenant") not as "relationship," "pact," or "agreement," but as "obligation" or "designation."[1] M. Weinfeld, who supported Kutsch's definition by citing terms paralleling *běrît* in the ancient Near East, points out that Kutsch's definition lays to rest "a lot of misunderstandings and pseudo-ideologies." He explains:

> Thus W. Robertson Smith's notion about the covenant as "the bond of truth and life fellowship" or the idea of "community of *sacra*" hidden in the blood falls to the ground. The blood in the covenantal ceremony does not serve as a symbol of holy communion, but, as can be learned from Aeschylus quoted by Kutsch, constitutes the dramatization of the punishment which will befall the one who violates the oath: his blood will be shed. The same applies to Wellhausen for whom the covenant is some kind of *bond between God and the people* which was reinterpreted by the Prophets.[2]

Weinfeld summarizes Kutsch's specific meanings for Hebrew *běrît* as follows:

A. A commitment by the subject of the *běrît*. That is, a promise given by the subject (mostly sanctified by oath).
B. An obligation imposed by the subject of the *běrît* upon someone else.
C. A mutual obligation by which two parties make pledges one to another.
D. A mutual obligation sponsored by a third party.

The biblical series of covenants between YHWH and man, or Israel—the concern of this paper—belong to the first two definitions. Both may be called unilateral because YHWH either binds himself to serve his servants (class A) or binds his servants to serve him (class B). In neither case does the covenant's existence depend on pledges by both parties. Class C may be called bilateral because the covenant contains terms that indicate duties incumbent upon both parties.

D. N. Freedman conveniently calls the class A covenant "a covenant of divine commitment" and the class B covenant "a covenant of human obligation."[3] Weinfeld labels them more succinctly "grant" and "treaty" respectively. He writes:

> While the "treaty" constitutes an obligation of the vassal to his master, the suzerain, the "grant" constitutes an obligation of the master to his servant. . . . The "grant" serves mainly to protect the rights of the *servant*, while the treaty comes to protect the rights of the *master*.[4]

In this paper I also use the terms *oath* for YHWH's commitment to the beneficiary and *law* for the obligations imposed by him on Israel.

Class A may be called unconditional in the sense that no demands are made on the superior party, and class B, conditional in the sense that the superior party promises to reward or punish the inferior partner for obeying or disobeying the imposed obligations. So defined, the distinction is valid, but the terms *unconditional* and *conditional* may be misleading. Some have mistakenly thought that class A contains no conditional aspects with reference to the beneficiary, and class B no unconditional aspects. I hope this paper will correct any mistaken notions.

The first kind of covenant — the grant — includes the covenants with Noah (Gen 9), the Patriarchs (Gen 12:1–3, 15, 17; 22:15–18; 26:3–5; 28:13–15), Phinehas (Num 25), and David (2 Sam 7 = 1 Chr 17; Ps 89:4, 29, 34, 39; Jer 33:21; passim). Covenants of the second type — the treaty — include those given by YHWH to Adam[5] in the Garden of Eden and to Israel at Sinai and Moab (Exod 19, Lev, and Deut). The latter was renewed at Shechem by Joshua (Josh 24) and again in the days of Jehoiada (2 Kgs 11:17; 2 Chr 29:10), Josiah (2 Kgs 23:3), and Ezra–Nehemiah (Ezra 10:3).

Scholars committed to the documentary hypothesis usually refer to the covenant made at Sinai as the "Sinaitic covenant" and to the one made at Moab as the "Deuteronomic covenant," the covenant book par excellence according to J. Muilenburg.[6] For the purpose of this paper, I will group these two covenants together and call them the "Mosaic covenant." (I do not mean to imply that the two share a common form.)[7]

Covenants between men usually belong to class C, in which the situation is effectively bilateral.[8] None of the covenants involving YHWH belong to this category. Class D is not pertinent for this study either.

Instructively, YHWH's grants feature most prominently gifts of offspring and land, matching the prominent gifts of house (that is, dynasty) and land by the suzerain in the Hittite and Syro–Palestinian political reality.

The distinction between *grant* and *treaty* is essential in understanding biblical theology, but scholars often fail to understand the terms' complementary relationship. For example on one hand, J. D. Levenson accuses C. Shedl, R. de Vaux, and A. H. J. Gunneweg of improperly integrating the Davidic and Sinaitic covenants by subordinating the Davidic to the Sinaitic. On the other hand, he accuses J. Bright and G. E. Mendenhall of improperly segregating the two covenant forms by pitting them against one another. Levenson himself, however, errs by radically divorcing them.[9]

In this paper I aim to study, primarily, the phenomenon of conditionality within irrevocable grants, a study I hope will clarify the relationship between YHWH's oaths to Abraham and David and the obligations He imposed on Israel. I will argue that YHWH's grants and treaty do not rival or exclude, but complement one another. If a more accurate biblical theology can be written as a result, then I will have achieved my purpose in this attempt to honor Professor R. K. Harrison.

A contribution of this study may be that it will help lay to rest the notion that the Deuteronomist, the redactor of Deuteronomy through the Book of Kings, reinterpreted the grants to Abraham and David by putting conditions on them.[10] This result would be especially appropriate in view of Harrison's interests.

I will begin the study with an analysis of the unconditional and conditional aspects of the grants given to Noah, Abraham, and David; I will then analyze the same features in the treaty imposed on Israel; finally, I will analyze the new covenant which successfully resolves the tension between YHWH's oaths and Israel's obligations. I will not attempt to reconstruct a hypothetical genesis of the covenant idea within Israel, a will-o'-the-wisp enterprise at best,[11] apart from noting that most scholars recognize that *covenant* was consciously applied to YHWH's relationship with Israel from the earliest times. Furthermore, the Pentateuch deserves to be interpreted as a unity.[12]

Finally, by way of introduction, I will treat my subject thematically, not lexically, even though this treatment exposes the study to the danger of subjective selection and arrangement of material.[13] The reader must judge whether I achieve objectivity.

GOD'S COVENANT WITH NOAH

Unconditional Aspects

D. J. McCarthy notes: "No *berît* is one-sided unless the obligation is incumbent on one party and one party makes the *berît*."[14] According to this definition, God's covenant with Noah is one-sided; it is unilateral and unconditional in the sense that no demands are made on Noah.

God's covenant with Noah involves all mankind. Strictly speaking, it involves a divine commitment both to the creation and to man. Note that its prominent features are land and offspring. With respect to land, God promises never again to curse the ground or destroy all living creatures as he did in the Flood, but to give the earth its seasons and harvest as long as it endures (Gen 8:21–22). With regard to offspring, he promises to make man fruitful and give him dominion over every living creature (9:1–4). Although God holds man accountable to exact capital punishment (9:5–6), the promises are not contingent upon it. Because of God's commitment, man can confidently multiply and increase on earth (9:7).

God's promises to both the creation and man are explicitly not contingent on man's behavior:

> Never again will I curse the ground because of man, even though every inclination of a man's heart is evil from his childhood.

(Gen 8:21)

The sign of God's commitment to all life (compare Gen 9:12–13, 17), the rainbow, functions to remind God, not man, of God's promise. God proves his commitment by not reneging on his promise after Noah gets drunk and involves himself and Ham in sexual impropriety (9:20–24). To be sure, Canaan will be cursed with slavery, but the earth is not cursed.

Conditional Aspects

The pleasing aroma. McCarthy[15] emphasizes the important point that the making of a covenant does not initiate a relationship, but rather formalizes and gives concrete expression to one already in existence. In every covenant of divine commitment, the beneficiary first creates a spiritual climate leading to the commitment. As in the royal grants in the ancient Near East, God also grants gifts pertaining to land and progeny to Noah, Abraham, and David, because they excelled in loyally serving him.[16] By building an altar to YHWH and making pure sacrifices, Noah prompted YHWH to grant the covenant: YHWH smelled the pleasing aroma and said in his heart: "Never again will I curse the ground" (Gen 8:20).

Earlier (6:9) we were informed that Noah was a righteous man (*ʾîš ṣaddîq*), blameless (*tāmîm*) in his generation. By faith he obeyed God and built the ark as instructed. Without those qualities, his sacrifice would not have pleased YHWH. In a very real sense, the covenant came about because of Noah's spiritual virtues. If a covenant does not establish a relationship, it nevertheless represents the climax of an already existing spiritual relationship. As we will see, there are local exceptions to this covenant; however, we may assume, on the principle of spiritual reciprocity, that the promises given to mankind flourish best among creatures pleasing to God.

Unique blessings and curses. The Creator's oath to all mankind never again to *universally* "curse the ground" (*qallēl . . . hăʾădāmâ*) because of man's sin (8:21), and to give the earth "seedtime and harvest" (*zeraʿ wĕqāṣîr*) (8:22), does not exclude local exceptions. God may *locally* manipulate life within the created order. On the one hand, with respect to the elect nation, he controls the rain and harvest in the promised land so as to encourage his people to obey the law mediated through Moses (Deut 11:13–17; 28:1–6, 15–24)—he promises to bless them exceptionally when they keep it (see the Abrahamic covenant below). On the other hand, he blesses the nonelect (that is, fills them with the potential of life) when they bless the elect (that is, pay them respect as the mediators of life) and curses (*ʾārar*) them when they curse (*qālal*) the elect (compare Gen 12:2–3, 17; 20:3; 26:10).

Famines and other devastations. Finally, there exist providential local famines apart from moral considerations (see Gen 26:1; passim), and local judgments for flagrant immorality when the elect are not involved, as in the case of Sodom and Gomorrah (see Gen 19).

Conclusion

God's grant of seasonal harvest and blessing are in space and time universally irrevocable, but locally and temporarily conditional upon moral behavior or providential acts. Both the irrevocable and conditional aspects of the covenant further man's spiritual life. The theological certainty that the stage for redemption is in place until the end of time allows man to live confidently and to follow God in hope. But the historical variations warn him to walk softly before his Creator.

GOD'S COVENANT WITH ABRAHAM

Unconditional Aspects

A covenant of divine commitment is well illustrated in Genesis 15. N. M. Sarna[17] analyzes the chapter as having two parts (vv 1–6 and 7–21) that share a common form: a divine promise (vv 1, 7) followed by Abraham's question (vv 2–3, 9), concluding with a divine response confirming the promise by a sign (vv 4–6 and 10–21). The first six verses deal with the promise of patriarchal progeny, the rest with possession of the promised land.

The Creator confirms his promise regarding an innumerable offspring by visually displaying the stars in the heavens and the sand on the shore. He ratifies the covenant to give Abraham the promised land by symbolically passing as a smoking firepot and flaming torch among the three slaughtered animals, symbolizing a threefold oath, and provisionally identifying himself with the slaughtered animals' fate. To judge from ancient Near Eastern parallels, Jer. 34:18–20 and Aeschylus, as YHWH passes among the slaughtered animals he is saying in the boldest symbolism: "May it be done to me as it has been done to these animals, if I do not fulfill my promise." Significantly, only YHWH makes promises, and only he passes between or among the butchered parts, demonstrating that this is a unilateral covenant.

The fulfillment of the covenant to Abraham and his descendants, the beneficiaries, depends on YHWH's faithfulness, which, as Freedman notes,[18] is axiomatic.

YHWH assumes this covenant regarding the offspring of Abraham and their land when he promises to make Abraham into a great nation that will bless others (Gen 12:1–3). He confirms the promises in Genesis 17, adding that Abraham will become the father of a multitude of nations, that He will be their God, and that these promises are forever *('ôlām)* (17:8). (We need to remind ourselves that even if Genesis 15 and 17 stem from different sources, the text we have in hand is meant to be read as a unity.) YHWH swears in Gen. 22:15–18 to fulfill this covenant, adding that Israel will defeat her enemies. The divine commitment is repeated to Isaac (26:24) and Jacob (28:13–15).

In sum, YHWH commits himself unilaterally to fulfill these promises to the Patriarchs, presenting them as irrevocable by promising, ratifying, swearing to, and confirming his promises in covenants (compare Heb 6:13–17).

Conditional Aspects

The oaths presume an existing spiritual relationship. Here too we find the principle of spiritual reciprocity at work. YHWH commits himself to these promises in response to Abraham's exceptional faith. Gen. 12:1–3 shares a common form with Genesis 1: Announcement, "And God said" (Gen 1:2, 6, etc., and 12:1), followed by imperatives, "Let there be . . . " (1:3, 6, etc.) and "Go" (12:1), followed by a report of fulfillment, "So God made . . . " (Gen 1:6) and "and Abraham went" (12:4). The pattern, however, differs from Genesis 1 in that God adds six promises:

> I will make you into a great nation . . . bless you . . . make your name great . . . bless those who bless you, and whoever curses you . . . curse; and all peoples on earth will be blessed through you.

These promises appear between the imperative and the report of their fulfillment, so that Abraham's obedience to the command becomes a faithful response to the promises. Had he not acted on his faith, presumably the promises would not have taken effect. Moreover, were the order of promise and report reversed, the notion of contingency would have been significantly reduced.

The promise to confirm the covenant in Gen. 17:2 is preceded by the command "Walk before me and be blameless" (17:1), clearly hinting at a connection between Abraham's ethical behavior and YHWH's fulfillment of the covenant with him. The oath in 22:16–17 is explicitly grounded in Abraham's exceptional loyalty and obedience to YHWH:

> I swear by myself, declares YHWH, that because you have done this *[kî ya'an 'ăšer 'āśîtā 'et-haddābār]* and have not withheld your son, your beloved son, I will surely bless you.

YHWH connects his promises in Genesis 15 regarding the offspring and land with Abraham's acts of faith, by introducing them with the statement: "Your reward is very great" (15:1).

In short, the oaths do not initiate a relationship, but reciprocate Abraham's loyalty. This explicit connection between Abraham's faith and the divine commitment may imply that for his descendants to qualify for these blessings they too must create the same spiritual climate. The following contingencies connected with YHWH's promises to Abraham tend to justify this notion.

The beneficiaries are to be devoted to YHWH. The confirmation of the covenant in Genesis 17 clearly falls into two parts: "As for me . . . " (17:4–8) and "As for you . . . " (vv 9–14), but this dialectical tension must not be resolved in such a way as to make the promises mutually dependent on one another in the sense that if one party fails, the other is relieved of responsibility. The first part unequivocally commits YHWH to fulfill his promises to give Abraham an enlarged progeny including kings (vv 4–6), to be his and their God (v 7), and to give his descendants the land of Canaan forever (v 8). The second part places conditions upon the beneficiaries. Only Abraham's circumcised descendants will participate in the grant. Here we enter into the mystery of divine sovereignty and human accountability. YHWH will fulfill his promises but not apart from faith on the part of their beneficiaries. The tension can be seen, in part, in this divine promise to Abraham: "to be your God and the God of your descendants after you" (17:7). The full meaning of this addition to the covenant is "I will be your God and you will be my people," an expression suggesting the marriage of the two parties. Weinfeld says,

> The marriage contract formula known to us from the Near East, "I will be to you a husband and you will be to me a wife," stands in fact behind the statements *[wĕhāyîtî lākem lēʾĕlōhîm wĕʾattem tihyû lî lĕʿām]* which occur in the context of *bĕrît* (Lev 26:12; compare Exod 6:7; Deut 29:12–13; Jer 31:33).[19]

The prophets exploit the metaphor and picture YHWH as putting away his wife when she proves herself unfaithful to him (Hos 2:2–13; Jer 3:1–3; passim). Nonetheless, because of YHWH's faithfulness to Abraham, the prophets do not envision God as divorcing Israel so that he could never take her back (compare Isa 50:1–3; 49:14–26; Mic 7:18–20; passim). Through YHWH's sovereign grace, a loyal remnant always exists, giving hope for a full realization of the grant.

YHWH explains that his grant extends only to those within Abraham's household who behave ethically:

> For I have chosen him, in order that he may direct his children and his household after him to keep the way of YHWH by doing what is right and just, so that YHWH will bring about for Abraham what he has promised him.
>
> (Gen 18:19)[20]

Moses, equating the "way of YHWH" with the law mediated through him, confirms the principle:

> You are standing here in order to enter *[ʿābar]* into a covenant *[bĕrît]* with YHWH your God and into his oath *[ʾālâ]* which YHWH your God is making *[kārat]* with you today in order that he may *establish [hēqîm]* you today as his people and that he may be your God, just as he spoke to you and he swore to your fathers, to Abraham, Isaac, and Jacob.
>
> (Deut 29:10–13)

The author of the Pentateuch views the two kinds of unilateral covenants, oath and law, as mutual complements defining the relationship between YHWH and Israel. The oath gives theological certainty of an enduring relationship; the law gives a moral quality to it.

I will discuss the resolution of the dialectical tension between YHWH's irrevocable, and yet qualified, commitment to Israel more fully in connection with the discussion on the New Covenant. Let it suffice to note that YHWH must elect true Israel to guarantee his irrevocable promises to the Patriarchs.

The uncircumcised are to be cut off. The second half of the covenant in Genesis 17 states that YHWH's covenant with the Patriarchs extends only to those within Abraham's lineage who embrace their father's faith, and it reaches beyond them to foreigners that share in it:

> As for you . . . every male among you shall be circumcised . . . including those born in your household or . . . those not your offspring. . . . Any uncircumcised male, who has not been circumcised in the flesh, will be cut off from his people [that is, excommunicated from the covenantal community and exposed to death from a divine agency].
> (Gen 17:9–14)

Elsewhere the Lawgiver clarifies that the circumcision in the flesh functioned symbolically as a circumcision of the heart (Deut 10:16; 30:6).

Conclusion

YHWH irrevocably committed himself to give Abraham an innumerable progeny and make him a father of many nations, to give him and his descendants the promised land forever, to be their God, and to bless others through them. His grant, however, extends only to Abraham's spiritual progeny. Paul's distinction between spiritual and natural Israel is firmly rooted in the Pentateuch. Paul puts it this way: "For not all who are descended from Israel are Israel" (Rom 9:6).

Though conditional on human obligations, YHWH's grants to the Patriarchs are unilateral because they do not depend on Israel's pledge to fulfill obligations. The irrevocable oaths to the Patriarchs, qualified to extend only to a loyal progeny, logically entail that YHWH must sovereignly and graciously elect Abraham's seed. Without these attributes and activity, the promises would fail.

GOD'S COVENANT WITH DAVID

Unconditional Aspects

YHWH's grant to David places no obligations on David for its enactment or perpetuation. It is unilateral, and in that sense unconditional.

R. A. Carlson[21] divides the grant into two parts—promises to be realized during David's lifetime (2 Sam 7:8–11a) and promises to be fulfilled after his death (7:11b–16). The two halves are formally divided from one another by breaking YHWH's address delivered in first person in verses 9–11a and 12–16 with a statement in third person, "YHWH declares to you" (v 11b), and by locating the promises given in verses 12–16 in the time, "When your days are over and you rest with your fathers" (v 12a).

YHWH promises three things to David before his death: a great name (v 9; compare 8:13), a place for the people (v 10; compare the catalog of David's victory within and beyond the promised land in chap 8), and rest (v 11; compare 1 Kgs 5:4). Promises to be realized after his death include an eternal house (an everlasting dynasty, vv 12 and 16), and an eternal throne and kingdom (vv 13 and 16).

Perhaps no external sign, such as a rainbow (see Gen 9:12–13), circumcision (17:11), or sabbath (Exod 31:13, 17), is needed, because anything in addition to the promised son(s) would be superfluous.[22] David accepts the promises as certain, with no obligations imposed on him: "For the sake of your word and according to your will, you have done this great thing and made it known to your servant" (2 Sam 7:21).

Significantly, the author of Samuel tells of David's sin with Bathsheba (2 Sam 11–12) immediately after narrating the covenant, for the same reason that the author of Genesis juxtaposes the stories of Noah's covenant and drunkenness. By this arrangement he subtly instructs us that the beneficiaries' darkest crimes do not annul the covenants of divine commitment.

Conditional Aspect

Favor is based on the prior spiritual relationship. Like Noah and Abraham, David, through his loyalty to YHWH, had created the spiritual climate favoring this covenant. YHWH grants David an eternal house (dynasty) because David desired to build YHWH an enduring house (temple). YHWH connects David's loyalty with the promises by calling David "my servant" (2 Sam 7:8). Once again we see the principle of historical relationship and spiritual reciprocity in effect, and we can assume from the following condition that David serves as a paradigm of the kind of individual that historically experiences the covenant's provisions.

Son of God. The irrevocable and conditional aspects of YHWH's grant to David are brought together under the evocative imagery of sonship:

> I will be his father, and he will be my son. When he does wrong, I will punish him with the rod of men, with floggings inflicted by men. But my love *[ḥesed]* will never be taken away from him, as I took it away from Saul, whom I removed from before you.
>
> (2 Sam 7:14–15)

The phrase "I will be his father, and he shall be my son" forms an adoption formula[23] that provides both the judicial basis for the gift of the eternal dynasty (compare Pss 2:7–8; 89) and the qualification that disloyal sons will lose YHWH's protection (compare 1 Kgs 6:12–13; 9:4, 6–7).[24] YHWH granted both Abraham and David an eternal progeny and fief. Loyal sons (those that fulfilled the stipulations of the treaty with Israel) would fully enjoy the fief; disloyal sons would lose YHWH's protection and, if they persisted in their wrongdoing, the possession of the fief itself. The fief, however, would never be confiscated—a promise that opens up the hope that YHWH would raise up a loyal son.

David is under curse. Although the covenant is irrevocable, David himself is punished for his crime. Nathan threatened: "This is what YHWH says: 'Out of your own household I am going to bring calamity upon you' " (2 Sam 12:11).

Conclusion

Freedman effectively summarizes the tension between unconditional commitment and conditional benefits in the Davidic covenant:

> The fate of individual kings or claimants was not guaranteed, but in the end the divine promise would be fulfilled. Historical contingency was balanced by theological certainty concerning the place of the house of David in the destiny of the nation.[25]

A. Gileadi makes the same point:

> Although the conditional aspect of the Davidic covenant—the question of the king's loyalty to YHWH—could affect Israel's protection by YHWH for better or worse, the covenant's unconditional aspect—that of an enduring dynasty—left open the possibility of YHWH's appointment of a loyal Davidic monarch in the event of a disloyal monarch's default. YHWH's protection of his people, by virtue of the Davidic covenant, could thus be restored at any time.[26]

Note that the explicit condition put upon the Davidic covenant, extending the irrevocable grant only to a faithful son who keeps the obligations of the treaty, is found not only in putative D (compare 1 Kgs 2:4; 6:12–13; 8:25; 9:4ff.) but also in the apparently ancient Psalm 132:

> YHWH swore an oath to David,
>   a sure oath that he will not revoke:
> One of your own descendants
>   I will place on your throne—
> if your sons keep my covenant
>   and the statutes I teach them,
> then their sons will sit
>   on your throne for ever and ever.
> (vv 11–12)

The Abrahamic, Davidic, and Mosaic covenants function as complements of one another in defining true Israel. Though unilateral, these covenants are as inseparable as the strands that make up a rope.

GOD'S COVENANT WITH ISRAEL
AT SINAI AND MOAB

Unconditional Aspects

The law is unilateral with reference to Israel and unconditional with reference to YHWH. YHWH's covenants with Israel, mediated through Moses at Sinai, augmented on the way from Sinai to Moab (see Num 19), and supplemented at Moab (compare Deut 29:1), call upon Israel to pledge herself to Him without obligating Him by a like pledge to Israel. The treaty is unilateral with reference to Israel and unconditional with reference to YHWH.

The similarities between Deuteronomy and the suzerainty treaties of the Hittites in the second half of the second millennium, and to those of the Assyrians in the first half of the first millennium, are too well known to be rehearsed here. In the first essay establishing this analogue, Mendenhall notes that treaties are unilateral on the part of the vassal. Contrasting the Mosaic covenant with YHWH's grants, he writes:

> The covenant of Moses, on the other hand [sic] is almost the exact opposite. It imposes specific obligations upon the tribes or clans without binding Yahweh to specific obligations, though it goes without saying that the covenant relationship itself presupposed the protection and support of Yahweh to Israel.[27]

The rewards and penalties for obedience and disobedience, couched in the form of blessings and curses, serve as encouragement to the recipients of the covenants not to renege on their commitment. The covenant itself, however, is not bilateral—it does not consist of two parties making pledges to one another to keep mutual obligations.[28]

The law is eternal and irrevocable. The suzerainty treaties were meant to be kept into the remote future. For example, the Hittite king Mursilis, who calls himself in the preamble of his treaty "the great king," stipulates to Duppi-tessub, his vassal in Amurru: "But you, Duppi-tessub, remain loyal toward the king of the Hatti land, the Hatti land, my sons [and] my grandsons forever!" Similarly, YHWH's law is said to be eternal. For example, one reads again and again of lasting *('ôlām)* ordinances (Exod 12:14; passim). Isaiah complains:

> The earth is defiled by its people;
> they have disobeyed the laws;
>   violated the statues
>   and broken the everlasting [*'ôlām*] covenant.
> (Isa 24:5)

Jesus said:

> I tell you the truth, until heaven and earth disappear, not the smallest letter, not the least stroke of a pen, will by any means disappear from the law until everything is accomplished.
> (Matt 5:18)

In short, YHWH's law is as irrevocable as his oaths are. Its absolute and eternal obligations do not stand or fall on Israel's loyalty or disloyalty to them. In this sense the Mosaic covenant is also unconditional.

Conditional Aspects

Carried on eagle's wings. The Mosaic covenant also comes as the climax of a long spiritual relationship between YHWH and Israel. Like the Noahic, Abrahamic, and Davidic covenants, it is an expression of spiritual reciprocity. The Hittite kings encouraged vassals to reciprocate their love by rehearsing the gracious relationship between them in the historical prologues of their treaties.

The point stressed is the overlord's kindness. D. R. Hillers shrewdly adds: "Parenthetically, if the history were to create any sense of obligation, it had to be substantially accurate."[29] E. Gerstenberger notes: "The treaty relationship frequently was couched in kinship terms. The concepts of 'brotherhood' *(aḫḫutu)* played a prominent role in this regard."[30]

Likewise, YHWH aimed to move Israel to accept his treaty by reminding her of his loyalty to the Patriarchs. Faithful to his promises to her, he had made Israel into a nation by miraculously increasing her and by delivering her from Egypt. He summarizes that history with a memorable metaphor:

> You yourselves have seen what I did to Egypt, and how I carried you on eagles' wings and brought you to myself.
>
> (Exod 19:4)

In sum, the law is conditioned by a history of a gracious relationship on the part of the overlord and rests on the principle of spiritual reciprocity.

Law is based on love of God. The ancient Hittite treaties, parallel in form and substance to the Mosaic covenant, reveal the great king promising his vassal protection against external and internal enemies, and guaranteeing the succession of his dynasty. W. Eichrodt notes: "[These statements] show plainly the mutuality of the new relationship, even though it is initiated and legalized by the king alone."[31]

On the basis of the parallels between these treaties and Mosaic law, K. Baltzer[32] notes that the substance of the law consists in loving God; W. Moran[33] argues convincingly that this love meant Israel would faithfully and devotedly dedicate herself to YHWH's service. R. Clements cautions that we must not think this command is mere legal terminology, empty of spiritual sentiment:

> The value of Moran's observations and comparisons cannot be discounted, but it must be strongly urged that the deuteronomic demand for love to God is wholly consonant with the character and aim of the work as a whole. An appeal to a right attitude to God fits closely into the scheme which asserts the spiritual and moral nature of all divine service.[34]

The love mandated from Israel of necessity depends on YHWH's sublime attributes and acts, frequent themes of Deuteronomy. Regarding the language of Deuteronomy, Eichrodt, in an insightful article, writes:

> [It] is not that of law but that of the heart and conscience. . . . Those who speak to us in the pages of Deuteronomy are men who know that a national law can never attain its goal so long as it remains a system reluctantly endured and effective only by compulsion; it must be founded on the inward assent of the people.[35]

In sum, for the covenant to be effective it must be maintained; it rests on the basis of spiritual reciprocity. Eichrodt notes:

> In fact, everything depends on whether the God who founds the Covenant continues to remain for his people in overwhelming reality a present, living encounter, as he was experienced at the beginning, or whether he disappears behind the mechanism of a distributive justice, dispensing reward and punishment.[36]

Conclusion

The unilateral covenant eternally committing YHWH to Abraham and his descendants, and the unilateral covenant imposing obligations on Israel are, in fact, inseparable.[37] On the one hand, YHWH's faithful discharge of his promise to Abraham provides the spiritual basis for Israel to accept and keep the covenant with commandments. On the other hand, the commandments set forth the conditions that qualify one to become a beneficiary of YHWH's grant. Both oath and law are presented unilaterally.

In this way YHWH irrevocably commits himself to fulfilling his promises, but not apart from ethical behavior on Israel's part. This connection between the two covenants explains how the two apparently incompatible kinds of covenants—oath and obligation—could be made with the same people. Under the terms of the *oath*, YHWH committed himself forever to Israel as a whole; under the terms of the *obligation*, he could discipline them individually, even to the point of putting them under curses.

Through the Davidic covenant, one man came to represent the people. Gileadi clarifies the relationship between the Mosaic and Davidic covenants: "The Davidic covenant did away with the necessity of all Israel—to a man—maintaining loyalty to YHWH in order to merit his protection."[38]

YHWH irrevocably committed himself to the house of David, but rewarded or disciplined individual kings by extending or withholding the benefits of the grant according to their loyalty or disloyalty to His treaty.

This dialectal arrangement also had distinct spiritual advantages. Israel kept YHWH's commands not on the basis of divine obligation but of divine benevolence. Israel could not put YHWH in her debt to fulfill his part of a bargain. The curses and blessings of the covenant that obliged Israel to keep YHWH's ethical demands gave Israel incentive to keep them. By these unilateral commitments, the relationship between YHWH and Israel was not contractual but covenantal—devoted and loving toward one another.

The arrangement, however, had one flaw: it could not compel the consent of Israel because of her hard heart, forehead of bronze, and stiff neck (Exod 32:9; passim). Because of this fundamental spiritual flaw—a flaw found in the human race as a whole (though exacerbated in Israel, according to Hebrew scripture)—the fulfillment of the promises to Abraham remained sporadic and partial. Although the covenant with commands was first given to all Israel, over the course of Israel's history its judicial leaders proved to be, by-and-large, faithless, which left only a remnant of true Israel—those true to the spiritual nature of the covenants, be they oath or law. The threatened curses, rather than the promised blessings, were fulfilled.

The two kinds of covenants, grant and treaty, are both eternal because both are founded on eternal attributes of YHWH—the former on his faithfulness, the latter on his holiness. Anticipating Israel's fracture of the treaty (which would disqualify her from the blessing of the grant), both putative P (Lev 26:44–45) and D (Deut 31:1–10) resolved the tension by predicting the restoration of the nation after its judgment. After predicting maledictions, P reads:

> Yet in spite of this, when they are in the land of their enemies, I will not reject them or abhor them so as to destroy them completely, breaking my covenant with them. I am YHWH their God. But for their sake I will remember the covenant with their ancestors.
>
> (Lev 26:44–45)

D resolves the tension between the working-out of the two covenants in a similar way but also anticipates the new covenant by promising that upon her return Israel will be given a new heart:

> When all these blessings and curses I have set before you come upon you . . . and when you and your children return to YHWH your God and obey him with all your heart . . . , then YHWH your God will restore your fortunes. . . . YHWH your God will circumcise your hearts . . . so that you may love him with all your heart.
>
> (Deut 30:1–6)

Note that both putative P and D put conditions on the irrevocable grant and work out the historical tension in the same way. No purpose is served by arguing that Deut. 31:1–10 is a later addition. The deuteronomic literature does not threaten the annihilation of the nation for failure to keep the treaty any more than does P.

As D anticipated, another arrangement had to be sought to bring the everlasting promises to the Patriarchs and to David to fruition by keeping the conditions of the treaty.

THE NEW COVENANT

As anticipated in these passages from the Pentateuch, Israel's history, always torn between what had been projected for Israel's history and what had been realized, provoked an acute tension between the two kinds of unilateral covenants. On the one hand, YHWH's oaths committed him to bless Israel irrevocably. On the other hand, Israel's inability to keep his treaty (containing his eternal law, consistent with his unchanging character) disqualified the nation from participating in these blessings. Only an elect remnant within the nation kept the treaty. As a result, contrary to YHWH's desires, the nation was cursed, not blessed. A new arrangement had to be sought.

The prophets of the exile foresaw an escape from this dilemma. In the name of YHWH, they announced that YHWH would grant Israel a new covenant in place of the old treaty. This new covenant would contain the substance of the treaty—the eternal law of YHWH—but not its form. Instead of having the form of a unilateral treaty depending on Israel's obedience, it would take the form of a grant, like the Abrahamic and Davidic covenants. YHWH would put his law in Israel's heart.

In setting forth this new covenant arrangement, Jeremiah unmistakably shows its continuity with the provisions of the old law:

I will put my law in their minds. . . . No longer will a man teach his neighbor, or a man his brother, saying, "Know YHWH."

(Jer 31:33–34)

The "law" in view here is unquestionably the Mosaic treaty. It is summarized by the expression "Know YHWH." H. B. Huffman[39] points out that Near Eastern kings use the verb *to know*, as well as the verb *to love*, as a treaty term. The former has two technical legal senses: to recognize as legitimate a suzerain or vassal, and to recognize treaty stipulations as binding. For example, the Hittite king, "the Sun," in a treaty with Huqqanas stipulated: "And you, Huqqanas, know only the Sun regarding lordship. Moreover, do not know another lord! Know the Sun alone!"

In short, the new covenant assumes the content of the old Mosaic treaty. But its form is like that of YHWH's grants to Abraham and David. Unlike the Mosaic treaty that rested on Israel's willingness to keep it, YHWH will unilaterally put his law in Israel's heart:

"The time is coming," declares YHWH, "when I will make a new covenant with the house of Israel and with the house of Judah. It will not be like the covenant I made with their forefathers when I took them by the hand to lead them out of Egypt, because they broke my covenant, though I was a husband to them," declares YHWH. "This is the covenant I will make with the house Israel after that time," declares YHWH. "I will put my law in their minds and write it on their hearts."

(Jer 31:31–33a)

As a result, the intention of the Abrahamic covenant will finally come to fruition:

"I will be their God, and they will be my people. . . . They will all know me, from the least of them to the greatest."

(vv 33b–34)

Under this arrangement there is no possibility of curses. Rather, the covenant will be preceded by forgiveness: "For I will forgive their wickedness and remember their sins no more" (v 34b).

NOTES

1. Ernst Kutsch, *Verheissung und Gesetz, Untersuchungen zum sogennanten "Bund" im Alten Testament (BZAW, 131),* (Berlin–New York: Walter de Gruyter, 1973).
2. Moshe Weinfeld, "Bᵉrith—Covenant vs. Obligation," *Bib* 56 (1975): 123–24; Moshe Weinfeld, "Bᵉrith," *TDOT*, 2:255–56.
3. David Noel Freedman, "Divine Commitment and Human Obligation: The Covenant Theme," *Int* 18 (1964): 420.
4. Moshe Weinfeld, "The Covenant of Grant in the Old Testament and in the Ancient Near East," *JAOS* 90 (1970): 185.

5. Although the Bible does not formally express the relationship between YHWH and Adam by the term *covenant*, yet in substance the relationship meets our definition of the word.

6. James Muilenburg, "The Form and Structure of the Covenantal Formulations," *VT* 9 (1959): 350.

7. See Dennis J. McCarthy, *Treaty and Covenant: A Study in Form in the Ancient Oriental Documents and the O.T., AnBib* 21 (Rome, 1963). Although he modified the analysis of Alt and Mendenhall, McCarthy still considers the commandments as an integral part of the covenant at Sinai, though not as an element of a treaty formula (158, n. 11; 163–64; 172–73).

8. For examples, see Dennis J. McCarthy, "*Bᵉrit* and Covenant in the Deuteronomistic History," *SVT* 3 (1972): 65–85.

9. Jon D. Levenson, "The Davidic Covenant and Its Modern Interpreters," *CBQ* 41 (1979): 215.

10. Compare Weinfeld, "Covenant of Grant," 195.

11. Dennis J. McCarthy, "*Bᵉrit* in Old Testament History and Theology," *Bib* 53 (1972): 110–21, esp. 121.

12. See D. J. A. Clines, "The Theme of the Pentateuch," *JSOT* (1978).

13. Instructively, with reference to the Davidic covenant, the term *bĕrît* is found in poetic texts (Ps 89:4, 29, 35) but not in prose accounts (2 Sam 7).

14. McCarthy, "*Bᵉrit* in Old Testament History," 84.

15. Dennis J. McCarthy, "Covenant-Relationships," in *Questions Disputées d'ancien Testament*, ed. C. Brekelmans (Gembloux, Belgium: J. Duclot, 1974), 91–103.

16. Weinfeld, "Covenant of Grant," 185.

17. Nahum M. Sarna, *Understanding Genesis*, 3d ed. (New York: Schocken Books, 1974), 120–22.

18. Freedman, "Divine Commitment and Human Obligation," 425.

19. Weinfeld, "Bᵉrith — Covenant vs. Obligation," 125.

20. I am indebted to Avraham Gileadi for calling my attention to this important text. Note that this condition put upon the grant is found not in putative D but J.

21. R. A. Carlson, *David and the Chosen King* (Uppsala, Sweden: Almquist and Wiksell, 1964), 111–14.

22. Avraham Gileadi, in "The Davidic Covenant: A Theological Basis for Corporate Protection," in this volume, suggests that YHWH's presence in Zion constitutes the sign of the Davidic covenant. That may be, but in contrast to the other biblical covenants, YHWH does not explicitly confirm his grant to David with a sign.

23. See C. Kuhl, "Neue Dokumente zum Verständnis von Hos. 2:4–15," *ZAW* 52 (1934): 102ff.; Weinfeld, "Covenant of Grant," 190.

24. See Gileadi, "Davidic Covenant."

25. Freedman, "Divine Commitment and Human Obligation," 426.

26. Gileadi, "Davidic Covenant."

27. George E. Mendenhall, "Covenant Forms in Israelite Tradition," *BA* 17 (1954): 62.

28. See George E. Mendenhall, *Law and Covenant in Israel and the Ancient Near East*, Biblical Colloquium, Pittsburgh, 1955 (= *BA*, 1954); Walter Beyerlin, *Herkunft und Geschichte der ältesten Sinaitraditionen* (Tubingen, West Germany: Mohr, 1961) (English translation, Oxford: Oxford University Press, 1965); K. Baltzer, *Das Bundesformular, WMANT* 4 (1964) (English translation, Oxford: Oxford University Press, 1971); Delbert R. Hillers, *Covenant: The History of a Biblical Idea* (Baltimore and London: Johns Hopkins University Press, 1969).

29. Hillers, *Covenant*, 31.

30. Erhard Gerstenberger, "Covenant and Commandment," *JBL* 84 (1965): 40.

31. Walter Eichrodt, "Covenant and Law," trans. Lloyd Gaston, *Int* 20 (1966): 310.

32. Baltzer, *Das Bundesformular*.

33. William Moran, "The Ancient Near Eastern Background of the Love of God in Deuteronomy," *CBQ* 23 (1963): 77 – 87.

34. Ronald E. Clements, *God's Chosen People: A Theological Interpretation of the Book of Deuteronomy* (Valley Forge, Pa.: Judson Press, 1969), 65.

35. Walter Eichrodt, *Theology of the Old Testament* I (London: S.C.M. Press, 1961), 91.
36. Walter Eichrodt, "Covenant and Law," 315.
37. Eissfeldt and Cross deny this relationship has a historical basis (see Frank Moore Cross, Jr., "Yahweh and the God of the Patriarchs," *HTR* 55 [1962]: 225–59; Frank Moore Cross, Jr., *TDOT*, 1:255ff.; Frank Moore Cross, Jr., *Hebrew Myth and Canaanite Epic* [Cambridge: Harvard University Press, 1973]). Cross claims that the Patriarchs worshiped the Canaanite god, 'El, and alleges that the Pentateuch deliberately distorts the historical situation.
38. Gileadi, "Davidic Covenant."
39. Herbert B. Huffman, "The Treaty Background of Hebrew Yada'," *BASOR* 181 (February 1966): 31–37.

11

The Prospect of Unconditionality in the Sinaitic Covenant

William J. Dumbrell

In recent years it has been commonplace in biblical studies to see the Sinaitic covenant account of Exodus 19–34 as a transaction different in type and effect from the divine covenant accounts of Genesis 15 and 2 Samuel 7. It is normally argued that the Abrahamic covenant and Davidic covenant are both "royal-grant" or promissory covenants in form, which assume no response from the beneficiary. Leaving aside the questions of form, which are always difficult to determine, a "royal-grant" assertion is certainly true of the Abrahamic covenant, though it provides a less adequate description of the Davidic.[1]

Be that as it may, a general distinction is then customarily drawn between these two covenants, which are said to exhibit one model, and the Sinai covenant, which is held to be essentially responsory—demanding a commitment from Israel. The Sinai covenant is normally said to echo yet another underlying pattern. In the case of the Sinai covenant, appeal has usually been made to the international treaty model, and therefore to all the elements of conditionality which in international arrangements surrounded the status of suzerain and vassal. Assertions of direct parallels between the treaties and the Sinai covenant, however, carry less conviction now than formerly.[2] This is not a point I propose to develop. However, the search for formal parallels between the biblical material and the environmental background which it may or may not be said to reflect is normally inclined to overlook the degree of difference between the original setting and the use to which Israel put them.

But a point that distinguishes the two promissory covenants from the Sinai is the place of law within the Sinai covenant. Law at once raises positively the questions of a response and at once, therefore, throws into real prominence an assumption of provisionality. Also undeniable is that the language of Exodus 19–34 is studded with an unambiguous air of provisionality. In light of all this, the case for unconditionality, or in the weaker sense the case for the prospect of unconditionality in the Sinai compact, would seem very difficult to establish.

The domain of biblical studies, however, is one in which paradox seems to abound. The task of this paper will be to make the point that basically the Sinai covenant contains not merely strong features pointing in the direction of unconditionality (or features from which, in the unfolding course of Israel's history, a notion of unconditionality might be drawn), but the Sinai covenant is a document essentially directed toward an unconditionality stemming from YHWH's intentions for Israel. Moreover, this directional emphasis is very clear from within the covenant material of Exodus 19–34 itself and is not superimposed upon a developing covenant framework later in Israelite history.

I first turn to the clear evidences of the significance of the Sinai covenant in the formation of Israel's eschatology; second, to obvious later indications of perpetuity; and finally, given the context of those eschatological hopes, to indications of unconditionality. I will return to Exodus 19–34 to seek the seeds of this development.

THE TENACITY ESCHATOLOGICALLY
OF THE SINAI COVENANT

The clearest evidences of Israel's eschatological dependence on the base of the Sinai compact comes, of course, in the material of the postexilic era, particularly in the new covenant theology of that period. Therefore Jer. 31:31–34 is concerned with transmuting the language of the Sinai covenant into the framework of a new covenant in which the Sinai covenant finds fulfillment. As I have noted elsewhere,[3] the language in that section is not so much that of replacement as of endorsement. What has been previously a potential would be brought to fulfillment. It is clearly also that of divine imposition, assuring a future for the Israel concerned, continuing a connection between covenant and law, and presupposing the continuance of the world role of Israel.

Much the same can be said of the restoration language of Ezekiel, who is more narrowly attached to the Jerusalem temple. Even here the prophetic eschatology that saw Jerusalem and its temple as the cosmic center (to which all nations would be drawn, and from which torah would emanate) was an eschatology that derived from the Sinai tradition's attachment to the temple. Israel's function as contemplated by the prophets—binding together covenant and law—is continued. The reconstruction program of Ezekiel 40–48 confirms the Sinai emphasis. Even though the city on view in this material is clearly Zion, the return to the theology of the conquest in these chapters, and thus to the underlying dependence on Sinai, is apparent.

The same can be argued for Isaiah. The Jerusalem eschatology of Isa. 2:2–4 is generated in Isaiah 40–55 in exodus/conquest/covenant terms. Again there is the interdependence with Sinai seen in Ezekiel, and again all stems from a new and creative divine initiative whereby the blessings of this new covenant will be imposed. The Hebrew canon ends with the Book of Chronicles, which closes with Cyrus' decree to rebuild the temple in Jerusalem. Thus the end of the canon anticipates the second exodus theology of Isaiah 40–55.

I have pointed out elsewhere[4] that since the books of Chronicles probably were written no earlier than 400 B.C., the second exodus "return" and the new covenant that must axiomatically follow—both Sinai features—had become translated into eschatological hopes after the failure of the Ezra–Nehemiah reforms. The Hebrew canon concludes, therefore, on the note of the future fulfillment of the program for Israel implicit in the Sinai covenant. This position could be argued for Malachi from another point of view. Malachi, which comes at the close of the Septuagint canon, concludes with the prospect of the return of Elijah, the twelve-tribed covenant revivalist. Elijah had been heavily cast into Mosaic Sinaitic form in 1 Kings 18–19; and it is he who must come with his message of covenant recall before the end comes.[5]

It would take us too far afield to continue the argument at this level. Nor indeed can I expend space on the place of the law except to offer the comment that the failure in the postexilic period that gave rise to the prominence of legalism was the removal of law from its covenant context. Consequently, endeavors to make the law an absolute became a way of life. This stood in apposition to the preexilic emphasis on the law as the expression of a more fundamental covenant relationship. In short, I will here simply note that from a Sinai perspective the repeated prophetic attempts during the classical period to return Israel to the covenant merely carried forward the dialogue between Moses and Israel given in Exodus 19–34. To these chapters I now turn.

EXODUS 19–34

Exodus 19:3b–6

For several reasons that I hope will become clear, these verses will form a key component of my presentation. From the inclusions formed by the formulaic statements of verses 3b and 6b, it is clear that this pericope is a self-contained unit. This unit requires detailed analysis, though for our purpose I do not propose to survey the history of the tradition that may underlie it. That will not necessarily lead to the solution of the problems concerning the theological use of the passage in its overall structure of Exodus 19–34. Verses 1–3a complete the movement of Israel to Sinai, the immediate goal of the Exodus (compare Exod 3:12), while verses 4–6 present the immediate purpose of the Exodus. Verse 4, in fact, offers an outline of the Book of Exodus; verse 5 gives the remoter purpose of the exodus redemption; the amplification of what was involved in Israel's choice, referred to in verse 5, occurs in verse 6. Let us look at these three verses in some detail.

In verse 4, three movements occur. They refer implicitly to (1) Israel's bondage: "You have seen what I did to the Egyptians"; (2) Israel's redemption: "how I bore you on eagles wings"; and (3) the immediate goal of the Exodus: "and brought you to myself," that is, to Sinai. In this threefold statement of YHWH's saving intervention in Israel's history we have a summary of the Book of Exodus. The book commences by depicting Israel as populous and feared for her potential, but enslaved. By the end of Genesis one-half of the twin Abrahamic promises of land and offspring has therefore been realized. A great nation is emerging, the people are there, only land is now required. It will be the function of the Book of Exodus to complete the transition by adding land to Israel — the offspring of the fathers — through the exodus redemption. YHWH will move Israel from slavery by intervening protectively, as verse 4 alerts us to. But the movement in the Book of Exodus also takes us from an Israel enslaved to one concerned, at the conclusion of the book, with building the tabernacle at Sinai, with constructing the cultic system.

In short, within this great book we are moving from slavery to worship, effected by means of the exodus redemption. It is clear that in its third movement verse 4 ("and I brought you to myself") has a worship structure at Sinai in view, in this way potentially carrying us through to the close of the book where the glory of YHWH suffuses the newly constructed tabernacle (Exod 40:35). Verse 4 is thus not merely operating as a review of the antecedent state of the relationship, as some have supposed — as a sort of historical prologue, to use the treaty analogy. The verse is a comprehensive review of God's intention for Israel, to be expressed through the exodus encounter. Now that Sinai has been reached, Israel is to be transformed into a worshiping people of God. The remainder of the book makes this clear. Worship in YHWH's presence, then, is the great and immediate goal to which the exodus redemption is directed. And all of Israel's aspirations would be ever bound up with that concept. The particular nature of Israel's role will be expanded on in verse 6; but in verse 4 the potential which the new relationship had aimed to establish is ready to be expressed.

Verse 5 is a much more profound theological statement of what is implicit in the new relationship, of the kingship of God the new relationship will express. While the potential is conceded in verse 4, conditions are introduced in verse 5. The twin conditions of "obeying my voice" and "keeping my covenant" are probably synonyms,[6] the second element ("keep my covenant") more clearly defining the first and locating the concept of obedience within a legitimizing framework.

Here, however, one must tread carefully. What covenant is in mind? Nothing definitely covenantal has been advanced in the book so far. Indeed, to this point the notion of a covenant has been associated only with the Abrahamic covenant in Exod. 6:1–8.[7] Most suggest the reference to covenant in verse 5 is prospective and looks forward to the Sinaitic covenant, which is about to be concluded. What argues against this, however, is the fact that the phrase "keep my covenant" (relative to a human response to a divine covenant) is used in the Hebrew Bible only where obedience to a prior divine commitment is being restated (compare the fairly exact parallels incorporating the use of *bĕrît* and *šāmar* in Gen 17:9–10; 1 Kgs 11:11; Ezek 17:14; Pss 78:10; 103:18; 132:12). This and other factors that will emerge make it probable that the covenant referred to is something preexisting. This can, of course, only be the patriarchal covenant with which continuity had been carefully forged by Moses' call in Exod. 3:13–15. The implications of this will be discussed later in the essay.

The term *sĕgŭllâ* found at 5bA, bound up with the associated prepositional phrase "among all the peoples," is one important factor in defining Israel's role. This term has been thoroughly treated in many reviews in recent years,[8] and we may accept its basic meaning as "property abstracted for special use," or the like. Most further biblical references to this term (Deut 7:6; 14:2; 26:18; Ps 135:4; Mal 3:17) depend on this exodus context. Two, however, call for our special attention; both of them spring from noncovenantal settings.

In Eccl. 2:8, a *sĕgŭllâ* is a special piece of crown property. But the reference at 1 Chr. 29:3 is even more interesting. There, David declares his intention to devote himself to the building of the temple. He will use not merely the empire's resources that are at his disposal but also his personal property, his *sĕgŭllâ*. All the empire is his, but amid that general ownership there is still the concept of a further, special attachment.

Clearly, as H. Wildberger and others have pointed out,[9] the term functions as an election word in Exodus 19. This is all the more so since the prepositional phrase "among all peoples," which follows it, plainly adds a separative emphasis. Hebr. *min*, "among," can hardly be comparative here (that is, "rather than"), for, as R. Mosis[10] points out, the tenor of verse 6 confirms the elective note and thus the separative note contained in *min:* Israel is not a priestly nation elevated above the normal world; rather by her separation Israel will "come to be" (*hāyâ*, v 6) a priestly nation. The notion expressed in 5b is the universal sovereignty of YHWH over all peoples, a sovereignty expressed in his choice of Israel, who are now electively God's.

Sĕgŭllâ, therefore, not only indicates the fact of choice, but the implications of choice. Israel is now "royal property." The term at once refers to YHWH's sovereignty and Israel's vassalship—certainly to the assertion of YHWH's kingship of Israel. For the moment we need take this no further.

The causal clause in 5bB, "for all the earth is mine," lacks a verb and thus throws up the bare nature of the fundamental relationship of all peoples to YHWH, stemming from the Creation. Taken from these *ʿammîm*, "peoples," Israel is to "become" a *sĕgŭllâ*, etc.[11] A superficial reading often makes this final phrase of verse 5 anticlimatic and almost parenthetical, and some modern versions print it that way. Read that way, it almost seems an aside, an apology for YHWH's choice of Israel. However, the phrase betokens ownership. W. Beyerlin,[12] who takes the somewhat weaker view of this phrase, suggests that the causal clause of 5bB is an affirmation of YHWH's right to choose: "You above all shall belong to me. The right to choose you is based on the fact (*kî*) that the whole earth and therefore all peoples belong to me."

It is doubtful, however, whether this is the most felicitous explanation of the function of this phrase. YHWH chooses, biblically, because he is YHWH, not because he is accountable. No reasons for his series of mysterious divine choices within history are ever offered other than here—if this be an exception. What passes for reasons are more readily seen to be tautologies (compare

Deut 7:6ff.). It is much more likely, then, that the *kî* clause functions not as the assertion of the right to choose but as the *reasons* or *goal* for choice.

Verse 6 begins with *wĕ⁾attem*, "and you," suggesting by the *waw* a slight break (compare LXX *de*) with what has preceded. Verse 6 explicates the content of *sĕgullâ* but adds nothing that is not potentially in the noun already. It is doubtful, therefore, whether E. S. Fiorenza[13] and others should be considered correct in defining verse 6 as the climax of the three verse movement. Verse 6 outlines what is to be Israel's response to YHWH's redemption — the worshiping community referred to in verse 4. Verse 5, on which the account pivots, deals with the exodus redemption in terms of divine choice and eschatological goals.

In this context the translation of the *kî* in 5bB is of some importance. It may well have a summarizing role,[14] and I basically agree with Mosis in this. However, I disagree with his suggestion that 6a is merely a restatement of the content of *sĕgullâ*.[15] The *kî* of 5bB brings that point's argument to its conclusion and states the final goal YHWH has in mind: Israel is called; she is to be a worshiping community. The nature of her election is identified.

The goal YHWH has in mind — the recognition by all peoples of his lordship — is the important note on which verse 5 ends. The election of Israel has the world in view; it is not an end in itself. The present alternative to such an Israel is simply a world of politically nondescript, loosely structured "peoples." The model of divine rule over Israel is to be the model of YHWH's universal lordship. Verse 5bB makes the point that the eschatological goal toward which the history of salvation is directed is the acknowledgment of the reality of divine kingship by the world outside Israel. This is implicit in the phrase "for all the world is mine." In view of the universality of the context, the term *⁾āreṣ* (5bB) cannot be restricted merely to Canaan. Verse 6 will continue with the application of Israel's function.

This brings us to 6a and the minefield represented by *mamleket kōhănîm*. I believe these words are synonymously parallel to *gôy qādôš*, but I admit that the phrase is an interpretive crux. I cannot in this paper review the wider range of options that have been presented to provide translations of these two terms. The main difficulty in *mamleket* is whether the term is absolute or a construct, and in defining it within either of those two relationships.

R. B. Y. Scott, who with others[16] has presented the interpretative options available to the translator, has opted for a rendering "a kingdom set apart like a priesthood in the ancient world is set apart." This seems to capture the sense the passage demands. The concept of kingly rule has already been presented in *sĕgullâ* and is dominant in the passage. One might expect that 6a, in elaboration of *sĕgullâ*, should emphasize this royal note. This makes it somewhat unlikely that *mamleket kōhănîm* simply represents one-half of the equation to which *gôy qādôš* is to be added in order to construct the whole of Israel.[17] It seems intrinsically more probable that the second term, *gôy qādôš*, "holy nation," explains and clarifies *mamleket kōhănîm*. *Mamleket*, it is generally agreed, refers to the institution of kingship as such, not to the holder of the office. Royal authority, power to exhibit such authority, and the status conferred by it are all within its normal semantic range. After a very careful examination of the relationship of the two terms, Fiorenza takes *kōhănîm* as the attribute, leaving us therefore with a translation of "priestly royalty."[18] This is certainly nicely paralleled by what follows.

The curious term in the phrase *gôy qādôš* is the noun *gôy*. The adjective *qādôš* strikes the continued note of separation and purity we have detected throughout this passage. This is expected and consistent, although the political term "nation," *gôy*, is somewhat puzzling in such an elevated context. This is especially the case since the normal election term used of Israel is the familiar *'am*.[19] *Gôy* has political superstructures in mind: national boundaries, political associations, cultural factors, etc. Perhaps the usage is natural here because the context deals with Israel's call to move onto the international scene. But in view of the nearby use of *'ammîm* in reference to the remainder of the world, perhaps more is being said.

Israel, within this passage, is being called to be a kingdom and that directs us to political realities. The point perhaps being made is the same point made in Gen. 12:2, where *gôy* is used of Abram's seed. In contradistinction to it the remainder of the world are merely "clans," *mišpĕḥōt*. Gen. 12:2–3 implies that outside the structure imposed by a kingdom of God there can really be no concept of an acceptable political model. Israel is thus being called onto the world stage in Exodus 19 to be a light to the Gentiles. While ultimately she will be assigned to this role only after a new exodus, this role is nonetheless implicit in her present initial political calling by YHWH.

Of course "priestly kingdom" implies not merely separation from society but the embodiment of those values intrinsic to the developing priesthood in Israel. Purity and holiness are intended, but above all a worshiping community whose heart is her relationship with her patron. A priestly kingdom is first a worshiping company of priests, who are also kings, an ideal governmental entity meant to be attractive by its distinctiveness, meant to provide a model of what true political alignment in the world must lead to. Israel is to be the community who by her manner of life displays the political harmony intended by YHWH for all of human society.

Moses and the Giving of the Legal Codes

Exod. 19:7–8 registers the assent of the elders and people to the divine proposals of Exod. 19:3b–6. The element of "doing" in these verses underscores the note of provisionality to what was previously promised. On the other hand, the phrase "if you obey my voice/keep my covenant" (v 5) preceded the promise.

I will now survey the remainder of Exodus 19–34 to establish whether this presentation given to Israel at Sinai will provide a basis for the doctrine of unconditionality within the covenant relationship of the Old Testament. The remainder of Exodus 19 is given over to special preparation for the divine theophany, in the course of which the law codes, the Decalogue, and the covenant codes (or case law) will be delivered. The Decalogue, the basis of Israel's system of jurisprudence, from whose code everything else stems, comes in Exod. 20:1–17. As Exod. 20:1 makes clear, it is given within a framework of grace. Its context tells us that it is given to each Israelite separately as well as corporately.

The position of Moses in all this is an elevated, important one, but not essentially mediatorial at this point in time. True, Exod. 20:18–21 seems to call upon Moses to play such a role, but this is at the request of the people. It is not initiated by YHWH. It is a request that stems from fear, and this fear is at once allayed by Moses. What follows in Exod. 20:22 is an admonition by YHWH to Moses for Israel. Then in Exodus 21–23 another legal code, of a different type to the Decalogue in Exod. 20:1–17, is given through Moses.

The formal differences between the two codes, now well known and accepted, probably need no elaboration. The case law of Exodus 21–23 contains contingent elements and provides penalties for specific offenses, and speaks to a mundane background of crime and punishment that is foreign to the lofty, imperatival delivery of Exod. 20:1–17. The Decalogue seems intended to reflect what flows naturally out of the relationship effected by redemption. It provides, by its specifics, the parameters within which the relationship will operate. It also offers the guidelines that determine whether the relationship will have been breached. Law, in this sense, results from covenant but is not its precondition. There is no indication that it can be performed independent of accepting the full implications contained in the covenant relationship.

The covenant codes of Exodus 21–23 are not so grounded but follow upon admonitions to avoid the dominant national sin of the Bible: idolatry, the root of all evil. While the Decalogue came unmediated, the covenant codes were given through Moses. Rather than stressing Moses' mediatorial role at this point, the distinction between the codes is probably meant to underscore the essential character of the one type of law and the derivative nature of the other.

The Decalogue also directs us to the values that will reflect the ideal acceptance of the relationship, while the covenant codes remind us of Israel's murmuring as she approaches Sinai, tempering the idealism implanted by Exodus 19–20 by reality. Thus, by the present editorial arrangement of these codes, we are reminded that both the challenges of Exodus 19–20 and the references to potential social failures in Exodus 21–23 are tensions normal to Israel in the Hebrew Bible. They do not, however, necessarily speak for concepts of unconditionality on the one hand and provisionality on the other, within the covenant framework. The schematic differences that would indicate this offer evidence that is too simplistic.

We may note that Moses is thrown into further prominence by his role in Exodus 24, particularly by his separation from the people at Exod. 24:1–2. The fact that at the ratification of the covenant in 24:1–11 seventy elders with Aaron, Nadab, and Abihu accompany Moses up the mountain and eat in the divine presence, makes it clear that all Israel is still considered capable of being addressed without the services of a mediator, and on a most intimate level. The note of promise is still hopefully there. Thus, at the end of

Exodus 24, when Moses finally goes up the mountain into the more immediate divine presence (to reduce the commandments to writing), whatever mediatorial role he has assumed up to this point has only been very summarily exercised. So far, the ideal that is to be Israel has been very carefully presented in Exodus 19–20, but the material of Exodus 21–23 has drawn attention to basic realities inherent in Israel's national nature.

Blueprint for the Tabernacle

Exodus 25–31 is often overlooked in an assessment of the material in Exodus 19–34, but it is clearly a part of the whole. It comes directly after the ratification of the covenant and must, in some sense, be said to interpret it. The blueprint for the tabernacle is given to Moses in terms of a heavenly *tabnît*, "pattern" (Exod 25:9). This means, of course, that not only is the true builder YHWH himself but that the true tabernacle is that which already exists in heaven. This explains the extraordinary function exercised in Israel's history by the tabernacle and also the importance of its later replacement, the Jerusalem temple.

Of course, the provision of the tabernacle attaches a degree of visibility to the divine presence while Israel is on the march to Canaan. But more than that, the position of these chapters in the total composition of the book should be noted. They are not, as often supposed, a pedestrian priestly insertion. Nor are they a digression within the total presentation of the book's movement. What they stress, or rather, what the tabernacle symbolizes, is the idea of YHWH's rule, adopted by the ratification of the covenant in Exodus 24 to which I referred. As a copy of the heavenly, the tabernacle seeks to replicate the heavenly dwelling. Put summarily, the tabernacle is the earthly palace of the heavenly king, and the gradations of approach within the tabernacle — the manner of its service, the vestments of its officials, etc. — all underscore this point.[20]

At the same time, the building of the tabernacle keeps before us the goal of the Exodus, which was the worship of YHWH as Israel's sovereign. This aim is what will constitute Israel's claim to be a "priestly royalty," a community directed by YHWH. Ratification of the covenant in Exodus 24 has meant the acceptance of YHWH's kingship. This in its turn must lead to the acknowledgment of that kingship. The gradation by which the worship structure is presented within the tabernacle, its approaches, etc., constitute the protocol by which the worship itself must be preserved — bearing in mind the divine nature of YHWH who is to be worshiped. After an interruption, which is the sin of the golden calf, and after a renewal of the covenant, this note of the importance of the institution of worship within Israel is the flourish on which the Book of Exodus concludes.

More than that, we remind ourselves of the credal statement of Exod. 15:1–18, which concludes on the note of the divine presence in the promised land, and of divine kingship (vv 17–18), establishing Israel's land as the world center (the "mountain"[21]) where YHWH has chosen to enthrone himself. Clearly

the promised land was to be a "sanctuary" (compare Ps 78:54) in which
YHWH's kingship would be honored.[22]

Bound up with this notion of the promised land, ideally occupied, is, as
we well know from the Book of Deuteronomy, the biblical concept of rest. The
great promise given to Israel in the Bible is that of "rest," *měnûḥâ*, in God's
presence in the land. "Rest" thus results from the proper response to divine
kingship. The building of the tabernacle in the Book of Exodus is the proper
response in this context. It is interesting that the sabbath, a major concept
bound to the biblical idea of rest, is brought into close contact with the building of the tabernacle. I will take this point a little further to explain the full
extent of the idealism with which Israel is being confronted.

Others have noted that the directions given to Moses regarding the construction of the tabernacle, etc., close with an injunction to keep the sabbath
(Exod 31:12ff.), while the account of the actual erection of the tabernacle
begins on the same note of sabbath observance (Exod 35:1ff.). B. S. Childs
sees tabernacle and sabbath as simply two sides of one associated reality.[23] The
reason for this is easily known. One possible meaning of the biblical concept
of sabbath, a major one, is that it is the day that "completes" a series; it brings
the week to an end. In this sense it is the goal to which the week is directed.
Likewise, the seventh day of creation is the day which "completes"[24] the creation sequence, and in that sense it constitutes a goal. Finally, in the fourth
commandment of Exod. 20:11, the notion of "rest" (Hebr. *nwḥ*) is connected
with the sabbath (Hebr. *šbt*) by its insistence that the goals set by creation be
remembered by resting on the seventh day.

The conjunction of tabernacle and sabbath involving "rest" makes it perfectly clear what the goals are which the building of the tabernacle will endorse.
It will be an acknowledgment of YHWH's kingship that leads to "rest" for his
covenant people. At the same time these goals remind Israel of YHWH's purpose for the world. The function of the sabbath is to endorse the goal to which
Israel's history is directed. The recommissioning of the tabernacle after the
golden calf episode makes it clear that the covenant renewal of Exodus 34 has
brought all these values back as possibilities. The tabernacle, as the point from
which divine world rule is exercised, is, as I have noted, the emphasis upon
which the Book of Exodus concludes.

The Role of Moses in Exodus 33–34

Surprisingly, after Exodus 32 there follows (in Exod 33:1–6) the repetition
of the Abrahamic promises, the basis on which Israel has been called into
being. After the heinous sin of the golden calf, this seems unexpected. But
the renewal of the covenant was without substance, for the narrative takes an
ominous turn in Exod. 33:3b when YHWH announces that he himself will not
go with the people. This at once reduces Israel to a mere *gôy*, a potential
geopolitical unit only; and now the weighty instrumentality of Mosaic mediation comes into play for the first time in the account. The future of Israel, the

fate of the Sinai convenant in Israel's experience, will be determined in these two chapters by the efficacy of Moses' mediatorial office, now positively assumed.

The tent episode of Exod. 33:7–11 is difficult to interpret. We are not dealing with the tabernacle here, since it has not yet been constructed. Probably what is on view is an oracular tent of some type.[25] The mention of the tent is designed to concentrate our attention on the figure of Moses from this point on. The account of the veiled Moses with which the covenant narrative ends (in 34:29–35) is anticipated by this encounter with the nature of the relationship in which YHWH and Moses speak openly, "face to face" (Exod 33:11). Moses is now the recipient of the "presence" withdrawn from Israel!

This separation between Moses and the people is emphasized by the repeated words in 33:7 of "outside the camp."[26] The direct intercession of Moses follows in verses 12–17, in which Moses alone[27] is now promised "rest"—the blessing that was to have been Israel's in the promised land. Remarkably, Moses is prepared to operate within this limitation and he accepts the fact that between YHWH and Israel a significant distance now exists. YHWH's presence must therefore now be mediated; it cannot any longer be generally received. It will go with Moses, and by going with Moses it will still distinguish Israel as the people of God. This much and this much only is conceded in verses 12–17 by YHWH.

In verses 18–23, Moses pleads for a theophany, his own theophany, as opposed to Israel's of Exodus 19. Upon this the second giving of the law will follow. This request is not fully granted, and the hidden dimension of YHWH in the Old Testament (his glory) is not encountered. The similarity of Exod. 33:19 to Exod. 3:13–15 has often been commented upon. Here it is Moses who receives the "name," though the essence of God himself—his glory—remains undisclosed. Israel is still to be set apart, since YHWH will go with her. But the doubt of her personally experiencing YHWH in her midst, who will accompany her on the march (see v 17), still remains.

The theophany, and Moses' response to it (Exod 34:1–7), marks the turning point in the narrative. Moses' comments in verses 8–9 about the theophany make the situation clear. Even though YHWH's forgiveness has been extended to granting his presence with Israel on the march, the personal distinctiveness of Moses (v 9) is still the reason for the second action of covenant renewal. It is a demonstration of YHWH's ḥesed (v 6), something beyond what might have been expected,[28] because Israel has been undeserving.[29] The marvels (v 10) that YHWH will do before all the people will, it seems, signify the renewal of his covenant with Israel through Moses.[30] The Septuagint, in verse 10, makes Moses the primary recipient of the covenant. It reads: *tithēmi soi diathēkēn*. This is probably secondary, although the function of the verse is to anticipate that the covenant renewal for Israel which follows takes place through Moses alone.[31]

A summary of conditions bound up with renewal of the covenant, with emphasis on warnings against idolatry, follows in Exod. 34:11–26. Israel's dependence on Moses is stressed by the substantial continuance of the second person singular throughout the course of this covenant address. But in verse 27 we find Israel now included in the covenant. It is therefore only in accordance with the warnings delivered through Moses in verses 11–26 that the covenant can be renewed. The actual act of renewal is recorded in 27b, whereby YHWH, the presumed subject of this half-verse, refers to the preconditions for renewal delivered in verses 11–26. YHWH[32] then rewrites the Decalogue (v 28b; compare v 1) that is to form the basis of the covenant, and Moses comes down from the mountain with the tables. Exod. 34:11–26 is not in itself a covenant renewal statement, and the attempt to derive a Decalogue from these verses has been fruitless.[33]

The implications of the renewed covenant, and its limitations for Israel, are contained in verses 29–35. Here should be noted the extreme emphasis on Moses. The important position that this narrative of the veiled Moses occupies in the total context of the covenant exposition deserves comment. By its conclusion of the extended covenant account (Exod 19–34), this narrative presumably summarizes the condition of Israel in terms of the Sinai covenant. At the same time the prospects are implicitly under review for this people of YHWH as they move under Mosaic leadership into the promised land.

In Exod. 34:29–35 the mediatorial role of Moses is designedly amplified. The glory that suffuses Moses' face as he comes down from the mountain with the two tables of stone terrifies Aaron and Israel (v 30). Moses then allays their fears and summons them to him (v 31), indicating by this summons that the radiance on his face is not something they must quail before, awesome as it is. Rather, it underlies the intimate relationship Moses enjoys with YHWH. The leaders first approach, then the congregation is summoned (v 32), and the tenor of YHWH's commandments, apparently those of Exod. 34:11–26, is conveyed to Israel.

After speaking with Israel, Moses veils his face. Fear, as a primary factor, does not underlie this veiling, since in the following account Moses is unveiled both when delivering revelation and (in the presence of YHWH) when receiving revelation. He is veiled only when he is not acting as receptor or mediator. This would seem to indicate that, dangerous as it was, the glow on Moses' face was more of a sign than a threat. We cannot assume that the veil is put on to hide an evanescent glory; this assumption enjoys support neither from this context nor from traditional rabbinic exegesis. What seems to be emerging from this passage (in which the emphasis is placed on Moses as the carrier of Israel's traditions) is that Moses' shining face authenticates the covenant renewal activity and the delivery of the divine word.

UNCONDITIONALITY IN THE SINAI COVENANT

We are now in a position to see where the prospect for unconditionality in the Sinai covenant lies. The narrative of Exodus 19–34 makes it clear that it could not lie with a national Israel. She had proved herself unworthy in Egypt, and on the march to Sinai she had "murmured." Even after the theophany there had been the golden calf! One could not with any confidence approach the future of this nation with hope.

But the role of Moses in this episode shows us not only how the covenant concept could be preserved but that it could, at least in a limited sense, from the outset bear the hallmark of unconditionality. God has raised up for himself a Moses from the debacle that was Israel on Sinai. In this Moses the covenant hopes would be fostered. But Moses was simply representative of a faithful Israel of that and future periods. God would continue to move upon the hearts of pious men and women in Israel through whom the reality of the concept of the worshiping community, drawn together at Sinai, would endure. In brief, the prospect for the unconditionality of this national covenant lay not in the nation with whom it was made but in the remnant that would emerge from this nation.

Yet a point now needs to be made from the material of Exod. 19:3b–6. The separation of Israel from her broad cultural environment, her invitation to obey a covenant already existing, her call to be a light to lighten the Gentiles – the model for the world that her role would provide – all of this is confessedly Abrahamic in its tenor. As the continuity of the exodus narratives suggests (compare Exod 3:13–15; 6:1–8), the Sinai covenant was in fact a particularization of Gen. 12:1–3 in the experience of Israel. Like Abram, Israel was called outside of the land that would be hers. Like Abram, Israel would be a great nation (*gôy*), occupying a "promised land." Like Abram, the world would find its source of blessing in this Israel.

At once, then, a further factor emerges that endorses more than just a *limited* concept of unconditionality. The strand of covenant theology that began with Abram continues with Sinai. It will add kingship to its ambit with 2 Samuel 7. Its direct unconditionality, because it is divinely imposed and sustained, will emerge in Jer. 31:31–34. On two counts, therefore – the remnant on the human side and divine design on the other – a worshiping company among whom God would dwell was bound to emerge. They will be priests and kings. The fact that this is projected early, or that its fulfillment is pointed to only at the close of the canon, should not disturb us. For the notion the Sinai covenant in its very erection enshrines is, as I have pointed out, fundamentally eschatological.

I can now briefly sum up the issues. YHWH's vocational call to Israel in Exod. 19:3b–6 was for Israel to become an ideal worshiping community. The endorsement of the covenant, the law which was to express the relationship, and, in particular, the building of the tabernacle by which YHWH's kingship would be recognized by Israel were all calculated to further this ideal. Given expression, these elements would make the promised land a place in which YHWH's "rest" would be experienced by Israel.

However, Israel's journey to the mount and her national apostasy at Sinai indicate even at that stage that no hope could be reposed on the nation. The mediatorial role of Moses that developed during the Sinai experience was a forerunner of later ministries in Israel's history that would seek to return her to the ideal. But Moses was also an indication at Sinai that the divine intent to raise up an ideal worshiping entity would stand. Since we do not see this happening with the nation of Israel anywhere in the Hebrew Bible, to that extent the element of provisionality within the Sinai covenant has prevailed. But we do see the erection of a people of God begun with Abraham and continuing with Moses. This continuity finds full expression in the later "remnant" covenants of the Hebrew Bible that continue the basic Abrahamic promises. The factor of unconditionality which has always existed in the Sinai covenant is thereby realized.[34]

NOTES

1. There are certainly conditional features about the Davidic covenant. On the whole question, refer to my article "The Davidic Covenant," *Reformed Theological Review* 39 (1980): 40–47.
2. A convenient point of reference here is D. J. McCarthy's review of the relationship between the Sinai covenant and the vassal treaties in *Treaty and Covenant, AnBib* 21A (Rome: Biblical Institute Press, 1978), 273–76.
3. William J. Dumbrell, *Covenant and Creation: An Old Testament Covenantal Theology* (Exeter: Paternoster, 1984), 174–85.
4. William J. Dumbrell, "The Purpose of the Books of Chronicles," *JETS* 27 (1984): 3:257–66.
5. Of course, the announcement of the coming of an Elijah is not a promise of unconditionality. However, it does result in unconditionality, because, according to Jeremiah, the new covenant is directly associated with the Sinaitic covenant.
6. Paul Kalluveettil, *Declaration and Covenant, AnBib* 88 (Rome: Biblical Institute Press, 1982), 157, n. 149.
7. We may leave aside the somewhat complicated matter of the name of the deity in Exod. 6:1–8. For a recent treatment of the issue involved, however, note G. J. Wenham, "The Religion of the Patriarchs" in *Essays on the Patriarchial Narratives*, ed. A. R. Millard and D. J. Wiseman (Leicester: Inter-Varsity Press, 1980), 157–88.
8. E. S. Fiorenza's coverage of this discussion is admirable (compare *Priester für Gott: Studien zum Herrschafts—und Priestermotiv in der Apokalypse*, Neutestamentliche Abhandlungen, Neue Folge 7 [Muenster: Aschendorff, 1972], 138–41).
9. H. Wildberger, *THAT* 2 (Munich: Chr. Kaiser, 1970), 142–44, and the literature which he there cites.
10. R. Mosis, "Exod. 19:5b–6a: Syntaktischer Aufbau und lexikalische Semantik," *BZ* 22 (1978): 19.
11. Note the use of the finite verbs in 5a, 6a; Mosis, "Exod. 19:56–6a," 23. Mosis points to the importance of the nominal sentence 5bB surrounded by the use of *hāyâ* in 5bA and 6a. The nominal sentence notes the fact, the verbal sentences the responses to be developed by this fact.
12. W. Beyerlin, *Origins and History of the Oldest Sinaitic Traditions* (Oxford: Blackwell, 1961), 71.
13. Fiorenza, *Priester für Gott*, 126–27.
14. The Hebrew particle *kî* has a wide range. It can be explicative, causal, emphatic, interpretive (compare Mosis, "Exod. 19:5b–6a," 16, and the references there cited). Here it must be used in a causal sense.

15. Mosis, "Exod. 19:5b–6a," 14. Verse 5 presents the election of Israel, verse 6 the function of Israel within the framework of this election.
16. R. B. Y. Scott, "A Kingdom of Priests" (Ex XIX 6), *OTS* 8 (1950): 213–19.
17. W. L. Moran argues this, building upon the earlier arguments of W. Caspari (compare Moran, "A Kingdom of Priests," in *The Bible in Current Catholic Thought*, ed. J. S. McKenzie [New York, 1962], 7–20).
18. Fiorenza, *Priester für Gott*, 141–42.
19. For the Old Testament sense of Hebr. *gôy* ("nation"), see R. E. Clements, *Theological Dictionary of the Old Testament* (Grand Rapids, Mich.: Wm. Eerdmans, 1975), 2:426–33.
20. On the question of approach to the deity with the tabernacle/temple structure, see M. Haran, *Temples and Temple Service in Ancient Israel* (Oxford: Clarendon, 1978), 205–25.
21. Underlying the reference to the sanctuary as a mountain in Exod. 15:17 is the older worldview of the chosen mountain as the meeting point between heaven and earth. Palestine is being presented in this verse in just these terms — as the place of revelation where heaven and earth will in this sense meet. On the whole question, note R. J. Clifford, *The Cosmic Mountain in Canaan and the Old Testament* (Cambridge, Mass.: Harvard University Press, 1972), 137–39.
22. It is sometimes suggested that Jerusalem centrality, later to appear, is on view in this verse. The antiquity and context of the poem speak against this, and probability and morphology against Kadesh. Palestine as the goal in mind seems the natural choice.
23. B. S. Childs, *The Book of Exodus* (London: S.C.M. Press, 1974), 541–42.
24. On the meaning of *šbt*, consult G. Robison, "The Idea of Rest in the Old Testament," *ZAW* 92 (1980): 32–42. While the root can and does mean to "cease" or "stop," what "completes a sequence" provides a dominant note in it.
25. M. Haran, *Temples and Temple Service in Ancient Israel*, 260–71, has argued this.
26. R. W. L. Moberly, *At the Mountain of God: Story and Theology in Exodus 32–34* (Sheffield: JSOT Press, 1983), 63–66, indicates what role Exod. 33:7–11 plays in the theme of Israel under God's judgment in Exodus 33–34.
27. The promise of divine rest is given in verse 14 to Moses alone (*lāk*). This is critically important in evaluating what follows, since it is the key promise of the Exodus.
28. This covenant use of *ḥesed* in the sense of forgiveness is taken up and discussed by K. D. Sakenfeld in her article "The Problem of Divine Forgiveness in Numbers 14," *CBQ* 37 (1975): 317–30.
29. On the possibilities contained within the *kî* of verse 9, compare Moberly, *At the Mountain*, 88–90. He opts for (and I agree) "even though."
30. Moberly seems to be correct when he refers to marvels to be wrought at to the covenant about to be renewed (*At the Mountain*, 94). The restoration of Israel is the fearful thing which will happen.
31. It seems more natural to preserve Moses as the object of verse 10 in both halves. We have so far had no indication of YHWH's willingness to draw closer to Israel other than through Moses. The second person singular is substantially sustained through verses 11–26, and it is somewhat artificial to suppose that in them Israel and not Moses is addressed.
32. There seems to be a change of subject within verse 28: 28a rounds off 11–27, but 28b changes the implied subject to YHWH since the Ten Words are in mind.
33. The view that Exodus 34 had contained a "J" ritual Decalogue has been a popular but unproven one. Childs (*Exodus*, 605–7) points to the erosion of confidence in this once widely held view (see Moberly, *At the Mountain*, 101–6).
34. The aim of this paper has been to examine the interrelationships of Exodus 19–34 as we now have them and thus to lay bare the theological thrust which the final form of the narrative conveys. Doubtless, the questions of underlying traditions and their redaction, etc., are valid questions, but since they do not shed any obvious light on the point conveyed by Exodus 19–34 as a whole, they are questions I have not taken up.

12

The Davidic Covenant:
A Theological Basis
for Corporate Protection

Avraham Gileadi

In biblical studies, the Davidic covenant has largely been treated separately from what is called "Zion ideology" and from the corollary idea of Zion's inviolability. Yet the two are closely intertwined. Two passages in the Book of Isaiah, linked rhetorically by a common phrase, shed light on the relationship between the Davidic covenant and Isaianic Zion ideology:

> I will deliver you and this city
>   out of the hand of the king of Assyria;
> I will protect this city.
> (Isa 38:6)
>
> I will protect this city and save it,
>   for my own sake
>   and for the sake of my servant David.
> (Isa 37:35)

Since these passages appear as one in 2 Kgs. 20:6, their division in the Book of Isaiah seems intended to link two separate historical incidents—the threat of Jerusalem's destruction by Assyria in Isaiah 36–37 and the threat of Hezekiah's death from a mortal illness in chapter 38—to a common context of Hezekiah's fidelity to YHWH. In one instance, while praying before YHWH, Hezekiah acknowledges that YHWH alone rules over all kingdoms of the earth (37:16–20); Hezekiah is a king who turns to YHWH, the all-powerful, in times of distress. In the other instance, also while praying before YHWH, Hezekiah asserts that he has been entirely faithful to him; Hezekiah is a king who has "done what is good" in YHWH's sight (38:3).

When the two passages are read together, the idea of protection of king and people by YHWH is represented as stemming directly from YHWH's relationship to David. Vital to this covenantal bond is the fidelity of the king. The "city" in these passages—Zion/Jerusalem—represents "the remnant [of YHWH's people] that is left" (37:4); the place protected by YHWH is the habitation of "the living" who acknowledge YHWH's faithfulness (38:19). In both instances, this context of protection heightens YHWH's relationship to David. For we will see that in seeking YHWH's protection of his people, Hezekiah considered himself answerable for the terms of the Davidic covenant.

TREATY BACKGROUND

As observed by M. Weinfeld, P. J. Calderone, F. C. Fensham, and others, YHWH's covenant with David reflects the salient points of Hittite and Neo-Assyrian suzerain–vassal agreements.[1] A summary of resemblances between the Davidic covenant and suzerain–vassal relationships follows:

1. In the Covenant of Grant, the suzerain or "great king," on demonstration of the exceeding loyalty of a vassal king, may bestow on him the unconditional right of an enduring dynasty to rule over a particular city–state.[2]
2. The establishment of a "father–son" relationship between the suzerain and the vassal (by means of a declarative adoption formula) creates a legal basis for the gift of an enduring dynasty;[3] alongside the vassal's covenantal designation as "son" of the suzerain, he is also known as his "servant."[4]
3. As part of ancient Near Eastern treaty formulary, the great king guarantees the protection of the vassal or his ruling heir by undertaking to annihilate a common enemy — provided the current ruler is loyal to the great king, does not recognize another as great king, and reports any evil word against the great king.[5]
4. The suzerain undertakes to protect the people of the vassal by virtue of the suzerain's agreement with the vassal, though on occasion the suzerain may contract an agreement directly with the people of the vassal. In such an instance, the separate agreement between the suzerain and the people serves as the complement of the suzerain's (primary) agreement with the vassal.[6]
5. In the Covenant of Grant, the curse formulary is directed against those who violate the rights of the vassal or his ruling descendants.[7] If a vassal is himself disloyal, he will be disciplined by the great king, often to be replaced by an heir of the dynasty loyal to the great king.[8]

THE DAVIDIC COVENANT

The combined findings of Weinfeld, Calderone, and Fensham reveal that, against its ancient Near Eastern background, one of the Davidic covenant's chief points of departure from other covenants of YHWH with his people or with individuals is the concept of protection. The validity of the protection clause in ancient Near Eastern treaties, although it could depend directly on a people's relationship to a suzerain,[9] depended primarily on a sound relationship being maintained between a vassal king and a suzerain.[10] In language similar to that of the Neo-Assyrian grant,[11] when David "walked before [YHWH] in truth, loyalty, and uprightness of heart," YHWH "kept *ḥesed* [a synonym of *covenant*][12] with him" (1 Kgs 3:6). On the other hand, when David transgressed against YHWH, as in his peremptory census of Israel (2 Sam 24:1), YHWH's protection of Israel broke down (2 Sam 24:13).

So in regard to YHWH's agreement with Solomon: if Solomon would "walk in my statutes, perform my laws and keep all my commandments," YHWH would "perform my word with you which I spoke to your father David" and "dwell among the children of Israel and not forsake my people Israel" (1 Kgs 6:12–13). But if Solomon would not walk before YHWH "as your father David walked, in integrity of heart and with uprightness," and would "not keep my commandments and statutes," YHWH would "cut off Israel out of the land that I have given them" and Israel would be "a proverb and byword among all people" (1 Kgs 9:4, 6–7). In Davidic covenant theology the fate and welfare of the nation hinged on the king's loyalty to YHWH.

Not surprisingly, the movement from a charismatic war leader in Israel to a full-fledged dynastic monarch occurred in response to a need for national protection. Israel's reaction to the objections of Samuel concerning a king was "We will have a king . . . that our king may . . . go out before us and fight our wars" (1 Sam 8:19–20). Saul's ire at the rumor that he killed Philistines by the thousands, but David by the tens of thousands (1 Sam 18:8), dramatizes the idea of the king as a divinely sanctioned and divinely prospered warlord. Like Saul's, David's first appointment to kingship was for the sake of Israel's protection, he becoming the means whereby YHWH "cut off all your enemies out of your sight" (2 Sam 7:8–9). Abner's appeal to the people to accept David as king was founded on the premise that "YHWH has spoken of David, saying, 'By the hand of my servant David I will save my people Israel out of the hand of the Philistines and out of the hand of all their enemies' " (2 Sam 3:18; compare 5:2).

David's second appointment by YHWH, as noted by Calderone (though he misses its intent),[13] was a confirmation of his first appointment and constituted the promise to a victorious ruler of an enduring dynasty over a particular people and place (compare 2 Sam 7:10–12; Ps 89:19–29). But the key idea behind David's second calling, that which lent an element of permanence to Israel's establishment in the land, was that thereafter those loyal to the Davidic king merited YHWH's protection by proxy so long as the king maintained loyalty to YHWH. Although the conditional aspect of the Davidic covenant — the question of the king's loyalty to YHWH — could affect Israel's protection by YHWH for better or worse, the covenant's unconditional aspect — that of an enduring dynasty — left open the possibility of YHWH's appointment of a loyal Davidic monarch in the event of a disloyal monarch's default. YHWH's protection of his people, by virtue of the Davidic covenant, could thus be restored at any time.

THE SINAITIC COVENANT

All of this has a bearing on why the earlier Sinaitic covenant—which follows the pattern of a separate and thus secondary agreement between a suzerain and a people—could be cited in support of the Davidic covenant (2 Sam 7:23–25). Through the unconditional Davidic covenant, YHWH has "confirmed to yourself your people to be your people for ever, and you, O YHWH, have become their God" (2 Sam 7:24). In accordance with suzerain-vassal agreements in general, a protection clause in the Sinaitic covenant would have been operative only if all Israel—as YHWH's vassal—were loyal to him. This appeared to be the case during the initial phase of Israel's conquest of Canaan under Moses and Joshua, when Israel was consistently victorious against her enemies. However, in an instance of one man's transgression by confiscating a Babylonian garment and a sum of money (Josh 7:21), all Israel was imputed with guilt in breaking the covenant (Josh 7:11) and Israel in general suffered reverses in battle (Josh 7:4–5, 12–13). Upon destruction of the offender and his house, YHWH's protection of his people was restored (Josh 7:24–8:1).

After the conquest of Canaan when Israel's loyalty to YHWH lapsed, YHWH's protection of his people also lapsed. By the time of Samuel and Saul, the Philistines threatened the very existence of Israel. The institution of the Davidic covenant, vested in a vassal loyal to the suzerain, constituted an earnest of protection, vouchsafed but virtually impossible to realize in the Sinaitic covenant. The suzerain–vassal model as a legal framework for both the Sinaitic and Davidic covenants validated the basis on which YHWH's protection was to be obtained. There now existed no provision for national protection other than within the framework of a suzerain–vassal type of relationship with YHWH. But the Davidic covenant did away with the necessity that all Israel—to a man—maintain loyalty to YHWH in order to merit his protection. In the analogy of suzerain–vassal relationships, David's designation as YHWH's "son" and "firstborn" (2 Sam 7:14; Pss 2:6–7; 89:27) legitimized him as Israel's representative—as the embodiment of YHWH's covenant people, also called his "son" and "firstborn" (Exod 4:22). With regard to Israel's protection, the Davidic covenant superseded the Sinaitic covenant, but only because of Israel's regression in her loyalty toward YHWH (compare 1 Sam 8:7). Henceforth, the king stood as proxy between YHWH and his people.

ZION IDEOLOGY

Appended to the Davidic covenant, therefore, was the idea of Zion as a safe place (Isa 37:33). YHWH's permanent dwelling among his people constituted, in effect, the sign of the Davidic covenant (compare 1 Kgs 6:12–13; Ps 132:11–14). The progression from Sinaitic to Davidic covenant thus coincided with the idea of the temple as YHWH's fixed abode. Zion became inviolable, because in Zion dwelt the "great king" (Ps 48:2), Israel's divine protector (compare Ps 76:2–3).

In that light, the Isaianic passage "I will protect this city and save it, for my own sake and for the sake of my servant David" (Isa 37:35) is an affirmation of an extant suzerain–vassal type of relationship between YHWH and a loyal Davidic ruler, heir of the dynastic promise. As mentioned, the expression "this city" contextually denotes both Jerusalem and Mount Zion (Isa 37:22, 32), the former designating the place that was ultimately to remain under Davidic jurisdiction (compare 1 Kgs 11:13), the latter the abode of YHWH himself (Isa 8:18). The phrase "for my own sake and for the sake of my servant David" signifies that the terms of covenant are being met by both parties. Hezekiah's loyalty to YHWH, evidenced by the statement "I have walked before thee in truth and in integrity of heart, in doing what is good in thy sight" (Isa 38:3), was confirmed by Hezekiah's recovery from a mortal illness (38:21) and by YHWH's extension of his life by fifteen years (38:5). Hezekiah's illness itself suggests his loyalty to YHWH, both the idea of doing "good," $t\hat{o}b$ (38:3), and being "sick," $h\bar{a}l\hat{a}$ (38:1), denoting covenantal loyalty in Near Eastern treaty language.[14] Hezekiah's summons of Isaiah at the Assyrian threat to Jerusalem (37:2) was for the purpose of reporting the king of Assyria's "evil word" against YHWH (37:4, 17). YHWH's twofold response was the annihilation of a common enemy — the Assyrian king and his army — and the infliction of covenant curses on those who violated the rights of YHWH's vassal (37:36, 38).

These events have an antithesis in the Book of Isaiah in remonstrance of the opposite phenomenon — that of a vassal's disloyalty.[15] YHWH's unconditional promise to Ahaz that Aram and Ephraim's scheme to place a puppet ruler on his throne would never succeed (7:6–7) underlines the unconditional nature of the Davidic dynasty's perpetuity. The name of the proposed puppet ruler, the "son of Tabeal" (7:6), in treaty language means a "no-good/noncovenantal vassal." In its context of YHWH's unconditional promise to Ahaz, therefore, the name asserts that he was non-Davidic. In the same passage, the shattering of Ephraim as a nation, sworn to by YHWH (7:8), represents a covenant curse on those violating the rights of YHWH's vassal, Ahaz.

But by sending tribute monies to the king of Assyria and calling on his aid against Aram and Israel (2 Kgs 16:7–8), Ahaz rejected YHWH's suzerainty. By referring to himself as the king of Assyria's "servant" and "son" (2 Kgs 16:7), Ahaz made the king of Assyria his suzerain. In accordance with ancient Near Eastern treaty procedure, YHWH's first response was to choose another "son"/vassal, namely Immanuel/"God is with us" (7:14). His second response was to deny his protection to king and people: the king of Assyria would come "upon you and your people and your father's house" (7:17). As it transpired, Ahaz' unsuspecting rejection of the sign Immanuel (7:10–14) was nothing less than a rejection of the sign of the Davidic covenant. When YHWH is *with* his people, there is an assurance of his protection (compare Ps 46:5–7); when he is not, there is evidently no such assurance.

In sum, the conditionality of the Davidic covenant, expressed in the words "If his children forsake my law, and do not walk in my precepts" (Ps 89:30–31), could, as in Ahaz' case, affect adversely the protection of YHWH's people but not the continuity of the Davidic line. Although YHWH's people could be punished with the "rod," *šēbeṭ*, on account of a disloyal vassal, their king (compare Ps 89:32), the covenant with David of an enduring dynasty would remain intact (compare Ps 89:33–37; 1 Kgs 15:4–5). Thus, in the Book of Isaiah, Ahaz' repudiation of YHWH's suzerainty has as a direct sequel the punishment of YHWH's people by a "rod," *šēbeṭ*, a term that serves as an Isaianic metaphor of the king of Assyria (Isa 10:5). YHWH's promise to Ahaz of a loyal successor, a "son" who would choose the "good," *ṭôb* (7:14–15), was nonetheless unconditional and vouchsafed YHWH's renewed protection of his people in the future.[16]

NOTES

1. Moshe Weinfeld, "The Covenant of Grant in the Old Testament and in the Ancient Near East," *JAOS* 90 (1970): 184–203; Philip J. Calderone, *Dynastic Oracle and Suzerainty Treaty* (Manila: Ateneo University, 1966); F. Charles Fensham, "Clauses of Protection in Hittite Vassal–Treaties and the Old Testament," *VT* 13 (1963): 133–43.
2. Weinfeld, "Covenant of Grant," 185, 188, 193, 201; Calderone, *Dynastic Oracle and Suzerainty Treaty*, 18–19, 34, 52.
3. Weinfeld, "Covenant of Grant," 190–92, 194; Calderone, *Dynastic Oracle and Suzerainty Treaty*, 53–55.
4. Weinfeld, "Covenant of Grant," 185; Calderone, *Dynastic Oracle and Suzerainty Treaty*, 70–71.
5. Fensham, "Clauses of Protection," 136–37, 140; Calderone, *Dynastic Oracle and Suzerainty Treaty*, 19–21, 30–31, 35, 44.
6. Calderone, *Dynastic Oracle and Suzerainty Treaty*, 21–25, 49–50.
7. Weinfeld, "Covenant of Grant," 185; Calderone, *Dynastic Oracle and Suzerainty Treaty*, 18.
8. Weinfeld, "Covenant of Grant," 189–90.
9. As in a twin agreement between a suzerain and a people; compare the Hittite treaties with the Mittani and Hayasa peoples (Calderone, *Dynastic Oracle and Suzerainty Treaty*, 22, 49–50).
10. Fensham, "Clauses of Protection," 138–40; Calderone, *Dynastic Oracle and Suzerainty Treaty*, 24–25, 31, 33. Although the Neo-Assyrian grants, unlike their Hittite models, make no specific mention of a vassal's protection, such was nonetheless an integral part of the agreement, as numerous historical examples show (Calderone, *Dynastic Oracle and Suzerainty Treaty*, 28–29). The feudal nature of Hittite covenants has been pointed to by Jacques Pirenne, "La politique d'expansion hittite envisagée à travers les traités de vassalité et de protectorat," *ArOr* 18 (1950): 373–82.
11. See Weinfeld, "Covenant of Grant," 185–86.
12. Moshe Weinfeld, "Bᵉrîth," in *TDOT*, ed. Botterwick and Ringgren (Grand Rapids, Mich.: Wm. Eerdmans, 1977), 2:258–59.
13. Calderone, *Dynastic Oracle and Suzerainty Treaty*, 46, 59–60.
14. See, respectively, M. Fox, "Tôb As Covenant Terminology," *BASOR* 209 (1973): 41–42; Weinfeld, "Bᵉrîth," 259; 1 Sam. 22:8; Amos 6:6, cited by Weinfeld, "Covenant of Grant," 187. See also the synonymity of "good," *ṭôb*, and "truth/loyalty," *ʾemet*, in Isa. 39:8, and the historical significance afforded a monarch's recovery from illness in Isa. 39:1.

15. The antithesis between Hezekiah and his people and Ahaz and his people forms part of a complex, seven-part structure of the Book of Isaiah that is outlined in my forthcoming book, *The Literary Message of Isaiah*.

16. These conclusions tend to discredit the rather weak arguments of J. H. Hayes, and others, that the origin of Zion's inviolability is to be found in pre-Israelite (Jebusite) traditions concerning Jerusalem (John H. Hayes, "The Tradition of Zion's Inviolability," *JBL* 82 (1963): 419–26). That possibility appears feasible only if the idea of divine protection in pre-Israelite Jerusalem duplicated or perhaps precedented Davidic covenant theology. J. J. M. Roberts, in "The Davidic Origin of the Zion Tradition," *JBL* 92 (1973): 329–44, offers more plausible arguments for basing the Zion tradition in general in the Davidic–Solomonic era.

13

Alienation and Restoration:
A Jacob–Esau Typology

Gary V. Smith

One of the theological foundation blocks of Israel's faith was the belief that YHWH's relationship to his people was unique. He set them apart from all the other nations to be his special possession, his chosen people, a holy nation (Exod 9:5–6; Deut 7:6). Moses believed that God's presence with the people made them distinct from the other families of the earth (Exod 33:16). With Israel YHWH made a covenant, which included a land flowing with milk and honey, a future of rest and prosperity, and a status above all other nations (Deut 26:18–19; 28:1).

This favored status required a commitment to holiness and distinctiveness from the ways of the other nations. Because Israel was a holy or separate nation, the Israelites were not supposed to worship the gods of the nations (Deut 29:15–18; Ezek 20:7), eat unclean food as did the neighboring peoples (Lev 20:23–25), follow the customs of Egypt or Canaan (Lev 18:3; 20:23), practice any of the abominable sexual acts of the Canaanites (Lev 18:20–24, 30), or imitate the worship habits of the nations by consulting sorcerers or diviners (Deut 18:9–14). The Israelites were not allowed to intermarry with the nations they defeated, because these people could teach the Israelites to worship gods other than YHWH or to follow their sinful ways (Exod 34:11–17; Deut 7:2–5; 20:16–18). W. Zimmerli maintains that Israel's covenant relationship to YHWH enabled the Israelites to define their identity and develop a unique way of life.[1]

In spite of the focus on the importance of the covenant and the distinctiveness of YHWH's people, Israel did not remain unique, and YHWH's involvement was not just with Israel. If one centers on the special status of Israel's covenant relationship, there seems to be no clear relationship between YHWH and the other nations. It seems that Israel and YHWH are united in their opposition to these nations and the forces of evil they embody.

However, this explanation of Israel's theology is too simplistic. Equally inadequate is J. McKenzie's explanation that "the nations have no places in YHWH's world scheme" or his conclusion that since YHWH had no covenant

with the nations "his purpose in the history of the nations was impossible at
this phase of biblical theology to discern. The rise and fall of the nations . . .
is in the last analysis as meaningless as the rise and fall of animals."[2] New ways
of looking at the parallels and contrasts between Israel and the nations are
needed. In reality, Israel despised her birthright and became more and more
like the nations. In this backslidden state, Israel and the nations are alienated
for many of the same sins, their judgments are often identical, and even their
hopes of future restoration are intimately intertwined.

A typological analysis[3] of common thematic treatments of God's complex
dealings with the nations over several periods of history provides a number of
significant insights into prophetic theology concerning the nations. Although
considerable emphasis has been given to the analogy between the Exodus of
the past and God's great act of deliverance in the new Exodus of the future,[4]
the numerous thematic analogies between early and later prophetic traditions
about Israel and the nations have received scant attention. These prophetic
traditions are sometimes very similar, but frequently a theme will be expanded,
slanted, refined, or transformed in its later setting. The new theme is not a
repetition of the old, but a reliving of the past in a radical new, but analogous, way. The extent and the development of traditions vary from prophet to
prophet,[5] but the recognition of connections between these traditions was fundamental to the task of explaining God's future plans for Israel and the nations.
The Jacob–Esau narratives display a number of these themes, which are picked
up and given broader application in the prophetic books.

THEMES IN THE JACOB/ESAU–
ISRAEL/NATIONS CONFLICT

The explanation of mankind's division into nations in the Table of Nations
of Genesis 10 expresses an ancient view of the original solidarity of all nations.
The author's perspective is universal; an acceptance of all nations without
judgment is evident. There is no mention of Israel and no reference to God's
directing nations to their allotted place (contrast Deut 32:8 and Acts 17:26).[6]
The division of mankind into separate nations at the tower of Babel (Gen
11:1–9) and the promise to Abraham that "I will make of you a great nation"
(Gen 12:2) set the stage for a broad distinction between the offspring of Abraham
and the nations.

J. Muilenburg reminds us that these initial points of discontinuity must
be balanced by the continuity of the blessing from Abram to "all the families
of the earth" (Gen 12:3).[7] From Abram himself, "many nations" would arise
(Gen 17:4–6). Yet only the seed of Jacob was specifically set apart to receive
the blessing of Abraham (Gen 28:1–4). At this fundamental juncture, the
Jacob–Esau relationship establishes a number of primary motifs that serve as
the basis for a typological analysis of the Israel–nations relationship. For *Jacob*

is a later synonym for Israel, and *Edom* (Esau) becomes a representative of the nations.[8]

It is generally agreed that one of the broadest themes in the Jacob–Esau narrative is conflict or alienation.[9] Conflict existed between the boys when they were in their mother's womb (Gen 25:22), and its continuation is foretold in the divine word that the older would serve the younger (Gen 25:23). Conflict and alienation infiltrate the selling of the birthright (Gen 25:29–34); Jacob's stealing the blessing ends with a desire for revenge (Gen 27:41–44). The threat of conflict fills the air when Jacob meets Esau and his four hundred men (Gen 33).[10] P. D. Miscall finds within the Jacob and Joseph stories three basic plot analogies: (1) they both deal with brothers who deceive their fathers; (2) a younger brother is exiled to a foreign land and gains great wealth; and (3) an eventual reunion and reconciliation takes place between brothers.[11]

Although G. W. Coats denies that reconciliation took place between Jacob and Esau, M. Fishbane's and Miscall's contrary analyses are more convincing.[12] Fishbane's study also draws attention to three areas of dialectic tension within the Jacob cycle — fertility or barrenness, the blessing or curse, and life in the land or exile — which are central to the promise theme in the patriarchal narratives.[13] These themes are important in defining the status of individuals and nations in the Pentateuch, as well as in the ancient Near East as a whole. Thus it is not surprising that these Jacob–Esau themes reappear in prophetic texts dealing with the relationship of Israel and the nations.

Jacob's characterization begins with a struggling alienation between brothers, and the subordination of the older to the younger (Gen 25:22–23). Themes of prosperity, possession of the land, "I am with you," and the return to the land are essentially positive (Gen 28:1–4, 15, 20; 31:2–5; 32:9–12). In contrast, Esau is characterized as one who despises his birthright (Gen 26:34–35; 25:34), is careless in marrying foreign wives (Gen 27:46), lives by the sword away from the fatness of the earth (Gen 27:39–40), and is bent on revenge (Gen 27:41–45).

Of course, these pictures are incomplete, for Jacob was deceitful (Gen 27:36), in effect, becoming Esau. He became the firstborn — Esau — by dressing like his brother and swearing that he was Esau, thus deceiving his father and taking the birthright (Gen 27:10–12, 15–16, 19–24). When Jacob met Esau again, Jacob played the role of Esau (according to the blessing), calling himself "the servant of his lord Esau" (Gen 32:4, 18, 20) and admitting that he was unworthy (literally "a little one," not the greater) out of fear for his life.

Jacob's struggle with God breaks Jacob's will, causing him to recognize God's control over his life and making reconciliation between the brothers possible. Jacob no longer stays at the back but moves to the front of his company. He bows to Esau seven times, seeking his favor; and he gives Esau part of the blessing that God has graciously bestowed on him (Gen 33:3, 8, 10–11). God's miraculous intervention in the Jacob–Laban conflict (Gen 31:7, 24, 29), and in the Jacob–Esau conflict (Gen 32:24–32), brings about a healing of relationships. J. P. Fokkelman sees Jacob, following this, as a true servant of God, and thus an instrument to renew broken relationships.[14]

The relationship of Israel (Jacob) to Edom (Esau) and the nations is dealt with in Jacob's blessing on Judah. Judah's hand will be on the neck of his enemies and the nations will obey him (Gen 49:8–10). YHWH promises victory over Israel's enemies (Exod 23:22–33), if YHWH's people will obey his voice. Balaam also predicts the destruction of Israel's enemies (Num 24:8–9), including Moab, Edom, Amalek, and several other nations (Num 24:17–24). The blessings enumerated in the books of Leviticus and Deuteronomy describe in detail the implementation of Jacob's blessing upon Israel (Lev 26:2–6; Deut 28:11–13). If Israel will keep YHWH's covenant, he will desolate the nations that are her enemies (Lev 26:7–8; Deut 28:7).[15]

On the other hand, if Israel does not listen to YHWH's voice, if she despises her birthright and lives like the other nations, then the curse of her enemies will fall on Israel instead. Israel will not enjoy the fatness of the earth but will be alienated from God and defeated by her enemies (Lev 26:17, 30–33, 38; Deut 28:25, 36–37, 48–49, 64–65). Nonetheless, in spite of defeat, God will intervene and reconcile Israel; he will return Israel to her land when she humbles herself and returns to him (Lev 26:40–44; Deut 30:1–7).

The pre-Mosaic Jacob–Esau themes of struggle and alienation, blessings of prosperity and the land, exile and return have clear analogies in the Israel–nations comparisons. Israel could choose the way of the nations (or Esau) and despise her birthright, but her only hope for redemption from these deceptive ways (the ways of Jacob) is through the miraculous intervention of God.

PROPHETIC USE OF THE JACOB–ESAU THEMES
FOR ISRAEL, EDOM, AND THE NATIONS

The prophetic reinterpretation of the interplay between Israel and the nations is developed according to the several purposes of each prophet. Analogies with the Jacob characterization—as it concerns all Israel—function at various levels of complexity and sophistication. Because Jacob is the father of all Israel, *Jacob* becomes a synonym for the nation.[16] In Ps. 24:6, those who seek YHWH are called Jacob, whereas Amos and Micah condemn the pride and rebellion of Jacob (Amos 6:8; Mic 1:5). Some prophets move beyond the simple use of the name *Jacob* to an elaborate application of Jacob's characteristics to the nation that walks in his footsteps. There are analogies between Jacob the individual and Jacob the nation regarding their sinful tendencies, their judgment, and their need for reconciliation in order to receive God's blessing. The analogies are not systematically designed, but the immediate proximity of such comparative statements leaves no doubt about the double application of a prophet's words.

Jacob

Thus, Hos. 11:12–12:14 uses the Jacob typology to convey the current status of the people.[17] The backsliding tendency that characterizes Israel consists of her being deceitful in religious and political relationships (Hos 11:12–12:1). The text is not, as P. R. Ackroyd maintains,[18] a positive statement of the Jacob tradition but a lawsuit (Hos 12:2) based on Jacob and the nation's parallel deceitfulness.[19] The accusation is that Jacob struggled to deceive his brother Esau (Hos 12:3a; compare Gen 25:22–26) and contended[20] with God (Hos 12:3b–4a; compare Gen 32:23–32), just as the nation Jacob was struggling to maintain its political status by dealing deceitfully with the other nations and with God (Hos 11:12–12:1).

The pronouns in verse four are notoriously difficult, but A. Bentzen believes Jacob is weeping while wrestling with God at Penuel,[21] while Holladay connects this to his weeping before Esau the next day.[22] Both understandings focus on Jacob's humility and inability to handle his situation deceptively. The Jacob typology thus functions as an exhortation for the nation to follow Jacob's example — for through humility and honesty he prevailed and made reconciliation with God and with his brother Esau.[23] This reconciliation is celebrated by recalling the intervention of God (Gen 28, 35; Hos 12:4–5), which is the only hope for the nation of Jacob. Israel must return to God as Jacob the individual returned (Hos 12:6).

In the next section Hosea criticizes Israel's adoption of the deceptive economic practices of the Canaanites (Hos 12:7–11). These practices led to pride and the claim that no injustice or oppression was involved. Although Jacob is not mentioned, one is immediately reminded of Jacob's ability to gain great wealth at Laban's expense and his claim that he did no wrong (Gen 30–31). The direct Jacob analogy is picked up again in the last few verses of the chapter in which Jacob is compared to YHWH. Jacob's flight to Aram and his years of watching sheep to pay for his wives (Gen 27:43; 29:15–30; 30:26) indicate a life of fear, exile, and slavery — the consequence of his deception of Esau.[24] YHWH's deeds are just the opposite; he delivered the people from slavery, fear, and exile in Egypt through Moses (Hos 12:12–13). The implication is that one should follow YHWH, not Jacob, if one wants to avoid judgment.

Jeremiah in his accusation against Judah makes a brief comparison with Jacob (Jer 9:4). Deceit, lying, and falsehood characterize both the nation's dealings with YHWH and the people's behavior toward one another (Jer 9:3–8). Because of these dealings, Judah will be laid waste, alienated from God, and scattered among the nations; and no one will dwell in her cities (Jer 9:9–15).

Esau

The prophets similarly use Esau as a symbol of the nations. The connection between Esau and Edom is based on the "red stew" ()ādōm) for which Esau sold his birthright (Gen 25:30). Because Esau is Edom (Gen 36:8), and Esau is the father of the Edomites (Gen 36:9, 43), it is quite natural for the prophets to see Edom as a type for "mankind,")ādām. The extended use of

Edom as a symbol for the nations is partly related to the identical consonantal construction of the names *Edom* and *ʾādām* — "man/mankind." The Septuagint rendering of Amos 9:12 (compare Acts 15:17), "the remnant of mankind" (versus the Masoretic rendering "remnant of Edom"), illustrates this.[25] The close relationship between Edom and "all the nations" in Amos 9:12 points to the representative role Edom could play in prophetic eschatology.

The prophecy of Isaiah includes two passages in which Edom, the arch-enemy of Israel, is used as a symbol for the wicked nations (Isa 34 and 63:1–6).[26] The evil nations are depicted as a single eschatological foe caught in the midst of YHWH's universal judgment. J. Muilenburg sees Isa. 34:1–9 as a unit with four themes (wrath, vv 2–4; sword, vv 5–6d; sacrifice, vv 6e–7; and the day of YHWH, vv 8–9), each introduced by "for."[27] The scope of the message concerns the entire earth (Isa 34:1), all the nations (34:2), all their hosts (34:2), as well as all the hosts of heaven (34:4)—not just the small nation of Edom. Edom represents the nations that are under the ban (compare v 2c with v 5c), whose blood will fill the earth (compare v 3 with vv 6 and 7c) when all will be destroyed (compare vv 4 and 7). The earth will return to its former state (compare Jer 4:23–27), empty and without form (compare Gen 1), without kingdoms of men or their rulers (Isa 34:11–12). This passage gives no hope to the wicked nations, which are symbolically called Edom. Images from the total destruction of Sodom appear in 34:9 and the eternality of their damnation is expressed in 34:10. Alienation will exist both day and night; it will last forever, for all generations, even forever and forever.

Isa. 63:1–6 follows a similar pattern: Edom herself (63:1) quickly falls into the background as a symbol of YHWH's broader emphasis on "the peoples" of the earth (63:3a, 6a), those whose lifeblood will be poured out (63:3b, 6b) on YHWH's day of vengeance. Here we find YHWH coming from his eschatological judgment of the wicked nations who have opposed him and his elect. His treading of the wine press, and the nations' drinking of YHWH's cup of wrath are found in similar eschatological passages of total judgment on the nations in Joel 3:12–14 and in Rev. 14:19; 19:15. The wicked nations which are annihilated by YHWH are designated by Isaiah as "Edom." This destiny is directly opposite the great salvation that YHWH will bring to his holy people, spoken of in Isaiah 60–62.

Obadiah's short prophecy centers on a condemnation of the nation Edom, but the paradigm of alienation is expanded to a universal eschatological judgment upon "all nations" (vv 15–16).[28] Once again the wicked nations drink the cup of God's wrath and suffer total destruction while those on Mount Zion will be saved (Obad 17, 21) when YHWH establishes his sovereign rule over the world. M. Woudstra demonstrates how the judgment on Edom in Ezek. 35:1–15 uses Esau's characteristics in YHWH's accusation against Edom. Enmity, the sword (35:5), anger, envy, and hatred (35:11) characterize both. But Israel's hope (Ezek 36) is not just based on the defeat of the small nation of Edom, for YHWH's anger will go out "against the rest of the nations and against Edom" (36:5).[29] Since "the whole earth," together with Edom, rejoiced at Israel's desolation (35:14–15), they will suffer the same punishment.[30]

ALIENATION OF ALL EVIL NATIONS

The Jacob/Esau–Israel/nations relationship works on a third level of theological comparison. It moves beyond the direct use of the names *Jacob* and *Esau* and beyond the limits of Israel and the nations. These passages are typologically related to those in which deceitful Jacob becomes Esau. The prophets viewed the apostate tendencies of Israel as a denial of the true characteristics of Jacob and an accommodation of the customs of the nations (compare 2 Kgs 17:8, 15, 19, 33). In some prophetic accusations and judgmental pronouncements, there is a continuity in the traditions that are applied to Israel and the nations, rather than a distinction based on national identities. This continuity provides a model for understanding another aspect of prophetic theology regarding the nations and gives a broader understanding of YHWH's rule of all mankind.

S. Erlandsson's study of Isaiah 13–14 has drawn attention to the rhetorical use of words and phrases from this passage in the rest of the Book of Isaiah. The motifs of pride, the day of YHWH, wrath, slaughter, devastation, lamentation, terror, and cosmic changes are used repeatedly in the Book of Isaiah as well as in other prophetic books.[31] An analysis of these factors shows that apostate Israel (like deceptive Jacob) acted like the nations (like Esau) and will suffer the same consequences of alienation from God.

Isaiah accuses the king of Assyria of arrogance (Isa 10:12; 37:23, 29), the king of Babylon with a desire to raise his throne above God's (Isa 14:11–15), the nation of Babylon of haughtiness (Isa 13:11), Moab of pride and idle boasting (Isa 16:6; 25:11), and Tyre of pride in her beauty (Isa 23:9). The sinful house of Jacob has followed the example of the wicked nations (Isa 2:6–11) and, because of its pride (Isa 5:14–16), will be judged. Isaiah gives a universal application to YHWH's hatred of pride by announcing that everything that is lifted up (the cedar, mountains, high towers, ships, and man) will be brought low before the splendor of YHWH's majesty (Isa 2:12–22). Alienation from God is determined by one's pride, not by national identity or past covenantal relationship to YHWH.

The prophet Jeremiah predicts YHWH's judgment on the "circumcised who are uncircumcised" and groups Judah with Egypt, Edom, Ammon, Moab, and those who live in the desert: "For all these nations are uncircumcised, and all the house of Israel is uncircumcised of heart" (Jer 9:25–26). The prophet's treatment of the apostate nation Jacob as one of the nations is evident in his use of the same extended judgment against Babylon (Jer 50:41–43) and Zion (Jer 6:22–24), and by his use of the same oracle against the wicked in Judah (Jer 23:19–20) and the wicked who are against Judah (Jer 30:23–24). Many of the same motifs appear in Jeremiah's judgment speeches against Judah and the nations. Judah's alienation from God will result in the nation's becoming a desolation, an object of perpetual hissing (Jer 18:16; 19:8; 29:18). But the same fate is also applied to Edom (Jer 49:13, 17), Babylon (Jer 50:3, 13, 23; 51:37), and "all the nations" (Jer 25:9–26).

Amos and Isaiah compare the fall of apostate Israel to God's overthrow of Sodom (Amos 4:11; Isa 1:9; compare Deut 29:23), and Isaiah and Jeremiah use the Sodom imagery to depict the fall of Edom (Jer 49:18; compare Isa 34:9–10), Babylon (Isa 13:19; Jer 50:40), and the nations (Isa 34:9). The cup of YHWH's wrath is given to wicked Israel (Isa 51:17–20; Jer 25:15–18), but also to Edom (Jer 49:12), Babylon, and all the evil nations (Isa 51:21–23; 63:6; Jer 25:26–27). The day of YHWH will see YHWH's judgment fall on his own (apostate) nation (Amos 5:18–20; Zeph 1:7; Joel 1:15; 2:2; Ezek 7:19) and on all the nations alike (Joel 3:14; Ezek 30:3–5). These parallel descriptions indicate that the prophets had a typological characterization of "Edom" containing several traditional themes which could be applied to any wicked nation that opposed YHWH.

The final restoration of positive relations between Jacob and Esau has parallels in the restoration of the righteous in Judah and the righteous among the nations. The intervention of YHWH in both situations is the key to the new day of salvation. The restoration of the fortunes of YHWH's people will take place when YHWH gathers all the righteous from Israel and the nations[32] to himself at Mount Zion (Isa 2:1–4; Mic 4:1–4; Jer 3:14–18).

But the prophetic theme associated with "Edom" was alienation and destruction. The prophets understood that God will destroy the earth and all evil peoples who reject him (Isa 24:1–6, 17–22; 66:24). They will be forever alienated from God. They are "Edom" and will inherit disgrace and everlasting contempt (Dan 12:2).

CONCLUSION

This study of the Jacob–Esau typology has shown that the deceptive ways of Jacob were a denial of God's dominion over the affairs of the human family. Similarly, the apostate nation Israel, the sons of Jacob, frequently trusted in deceptive political alliances, failing to recognize YHWH's sovereign control over other nations. The lives of Jacob and Esau are paradigms of the conflicts that all men and nations face. Will men and nations despise God's promises and trust in their own ability to control him and their world? Or will they confess that God rules over all mankind? YHWH, the God of Jacob and Israel, graciously gave his covenant people a unique position, but he is also a God who will judge "Edom." A true biblical theology must encapsulate the breadth of the biblical revelation about YHWH's rule as well as the foundational nature of its significance.

NOTES

1. W. Zimmerli, *Old Testament Theology in Outline*, trans. D. E. Green (Atlanta: John Knox, 1978), 43–58; G. E. Wright, *The Old Testament against Its Environment* (London: S.C.M., 1950), 39–59, 86–87.

2. J. L. McKenzie, *A Theology of the Old Testament* (Garden City, N.Y.: Doubleday, 1974), 167, 172.

3. G. von Rad, "Typological Interpretation of the Old Testament," in *Essays on Old Testament Hermeneutics*, ed. C. Westermann (Richmond, Vir.: John Knox, 1963), 17–23; D. L. Baker, *Two Testaments: One Bible* (Downers Grove, Ill.: Inter-Varsity Press, 1976), 239–70.

4. B. W. Anderson, "Exodus Typology in Second Isaiah," in *Israel's Prophetic Heritage* (New York: Harper and Row, 1962), 177–95; J. Fischer, "Das Problem des neuen Exodus in Isaias c. 40–55," *TQ* 110 (1929): 111–30; M. Fishbane, *Text and Texture* (New York: Schocken Books, 1979), 121–40.

5. W. Zimmerli, "Prophetic Proclamation and Reinterpretation," in *Tradition and Theology in the Old Testament*, ed. D. A. Knight (Philadelphia: Fortress Press, 1977), 69–100.

6. G. von Rad, *Genesis* (Philadelphia: Westminster Press, 1972), 144.

7. J. Muilenberg, "Abraham and the Nations," *Int* 19 (1965): 392–98.

8. M. H. Woudstra, "Edom and Israel in Ezekiel," *CTJ* 3 (1968): 21–35.

9. T. L. Thompson, "Conflict Themes in the Jacob Narratives," *Semeia* 15 (1979): 5–26; M. Fishbane, "Composition and Structure in the Jacob Cycle (Gen 25:19–35:22)," *JJS* 26 (1975): 15–38; G. W. Coats, "Strife without Reconciliation: A Narrative Theme in the Jacob Traditions," in *Werden und Wirken des Alten Testament* (Gottingen, West Germany: Vandenhoeck and Ruprecht, 1980), 82–106; J. P. Fokkelman, *Narrative Art in Genesis* (Amsterdam: van Gorcum, 1975), 86–239; M. R. Hauge, "The Struggles of the Blessed in Estrangement I," *ST* 29 (1975): 1–30, 113–46.

10. In addition to the Jacob–Esau conflicts, there is conflict between (a) Isaac and Rebekah; (b) Laban and Jacob over marriage arrangements, payment for labor, departure plans, and the household gods; (c) Jacob's two wives; and (d) Jacob and God at Penuel.

11. P. D. Miscall, "The Jacob and Joseph Stories As Analogies," *JSOT* 6 (1978): 31–32.

12. Coats, "Strife without Reconciliation," 103; Fishbane, "Composition and Structure in the Jacob Cycle," 32; and Miscall, "Jacob and Joseph Stories As Analogies," 31–32.

13. Fishbane, "Composition and Structure in the Jacob Cycle," 35–37.

14. Fokkelman, *Narrative Art in Genesis*, 231.

15. F. C. Fensham, "Clauses of Protection in Hittite Vassal-Treaties and the Old Testament," *VT* 13 (1963): 133–43.

16. See 1 Chr. 16:13; Pss. 14:7; 53:6; 79:7; Isa. 40:27; 41:8, 14; 42:24; Jer. 5:20; 30:10; 46:27; Mal. 1:2.

17. The interpretation of Hos. 11:12–12:14 bristles with a multitude of textual, redactional, and interpretive problems (see T. C. Vriezen, "Hosea 12," *Nieuwe Theologische Studien* 24 [1941]: 144–49; M. Gertner, "Appendix: An Attempt at an Interpretation of Hosea XII," *VT* 10 [1960]: 272–84; P. R. Ackroyd, "Hosea and Jacob," *VT* 13 [1963]: 245–59; W. H. Holladay, "Chiasmus, the Key to Hosea XII:3–6," *VT* 16 [1966]: 53–64; E. M. Good, "Hosea and the Jacob Tradition," *VT* 16 [1966]: 137–51).

18. Ackroyd, "Hosea and Jacob," 245. This does not describe the nation's deceitful relationship to the prophet, as H. W. Wolff maintains in *Hosea* (Philadelphia: Fortress Press, 1974), 209–10. Nor is it a dialogue between the prophet and the people, as in T. C. Vriezen, "La Tradition de Jacob dans Osée XII," *Oudt. St.* 1 (1942): 64–78.

19. See Gen. Rabba 70.18 on Gen. 29:25, which refers to Hos. 12: "Your pattern is like that of Jacob your ancestor."

20. Not "ruled, commanded" (Gertner, "An Attempt at an Interpretation of Hos XII," 272–78, and Wolff, *Hosea*, 212).

21. A. Bentzen, "The Weeping of Jacob in Hosea XII:5a," *VT* 1 (1951): 58–59, sees Jacob's weeping as part of his struggle with God in Gen. 32:23–33, while Good, "Hosea and the Jacob Tradition," 144, relates the weeping to the oak of weeping at Bethel in Gen. 35:8.

22. Holladay, "Chiasmus, the Key to Hosea XII:3–6," 55–58.

23. J. L. Mays, *Hosea* (Philadelphia: Westminster, 1969), 164.

24. It is commonly held that verse 12 includes an accusation against Jacob's (the nation's) service at the sexual rites of the Baal centers, but this is not at all clear.

25. J. de Waad, *A Comparative Study of the OT Text in the Dead Sea Scrolls and in the New Testament* (Leiden, Netherlands: Brill, 1965), 26.

26. Edom is interpreted as a symbol of the nations by C. C. Torrey, *The Second Isaiah* (New York: Scribner's, 1928), 122–23, 279–81; J. Muilenburg, "The Book of Isaiah," *IB, V* (Nashville, Tenn.: Abingdon, 1956), 354–55, 724–26; E. J. Young, *The Book of Isaiah III* (Grand Rapids, Mich.: Wm. Eerdmans, 1972), 476; and C. Westermann, *Isaiah 40–66* (Philadelphia: Westminster, 1969), 384, but others emend Edom to "red" (Legard) or "man" (Kissane).

27. J. Muilenburg, "The Literary Character of Isaiah 34," *JBL* 59 (1940): 342; B. C. Cresson, "The Condemnation of Edom," in *The Use of the Old Testament in the New and Other Essays*, ed. J. M. Efrid (Durham, N.C.: Duke University Press, 1972), 133–48.

28. L. C. Allen, *The Books of Joel, Obadiah, Jonah and Micah* (Grand Rapids, Mich.: Wm. Eerdmans, 1976), 160–62; H. D. Hummel, "The Old Testament Basis of Typological Interpretation," *BR* 9 (1964): 45; B. Childs, *Introduction to the Old Testament As Scripture* (Philadelphia: Fortress Press, 1979), 414–15.

29. Although some consider Ezek. 36:3–5 to be a later addition, and the specific reference to Edom in these verses to be an even later addition, the use of Edom as a representative of the nations and the context of Ezekiel 35–36 argue against this conclusion (see K. W. Carley, *The Book of the Prophet Ezekiel* [Cambridge: Cambridge University Press, 1974], 239; W. Zimmerli, *Ezekiel 2* [Philadelphia: Fortress Press, 1983], 233–34).

30. Woudstra, "Edom and Israel in Ezekiel," 21–35.

31. S. Erlandsson, *The Burden of Babylon* (Lund, Sweden: Gleerup, 1970), 128–53. In a later chapter he specifically focuses on the interrelationship between Jeremiah 50–51 and Isaiah 13–14.

32. Not just the Israelites among the nations, as proposed by D. E. Hollenberg, "Nationalism and 'The Nations' in Isaiah XL–LV," *VT* 19 (1969): 23–36. See the discussion of universalism and the nations in R. Martin-Achard, *A Light to the Nations* (London: Oliver and Boyd, 1962), and D. Christensen, "A New Israel: The Righteous from among All Nations," in this volume.

14

Historical Selectivity:
Prophetic Prerogative or
Typological Imperative?

Alfred E. Krause

Biblical scholarship exemplifies the uniquely human ability to reason from incomplete data. Indeed, the field of study offers ample grounds for humility. One of R. K. Harrison's contributions has been a powerful expression of this humility, in his recognition that all our hypotheses are at best possibilities.

History may consist of any of three things:
1. the sum of day-to-day human experiences (mundane history)
2. the remembrance and recording of human experiences (descriptive history)
3. the use of past experience and its records to understand the present or future (systematic or analytical history).

Obviously, any record of history involves a degree of selectivity. Historians pick and choose among events or experiences, retaining the most interesting or meaningful ones, just as we all do in the process of memory. A battle is not intrinsically more important than a good harvest, but it is usually more dramatic, more likely to be remembered. The highest degree of selectivity is reached in systematic or analytical history. There the attempt to uncover meaning may cause an emphasis on certain events and the total omission of others.

Historical selectivity in the classical prophetic writings comprises any major deviation from an assumed plane of descriptive history as perceived by the prophet, his contemporaries, or the reader today. Such deviation may include highlighting events a prophet wishes to emphasize, even if it entails refusal to discuss other events that we (or the prophet's contemporaries) might consider important.

A prophet might also exercise selectivity by predicting things that did not occur or had little chance of occurring on the plane of history. This futuristic projection can be viewed in several ways. For example, many scholars accept the hypothesis that the classical prophets offered moral, theological, and historical views that were new or unprecedented. Acceptance of this often leads to the conclusion that their prophecies derived entirely from the events of their own times and are therefore concerned solely with those events. Some of the most articulate views of history extending outside the prophets' own times, such as are found in Hos. 14:1-9, Amos 9:8-15, and Mic. 4:1-8, would then be considered exilic redactional additions, not at all characteristic of classical prophetic thought.

Under such scholarly hypotheses the prophets appear to have had little to offer the people of their day beyond an elevated morality cloaking sheer guesses about contemporary politics. According to such views, it follows that the erratic prophetic messages might indeed have been trying or even disagreeable to a believing audience.[1] Their hearers would have found it difficult or impossible to distinguish true from false prophecy.[2] Under such circumstances, typology, eschatology, and even hermeneutics could become tools for reverently covering the prophets' erring tracks.[3] Taken together, these views and their corollary could be called "prophetic prerogative"—a prophet's right to say what he wants, to omit, deviate, or embellish as he sees fit. But such a "prerogative" has been misunderstood and can easily be misused. Seen, for example, together with the *vaticinia ex eventu* view of prophecy, they form a Procrustean bed: any prophecy accurate or consistent with the events of the prophet's own time must have occurred *after* those events; any prophecy inconsistent with the time demonstrates the alarming unreliability of prophecy. The sum is a no-win view of prophecy, a view that denies a prophet credit for even the common insight of his contemporaries. It demonstrates the hazards of mixing arguments that are in part mutually exclusive.

If, however, the prophets wrote within an established tradition of viewing historical events in terms of a moral context, they may have been historically selective for a purpose. If they expressed themselves in a highly stylized manner, their apparent selectivity might sometimes reflect our misunderstanding of their utterances. If the prophets habitually or traditionally linked present conduct to future events in analogic or causal relationships, what I have called historical selectivity might sometimes constitute only a disposable anchor for structure or typology or even eschatology. A perspective of this sort may suggest a meaning for a given case of historical selectivity that is primarily typological—using a contemporary event as an analogy of a much more important one in the future. When this happens, the necessary shaping and emphasis of the prophet's description of the contemporary event (to make it a more precise analog of the future) may be called "typological imperative." This does not detract from the event itself, but highlights precisely those aspects of it that may apply on a secondary level.

Like prophetic prerogative, typological views of prophecy may be grossly misused or misunderstood. The Fathers of the early Christian era, especially Origen, brought a hermeneutic to scripture which included typological significance for *every* passage. This had the unfortunate effect of alienating prophecy from its historical context, often reducing hermeneutics to a calculated scramble for prooftexts.

On the contrary, within the limited resources of our knowledge, the task of scholarship should be to learn as much as possible about the prophets' messages in relation to their past, present, and future. Wherever possible, evidence should determine both the extent of selectivity and its possible motivation. This necessary evidence can be obtained in part from archaeological sources and documents, but also from our more complete understanding of the prophetic texts.

This essay offers a brief survey of historical selectivity in classical prophecy, with representative case studies. It is necessarily limited in scope and is by no means conclusive. Its thesis, developed from the summarized evidence, is that classical prophetic writings are part of a literary and intellectual continuum, possessing a common message and means of expression. At times, this message and its means of expression required deliberate historical selectivity by the prophets, and at times they only created the illusion of such selectivity.

THE SONG OF MOSES AND THE ANTIQUITY OF THE PROPHETIC FAITH

Dating

Harrison has been persuasive in his arguments for a generally Mosaic authorship of Deuteronomy.[4] While others, notably M. G. Kline,[5] have seconded him, the bulk of scholarly opinion has favored a seventh-century date for Deuteronomy in its final form. However, a similar late dating of important portions of the book, especially the Song and Blessing of Moses (Deut 32:1–43; 33:1–29), has been questioned frequently. Very few scholars support an origin as late as King Josiah's time for the Song. Opinions are generally divided between those who favor the sixth century B.C. or later (on the grounds of assumed wisdom influences and exilic ideas) and a substantially larger group who favor a much earlier date, extending from proto-deuteronomic times back to the Conquest.

Among scholars who support a late date for the Song is A. D. H. Mayes, who describes it as "undoubtedly exilic or postexilic." He notes the presence of wisdom elements in Deut. 32:1–4, although these are also found in Ps. 78:1–6. He cites G. E. Wright's form-critical analysis and Wright's mild objection to a purely linguistic means of dating the Song. Mayes does not mention, however, that Wright himself favored a date almost three hundred years before the exile and believed the Song to be clearly of a northern origin. Remarkably, Mayes cites D. A. Robertson's warning that the author may have consciously written the Song in archaic language, and Mayes suggests that Robertson offers "the most thorough study of its vocabulary and morphology." Again, however, he does not mention that Robertson himself, in spite of his caution, dates the Song to the tenth or eleventh centuries B.C.[6]

G. Fohrer dates the Song to early or middle exilic times. He too cites the "wisdom" phrases in Deut. 32:1–4. He is also one of the few scholars to claim that the "unpeople" (Deut 32:21) are identifiable from internal evidence; he feels they are clearly Babylonian and adds, "It is a real question why the exilic origin of the Song was ever in doubt."[7] G. von Rad, although favoring an exilic date, is somewhat more flexible. He cites the wisdom phrases but notes that they are also found in Psalm 78, Judges 5, and Isaiah 28. He notes that some important ideas, such as the responsibility of heavenly beings in managing nations (Deut 32:8–9), can also be found in 1 Kings 22 and Psalm 82. YHWH's "finding" of Israel in the desert (Deut 32:10) appears elsewhere as late as the time of Jeremiah (Jer 31:2) but as early as Hosea (Hos 9:10).[8] Von Rad notes the description of internal deliberations of God in a matter of salvation (Deut 32:26–27) but indicates parallel examples exist in Hosea and Genesis. He finds the identification of the "unpeople" highly uncertain; his objection to O. Eissfeldt's identification of the "unpeople" as the Philistines rests on Eissfeldt's eleventh-century date, which von Rad considers "barely defensible."[9]

In contrast to the above scholars, W. F. Albright, Wright, P. J. Skehan, Eissfeldt, H. W. F. Saggs, J. A. Thompson, F. M. Cross, D. N. Freedman, J. Bright, D. A. Robertson, C. Schedl, G. E. Mendenhall, P. K. McCarter, W. J. Moran, and Harrison support a date earlier than the eighth-century B.C. These scholars use a wide range of methods, mostly linguistic, to date the Song.[10] Eissfeldt emphasizes the Song's similarities of language, theme, and structure to Psalm 78 and suggests that both were a reaction to a single catastrophe: the Philistine destruction of the sanctuary at Shiloh (1 Sam 4:3–11).[11] Albright considers the poetic style intermediate between that of the Songs of Miriam or Deborah and the tenth-century lyric style of the Lament of David (see 2 Sam 1).[12] Both Albright and Eissfeldt date the Song of Moses to the eleventh or twelfth centuries B.C.

Wright does not accept Eissfeldt's identification of the "unpeople" as the Philistines but emphatically rejects an exilic or postexilic date for the Song. Deut. 32:26–30 implies that the people are not in exile but merely oppressed. Wright also suggests that uncertainty about the dating of wisdom literature means that any dating of the Song from supposed wisdom elements "must be abandoned as without merit." As a result of his dating the RIB/lawsuit's incorporation into covenant-renewal liturgy in the Northern Kingdom, Wright places the date of the Song in approximately the ninth century. This would be near the time of Omri and Ahab, in which the prophetic concept of Israel as the object of divine retribution emerged. This would make the Aramaeans the "unpeople," but Wright suggests that other dates are possible.[13]

Saggs is particularly critical of the use of wisdom elements to date the Song. He notes that wisdom literature was international in scope and includes many examples from Egypt and Mesopotamia as early as the second millennium B.C. Some of these texts survived largely unchanged over periods of a thousand or more years.[14] Based on his system of dating Hebrew poetry by the mixture of divine names, Freedman estimates a date no later than the ninth century and possibly as early as the tenth.[15] The results of his dating system often coincide strikingly with those of D. A. Robertson.

My purpose has been to show that modern scholarship generally favors a date for the Song of Moses earlier than the middle eighth century B.C. This opinion is unusual in that it arrives at substantial agreement through heterogeneous linguistic and literary-critical methods. If we add to the results of these modern methods the earlier, more controversial views of T. Oestreicher, E. Robertson, and R. Brinker on the dating of Deuteronomy as a whole,[16] we can reasonably claim that a majority of twentieth-century scholars' opinion supports a date for the Song no later than 800 B.C., and possibly much earlier.

Content

The scholarly consensus about the date of the Song of Moses may significantly affect our views of Hebrew prophecy, for the Song presents a classic prophetic warning. Future events may be expressed in an early form of prophetic perfect. YHWH is a being of absolute moral perfection (Deut 32:3–4). His past assistance to Israel (vv 7–14) leads to his people's wealth, to which they respond with complacency and unfaithfulness, especially idolatry (vv 15–18). YHWH will therefore use an unnamed people that are "no people" *lōʾ ʿām* (v 21) — a generic opponent — to punish Israel. Israel's conduct deserves scattering and annihilation, but this would have too harmful an effect on the surrounding nations (vv 26–27).

Moses further denounces gentile ignorance and spiritual defects (vv 29–33). He emphasizes that only YHWH has the power to intervene and act in history (vv 34–36). YHWH can inflict death and restore to life (v 39). His retribution is aimed at both unfaithful Israelites (vv 15–19) and nations who perform evil or destructive deeds (vv 32–35). The Song closes with a great shout of rejoicing, in which angels or other divine beings (*bĕnê ʾĕlōhîm, ʾelōhîm*, or equivalent, in LXX and Qumran Cave 4 fragments only), Israelites, and the nations are encouraged to join in praise of YHWH; for YHWH will avenge his people's blood, reward his enemies with the consequences of their deeds, and cleanse his people and their land (v 43).

The happy culmination to YHWH's cycle of intervention in history, which involves punishment first of Israel and then of her enemies (an apparent *vorher-nachher* pattern), may reflect popular eschatology. The rejoicing of nations and Israelites in a restored moral order anticipates views of the nations often considered exilic. Its position at the end of the Song, however, encourages an early eschatological view.[17]

Thus, if the many linguistic arguments about the Song of Moses are correct, by the time of Amos, for example, the concept of a perfect YHWH intervening in history on moral grounds may have been at least two generations old and may have extended back to the Conquest. One might then expect such a concept to have influenced the classical prophets and the record of their times.

I will briefly sketch the message and means of expression of the classical prophets, especially in the light of the Song of Moses, and suggest how prophetic faith and its expression could, on their part, create real or apparent historical selectivity in their writings.

SILENCE ON QARQAR

One telling example of historical selectivity in reverse—silence about a major event—occurs in the time of Elijah, Elisha, and Micaiah ben Imlah, the time suggested by Wright for the origin of the Song of Moses. No biblical prophet or historian mentions the battle of Qarqar in 853 B.C., and yet Qarqar was possibly the largest battle in which Israelite forces were ever engaged. Whether it resulted in an Assyrian defeat or a bloody draw (Harrison and C. Herzog strongly support the former),[18] the marshalling of four thousand chariots by the Western Semitic alliance against Shalmaneser III was the crowning success of Omri and the other architects of the alliance. To pass over the greatest battle in Israelite history, one foreshadowing a quarter-millennium of involvement with Assyria, is to show a sharply defined view of what is important in Israel's history.

By way of analogy of what was considered historically significant, the Song of Moses describes four possible configurations in Israel's experience: (1) victory and prosperity when the people are faithful to YHWH (Deut 32:11–14); (2) defeat and oppression when the people are unfaithful (vv 21–36); (3) a general cleansing of the unrighteous within and outside of Israel (vv 34–42); and (4) a restored moral order that is equally a source of joy to Israelites and to the nations (v 43). In this context, gentile culture, especially religion, is considered fundamentally destructive (vv 28–33).

In terms of Israel's relationship to YHWH—the major variable underlying these four scenarios—Qarqar was hardly relevant. The gathering of four thousand chariots required compromises: political marriages for Phoenician princesses and increased religious and cultural syncretism among Western Semitic peoples.[19] From a Yahwist viewpoint (the viewpoint of the Song of Moses and of Elijah), the policies of Omri and Ahab placed everything unique and worthy of preservation in Israel at risk in return for a momentary martial success. Qarqar illustrated neither YHWH's ability to rescue a righteous Israel *(Heilsgeschichte)* nor his ability to punish an unrighteous Israel *(Unheilsgeschichte).*

Ahab's recorded battles, on the other hand, namely his early successes in the Golan and his death at Ramoth–Gilead, are specifically linked to his relationship with YHWH and YHWH's messengers. This silence over Qarqar may thus be an example of one important aspect of historical selectivity: prophetic indifference based on the irrelevance of an event external to YHWH's purposes.

AMOS USES "DEUTERONOMIC" TOOLS

In comparing the message and expression of the Song of Moses with those of the classical prophets, it would be wise to remember the advice of Mendenhall: "An analogy should not be expected to be an identity."[20] The fact that a given prophet agreed with many of the concepts expressed in the Song, and expressed his own message in some of the same ways, does not mean he was certainly aware of the Song (if it was then extant), but it does suggest the existence of a continuum of Yahwist thought that could be the origin of a common message and form of expression in both Song and prophet.

The prophet Amos expresses a moral and historical outlook not unlike that found in Deuteronomy 32. Like the Song of Moses, he does not preach repentance directly, although YHWH's stated aim for the punishments of Amos 4:6–11 is to encourage repentance. F. H. Seilhammer argues that Amos's use of technical covenant language shows that his warnings were in response to rebellion against a covenant and thus included a possibility of repentance.[21] God is clearly interested in the condition and behavior of all nations in both Amos and the Song of Moses: 'Elyon assigns boundaries to each nation (Deut 32:8–9; compare Amos 9:7), and YHWH observes and rewards the misdeeds of all nations (Deut 32:29–42; Amos 1:3–3:2). Albright speculatively emends Amos 2:1 so that the crime of Moab becomes human sacrifice: "They burn the bones of human sacrifices for demons."[22] If this emendation is valid, the verse would deserve comparison with Deut. 32:17: "They sacrificed to demons."

Like the Song, Amos uses generic descriptions. Warfare inflicted by an unnamed people is to be the means of punishment in the poem of judgments (Amos 1:3–2:16; compare 3:11; 6:14; Deut 32:21). Place names are also used in a generic sense. Samaria sometimes refers to the entire Northern Kingdom, but usually means the ruling elite of its capital (Amos 4:1; 6:1; 8:14). Bethel is a place Amos visits and is encouraged to leave, but it also represents the deficiencies of the syncretist cult of the sanctuaries, especially the substitution of sacrifice and other cultic activities for righteousness (Amos 4:4; 5:5; 7:12–13). In both Amos and the Song, Sodom and Gomorrah represent incorrigible wickedness (Amos 4:11; Deut 32:32).

Prophecies of cleansing and restitution in Amos (compare 9:8–15), some of which are considered exilic additions,[23] resemble concluding parts of the Song (Deut 32:36–43). The idea of Israelites rejoicing with the nations in the Song (Deut 32:43) parallels that of Israelites exercising leadership among the nations (Amos 9:12). Such parallels with the content of Deuteronomy 32 clarify an important question about Amos. The universal rejoicing in a restored moral order in Deut. 32:43, which suggests the existence of an early popular eschatology, may also indicate that the "day of YHWH" in Amos 5:18 is something weightier and more distant than the next New Year festival suggested by J. Lindblom and others.[24] At least, Amos' "day of YHWH" may be seen as a composite of Israel's punishment (Amos 5:18–20) and the retribution pronounced against the nations (1:3–2:3; compare 2:4–16). In sum, Amos shows us the need for caution in assessing instances of possible historical selectivity on the part of the prophets. As an example, without the Song of Moses for comparison, one could possibly conclude that Amos was claiming the nation would come to an end or collapse on New Year's Day.

TIME AND TYPOLOGY IN HOSEA

Preclassical prophecy offers many instances of typology—the use of past or present events as analogies of future events. The tearing of Ahijah's mantle foreshadowed the division of the kingdoms. At Elisha's command Joash struck the ground three times, an analogy to three future victories over Syria. Hosea, in classical times, uses typology as much as any of his predecessors, and it clearly functions as an instructive tool.

Hosea's family relations have been the subject of intense critical disagreement, including controversy over his exact relationship with Gomer, the reality of his marriage, and attempts to identify Gomer with the woman in Hosea 3.[25] What has never been in doubt is the idea that Hosea's family life is in some way an analogy of the relationship between YHWH and Israel. The periods of trial for Gomer(?) and Israel will both last a long time (Hos 3:3–4).

We do not know whether Hosea and Gomer actually married. Many argue seriously that they did not.[26] If they did not, Hosea used an imaginary event of his own time as an analogy of something that would occur "after many days" (3:4). If there *was* a real marriage, Gomer(?) may or may not have repented, as both she and Israel were expected to do. In either case, we see a kind of typology. If she did not repent, we witness human choice creating an instance of prophetic selectivity—an event that did not occur is still used typologically by the prophet. Hosea thus transforms the perception and use of time and history in prophecy. By way of comparison, time sense in the Song of Moses is basically linear, moving from a distant past to a far future. An important exception is the analogy between gentile culture and Sodom (Deut 32:32–33), in which a present phenomenon is likened to one well known from the past.

The analogy between Gomer and Israel, however, is only the centerpiece of a rich assortment of analogies and contrasts, unsurpassed in prophetic literature. As in the Song, analogies link the distant past with the prophet's own time (Hos 9:9; 10:9–10), but so do contrasts (12:3–9, 12–14; 13:1–2). In addition, analogies link the events of the recent past and the near future (10:14) and illuminate contemporary conditions as extensions of ongoing trends (9:15). Hundreds of years before Confucius or Aristotle, and millennia before Ibn Khaldun or Toynbee, Hosea offers examples of systematic history—planned use of the past to understand the present, and of past and present to project the future.

In several other respects Hosea shows important parallels to the thought and expression of the Song. YHWH's affectionate care for Israel (Deut 32:10–11) is also emphasized in Hos. 11:1, 3–4, 8. Both Moses and Hosea recall how YHWH "found" and cared for Israel in the wilderness (Deut 32:10; Hos 9:10).[27] In both the Song and Hosea YHWH is unwilling to carry out the annihilation of his people that justice demands (Deut 32:23–27; Hos 11:9). The conflict between justice and mercy is resolved in the same way: punishment followed by redemption (Deut 32:21–25, 36; Hos 11:6, 10–11)—a *vorher/nachher* pattern. Finally, the restored Israel of Deut. 32:36, 43 (compare Amos 9:11) also flourishes in Hos. 1:10–11:2; 2:18–20; 3:5; 14:5–8.

Such conceptual parallels are relevant to the question of the authenticity of Hosea 14, often considered an exilic addition.[28] Repentant Israel (Hos 14:2) realizes that YHWH's nature is exactly as described in the Song: YHWH's "ways" are just (Deut 32:4) and right (Hos 14:9); idolatry (Hos 14:3b) is as futile as the Song says (Deut 32:17). The images of agricultural productivity that close the chapter (Hos 14:5–8) are consistent with productivity imagery in Hos. 2:22–23 and Amos 9:13–15, while the Song states that YHWH will atone for both land and people (Deut 32:43). The concern for an extended future and the existence of a popular eschatology are important factors shaping how we view Hosea's treatment of the present.

Like the Song (compare Amos), Hosea makes use of symbolic or generic names. Samaria stands for the idolatrous Northern Kingdom (Hos 8:5–6). Egypt and Assyria stand for bondage (8:13; 9:6) and foreign domination (10:6; 11:5). Derogatory place-names are used to designate real places in generic ways: Gibeah ("height") stands for corruption in high places (5:8–9; 9:7–9). Beth-Aven ("place of iniquity") stands for the general corruption of the national syncretist shrine at Bethel and its cult (compare 4:15; 10:5, 15). Included are generic names that allude to YHWH's purpose: a valley associated with Jehu's coup (Jezreel—what YHWH has sown) becomes analogous to the time "after many days" when YHWH's purpose bears fruit (compare 1:4–5, 11).

Hosea's expansion of analogies between different time periods greatly increases the potential for historical selectivity. This is especially so since not all analogies fit perfectly. Thus, Hosea speaks of YHWH "finding" Israel in the desert (9:10), although he was clearly aware of Egypt and the Exodus, since he uses Egypt as a generic term for bondage. He also shows us one kind of analogy that is important for our purpose: the typological link between the near future, where the vagaries of human choice are still operating, and the long-term future, in which YHWH's purpose dominates and will inevitably be fulfilled (compare "Jezreel").

MICAH: REPENTANCE MANIFEST

Although there is growing recognition of the possibility that all of Micah may date from approximately the lifetime of the prophet,[29] the first three chapters are usually recognized as being largely his work.[30] These chapters culminate in a prophecy of the destruction of Jerusalem and her reduction to a wasteland (Mic 3:12). As a matter of fact, Jerusalem was besieged but not heavily damaged during the prophet's lifetime, although many Judeans were deported by Sennacherib. Jer. 26:16–19 describes how Micah's prophecy was remembered a century later as the force that moved Judah to support Hezekiah's reforms, thereby averting YHWH's promised punishment.

Such a contingency of repentance is not articulated in the Song of Moses, although there is the strong implication that persons ignorant of YHWH's nature and actions can learn from the past and change their present unsatis-factory conduct (Deut 32:5-7). Repentance is clearly recommended in Amos. What is uncertain there is whether it will really alter Israel's predicted future; those who avert calamity are depicted as but a remnant (Amos 5:3-4, 6). In Hosea, repentance is clearly the aim of YHWH's punishments (Hos 2:7; 14:1-4), but repentance is depicted as coming after them. Jeremiah, who owed his life to a popular understanding of the doctrine of repentance, clearly articulates the principle that a nation that repents can avert, at least for the present, the calamity pronounced against it (Jer 18:8). There is in Jeremiah, of course, a corresponding possibility for apostasy (compare 18:10), and it is that which triggers the cycle of divine intervention that also appears in the Song of Moses. This idea forms the basis for the various prophetic lawsuits, which include the Song itself; Micah 6; Isa. 1:16-20, etc.

A public that noted how repentance averted calamities pronounced by Micah would be likely to notice further that calamities followed a return to behavior YHWH had denounced. In this respect, all prophets concur with the principle articulated in the Song, namely, that unfaithfulness to YHWH leads to divine retribution but that YHWH's purpose cannot thereby be frustrated.

In other ways, too, Micah's message reflects the thought and expression of the Song as well as that of early classical prophecy. Micah 4 and 5 connect a restored moral order to the presence of Israelites among the nations, as found in Deut. 32:43 (compare Amos 9:12). The dew and rainfall imagery of the Song (Deut 32:2) is used to portray the spread of Israel among the nations at the time of her return, in Mic. 5:7. Meanwhile, as in the Song, Israel's current condition reflects former national practice, and current national practice will affect Israel's future condition (6:10-16).

In sum, although Micah exhibits many common elements of classical pro-phetic faith and its expression dating to the Song of Moses, one aspect of his message that relates particularly to historical selectivity is the possibility for immediate change (for better or worse) and the certainty that long-term change is needed to accomplish YHWH's ultimate purpose of universal peace wrought through Israel. In the interim, as suggested by the unsuccessful labor pains of Mic. 4:9-10, Judah was at least afforded the opportunity to bring forth a new future. These pains and such an opportunity would, however, return again, the next time with greater success (5:3).

SELECTIVITY IN ISAIAH

Isaiah's prophecies exhibit many similarities of thought and expression to the Song of Moses and the writings of the earlier classical prophets, suggesting that Isaiah's prophecies belong within the same continuum of ideas suggested so far. For example, Isaiah's opening declaration of YHWH's fatherhood of Israel and his assertion of the nation's apostasy (Isa 1:2-4) resemble similar assertions in the Song (Deut 32:5, 19). In the same opening chapter, Judah is punished by an unnamed people (Isa 1:7-9); likewise, punishment or blessing is predicated on conduct (1:19–20). Because the people have become corrupt, they have become YHWH's enemies (1:24) in the same sense as appears in the Song (Deut 32:19, 41). Both Isaiah and the Song look back to Sodom for an analogy of contemporary wickedness (Isa 1:10; Deut 32:32) and forward to a restoration of the moral order (Isa 1:26; Deut 32:43). Comparisons such as these (the list could extend throughout Isaiah) are helpful because they immediately suggest that Isaiah contains many of the factors already discussed that may provide a basis for historical selectivity.

Serious analysis of the use of history in Isaiah is complicated by the fact that while some prophecies can be placed in specific historic contexts, many others cannot, though they may address particular nations or places. Even when a prophecy suggests a specific audience or problem, it may still not be possible to identify a particular time frame. During Isaiah's lifetime alone the ruling aristocracy of Judah underwent three major reversals of ideology. There were numerous attempts, with and without the participation of Judah, to form international alliances against Assyria.

In spite of these difficulties, the Book of Isaiah teaches the prophetic faith and its peculiar view of history, using all the associated means of expression — historical analogies, generic names, possibilities of apostasy and repentance, and typology rooted in real or imaginary situations as well as in the near future. In addition, Isaiah uses hebraicized or demythologized versions of some traditional Near Eastern religious concepts as typological models.

In recent years A. Gileadi has suggested the existence of large-scale, multiple-level structuring of the whole Book of Isaiah.[31] His work suggests that the author or final compiler/editor of Isaiah made a calculated use of structural devices to a degree unmatched elsewhere in prophetic literature. Of course, many so-called poetic structures have often proven to be extremely tenuous and tell us more about the interests and expectations of the scholar than those of the author. Gileadi's structures, however, in general, are highly visible and quite persuasive. He traces, for example, the cycle of themes of apostasy, judgment, restoration, and salvation on a localized, repetitive scale in Isaiah as well as on a broad, overarching scale. This example of localized and broad structuring he duplicates in a number of other instances, underscoring the structural complexity of the book.[32]

Such structuring adds yet another variable to the study of historical selectivity. The treatment of any subject may also have to be viewed against a backdrop of an overall structure that attempts to establish parallels with events and ideas in other time periods. The use of structural and poetic devices itself does much to shape how past, present, and future are to be understood. Finally, and most familiarly, any study of Isaiah is complicated by the lack of critical consensus about the date and authenticity of a given passage. Isaiah 26, for example, has been dated to almost any time from the eighth century to the year 110 B.C.[33] All this is critically important to the study of historical selectivity, since every point outlined increases the uncertainty (and thus the potential for misunderstanding) of the historical context of a given prophecy.

The remainder of the paper examines three well-known prophecies, or silences of prophecy, that suggest themselves as instances of historical selectivity in Isaiah. For each one, the nature of the apparent selectivity is explained and evaluated in the light of the historicity of the events as well as of the prophetic faith and its means of expression, notably typology. Sources other than the prophetic writings may play an important role in establishing or disproving the existence of selectivity. Without the records of Shalmaneser III, for example, we might not have known there was a battle at Qarqar.

The Northern Exile

Isaiah's message to and about the Northern Kingdom involves the exercise of historical selectivity in one important way: his failure to prophesy or comment on the exile of the northern tribes, a major event of Isaiah's time.[34] The principal Isaianic verses that bear on the decline and fall of the Northern Kingdom include —

1. The poem of judgments in Isa. 9:8–10:4. This is generally believed to date from Menahem's payment of tribute in approximately 738 B.C.[35] It speaks of suffering, hunger, and punishment, but says nothing about the exile or scattering of the people — in contrast to Amos and Hosea.
2. The prophecy about Damascus and Ephraim (Isa 17), which is believed to date from some time after Pekahiah's assassination that drew Israel into the existing Philistine–Syrian alliance against Assyria, but before the actual invasion of Judah in 734 B.C.[36] It speaks of the destruction of the power of Syria and the Northern Kingdom, and the great reduction in population (17:4–6, 9), but is indefinite as to whether this reduction comes from death or exile.
3. The complex of prophecies concerning the Syro–Ephraimite crisis of 734 B.C., including Isaiah's two encounters with Ahaz (Isa 7:1–25) and the prophecy of Maher-shalal-hash-baz (8:1–15). The first of these is generally believed to date from the time of the crisis, while the prophecy of Maher-shalal-hash-baz is thought to come within a few years of the crisis.[37] These touch on the destruction of the Northern Kingdom (7:8, 16) but do not discuss the removal of the people from the land.
4. Parts of Isaiah 28. This chapter is less certain in date, although there is an allusion to troops battling to the end at the gates of Samaria (28:5–6). Again, there is a general sense of pending calamity (28:2–4), but no suggestion of an experience decidedly different from anything that has gone before (in the time of Aramaean domination).

With the exception of Isaiah 28, these are among the most securely datable portions of the book and are generally recognized as being Isaiah's own work.

To assess how the events of the northern exile were treated historically, it is worth reviewing what is currently known or conjectured about them. Recent studies suggest the incremental nature of vassalage to Assyria in general, and of the Northern Kingdom's captivity and resettlement beyond Damascus in particular.[38] In contrast, the deuteronomic historian and the Chronicler, both writing at a time when relations between the Samaritans and Jerusalem were not good, emphasize the complete turnover of peoples; popular views about the "ten lost tribes" reflect this outlook.

There were, however, numerous Assyrian resettlements of northern and southern Israelites. The first, under Tiglath-pileser III, followed Assyria's intervention into the Syro–Ephraimite crisis at the invitation of Ahaz. The deuteronomic historian speaks of whole tribes being carried off (2 Kgs 15:29), while most of Tiglath-pileser's inscriptions speak of the captivity of an indefinite but large number.[39] A. T. E. Olmstead cites a tablet containing specific numbers for deportations from Galilee and Gilead which total 16,751.[40] Much of the northern and eastern parts of the kingdom of Israel became an Assyrian province.

Another major round of deportations accompanied the fall of Samaria in 721 B.C. Sargon II records that he resettled 27,290 Israelites and then repopulated the city and rebuilt it, leaving it better than he found it.[41] H. H. Rowley suggests that this number could not have been more than a twentieth of Israel's population.[42] There were further deportations on a massive scale from occupied Judah during Sennacherib's invasion of 701 B.C.; the king claims that 200,150 people were carried off as "booty."[43] There were also further resettlements into northern areas of Israel. Ezra mentions extensive resettling in the time of Ashurbanipal of people from Elam and Babylonia (Ezra 4:9–10), probably occurring after the rebellion of Shamash-shum-ukin or the Elamite campaigns of 647 and 646 B.C.[44]

In spite of the viewpoints of the deuteronomic historian and the Chronicler, the recorded actions of Hezekiah and Josiah do not suggest on their part a sense that anything irrevocable had happened in the north. Hezekiah circulated his Passover invitation throughout the north, and while many people were hostile, many others attended (2 Chr 10, 13). Josiah attempted to extend his reforms to the north, destroying the northern places of worship and the syncretist shrine at Bethel, while accepting (or compelling) contributions for repairs to the temple (2 Chr 34:6–7). The deuteronomic historian suggests that the new settlers were willing to combine the worship of YHWH with their native cults (2 Kgs 17:24–41). Seen from a purely Yahwist viewpoint such as Isaiah's, the settlers' religious deficiencies (including idolatry, human sacrifice, and a largely non-Levitical priesthood) were almost indistinguishable from those of the people they replaced, or for that matter from those of Judah near the time of Hezekiah.[45]

It is valuable to consider how Isaiah might reasonably have viewed these events in terms of the prophetic faith and his own experience and how his reaction reflected his understanding of YHWH's message. Some elements of the prophetic faith in Isaiah closely resemble those of the northern prophets. Day-to-day injustice, idolatry, and the substitution of cultic activity for righteousness are concerns common to Isaiah (Isa 1:10–15), Hosea (Hos 8:11–13), and Amos (Amos 5:21–26). Like Amos and Hosea, Isaiah focuses on the deficiencies of the northern leadership (Isa 9:14–16; 28:7–8). Isaiah, however, is clearly committed to the Davidic covenant (Isa 9:2–7; 11:1–5) and Hezekiah's program for the rehabilitation of Judah. His role in the crisis of 734 B.C. showed him the northern monarchy directly attempting to overthrow that covenant and causing a Davidic king to make some remarkably bad choices.[46] Given these personal experiences and his general views of the northern monarchy, its aristocracy and priesthood (suggested in Isa 28:1, 8), Isaiah's reaction to the fall of Samaria may well have been complete acceptance or even indifference.

The account of Hezekiah's Passover also suggests that the removal of the northern leadership presented an opportunity for Hezekiah's resurgent Yahwism. If the description of foreign settlers in 2 Kings 17 is accurate, some of them may even have attended with the Ephraimites; this would certainly account for their unfamiliarity with the requirements for cultic purity (2 Chr 30:17–20). A sincere response by the northern settlers may have led to speculation that other Gentiles might become worshipers of YHWH. The possibility of an interest in Yahwism by the northern settlers, its consistency with a contemporaneous quasi-monotheism,[47] and a willingness of Yahwist leadership to tolerate or use it in the interests of Judah might impart a clearer meaning to prophecies in Isaiah 1–39 often considered exilic or postexilic. Relegation of any expression of interest in the religious condition of other nations to exilic times ignores the interest already expressed in the Song of Moses and the judgment poem in Amos. It further overlooks the incomplete nature of the conquest of Canaan and the work of assimilation that went on from the time of the United Monarchy.

Interest in the cultural or religious assimilation of new settlers was certainly not alien to this time. Saggs cites the inscription of Sargon II at Dar-Sharrukin:

> People of the four quarters—of strange tongues and different speeches, dwelling in mountains and plains—I took as spoil at the word of Ashur my Lord. I made them of one purpose. I made them take up their abode therein (in the new city). I sent natives of Assyria, competent in everything, as overseers and supervisors to instruct them in custom and to serve the gods and the king.[48]

Sargon II was the king who sent a Levite to teach the new settlers in Israel and who resettled the survivors of Samaria (2 Kgs 17:24–29). Hezekiah and Isaiah were certainly aware of the Assyrian method of dealing with foreign minorities (Isa 2:1–4 and Mic 4:1–8 cite a similar process of assimilation and education, but one without compulsion—a compulsion that Hezekiah, in any case, could not exercise in an Assyrian province).

Isaiah might thus even hope that the new mixture of foreign settlers and Ephraimite poor could become more righteous than the former kingdom. This could well be the intent of Isaiah 26. Although this poem is usually considered part of a postexilic "Isaiah Apocalypse" comprising chapters 24–27, at least parts of it are recognized to have been possibly much older.[49] Indeed, Isaiah 26 could very well have been a hymn of welcome to the guests at Hezekiah's Passover; that context harmonizes more nearly with the chapter than any known context before or after it. In that case, the fallen city on the hill would be Samaria; and the mixture of poor and Gentiles would be the exact population Hezekiah had to deal with. Verses 14–19 would recall the failure, repentance in exile, and eventual redemption of the departed aristocracy. The implied responsibility to teach "the inhabitants of the world" and keep them from falling (vv 9, 18) might be aimed at the new settlers. In both Isa. 9:3ab and 26:15a, YHWH "enlarges the nation," increasing the joy of the people and his own glory. The new people, who are described as "dwelling in darkness," could be both the uninformed Ephraimites and the equally ignorant new settlers. Elements of both may have accepted or refused Hezekiah's invitation (compare 2 Chr 30:9; Isa 26:10–11). Hezekiah's Passover invitation itself hints at the possibility of the return of the captives (2 Chr 30:6–9).

To summarize, Isaiah, living in a very unstable period of time, clearly foresaw an exile, since return from exile is a common Isaianic theme (Isa 11:11–16; 14:1–2; 27:11–12). As signified by the name of his son, Shear-jashub ("a remnant shall repent/return"), Isaiah linked the exile and return to the people's moral condition and their fidelity to YHWH's covenant with Israel (10:20–22). Isaiah was also a citizen of Judah and a believer in the Davidic covenant. He regarded the division of the kingdoms as harmful (7:27). Throughout his lifetime people from both kingdoms were going into exile; yet Hezekiah still attempted to reconcile north and south long after the fall of Samaria. Isaiah apparently viewed all Israel as one people, involved in a single exile that had begun for some and that may already have had consequences affecting other nations. Added to this was the conviction that Assyria herself would fall (10:16–19), with consequences for Israel similar to her release from Egypt (10:24–27).

The case of the northern exile thus teaches us several lessons about historical selectivity by the prophets. Our knowledge of history may be so encumbered with stereotypes (the ten "lost tribes" and an imputed narrow, ethnocentric view by the prophet) that we are unable to see the northern prophecies as a contemporary of Isaiah might. Records of the time and the internal evidence of Isaiah's prophecies suggest that his treatment of the northern tribes is a reasonable response to his own experience. That he viewed his experience in terms of the nature and will of YHWH common to the prophetic faith, using the distinctive means of expression associated with that faith, suggests that his failure to prophesy the exile was less an oversight than it signified the exile to be a foregone conclusion—consistent with the thought of the classical prophets, and as something already contemplated by YHWH in the Song of Moses.

Perhaps most significant in any kind of typological reinterpretation of Isaiah is the idea that Israel's exile, in the broader context of his prophecies, forms a presupposition. While other typological events, such as the exodus out of Egypt and release from Egyptian bondage, might repeat themselves in the future contexts of Israel's exodus and release from Assyria (10:24–27; 11:15–16), Israel's exile did not and would not serve as a type for the future. To an author who drew on the past to create analogies to both the present and the future, the exile was typologically relevant to neither. But the exile's ongoing reality would be the stage on which YHWH's universal redemption and restoration could be wrought, the stage on which YHWH would reconcile Israel and the nations.

My People Egypt

Isaiah 19, which deals with Egypt, consists of two principal parts. The first (vv 1–15), a poem of three strophes, describes YHWH's actions against Egypt — a series of punishments which include outbreak of civil war, rule by a tyrannical king, drying up of the Nile, withering of the bases of the Egyptian economy, and complete impotence by the Egyptian leadership in the face of crisis. The second (vv 16–25), a series of five prose oracles, tells how Egypt's crisis will eventually lead the Egyptians to turn to YHWH for deliverance.

R. P. Carroll cites the prose oracles as a prime example of the failure of prophecy: "It would be difficult to find a better example in the prophetic traditions of a prophecy that failed."[50] He argues that the obvious failure led to later hermeneutic and translation (LXX and Targums) limiting the blessing on Assyria and Egypt (v 25) to Israelites returning from exile in those countries.[51] The basis for this viewpoint is obvious: neither of these peoples approached a monotheistic consensus until the Christian era or the Arab conquest. Certainly the outcome foreseen in this prophecy scarcely resembles any events within the lifetime of Isaiah or any of the Hebrew prophets. For this seemingly odd use of history to be understood, establishing a plausible date and context is important.

A substantial body of scholarly opinion suggests the poem at least may date from the time of Isaiah or shortly thereafter. E. J. Young suggests that both poem and prose reflect the "time of troubles" accompanying the Ethiopian conquest of Egypt, and therefore date from about 715 B.C.[52] S. Erlandsson concurs with this, admitting other models are possible but finding no clear reason to place the prophecies outside Isaiah's lifetime.[53] O. Procksch also considers both parts to be Isaianic.[54] Eissfeldt rejects Isaiah's known lifetime for both parts but suggests that they could date from any time between Psammetichus I's revolt against Assyria in 660 B.C. and Cambyses' invasion in 525 B.C..[55] A. S. Herbert and Bright both accept any date between the lifetime of Isaiah and the reign of Xerxes for the poem but an indefinite postexilic date for the prose oracles.[56] A. Bentzen, E. A. Leslie, A. Weiser, R. B. Y. Scott, and the Jerusalem Bible all consider that the poem could be Isaianic.[57]

The prophecy thus exhibits qualities that may suggest more than one time period but do not clearly rule out Isaiah's own lifetime. In the case of the prose oracles, internal evidence is so general that many time periods are considered possible. A more detailed examination of the message of the prophecy may help to determine the historical context and the degree or purpose of prophetic selectivity.

The poem's first strophe announces YHWH's entry into Egypt, shaking the idols of the land and melting the hearts of the Egyptians (Isa 19:1). YHWH will cause a civil war among Egyptian brothers, neighbors, and cities (v 2). This will undermine Egyptian religious morale, causing the people to turn to the occult in desperation (v 3). Finally a fierce, cruel ruler will dominate Egypt (v 4).

The second strophe proclaims the destruction of Egypt's environment and economy. The Nile itself, or the impoundments that hold floodwater for irrigation, will dry up, along with wadis, canals, and other bodies of water (vv 5–6). Vegetation along canals and estuaries will wither, together with any crops sown in irrigated areas (v 7). The fisheries and linen industry will suffer greatly (vv 8–10). If we assume that it is not the literal river Nile that is said to dry up in verse 5, all these impacts are consistent with the disruption of the Egyptian agricultural economy through lack of proper maintenance and the curtailment of foreign trade; the waters could represent irrigation itself but would also represent the flow of commerce.

The third strophe challenges Pharaoh's advisors to discern YHWH's plan (vv 11–12). The Egyptian leadership has been deliberately misled, so the result is inevitable decline (vv 13–15). The term *pharaoh* (v 11) represents the distinctly Egyptian ruler, who may thus be a different person from the fierce ruler of verse 4.

The five prose oracles answer the question posed in verse 12, at the same time expanding on the theme of verse 1:

1. This "time of troubles" in Egypt will terrify the Egyptians, creating anxiety about what conqueror will next be moving through Judah (vv 16–17); the emphasis is apparently on the land of Judah and not on her people or government.
2. One result of these times will be five cities in Egypt who speak a mercantile *lingua franca* ("the language of Canaan") committing themselves to the worship of YHWH of Hosts. One of these cities will have a reputation for righteousness comparable to that expected from Jerusalem (v 18; compare 1:26); Gileadi translates the "City of Righteousness" based on LXX: *polis 'asedec.*
3. The Yahwist presence and example will result in a place for the worship of YHWH in central Egypt, with signs of commitment to YHWH extending to her borders; these external signs will testify of YHWH of Hosts throughout the land of Egypt (vv 19–20a). As a confirmation of his presence, YHWH will send a deliverer (a Moses?) to save the Egyptians who call on YHWH when their oppression becomes unbearable (vv 20b–d).
4. YHWH will thus make himself accessible to the Egyptians, who will obtain direct, personal knowledge of him; they will demonstrate this knowledge by offering sacrifice and by making and keeping vows to YHWH (v 21). The answer to the question posed to Pharaoh's advisors in verse 12 is thus that YHWH has a plan to "heal" (save) Egypt by

putting the Egyptians through trying times; taught by example, they will repent and turn to YHWH, who will respond to their pleas (v 22).

5. When this change occurs, Egypt will establish firm ties with Assyria; Egyptians and Assyrians will regularly enter within each other's borders, suggesting stable inter-cultural exchange (v 23). At the completion of this process, Israel will become an equal, "silent partner" in the Egyptian and Akkadian civilizations; commencing with Egypt, Israel will be the channel for YHWH's blessing of the entire world (vv 24–25).

J. H. Breasted argues that the poem of Isaiah 19 is an accurate account of political and economic conditions in Egypt for a full century before the Ethiopian invasion in 715 B.C. and for approximately sixty years afterward. Indeed he uses the poem as his principal description of that time to convey the national disintegration into autonomous city-states, the breakdown of law and order, the disruption of the national economy, and abandonment of any centralized program of public works.[58] Even after the invasion, the substantial independence of the Delta cities made Piankhi's conquest incomplete, and the successors of the Delta rulers were to prove willing tools of the Assyrian conquest. Esarhaddon and Ashurbanipal certainly showed themselves as fierce rulers with the sack of Memphis and Thebes, along with extensive deportations of Egyptians and settlements of foreigners.[59]

K. Butzer, in his study of the history of Egyptian irrigation, notes that Nile flood levels were at a prolonged cyclical minimum from about 1200 B.C. until the time of Herodotus. At any time, transient flood levels below cyclical norms could result in a 75 percent reduction in arable land. When such a shortfall occurred during a time when irrigation was neglected (due to incompetent government or civil war), it could produce catastrophic results, especially in the Delta. There is a large literature of lamentations and "penitential psalms" datable to flood failures during earlier low-flow periods in the Old and Middle Kingdoms.[60]

Psammetichus I, after expelling the Assyrians, made the resumption of foreign trade a major element in the revival of the nation. His long reign saw the foundation of many foreign trading colonies, including numerous Semitic enclaves. Neither he nor the other Saitic pharaohs could find a truly Egyptian basis for the revived commercial and military establishments; Greeks, Aramaeans, and Phoenicians were predominant in commerce and the military.[61] Later Egyptian civil wars, such as the one between Hophra and Amasis (568–565 B.C.), were briefer, and none was associated with a general breakdown of the Egyptian economy.[62] Other possible "fierce" foreign rulers in Egypt include Nebuchadnezzar (who never actually ruled Egypt), Cambyses (of whom there are some surprisingly favorable Egyptian views), and Artaxerxes III Ochus (who achieved the conquest of Egypt just eleven years before Alexander).

The substance and historical context of the poem, in the light of a general survey of Egypt's history, thus suggest a time beginning about 820 B.C. with the feudal breakdown of Egypt and concluding with its reunification under

Psammetichus I. The poem's content apparently reflects a balanced assessment of Egyptian conditions from a Yahwist point of view.

The meaning and relation of the prose oracles to the poem therefore become important. The oracles appear to respond to the question Pharaoh and his advisors cannot answer and to take the events of the poem as a given thing. The first prose oracles anticipate a time arising from the conditions of weakness so vividly described in the poem, a time when internal collapse leads Egypt to fear the major land power to the north moving through Judah to conquer Egypt. Although such fear existed in the times of the Assyrians, Babylonians, and Persians, only during the time of the Assyrian empire was the threat of invasion associated with Egyptian civil war and a general disruption of trade. (In this overall historical context, Nebuchadnezzar's siege of Tyre, near in time to the civil war between Hophra and Amasis, is a poor second choice.) Breasted denounces the Libyan dynasts' fatal inertia, which allowed Tiglath-pileser III to subdue Palestine unchallenged.[63]

Also during Assyrian times the major land power showed some awareness of the importance of foreign trade to the Egyptian economy. Saggs cites an edict of Sargon II strongly encouraging trade with Egypt. This might have reflected the alarm in Egypt about Assyrian control of Palestine and Phoenicia that led Shabaka to encourage uprisings in Palestine and Judah.[64] We cannot tell from the oracles who was to initiate the Israelite commercial colonies in Egypt. This could have occurred when Judah possessed substantial freedom of action, as she did under Hezekiah, but it could also have occurred on the initiative of the Egyptians themselves, or of the major land power.

The historic novelty of the prose oracles lies in the fact that they anticipate a complete reversal of the prevailing flow of religious influence in Isaiah's day. The reigns of Ahaz and Manasseh demonstrated a substantial growth of Assyrian/Akkadian, Aramaean, and even Egyptian religious and cultural influence in Judah. An outward flow of Yahwist influence, on the other hand, is often considered to be a distinctly exilic idea. It is therefore appropriate to examine this departure from contemporary experience in terms of what we have already seen of the prophetic faith and its means of expression to determine if the oracles represent an anachronism or a response to a challenge.

Erlandsson suggests that the description of Egyptian decadence in the poem had a specific purpose in Isaiah's time, expressing the same opposition to reliance on world powers expressed by Hosea (Hos 5:13-15; 7:8-11; 8:9-10; 14:3) and by Isaiah himself (Isa 20:6; 28:15; 30:1-5; 31:1-3). This would become a much more familiar theme in the generation of Jeremiah and Ezekiel.[65] The prose oracles likewise offer some thematic parallels to the earlier prophetic literature. Israel is still YHWH's "inheritance" (Isa 19:25), as in the Song of Moses (Deut 32:9), but Assyria and Egypt become "the work of my hands" and "my people." YHWH is thus clearly interested in the destiny and conduct of other nations — as he is in Amos 1:3–2:3. He foresees them joining with Israel in a final harmony of worship and values, also suggested in Deut. 32:43 and possibly Amos 9.

As in prophecies of a return of Israel's remnant, an eschatological context for the oracles is also plausible. The changes foreseen for Egypt and Assyria imply a highly developed form of the harmony hinted at in Deut. 32:43. This harmony involves a transformation of values so great that it forms the climax of the Song of Moses and of Amos (Amos 9:7–15). Micah sees the return of the remnant as the necessary prelude to the time when all nations will learn from YHWH (Mic 4:2). Elsewhere, Isaiah associates such a transformation of values with the return of Israel's remnant, her triumph over oppressors, and possibly a new covenant. In a climax to Israel's history that parallels the exodus, plagues, and covenant that marked the beginning of her history, the end of YHWH's anger against Israel (Isa 12:1) will be followed by an acknowledgment "among the nations" of his saving power (Isa 12:4–5; compare Mic 7:8–11, 14–20).

As implied by the context of the poem in chapter 19, the time of a transformation of such dimensions is often associated with significant changes in reliable natural phenomena as well as normal human behavior. The biblical account of Israel's exodus out of Egypt serves as an example. An eschatological context for the oracles is also feasible because Egypt and Assyria form common generic names of nations in classical prophecy to signify bondage past and future (compare Hos 9:3; Mic 5:5–7; 7:15; Isa 10:24, 26; 14:25; 27:13); they are even used as such in Zech. 10:10–11. Arguing from structural evidence, Gileadi regards Egypt and Assyria in Isaiah, along with Babylon and Zion, as typological arch entities whose actions relate as equally to an eschatological context as to a historical one.[66]

There thus exist three possible levels of history mingled in the poem and prose passages of Isaiah 19. There is a level specifically descriptive of conditions in seventh- or eighth-century B.C. Egypt. There is also a generic level, on which the message may be applicable to world powers who threaten bondage against Israel. And there is an eschatological level, on which the religious conversion of world powers in the prose oracles constitutes another manifestation of the final universal transformation also foreseen by the Song of Moses, Amos, Hosea, and Micah. According to the Song, this latter stage is reached after an initial demise of the nations in general (Deut 32:35); and according to the classical prophets, it is reached after an initial demise of Assyria and Egypt in particular (Mic 5:5–9; 7:15–17; Isa 11:10, 15–16). Together these three levels may form a continuum of time, beginning with the Egyptian "time of troubles" and extending to the final attainment of YHWH's purpose.

Such a synthesis of times and events is consistent with the central concept of the prophetic faith: YHWH is the only divine being with power to act and intervene. YHWH is a being of pure righteousness (Deut 32:4) who will intervene in history to bring about his divine purpose. Religion, morality, and systematic predictive history arise from and express the same thing in the prophetic faith: the personality of YHWH. YHWH's very perfection means that his justice and intervention, as in Hosea's Jezreel, are sometimes indistinguishable from normal cause and effect.

This natural linkage is of great importance in understanding the generic application of the prose oracles. Obviously, it would be naive to say that a nation more righteous than her neighbors will never lose a war to them. To say that a nation with culture or morality visibly superior to her neighbors may eventually transform them into her own image, however, defines one of the basic sources of power for cultures and civilization. That power allowed the culture of Babylon to dominate Assyria, that of Greece to transform Rome, and for three thousand years has been the major factor in allowing the Chinese to assimilate their neighbors and overwhelm their conquerors.

Viewed in this light, the prose oracles outline a plan to transform the religious establishment of the ancient world by a Yahwist counteroffensive. This plan would be largely indistinguishable from cause and effect, resembling the process by which Buddhism entered China in the late Han Dynasty and by which Christianity infiltrated the Roman Empire. Reduced to essentials, the Yahwist strategy of Isaiah 19 would consist of the following:

> Wait for a "time of troubles," when the people are more susceptible to a foreign ideology. Use commercial and cultural contacts, and live YHWH's laws until your people have a reputation for righteousness and some local residents have become participating Yahwists. Then, if times become sufficiently trying, a local leader (a Darius, Constantine, or Ashoka) will adopt Yahwism as the core of a program of national regeneration.

Such a plan need not involve anything as alien to Israelite thought as overt proselytizing. It uses only normal commercial contacts and a willingness to live a pure (Yahwist) code for an extended duration of time.

The prose oracles thus contain not only a statement of Yahwist doctrine but also an assessment of prevailing economic, social, and cultural conditions in or near Isaiah's time, as well as the opportunities they afforded. Some of these opportunities assumed certain actions and a high level of conduct by Yahwists in Egypt. While it is clear that the conversion of the Egyptians never took place, it is possible to examine Isaiah's time and the following centuries to consider the validity of the prophecy as an assessment of historic opportunity, that is, as an analysis of historic trends in itself. Such an examination need not prove or disprove "fulfillment" but need merely consider whether there was a real chance for Yahwism to impact the ancient world by cultural and economic contacts or through force of example.

As we have seen in Egypt, the "time of troubles" and the invasion from Assyria resulted in the accession of the Saitic pharaohs. Psammetichus I and his successors were noted for their openness to foreign cultures and innovation. After putting in a ceremonial morning's work as pharaoh, Amasis, for example, spent his afternoons relaxing as a Greek gentlemen among friends.[67] The Saitic reliance on foreign troops, technicians (like Hanno, circumnavigator of Africa), and merchants gave rise to large foreign communities in Egypt. By Ptolemaic times this had led to influential Jewish communities, such as that in Alexandria, and to the construction of the temple of Onias at Leontopolis (for which Josephus claims Isaiah 19 was offered to the Egyptians as justification).[68]

From the sixth century B.C. onward, the Persians maintained a large colony of Jewish mercenaries in Egypt at the town of Elephantine. Records exist from this colony, which maintained its own small temple. YHWH was worshiped there, but so were many of his attributes (such as "Righteousness"), in a manner resembling the worship of personified attributes of Ahuramazda in contemporary Zoroastrian thought. This was consistent with one approach to monotheism common in the ancient world: attribution of all forms of divine power to a single member of the pantheon, or the treatment of all other gods as manifestation of that one.

Breasted cites the concept of Ptah as the divine mind, the controlling intelligence whose will is carried out by gods, men, and all the forces of nature. He cites the testimony of Intef, herald of Thutmosis III, that the herald owed his success to the guidance of his heart, "the oracle of the god, which is in every body."[69] S. Smith cites a late ninth-century B.C. Assyrian inscription urging the reader to "trust in Nabu, and rely on no other god."[70] Wright notes that possession of power to intervene by a single divine being might be a valid definition of Hebrew monotheism.[71] Saggs cites an Assyrian text attributing all power to Ninurta and comments, "If by monotheism one means a belief that ultimately all divinity is one, then some Assyrians were certainly monotheistic."[72] It is notable that such views are found in the two nations whose religious conversion is contemplated in Isaiah 19.

Saggs also notes a pervading sense that "something was lacking" in the anthropomorphic pantheon of Assyria and Babylonia, at least by the sixth century B.C.. As one example, he cites the innovations of Nabu-na'id, especially the attempt to cultivate an innovative empire-wide worship of Sin, the moon god.[73] He also cites Nabu-na'id's colonization of six oases in the vicinity of Yathrib (Medina) with people from the western part of his empire ("Hatti-land"). Saggs notes that a thousand years later five of these six oases were inhabited by Jews, providing the population from which a later cultural "savior," Muhammed, formed his first impressions of monotheism.[74] Muhammed, judging from the Koran, was impressed by the ideas of these people, not necessarily by their example, which did not differ much from that of their neighbors.[75] Had these communities been recognizable for a superior culture and working morality, we might have witnessed a field test of Isaiah's plan for Egypt.

The poem and prose oracles of Isaiah 19 thus reflect cultural and religious opportunities of which there was certainly evidence for the discerning individual of Isaiah's day, and ample confirmation in later times. They represent a breakthrough in the use of history: analysis of past, present, and future conditions in the light of the major goals of prophetic Yahwism (*mah yā'aṣ yhwh*, v 12), together with a specific program for the attainment of those goals. The oracles also offer a striking example of political insight: analysis of conditions and opportunities at a time when the major land power of the Near East controlled the trade routes to Egypt. This situation would recur many times but was most apparent during the lifetime of Isaiah and the two generations immediately following, among which are the most likely dates for the oracles.

In sum, the prophecy suggests a course of action that might conceivably have led to the spread of Yahwism through the ancient world, though it relies implicitly on certain actions by the community of Yahwists. Among such actions was a program for economic and cultural contacts, especially a pattern of daily conduct on a par with Isaiah's vision of Jerusalem. We see no sign that this combination was achieved during the lifetime of Hezekiah or later. The major departure from the plane of history in Isaiah 19 thus reflects the choices of the prophet's contemporaries. The prophecy itself, coming at a time when the systematic study of society, economics, and religion was unknown, remains an astounding exhibition of insight, worthy of the name of inspiration in at least the secular sense.

The possibility for the fulfillment of YHWH's revealed word could certainly be seen in Isaiah's time and in later generations, so that there is, in fact, no significant degree of selectivity in the prophecy. The ultimate vision of Israel/Zion as mediator in the transformation of the world is central in Israel's thought and indeed in prophetic thought from the Song of Moses onward. YHWH's word, expressing his first purposes for Israel and mankind, could and would linger, accumulating potential energy, like water behind a dam. Monotheism might come to Egypt and Assyria sooner or later, but the ultimate transformation of history, of which monotheism was part and symbol, was certain.

Lastly, the prophetic historical outlook and eschatology, applied to the present, offered justification for a Yahwist ideology. The faithful Israelite who kept the law and endured could know that he was engaged in a fundamentally revolutionary act: a transformation of the world by righteous example, in close harmony with a Will that was at once love and justice.

The Burden of Babylon

Isa. 13:1–14:27, also called the Burden of Babylon, consists of two principal parts: a vision of Babylon's destruction and a song of mockery of a fallen king of Babylon. An assessment of historical selectivity in this material should take into account possible dates and contexts for the prophecy. If the Burden of Babylon is a structural unit dating from exilic or postexilic times, there would be evidence of perhaps inexplicable prophetic selectivity: Babylon in that period was not dramatically destroyed but survived her capture by Cyrus for centuries, entering a period of gradual decay after the time of Alexander.[76]

Isaiah 13 describes YHWH's marshalling an army of nations to carry out his plan for punishing the world (vv 1–5). The retribution will be cataclysmic, distinguished by changes in the heavenly bodies (vv 6–13). In verses 14–22 YHWH's anger is focused on a single place, evidently the city of Babylon named in verse 19; the city is to be attacked and destroyed by the Medes and will become a wasteland forever. Isaiah 14 describes events that could be associated with the general punishment of 13:6–13, the specific punishment of 13:14–22, or both. Israel's remnant, assisted by the nations, is to return to her own land and there rule over her oppressors (vv 1–2). A great taunt song will be sung against the "king of Babylon," in which Israelites, trees, and the dead rulers of the world will join in mocking the overthrown Tyrant (vv 3–11, 16–21). Forming part of this mockery is the famous lament for Helal ben Shachar

("Morningstar, Son of the Dawn"), who aspires to divine status but is instead cast down to the place of the dead (vv 12–15). The remainder of the chapter describes the final destruction of Babylon and her conversion into a swamp (vv 22–23). YHWH promises to destroy Assyria in his own land (vv 24–25). The prophecy contains YHWH's plan for the entire world (vv 26–27).

Many scholars believe in an exilic context for the Burden, because the mention of Babylon suggests that she is the dominant world power.[77] Babylon is mentioned in 13:1, 19 and 14:4, 22. Only 13:19, however, lies within the poetic text, and it emphasizes Babylon's cultural splendor, not her political power. Many other scholars consider all or parts of both chapters to be Isaianic, because internal evidence strongly suggests an Assyrian context.[78] Yet others consider the chapters to be compilations or reflections of entities that are deliberate composites.[79] All or part of 13:2–18 may be Isaianic, resembling preexilic warnings like Nah. 1:2–14 or Zeph. 1:14–18. The Tyrant may be Sennacherib or Sargon II (said to have suffered from a curse leading to his death and burial outside Assyria on campaign).[80]

Erlandsson notes that the prophecy of specific destruction in Isaiah 13 (vv 14–22) closely resembles the historic destruction of Ashur and Nineveh, especially in the extent of the devastation and the desertion of the site for ages. He further suggests that the destruction of Babylon in 14:22–23 forms an analogy of the preceding overthrow of the Tyrant.[81] Erlandsson also synthesizes the findings of several comparatively recent surveys of Assyrian, Babylonian, Medean, and Elamite history. The only true destruction of Babylon occurred under Sennacherib in 689 B.C. Further, the Assyrian kings Tiglath-pileser III and Sargon II had each "taken the hand" of Marduk to be recognized as "king of Babylon," a religious title. In 715 B.C. Daiukku (Deioeces) of the Medes conspired with Urartu against Assyria, only to be swept up by Sargon in the campaign of 714 B.C. and exiled to Syria, placing a major anti-Assyrian leader within a few days' journey of Jerusalem.[82]

Babylon was clearly the cultural center of the ancient Near East. Sennacherib's destruction of Babylon thus sent a wave of shock and horror through ancient Mesopotamia. This reaction may have promoted Esarhaddon's rebuilding of Babylon after 678 B.C. and his recognition of an Assyrian–Babylonian "dual monarchy" in the designation of his eldest son, Shamash-shum-ukin, as king or viceroy of Babylon (working with or under his brother Ashurbanipal).[83] Parts of the prophecy can be readily linked to specific events within this context. The conversion of Babylon to marshland (14:22–23) was carried out in detail under Sennacherib, who had drainage canals dug and diverted the river to flow over the site. Erlandsson and J. Brinkman feel that these events strongly suggest a historic setting for that part of the prophecy.[84] Sennacherib obtained oracles that Babylon would be uninhabited for seventy years, which Esarhaddon evaded only by an artful strategem.[85]

The song of mockery in Isaiah 14 (excluding, for now, the lament of vv 12–15) mentions a number of activities of the fallen Tyrant. These are typical of rulers of the dominant Mesopotamian land power from Ashurnasirpal II to Nabuna'id, although some are identifiable with specific individuals:

1. *Striking down nations, subduing peoples, making the earth shake and kingdoms quake (vv 6, 16)*. These are quite general descriptions and could apply to almost any victorious ruler. If they are intended to describe something resembling genocide, Ashurbanipal's Elamite campaigns are almost one of a kind.
2. *Cutting trees, especially in Lebanon (v 8)*. This was a prerogative of every major conqueror of Palestine and Syria. Sargon II also cut trees on a large scale in the Urartu campaign.[86] It is the theme of the boasting attributed to Sennacherib in Isa. 37:24.
3. *Creating wilderness, demolishing cities (v 17ab)*. The major examples of large-scale destruction are Ashurbanipal's Elamite campaigns of extermination; Sennacherib's Jerusalem campaign of 701 B.C., with its huge deportations; Sennacherib's destruction of Babylon, with equally large deportations; Nebuchadnezzar's destruction of Jerusalem; and Sargon II's devastation of Urartu.[87]
4. *Retaining captives (v 17c)*. This was typical of every Mesopotamian monarch from Ashurnasirpal to Nabuna'id.
5. *Destroying his homeland, murdering his own people (v 20bc)*. The only real examples of this are the religious dispute of Shalmanesar V with the city of Ashur, apparently leading to the king's downfall, and, especially, the Babylonian rebellion of Shamash-shum-ukin against Ashurbanipal. The latter rebellion apparently involved an attempt to orchestrate an invasion of Assyria by Elam and other powers. Both Shamash-shum-ukin's treason and Ashurbanipal's destruction could be included in this category. This assumes the presence of Assyrians among the ringleaders whose tongues were cut out before execution.[88]
6. *Ending of dynasties, massacring of descendants (vv 20d–21)*. This is of course an activity inflicted on and not by the Tyrant. Changes of dynasty were not uncommon during Neo-Assyrian and Neo-Babylonian times. Rulers who did not leave descendants or whose families died with them include Shalmanesar V, Shamash-shum-ukin, and Nabuna'id. Sennacherib's son and heir, Ashur-nadin-shum, was taken captive in 694 B.C. by the Elamite–Chaldean alliance (after five successful years as ruler of Babylon) and died in captivity. Brinkman suggests this as a motive for Sennacherib's harsh treatment of Babylon.[89]
7. *Building cities (v 21d)*. Founding or rebuilding cities was a major activity of Mesopotamian rulers, including Ashurnasirpal (Kalah), Sargon II (Dur-Sharrukin), Sennacherib (Nineveh), Esarhaddon (Babylon), and, more doubtfully, Nabuna'id (Haran and the many desert colonies).[90]

The activities of the anonymous "king of Babylon" in the taunt song thus clearly form a composite, combining the woes of 350 years of Neo-Assyrian and Neo-Babylonian imperial supremacy, as seen from the point of view of a smaller nation. While no one ruler can be associated with all listed activities, Israelites could have experienced or been aware of the sum of them as early as 715 and no later than 648 B.C. While many activities of Nebuchadnezzar and

Nabuna'id resemble those on the list, nothing is uniquely Babylonian or specifically datable to the sixth century, such as a clear-cut reference to the destruction of Jerusalem. Assyrian examples greatly outnumber Babylonian ones, but this is not surprising since the much longer span of Assyrian power offers several possible examples for almost every activity.

Isaiah's oracle about the siege of Jerusalem (37:22–35) supports an Assyrian context for both the taunt song and the lament for Helal ben Shachar. This prophecy, considered authentically Isaianic by Eissfeldt, Herbert, Scott, Young, and Harrison,[91] describes activities of Sennacherib resembling those of the Tyrant in chapter 14, in language similar to the description of Helal ben Shachar:

> Whom have you mocked and ridiculed?
>   Against whom have you raised your voice,
>   lifting your eyes to high heaven?
> Against the Holy One of Israel!
>   You thought: On account of my vast chariotry
> I have conquered the highest mountains,
>   the furthest reaches of Lebanon.
> I have felled its tallest cedars,
>   its choicest cypresses.
> I have reached its loftiest summit,
>   its finest forest.
> I have dug wells
>   and drunk of foreign waters.
> With the soles of my feet
>   I have dried up all Egypt's rivers![92]

That the lament of Helal ben Shachar, too, has a generic intent in a specifically Assyrian context, depicting an attitude characteristic of many Assyrian kings, is possible. Saggs cites a strong Assyrian confidence in human abilities and human importance in relation to the gods. He considers the self-adulatory statement of 10:13–14, for an example, an accurate but unsympathetic depiction of the Assyrian aspiration to power and their kings' state of mind. In particular, he cites the relief of Ashurnasirpal II and the Tree of Life as evidence of an outlook placing the very first Neo-Assyrian king on a level of equality with the anthropomorphic gods.[93] An Assyrian mythological text, the myth of Anzu, may offer some insight into the Lament. This myth is of great age, apparently dating from times before the Sumerian gods were envisioned in human form.[94] It was, however, still current at the time of Isaiah and the rebellion of Shamash-shum-ukin, as it is found in fragments from Ashurbanipal's library.[95] The myth describes a struggle for divine supremacy. Anzu, a bird-god (possibly an eagle), a Hermes-like messenger of Enlil, conceives the idea of seizing the Tablets of Destiny, the source of Enlil's power, and replacing him as supreme god. Only the Assyrian version of the myth explains Anzu's aspirations:

> As he continues to watch the father of the gods, the god of Duranki [temple],
>   he conceives the idea of taking over his office.

As Anzu continues to watch the father of the gods, the god of Duranki [temple],
    he conceives the idea of taking over his office:
I will seize the divine tablet of destinies for myself.
I will control the decrees of all the gods.
I will make my power absolutely secure and regulate all morality.
I will control all the supreme gods.[96]

This closely resembles Helal ben Shachar's intentions in 14:13–14:

You said in your heart:
    "I will rise in the heavens
        and set my throne above the stars of God;
    I will seat myself in the mount of assembly [of the gods],
        in the utmost heights of Zaphon.
    I will ascend above the altitude of the clouds;
    I will make myself like the Most High!"[97]

In both accounts the intent is expressed in four statements. In both, the
aspiration to power takes the form of supremacy over the divine assembly. The
objects of rivalry are similar: "the father of the gods" and "the Most High." In
14:12c Helal is said to have "commanded the nations," while Anzu seeks absolute power.

The outcome of the myth can be traced from only several sources, including earlier Babylonian ones. Anzu steals the Tablets of Destiny and flees to a
mountain in the North (Zaphon?). Eventually Ninurta, the divine warrior,
agrees to fight the nearly invincible Anzu. He kills Anzu only after using the
power of the winds to take away his wings.[98] Isa. 14:12a, d, 15 describes Helal
as "falling," being "cast down," and coming to the abode of the dead.

There is one other text with parallel ideas and language to this in an early
Babylonian source. This comes from the Babylonian creation epic, *Enuma
Elish*, at the moment when Tiamat, the dragon–mother of chaos, confers author-
ity on her generalissimo, Kingu:

I have cast the spell that exalts you above the assembly of the gods.
    I have given you full authority to command the gods.
You are truly supreme, my only equal!
Your work will prevail over all the supreme gods.

She gives him the Tablets of Destiny and fastens them on his breast:

Your commands will be unalterable.
    Your edicts will endure forever![99]

Tiamat's initial proclamation again consists of four statements and conveys
the idea of supremacy over the divine assembly and equality with the highest
divine power, or at least one of the contenders for that office.

It is interesting, therefore, that Sennacherib's destruction of Babylon was
the occasion for a new edition of the creation epic, in which Marduk, the
divine warrior of Babylon, is replaced by "Anshar," a Babylonian divine name
selected for the occasion as the Babylonian form of Ashur. W. H. Shea, in a
recent article, cites new evidence of inscriptions describing Sennacherib's second Palestinian campaign (about 688/687 B.C.), evidence which refers to "my

Lord Anshar" as the source of Sennacherib's authority. It is also immediately after the destruction of Babylon by Sennacherib that inscriptions from Egypt and Palestine begin referring to him as the "king of Babylon."[100]

Considered in this light, the internal evidence of Isaiah 14 and 37 suggests that the prophet was well aware of domestic Assyrian activity and ideological currents. The response to an arrogant king who described his own activities in terms of an Assyrianized account of a *chaos-kampf* or war in heaven might well serve as a taunt song or lament alluding to a Hebrew or hebraicized account of such a war. In this prophetic response, Sennacherib, instead of being the agent of the divine warrior, as found in one epic, really acts the part of the doomed opponent of the divine warrior. In this vein, to cite a further example, Isa. 8:8 combines chaos-beast imagery of water and flight to describe a king of Assyria spreading his "wings" (Anzu?) over the land of Immanuel in the interim before his demise (compare 10:12ff.). Other language that may have specific associations with the chaos-beast is found in Isa. 13:5, 8.[101]

In sum, the patterns of parallels among Anzu, Helal ben Shachar, and the poem relating to Sennacherib's siege of Jerusalem in 37:22–29 suggest a specifically Assyrian context for Helal ben Shachar. In each case the main statement describes the aspirations of a blasphemous usurper, acting on his own initiative. In each, the movement of the action is to the mountains northward. Such parallels strongly suggest that the author of 14:12–15 was aware of the Assyrian version of the myth of Anzu or something similar to it. Anzu appears as a common synonym for martial ferocity in Assyrian inscriptions, and apparently no extant text later than Assyrian times exists that expresses Anzu's aspirations.

Considered in light of Isaiah 21 and 22 (the Wilderness of the West and Arena of Spectacles prophecies), the lament of Helal ben Shachar and the Tyrant's murder of his own countrymen may reflect an important event, often overlooked by biblical scholars: the Babylonian rebellion of Shamash-shum-ukin. Bright and H. Winckler consider this rebellion a plausible context for Isaiah 21.[102] Significantly, Bright, B. Oded, J. M. Myers, and Brinkman consider the rebellion the most plausible context for the captivity of Manasseh and the rebuilding of Jerusalem's defenses (2 Chr 33:10–17).[103] Brinkman describes Shamash-shum-ukin as "the arch-rebel" and considers the rebellion and its aftermath the major factor in the decline of Assyrian power.[104]

If Manasseh, a loyal Assyrian vassal, were captured by the Kedarite raid in support of Shamash-shum-ukin's rebellion of 650 B.C., and endured Ashurbanipal's siege of Babylon as a hostage, we would have a coherent explanation for the account in 2 Chr. 33:10–17, the allusion to Anzu in Isaiah 14, and the combination of Babylonian and Kedarite prophecies in Isaiah 21.[105] Ashurbanipal might reasonably reward the liberated Manasseh with greater autonomy in defense and religious affairs. From an Assyrian viewpoint, equation of an attempt to seize royal power with an attempt to seize divine power would reflect the state of mind Saggs cites.[106] From a Yahwist point of view, an attack on the Davidic covenant would be a blasphemous aspiration, paralleling

Isaiah's dim view of the Syro–Ephraimite coalition against Ahaz. In that context a leader in anti-Assyrian prophetic circles might become personally absorbed in the progress of the rebellion (21:1–10) or even be approached for advice by Kedarite forces (21:16–17). A rebellion scenario for Isaiah 21 is consistent with as much as is known of Assyrian, Medean, and Elamite history.[107] It offers an additional reason why so much divine and prophetic anger might be aimed at Babylon in times of Assyrian domination.

Both internal and external evidence for the Burden of Babylon thus suggest several distinct historical contexts:

1. *A general prophecy of the punishment of the wicked and the return of the remnant.* This is the object of 13:2–14:2, 24–27. It resembles similar prophecies in Zephaniah and Nahum, both of which reflect conditions of Assyrian hegemony.
2. *An indefinite (composite) anti-Assyrian context.* The taunt song of 14:4c–11, 16–21 denounces typical Assyrian imperial activities.
3. *Sennacherib's siege of Jerusalem in 701 B.C.* This may be the subject of 14:12–15.
4. *Sennacherib's destruction of Babylon in 689 B.C.* This is the probable subject of 14:22c–23.
5. *The Rebellion of Shamash-shum-ukin (652–648 B.C.).* This is the possible subject of Isaiah 21 and may be the subject of both 14:12–15, 20 and the prophecies in 21:1–22:14. Both Shamash-shum-ukin and Ashur-nadin-shum offer further plausible occasions for celebrating the death of the king of Babylon within an Assyrian context.

In spite of the direct mention of Babylon, nothing ties the prophecies to a sixth-century B.C. Neo-Babylonian context. The labels on the city and on the king and his activities all say "Babylon," but the king and his activities are clearly Assyrian.

While the mention of Babylon could conceivably be a sixth-century gloss to the original text, or even possibly a code word for Assyria adopted by the Yahwist resistance during Manasseh's reign, it is more likely a recognition of the pivotal role of Babylon in Mesopotamian civilization. Isaiah was clearly aware of the transforming power of cultures (see Isa 19 discussion). Babylon was the cultural capital of a civilization that had successfully transformed her neighbors and overwhelmed her conquerors for perhaps 2500 years. Sumerian/Akkadian religious, political, and social institutions transformed Kassites, Assyrians, Aramaeans, and Chaldeans. In the face of this longevity, little inferior to that of Egypt, Neo-Assyrian power was a comparatively recent development. A. Toynbee, for example, considers Assyria only the proto-universal empire of the civilization of which Babylon was the symbol.[108]

Israel and her prophets were both immersed in and at war with Babylonian civilization and its Western Semitic cousins.[109] Just as YHWH, the divine warrior, was at war with the chaos-beast (which, in the *Enuma Elish* conferred its authority on its military representative, Kingu), so the cultural and theological antagonist of YHWH's people was Babylon, whose power was now vested in her military arm, Assyria. In both the Burden of Babylon and the *Enuma Elish*, the divine warrior fights with the ultimate source of opposition, leaving the military representative to be "mopped up." As has been noted, this juxtaposing of forces, particularly in the light of the prophetic faith and its means of expression, is suggested by the allusions to Assyrian and Babylonian mythology. The prophet uses such mythology to parody both Babylon and her king as forces of chaos.

This prophetic antagonism toward Babylon may also be demonstrated in the poetic structure of the material. From this we may be able to learn whether or not the assemblage of Assyrian and "Babylonian" prophecies was deliberate, in order to better estimate a historical context. There have been at least two significant attempts to link the prophecies of Isaiah 13 and 14 to larger-scale structures within the Book of Isaiah. T. K. Cheyne argues that the taunt song is a "clear parallel" to the prophecy about Sennacherib's siege of Jerusalem in Isaiah 37.[110] The parallel language and situations of Sennacherib and Helal ben Shachar are impressive and have already been discussed. The mockery of the king in both Isaiah 14 and 37 is a prophetic response to vaulting ambition expressing itself in mocking rivalry of YHWH. In both, the return of the remnant is a response to the humbling of the king. In 14:1–2, the remnant moves from other nations toward Israel, in 37:32 from Jerusalem to the depopulated countryside. Both, however, would be reasonable prophetic aspirations in view of Sennacherib's deportation of more than 200,000 people from rural Judah.

Gileadi finds in 14:1–23 (with a fragment of Isa 47) a verse-by-verse antithesis of 52:1–53:12. The contrast of the two poems deserves citing in detail:[111]

Isaiah 47:1-4; 14:1-23	*Isaiah 52:1-53:12*
47:1–4 Babylon is dethroned, disrobed, cast into the dust — retribution by Israel's God.	52:1–3 Zion is enthroned; clad in robes, she rises from the dust, redeemed by YHWH.
14:1 Israel returns to her land, joined by strangers.	4 Israel, in exile from her land, is oppressed by strangers.
2 Israel's authority is restored; she rules over her oppressors.	5 Israel's authority is taken away; she is ruled by oppressors.
3 YHWH acts to give rest from sorrow and bondage in that day.	6 YHWH acts to reveal his presence in that day.
4 Bad news for Babylon — the Tyrant's reign ends.	7 Good news for Zion — her God's reign of peace begins.
5 Babylon's king is cast down.	8 YHWH is reestablished as king in Zion.
6 The Tyrant strikes the nations in anger.	10 The nations see YHWH's arm acting to save.
7 There is rejoicing; the whole earth is at rest and in peace.	9 There is rejoicing; Jerusalem is comforted and redeemed.
8 The Tyrant who hewed down trees has departed.	11 Those who bear YHWH's vessels depart from Babylon.
9 The Tyrant is exiled to Sheol, in company with the dead.	12 Israel returns from exile, in company with her God.

10 The Tyrant is cast down, subject to reproach.

13 The Servant is exalted, acquires eminence.

11 The humiliated Tyrant formerly enjoyed eminence.

14 The eminent Servant formerly endured humiliation.

12 The erstwhile ruler of nations is lamented with awe.

15 The cleanser of the nations is regarded with awe.

13 The Tyrant (Helal ben Shachar) rises up to the heavens.

53:1–2 The Servant grows up from the earth.

14 The Tyrant aspires to be like the Most High.

3 The Servant accepts being the lowliest of men.

15 The Tyrant's humiliation is final.

4–5ab The Servant's humiliation is redemptive.

16–17ab The Tyrant causes havoc and destruction.

5cd The Servant causes peace and healing.

17c The Tyrant brings others into lasting bondage.

6 The Servant makes atonement for the sins of others.

18 The kings of the nations die with honor.

7 The Servant dies like a slaughtered lamb.

19 The Tyrant is slain for his own crimes.

8 The Servant is slain for the sins of his people.

20ab The Tyrant is left unburied because of violence he has committed.

9 The Servant is buried because he committed no violence.

20c–21 The Tyrant's offspring are slaughtered and will not continue.

10 The Servant sees his offspring continue.

22 The remnant of Babylon is condemned and wiped out.

11 Those vindicated by the Servant are many.

23 Babylon becomes an inheritance for marsh creatures.

12 Zion becomes an inheritance for the Servant and those he redeems.

In general, this structure of contrasting and parallel ideas is dramatic, an almost unanswerable demonstration that the assemblage of prophecies in 14:1–23 is linked to the composition of Isaiah 52 and 53. One of these would already have been in existence and regarded as a poetic and conceptual unit by the time the other was written or compiled. This structural juxtaposition of ideas is an even more dramatic demonstration of the prophetic opposition between "Babylon" and Zion. It is notable that at no point do the people or institutions of historical Israel appear in apposition to Babylon, but rather Zion: the idealized/ideological Israel. Potentially, Zion is the place or people where YHWH is king (52:8); Babylon is its antithesis (1:26–27; 2:3; 4:3, 5; 8:18; compare 52:8).

We may better understand the intended application of the seemingly composite and structurally linked Burden of Babylon by examining it in the light of the prophetic faith and its means of expression. In particular, Isaiah 13 and 14 contain important thematic parallels with the latter half of the Song of Moses. Isaiah describes in some detail the time when YHWH's intervention turns from the punishment of Israel by other nations to retribution against all

his enemies, particularly the oppressors of Israel. Common elements include
(1) analogic linkage of the current oppressor to Sodom (Deut 32:32; Isa 13:19);
(2) YHWH's hand as the source of retribution and the sign of his commitment
to intervene (Deut 32:39–41; Isa 14:26–27); (3) YHWH's long-term goal of the
destruction of the wicked (Deut 32:41; Isa 13:9) and rescue of the helpless
remnant (Deut 32:36; Isa 14:1–3); (4) a survey of factors making destruction
possible or necessary (Deut 32:35; Isa 13:9–11; 14:2–23); (5) the cataclysmic
nature of the destruction, even to Sheol (Deut 32:22; Isa 13:13; 14:15–17);
(6) ferocious vengeance on YHWH's enemies (Deut 32:40–43; Isa 13:5–8, 14–18);
(7) a dramatic reversal of fortunes for Israel (Deut 32:36–43; Isa 14:1–2);
(8) a final song of rejoicing in which Israelites are joined by many others
(Deut 32:43; Isa 14:4–8); and (9) hebraicized concepts of gentile religion
(Deut 32:7–8; Isa 14:12–15).

The Burden of Babylon also expresses four basic phases of the generic
cycle of history found in the Song of Moses and in classical prophetic writings.
These resemble but are not identical with the historical contexts discussed earlier. They include —

1. Contemporary international problems ranging from 701 to 648 B.C.
   (compare particularly the indictments in the taunt song with those of
   Amos 1:2–2:3).
2. The return of the remnant, marking the end of YHWH's anger against
   Israel (compare Mic 2:12–13; Isa 37:32).
3. The general destruction of the wicked; this may represent an eschatological time frame linked to the "day of YHWH" (Isa 13:6), which includes
   the alteration of reliable natural phenomena (compare Amos 8:8–9).
4. The conclusion of the process, when there is a final rejoicing in a restored
   moral order that extends beyond Israel (compare Mic 4:1–5; 7:8–20;
   Amos 9:7–15; Hos 2:18–22); in one form or another, all the classical
   prophets depict this time.

The deliberate assemblage of prophecies in the Burden of Babylon, attested
to by parallels with earlier and later writings, thus suggests that the time frame
which is the object of the passage actually consists of a range of times comparable to that found in the Song of Moses. It forms a continuum beginning
with the troubles of Isaiah's generation, and possibly the rebellion of 652 B.C.,
but extending through the whole course of Yahwist history to the return of the
remnant and the final purge and transfiguration of the earth.

Historical selectivity, the prophetic use of history to depict this process, is
thus pronounced in one respect, namely in the synthesis of several historical
contexts to portray Babylon's destruction and the activities of the Tyrant. In
another respect historical selectivity, and indeed the entire question of the
short-term fulfillment of the prophecy, becomes largely irrelevant. The prophecy transcends time. For that reason, whether individual segments of it were
written down before or after the contemporary events on which they are
based is unimportant. There are no localized pieces of *Heilsgeschichte* or
Unheilsgechichte; there is only generalized information about patterns of present

and future events throughout an overall continuum of time. Lindblom notes this deliberate imprecision in prophecy but does not attempt to explain its purpose.[112]

In the Burden of Babylon, the purpose is evidently to offer not predictive but projective prophecy. Taken as a whole, Isaiah 13–14 demonstrates (1) YHWH's basic cycle of intervention, as also outlined in the Song of Moses; (2) the validity of the cycle for contemporary conditions; (3) the relevance of other Isaianic writings, such as 10:12–19, which shows Assyria moving from a position as YHWH's tool to the object of his anger; and (4) a definition of the power which will cause suffering throughout the continuum and against which YHWH will intervene, namely, a dominant military power (Assyria), acting for an agent of cultural and religious orthodoxy (Babylon), under the rule of a hubristic ruler (Helal ben Shachar), and standing in opposition to Zion, to the return of the remnant, and to Zion's king.

Although there are clear grounds for accepting the validity of discernible segments of the Burden of Babylon as prophecy or history, the idea of prophetic prerogative is not so much disproven as rendered irrelevant. Instead, we see true typological imperative: the mixing and blending of contemporary experience, through the superimposition of established eschatological and historical views, to depict the forces that will shape the end of history. Since the author(s) and compiler(s) of Isaiah 13 and 14 apparently well understood the religious and political dynamics of the time, the Burden of Babylon also represents a systematic depiction of future trends in Yahwist history. It is a richer, more complex manifestation of the achievements we find in Isaiah 19 and in Hosea, and also hinted at in the Song of Moses.

In a civilization where much of divine behavior (as evidenced by the thousands of Baru oracles) was perceived as being arbitrary and capricious, the historical outlook of the Burden of Babylon was ennobling to man and subversive of both Eastern and Western Semitic orthodoxy. YHWH, as Lord of history, reconciles justice and mercy. A righteous man could hope to contact him and cooperate with his plan. Armed with such a knowledge of him, a just man could gain understanding from the past, thrust and purpose for the present, and hope for the future. Faith and reason combine to help him understand human destiny, to recognize that behind every turn of history there operates an All-knowing and All-powerful Divine Love.

NOTES

1. See Robert P. Carroll, *When Prophecy Failed* (New York: Seabury Press, 1979), 111–28.
2. See James L. Crenshaw, *Prophetic Conflict* (West Berlin: Walter de Gruyter, 1971), 49–62.
3. Carroll, *When Prophecy Failed*, 124–28.

4. Roland K. Harrison, *An Introduction to the Old Testament* (Grand Rapids, Mich.: Wm. Eerdmans, 1970), 636–62.

5. Meredith G. Kline, *Treaty of the Great King* (Grand Rapids, Mich.: Wm. Eerdmans, 1963), 27–44, esp. 41–43.

6. Andrew D. H. Mayes, *Deuteronomy*, New Century Bible Commentary (Grand Rapids, Mich.: Wm. Eerdmans, 1981), 380–93.

7. Georg Fohrer, *Introduction to the New Testament* (Nashville: Abingdon Press, 1968), 189–90.

8. Gerhard von Rad, *Deuteronomy*, OTL, trans. D. Barton (Philadelphia: Westminster Press, 1966), 196–97.

9. Ibid., 198–99.

10. William F. Albright, "Some Remarks on the Song of Moses in Deuteronomy XXXII," *VT* 9 (1959): 339–46; William F. Albright, *Yahweh and the Gods of Canaan* (New York: Doubleday, 1968), 17–19; Otto Eissfeldt, "Das Lied Moses Deuteronomy 32:1–43 und das Lehrgedicht Asaphs Psalm 78 samt einer Analyses der Umgebung des Moseliedes," in *Berichte über die Verhandlungen der Sächsischen Akademie der Wissenschaften zu Leipzig* (Leipzig, East Germany: Philologisch-Historische Klasse, Band 104, Heft 5, 1958), 13–15; G. Ernest Wright, "The Lawsuit of God: A Form–Critical Study of Deuteronomy 32," in *Israel's Prophetic Heritage*, ed. Bernhard W. Anderson (New York: Harper, 1962), 26–67; Patrick Skehan, "Qumran and the Present State of Old Testament Text Studies: The Masoretic Text," *JBL* 78 (1959): 22; Patrick Skehan, "A Fragment of the 'Song of Moses' (Deut. 32) from Qumran," *BASOR* 136 (1954): 12–15; Patrick Skehan, "The Structure of the Song of Moses in Deuteronomy," *CBQ* 13 (1951): 153–63 (Skehan does not suggest a specific date but considers the Song quite old); J. Arthur Thompson, *Deuteronomy: An Introduction and Commentary* (Wheaton, Ill.: Inter-Varsity Press, 1977), 296–98; Frank Moore Cross, Jr., *Canaanite Myth and Hebrew Epic* (Cambridge: Harvard University Press, 1973), 264; David Noel Freedman, "Divine Names and Titles in Early Hebrew Poetry," in *Magnalia Dei: The Mighty Acts of God*, ed. F. M. Cross et al. (New York: Doubleday, 1976), 77–80, 97; David A. Robertson, *Linguistic Evidence for Dating Early Hebrew Poetry* (New Haven, Conn.: Yale University Press, 1976), 153–55; George E. Mendenhall, "Samuel's Broken *RIB:* Deuteronomy 32," in *No Famine in the Land*, ed. James W. Flanagan and Anita Weisbrod Robinson (Claremont, Calif.: Scholars Press, 1975), 63–74; Claus Schedl, *History of the Old Testament* (New York: Alba House, 1973), 2:235 (Schedl does not actually date the Song but cites a scholarly consensus that it is one of the most ancient portions of the Pentateuch); John Bright, *History of Israel* (Philadelphia: Westminster Press, 1981), 147; P. Kyle McCarter, Jr., *I Samuel* (Garden City, N.Y.: Doubleday, 1980), 76; William J. Moran, "Deuteronomy," in *Jerome Bible Commentary* (New York: Prentice-Hall, 1968), 275.

11. Eissfeldt, "Das Lied Moses Deuteronomy 32:1–43."

12. Albright, *Yahweh and the Gods of Canaan;* Albright, "Song of Moses."

13. Wright, "Lawsuit of God," 66–67.

14. H. W. F. Saggs, letter to the author, dated 27 January 1986.

15. Freedman, "Divine Names and Titles."

16. Theodor Oestreicher, *Das Deuteronomische Grundgesetz* (Goutersloh, West Germany: C. Bertelsmann, 1923); R. Brinker, *The Influence of Sanctuaries in Early Israel* (Manchester, England: Manchester University Press, 1946), 189–228, esp. 205–11, 223–28; Edward Robertson, *The Old Testament Problem* (Manchester, England: Manchester University Press, 1950), 33–55, esp. 41–43.

17. This harmony among people is not necessarily specifically Hebrew, much less exilic. Many cultures have accounts of a past or future "golden age." H. W. F. Saggs (*The Greatness That Was Babylon* [New York: Praeger, 1962], 329) cites a Sumerian text describing how people of many nations (Sumer, Akkad, Assyria or Elam, and the Semitic nomads of the west) originally lived together in peace, giving praise to Enlil.

18. Harrison, *Introduction to the Old Testament*, 218; Chaim Herzog and Mordeca'i Gichon, *Battles of the Bible* (New York: Random House, 1978), 115–21.

19. See Brian Peckham, "Israel and Phoenicia," in *Magnalia Dei*, 236–37.

20. George E. Mendenhall, "Social Organization in Ancient Israel," in *Magnalia Dei*, 148.

21. Frank H. Seilhammer, "The Role of the Covenant in the Mission and Message of Amos," in *A Light unto My Path*, ed. Howard N. Bream, Ralph D. Heim, and Carey A. Moore (Philadelphia: Temple University Press, 1974), 446–47.

22. Albright, *Yahweh and the Gods of Canaan*, 240. The emendation from "King of Edom" to "Human Sacrifice" involves only a shift of vowels. *Šēdîm* ("demons") is found only in Ps. 106:37; Deut. 32:17; and Albright's reading of Amos 2:1.

23. Johannes Lindblom, *Prophecy in Ancient Israel* (Phildelphia: Fortress Press, 1962), 242, 281; Carrol, *When Prophecy Failed*, 18–19.

24. Lindblom, *Prophecy in Ancient Israel*, 316–18. A comparatively early date for Deuteronomy 32 could provide evidence for a preprophetic popular eschatology. Lindblom finds the lack of such evidence the principal objection to Gressmann's hypothesis. Deut. 32:43 may also contain the "eschatological remnant" that Carroll (*When Prophecy Failed*, 26–28, esp. 37) finds generally lacking.

25. Lindblom, *Prophecy in Ancient Israel*, 165–68, 243; John Mauchline, *IB*, 6:560–63; Henry McKeating, *Amos, Hosea, Micah*, Cambridge Bible Commentary (Cambridge: Cambridge University Press, 1971), 75–78.

26. Mauchline (*IB*, 6:560–63) summarizes the argument.

27. Foster R. McCurley, "The Home of Deuteronomy Revisited: A Methodological Analysis of Northern Theory," in *A Light unto My Path*, 298, cites dozens of seeming parallels of language and theme between Deuteronomy and Hosea, as developed by Hans Walter Wolff, "Dodekapropheten I: Hosea," 14 *BKAT* (1961).

28. See Lindblom, *Prophecy in Ancient Israel*, 391–92. However, Mauchline (*IB*, 6:559) and McKeating (*Amos, Hosea, and Micah*, 151–53) consider Hosea 14 authentic.

29. See A. S. Van der Woude, "Three Classical Prophets: Amos, Hosea and Micah," in *Israel's Prophetic Tradition*, ed. Richard Coggins, Anthony Phillips, and Michael Knibb (Cambridge: Cambridge University Press, 1983), 49–51. See also Otto Eissfeldt, *The Old Testament: An Introduction* (New York: Harper and Row, 1965), 409–12. Eissfeldt finds that nothing before Micah 7:7 is indisputably exilic.

30. Lindblom, *Prophecy in Ancient Israel*, 250–51; Rolland E. Wolfe, *IB*, 6:899–901, 921; McKeating, *Amos, Hosea, Micah*, 170.

31. See Avraham Gileadi, *The Apocalyptic Book of Isaiah* (Provo, Utah: Hebraeus Press, 1983), 171–88; and Avraham Gileadi, *The Literary Message of Isaiah*, forthcoming.

32. Gileadi, *Apocalyptic Book of Isaiah*, 174–76.

33. See Seth Erlandsson, *The Burden of Babylon* (Lund, Sweden: Gleerup, 1970), 47; A. S. Herbert, *Isaiah 1–39*, Cambridge Bible Commentary (Cambridge: Cambridge University Press, 1971), 143–44; R. B. Y. Scott, *IB*, 5:203, 234, 239.

34. Gileadi, *Apocalyptic Book of Isaiah*, 194–95.

35. Scott, *IB*, 5:234–35; Jerusalem Bible, 1157.

36. Scott, *IB*, 5:272; Herbert, *Isaiah 1–39*, 113; Jerusalem Bible, 1169.

37. Scott, *IB*, 5:222ff.; Herbert, *Isaiah 1–39*, 67–71; Jerusalem Bible, 1151–57.

38. See Saggs, *Babylon*, 240–43; Hermann Barth, *Die Jesaja-Worte in der Josiahzeit* (Neukirchen–Vluyn, West Germany: Neukirchener Verlag, 1977), 242–43.

39. *ANET*, 283–84.

40. Albert T. E. Olmstead, *History of Assyria* (New York: Scribner's, 1923), 201.

41. *ANET*, 284:10–17.

42. H. H. Rowley, "The Samaritan Schism in History and Legend," in *Israel's Prophetic Heritage*, 209.

43. *ANET*, 288. This is the second-largest deportation for which numbers are recorded, exceeded only by the 208,000 Sennacherib resettled from Babylonia.

44. See Erlandsson, *Burden of Babylon*, 91.

45. Rowley, "Samaritan Schism," 210–11.

46. See Avraham Gileadi, "The Davidic Covenant: A Theological Basis for Corporate Protection," in this volume.

47. Olmstead, *History of Assyria*, 164–66; Saggs, *Babylon*, 145–46; H. W. F. Saggs, *The Might That Was Assyria* (London: Sidgewick & Jackson, 1983), 203–4. There are comparable Egyptian texts attributing all divine activity to Ptah. Cleanthes' *Hymn to Zeus* (quoted by Paul) expresses this belief in an advanced form.

48. Saggs, *Assyria*, 125–29.

49. Scott (*IB*, 5:297–98) offers a postexilic model based on an assumed triumph over Moab; Herbert (*Isaiah 1–39*, 143–44, 155–56) suggests that substantial portions of chapter 26 could be earlier hymns imbedded in the so-called Apocalypse of chapters 24–26.

50. Carroll, *When Prophecy Failed*, 127.

51. Ibid., 127–28.

52. Edward J. Young, *The Book of Isaiah* (Grand Rapids, Mich.: Wm. Eerdmans, 1969), 2:13–26.

53. Erlandsson, *Burden of Babylon*, 76–80.

54. Otto Proksch, *Jesaja I*, Kommentar zum Alten Testament (Leipzig, East Germany: A. Deichert, 1930), 240ff.

55. Eissfeldt, *The Old Testament*, 321.

56. Herbert, *Isaiah 1–39*, 121–26; John Bright, "Isaiah," in *Peake's Commentary on the Bible* (London: Thomas Nelson, 1962), 502–3.

57. Aage Bentzen, *Introduction to the Old Testament* (Copenhagen: G. E. C. Gadd, 1964), 2:107; Elmer A. Leslie, *Isaiah* (Philadelphia: Abingdon, 1963), 67–69; Artur Weiser, *The Old Testament: Its Formation and Development* (New York: Association Press, 1961), 191; R. B. Y. Scott, *IB*, 5:278–80; Jerusalem Bible, 1171.

58. James H. Breasted, *A History of Egypt* (New York: Bantam Books, 1964), 444–48, 457–58.

59. Ibid., 464–70; Bustenay Oded, *Mass Deportations and Deportees in the Neo-Assyrian Empire* (Wiesbaden, West Germany: Ludwig Reichert Verlag, 1979), 122, 134. Oded cites deportations from Memphis under Esarhaddon; and to Memphis under Ashurbanipal; from Thebes and Unu under Ashurbanipal; and from Kirbit to "Egypt" under Ashurbanipal.

60. Karl Butzer, "Perspectives on Irrigation Civilization in Pharaonic Egypt," in *Immortal Egypt*, ed. D. Schmandt-Besserat (Malibu, Calif.: Urbana Press, 1978), 13–18.

61. Breasted, *A History of Egypt*, 474–75, 481–84.

62. Ibid., 491–92.

63. Ibid.

64. Saggs, *Assyria*, 178.

65. Erlandsson, *Burden of Babylon*, 76–80.

66. Gileadi, *Apocalyptic Book of Isaiah*, 194–98.

67. Breasted, *A History of Egypt*, 496.

68. Erlandsson, *Burden of Babylon*, 80; Bright, "Isaiah," 503; Josephus *Antiquities* 13.3.1.

69. Breasted, *A History of Egypt*, 298–300.

70. Sidney Smith, *Cambridge Ancient History* (Cambridge: Cambridge University Press, 1929), 3:29.

71. Wright, "Lawsuit of God," 32, n. 20.

72. Saggs, *Assyria*, 203–4.

73. Saggs, *Babylon*, 145–46.

74. Ibid., 148–49.

75. Koran, V.70–85ff.; LXII.5ff.

76. Lindblom, *Prophecy in Ancient Israel*, 199, n. 149; Crenshaw, *Prophetic Conflict*, 51, n. 39.

77. Among many: Scott, *IB*, 5:254–64, esp. 254–55, 258–59; Bentzen, *Introduction to the Old Testament*, 2:107; Eissfeldt, *The Old Testament*, 317, 319–20; Leslie, *Isaiah*, 119–26.

78. A. Robert and A. Feuillet, *Introduction to the Old Testament* (New York: Desclee, 1968), 287, 337; Barth, *Die Jesaja-Worte*, 135–40 (the theme of Barth's book is the discernible existence of an "Assyrian redaction," including many portions of Isaiah [notably chapter 14],

dating from the time of Josiah); Young, *Book of Isaiah*, 1:408–53, esp. 409–13; Erlandsson, *Burden of Babylon*, 165–66.

79. Herbert, *Isaiah 1–39*, 98, 102, 104; Gileadi, *Apocalyptic Book of Isaiah*, esp. 194–205; Scott, *IB*, 5:254, 259, 264. (Scott suggests a composite from several different times, with parts of the Song of Mockery possibly having an Isaianic origin. Although he considers an exilic date probable, he suggests a clearly generic application for chapter 14.)

80. Herbert, *Isaiah 1–39*, 102; Robert and Feuillet, *Introduction to the Old Testament*, 287.

81. Erlandsson, *Burden of Babylon*, 126.

82. Ibid., 82ff.

83. Olmstead, *History of Assyria*, 395–99, 405.

84. Erlandsson, *Burden of Babylon*, 91, 125–26; John Brinkman, in a letter to the author dated 8 November 1985.

85. Saggs, *Assyria*, 105; Olmstead, *History of Assyria*, 347–48; *ARAB*, 2:150–51 (destruction) and 2:242–43 (rebuilding).

86. Saggs, *Assyria*, 94–95. This is of course based on Sargon's famous memorandum to Ashur about the campaign of 714 B.C.; the text is in *ARAB*, 2:73–79.

87. Saggs, *Assyria*, 103, 114–16; Oded, *Mass Deportations*, 20–21, 41–45, 112.

88. For Shalmanesar V: Saggs, *Assyria*, 92, 189; Olmstead, *History of Assyria*, 206. For Rebellion: Olmstead, *History of Assyria*, 474–75; for Ashurbanipal's silencing of the "vulgar mouths": *ARAB*, 2:795.

89. John Brinkman, *Prelude to Empire: Babylon in the Seventh Century* (Philadelphia: University Museum, 1984), 61, 67–68, n. 321.

90. Saggs, *Assyria*, 105–6, 128, 187–89; Saggs, *Babylon*, 148–49.

91. Eissfeldt, *The Old Testament*, 5:157, 328–29; Herbert, *Isaiah 1–39*, 201, 203, 207–8; Scott, *IB*, 5:157, 368; Young, *Book of Isaiah*, 2:487–89.

92. Gileadi translation, *Apocalyptic Book of Isaiah*, 93–94.

93. Saggs, *Assyria*, 234, 264–65.

94. Ibid., 203, 235.

95. *ANET*, 111–17; *ARAB*, 2:156, 180, 229. Anzu is a synonym for martial ferocity in inscriptions of Ashurnasirpal II and Shalmanesar III.

96. James B. Pritchard, ed., *The Ancient Near East* (Princeton, N.J.: Princeton University Press, 1971), 2:17–26, contains a collated text of the myth.

97. Gileadi translation, *Apocalyptic Book of Isaiah*, 44–45.

98. *ANET*, 24–26

99. Ibid., 62–65.

100. William H. Shea, "Sennacherib's Second Palestinian Campaign," *JBL* 104/3 (1985): 410–18, esp. 406–11.

101. J. B. Geyer, "Twisting Tiamat's Tail: A Mythological Interpretation of Isaiah 13:5 and 8," *VT* 37 (1987): 164–79.

102. Bright, "Isaiah," 504–5; Hugo Winckler, *Die Keilsschrifte Sargons* (Leipzig, East Germany: Pfeiffer, 1889).

103. John Bright, *A History of Israel* (Philadelphia: Westminster Press, 1981), 311, 313–14; Bustenay Oded, "Judah and the Exile," in *Israelite and Judaean History* (Philadelphia: Westminster Press, 1977), 454–56; Jacob M. Myers, *II Chronicles*, Anchor Bible, 198–99; John Brinkman, in a letter to the author, dated 8 November 1985.

104. Brinkman, *Prelude*, 25, 37, 92–94, 103–4.

105. For Shamash-shum-ukin's motives and the danger of encountering even a single loyal vassal, see Robert W. Rogers, *History of Babylonia and Assyria* (Salem, N.H.: Ayer Co. Publishing, 1900), 2:242–43, 263–64. For these and the Kedarite raid, see Smith, in *Cambridge Ancient History*, 3:121–24; Olmstead, *History of Assyria*, 395–99, 400–3, 442, 472–74; *ARAB*, 2:302–3, 313–14, 335–36.

106. Saggs, *Assyria*, 234, 264–65.

107. For Medean attacks on Nineveh in 653 and 652 B.C., see Herodotus 1.102–3; Richard N. Frye, *The Heritage of Persia* (New York: New American Library, 1966), 94; Georges Roux, *Ancient Iraq* (New York: World Publishing Company, 1964), 275, 310–11; George C. Cameron, *History of Early Iran* (1936; reprint, New York: Greenwood Press, 1968), 177, 183; Albert T. E. Olmstead, *History of the Persian Empire* (Chicago: Phoenix Books, 1948), 29–31; R. Ghirshman, *Iran* (London: Penguin, 1961), 98, 119. For the role of Elamite palace revolutions, and the diplomatic negotiations accompanying each change of regime, see Walther Hinz, *The Lost World of Elam*, trans. from *Das Reich Elam* (New York: New York University Press, 1973), 150–51; Cameron, *History of Early Iran*, 190–96; Saggs, *Babylon*, 130–33; Brinkman, *Prelude*, 30, 96, 98–102; *ARAB*, 2:335–37.

108. Arnold Toynbee, *A Study of History* (New York: Galaxy Press, 1962), 1:78–79, 118–19, esp. 118, n. 1.

109. James L. Crenshaw, "The Human Dilemma and the Literature of Dissent," in *Tradition and Theology in the Old Testament*, ed. Douglas A. Knight (Philadelphia: Fortress Press, 1977), 235–36.

110. T. K. Cheyne, "Recent Study of Isaiah," *JBL* 15 (1896): 28.

111. See Gileadi, *Apocalyptic Book of Isaiah*, 181–83. All but the third and seventh parallels of the main body are antithetical.

112. Lindblom, *Prophecy in Ancient Israel*, 199.

15

A Holistic Typology of Prophecy and Apocalyptic

Ronald Youngblood

That prophecy and apocalyptic[1] are in some sense distinct from each other is a truism that will be taken for granted here. At the same time, however, it must be asserted as forcefully as possible that the differences between the two have often been grossly overdrawn at the expense of the undoubted similarities that exist between them. It is the thesis of this essay that the basic themes of Hebrew apocalyptic[2] are derived from and are developments of Hebrew prophecy and that the relationship between prophetic writings on the one hand and apocalypses on the other is one of harmony rather than of cacophony.

APOCALYPTIC DEFINED

The late E. J. Carnell used to remind the students in his systematic theology classes that "definitions are neither true nor false; they are merely useful." He meant of course that communication is only as precise as the extent to which the communicators agree on the definitions of the words they use. B. Vawter has made the helpful observation that "Hermann Gunkel protested that 'apocalyptic' was a word too readily used by authors who did not have an agreed definition of what it meant."[3] We are apparently no closer to a consensus on this matter than we were a century ago. Definitions of *apocalyptic* tend to be either so general as to be vacuous[4] or so specific as to eliminate from consideration a substantial number of erstwhile apocalypses.[5] In fact, many scholars despair of defining the term at all and resort instead to listing the characteristics that they feel apply most closely to apocalyptic as a religio–philosophical worldview and to apocalypse as a literary genre reflecting that worldview.

APOCALYPTIC CHARACTERIZED

An often-cited list of characteristics of apocalyptic is that of J. Lindblom:[6] artificial claims to inspiration, cosmological survey, division of time into periods, dualism, esoterism, mythology, numerology, pessimistic historical surveys, pseudo-ecstasy, pseudonymity, teaching of Two Ages, transcendentalism.[7] Needless to say, numerous others could be—and have been—added and/or suggested,[8] since there is virtually no end to the number of qualities that have at one time or other been assigned or attributed to that elusive entity known as apocalyptic.

The problem with all such lists (and the problem becomes more serious as a list lengthens) is manifold. No single apocalypse includes every item in the list, and in fact some well-known apocalypses contain very few of them. Some of the items tend to be more characteristic of later apocalypses than of earlier ones. Quite often, no attempt is made by a list's proponent to distinguish between what is essential to apocalyptic and what is incidental to it. And the differing lengths of and items within the various lists make us suspicious about the validity of the entire enterprise.

Attempts to differentiate between what is basic and what is secondary in apocalyptic[9] do not materially alleviate the dilemma, since it is impossible to secure agreement in these areas as well. One scholar's nomination of a secondary characteristic falls into the basic list of another, and vice versa.

Is there, then, no way out of this predicament? Are all attempts to define or characterize apocalyptic doomed to failure? By no means. Virtually all students of the subject agree on at least two features of Hebrew apocalyptic: it contains a strongly futuristic and/or eschatological dimension,[10] and its ultimate wellspring is Israelite prophecy.[11] For the purposes of this essay, I shall therefore attempt a working definition of Hebrew apocalyptic: it consists of one or more emphases within and developments of the eschatological aspects of Israel's prophetic movement.

APOCALYPTIC DATED

Since many features of canonical Hebrew apocalyptic are especially characteristic of noncanonical intertestamental apocalypses, Old Testament apocalypses (such as Isa 24–27; Daniel; Zech 12–14) are routinely dated quite late. It is therefore appropriate at this point to remind ourselves of the *caveat* expressed long ago in a similar situation by Robert Dick Wilson: "No one can maintain that because a word occurs only in a [demonstrably] late document the word itself is late for in this case, if a late document was the only survival of a once numerous body of literature, every word in it would be late, which is absurd."[12] It is becoming increasingly evident that much Hebrew apocalyptic is in fact quite early and that, for example, nothing in Isaiah 24–27 precludes composition in the late eighth or early seventh century B.C. The apocalyptic themes in Isaiah had to begin at some point in time; why not then?

The problems of isolating the origins of apocalyptic and of dating the various Hebrew apocalypses are admittedly complex.[13] As noted previously, definition and characterization enter the picture, as do preconceived notions about the very possibility of the existence of an apocalyptic *Weltanschauung* in the preexilic period. There would seem to be no formidable reasons, however, to deny the emergence of at least an embryonic form of apocalyptic to the time of Amos and Hosea or slightly earlier.[14]

APOCALYPTIC RELATED TO PROPHECY

The opinion that Hebrew apocalyptic is in some way related to Hebrew prophecy has become axiomatic in recent years.[15] Whether that relationship, however, concerns apocalyptic's origins in prophecy, or its development from prophecy, or its mutation of prophecy, or merely its similarities to prophecy will surely continue to be hotly debated.

The Greek word *apokalypsis* is used in the New Testament to refer to a present revelation or disclosure of something formerly hidden or to a future revelation or disclosure of something presently hidden (Luke 2:32; Rom 2:5; 8:19; 16:25; 1 Cor 14:6, 26; 2 Cor 12:7; Eph 1:17; 3:3; 1 Pet 4:13). The visionary aspect of the term is implicit in many of its New Testament contexts and becomes explicit in 2 Cor. 12:1 (compare also Gal 2:2). A particularly noteworthy use of *apokalypsis* is its frequent occurrence before *Iēsou Christou* (Gal 1:12), especially when it has reference to the *parousia* (1 Pet 1:7, 13; compare 1 Cor 1:7; 2 Thess 1:7). The phrase *apokalypsis Iēsou Christou* finally becomes virtually a technical expression—indeed, for all practical purposes the title of a book—in Rev. 1:1.

The author of the Book of Revelation—the Apocalypse, as we also call it—informs us at the beginning and end of his work that he considers it to be a *prophēteia* ("prophecy," Rev 1:3; 22:7, 10, 18–19; the words *apokalypsis* and *prophēteia* are found in the same context also in 1 Cor 14:6). This does not mean that prophecy and apocalyptic are identical, of course. But it does mean that John thought of his "apocalypse" as being in some sense a "prophecy"—and therefore, as Vawter puts it, "the association of apocalyptic with prophecy in the ancient mind should impose on us the obligation to be very clear in our own mind regarding the basis on which we distinguish the two."[16]

R. K. Harrison issues the further salutary warning that "it is important for a distinction to be drawn between biblical and non-biblical apocalyptic, and to avoid reading into the canonical Scriptures thought that either occurred in Jewish apocryphal and pseudepigraphal literature of a subsequent period, or that was foreign to the thought of Judaism altogether."[17] The idea that the origins of even Hebrew apocalyptic were foreign, and especially Persian, has become virtually *de rigueur* in some circles.[18] T. W. Manson has gone so far as to suggest that the Sadducees of the Intertestamental Period called their opponents Pharisees (which means simply "Persians," according to Manson) because the eschatological teachings of the latter bore unmistakable resemblances to those of Zoroastrianism.[19]

It would appear, however, that a developing consensus will finally lay to rest the insistence that Persian influence was a necessary element in apocalyptic. "The unfolding of Israelite concepts, as for example the development of the doctrine of resurrection, was always the chief factor in the variations of apocalyptic."[20] Since Hebrew apocalyptic did not emerge in a totally Israelite context, it is understandable that foreign influences would have a minor impact on it. But when all is said and done, "Hebrew prophecy and not some other source is the true origin from which apocalyptic sprang."[21]

Very few would deny, of course, that apocalyptic and prophecy represent two somewhat different worldviews or that apocalypses and prophetic writings are two reasonably distinguishable literary genres. Agreement concerning precisely what constitutes the differences and distinctions between the two forms is not easy to find, and scholars routinely demolish the best-laid arguments of their colleagues.[22] As it turns out, a number of basic themes are shared by prophets and apocalyptists, whereas the distinguishing characteristics (where present) are almost always matters of emphasis. Two cases in point are eschatology and ethics.

Prophetic eschatology tends to emphasize the redemptive and judgmental activity of God in short-term as well as in long-term contexts. The day of YHWH will come soon, and it will also come in the end times. By contrast, apocalyptic eschatology focuses almost exclusively on end-time divine activity.

Prophetic ethics is very much concerned about the divine demand for repentance, social justice, righteous conduct, etc. The prophets' all-consuming desire was to turn the people of their times back to obedience of Moses' laws as a reflection of YHWH's holy requirements. By contrast, ethics does not receive the same amount of attention in apocalyptic because of its teaching that the righteous suffering remnant will be the recipients of divine salvation in the *eschaton*. Emphasis tends to be placed on consolation rather than on condemnation.[23]

Apocalyptic, then, is prophecy continued, prophecy developed, prophecy adapted to new needs in new situations. It is, in the words of B. W. Anderson, "prophecy in a new idiom,"[24] and "the [Old Testament] prophets themselves became the first of the apocalyptists."[25] It should therefore come as no surprise to us that the prophets and apocalyptists of the Hebrew Bible should share—though admittedly with somewhat different emphases—what we have chosen to call a holistic typology of theological themes. I should like to conclude this essay by illustrating that thesis from an early Israelite apocalypse.

APOCALYPTIC IN ISAIAH 24–27

Vawter notes that Isaiah 24–27 "is commonly called 'the Isaiah apocalypse'; but some distinguished authorities . . . utterly reject this title."[26] H. H. Rowley, for example, excludes the section from his discussion of Hebrew apocalyptic.[27] Most scholars, however, assign Isaiah 24–27 to the genre of apocalypse.[28] But trying to be sensitive to those who are reluctant to call Isaiah 24–27 an apocalypse, and preferring to err on the side of caution, I will speak rather of apocalyptic *in* Isaiah 24–27 than of all of Isaiah 24–27 as an example of Hebrew apocalyptic.

"This section of Isaiah contains the largest concentration of apocalyptic elements."[29] It bears the same relationship to chapters 13–23 as Isaiah 34–35 does to chapters 28–33. "In each case an apocalyptic section provides a dramatic conclusion to the preceding chapters."[30] The prophetic oracles against the nations in chapters 13–23 are followed by a series of apocalyptic oracles against the whole earth in chapters 24–27.

Features often claimed as characteristic in the apocalyptic literary genre are relatively common in Isaiah 24–27. The eschatological day of YHWH, on which he will punish the wicked and bless the righteous, is alluded to once in each of the first three chapters (24:21; 25:9; 26:1), and four times in the fourth (27:1, 2, 12, 13),[31] for a total of seven times in all. The phrase "in that day" is used frequently elsewhere in Isaiah as well (see especially 2:11, 17, 20; 10:20, 27; 12:1, 4; 52:6). Judgment on the day of YHWH will be cosmic in nature; judgment will overtake the entire world (24:1–13, 18b–23; 26:20–21; see also 2:19, 21; 13:13; 63:3–6; 66:14–16; Zeph 1:18). Phenomena associated with that day include the darkening of and other visible changes in the sun and moon (24:23; see also 13:10; 60:19; Joel 2:10, 31; Amos 5:18, 20; Zeph 1:15); earthquake and thunder (24:18b–19; see also 13:13; Joel 3:16); the drying up and withering of the earth's plant life (24:4, 7; see also 15:6; 16:8; 19:7; 34:4); the divine descent as YHWH punishes the world's wickedness (26:21; see also 64:1; 66:14–16); and fire as an instrument of his judgment (26:11; see also 1:31; 33:11–14; 34:9–10).

Especially striking is the recurrent image of the destroyed city (referred to in each of the four chapters: 24:10; 25:2; 26:5; 27:10)—unidentified (deliberately, it would seem) and therefore probably paradigmatic of all sinful cities. Judgment against unrighteousness is inevitable, a fact underscored by employing a triple threat, sometimes with alliteration and assonance *(paḥad wāpaḥat wāpāḥ*, "terror and pit and snare"; 24:17–18a; see Jer 48:43–44; compare Amos 5:19). Isaiah uses the literary technique of merismus to emphasize that sinners of all classes will be judged (24:2; see also 1:6; 3:1–3; 41:19; Jer 7:9; for the priest/people pair in Isa 24:2, see Hos 4:9).

In short, the entire world is under a divine curse (24:6; see also Mal 4:6) with only a tiny remnant of its inhabitants left (24:13; 27:12; see also 13:12; 17:6). The godly survivors collectively declare their woe (24:16b) in terms reminiscent of Isaiah's lament at the time of his prophetic call (6:5).[32]

YHWH's judgment reaches its climax in 27:1, where mythological language (often claimed as a particularly characteristic feature of apocalypse) is used symbolically to stress the cosmic aspects of divine punishment. Leviathan, dragon of the watery chaos, was destroyed by Anath and/or Baal in the mists of the remote mythological past, according to an ancient Canaanite text that contains almost verbatim parallels to the phraseology of Isa. 27:1.[33] In Isaiah, however, Leviathan is effectively demythologized (in the best sense of that term) and becomes a symbol of YHWH's fiercest enemies in the eschatological future (see also 30:7; 51:9–10, where a monster called Rahab symbolizes Egypt; see further Ezek 29:3; 32:2). After their final defeat, YHWH rules on Zion, the holy mountain (24:23; 25:6–7, 10; 27:13; see also 2:2–4 [= Mic 4:1-3]; 11:6–9; 56:7; 57:13; 60:3–5; 65:25; 66:20; Zech 14:16), where he spreads an eschatological banquet for his faithful followers (25:6–8; compare Rev 19:9). Resurrection, both national and personal, is the order of the day (26:19 [contrast v 14]; see also Ezek 37:11–12; Dan 12:2; Hos 14:5), and Death, the great swallower (compare 5:14; Jonah 2:2; Hab 2:5),[34] will himself be swallowed up forever (25:8). Sorrow will cease (25:8; see also 35:10 [= 51:11]), and the righteous will be blessed by YHWH at the onset of the messianic age (27:6;[35] see also 4:2; 11:1, 10; 32:15; 44:3). Isaiah's apocalypse is justifiably punctuated by songs of joy at the anticipated deliverance of YHWH's faithful remnant (24:14–16a; 25:1–5, 9; 26:1–15; see also 12:1–3, 4–6; 42:12; 48:20; 52:7–10; 54:1; 63:7–64:12; 66:10). YHWH's anger against his people will be shown to have been brief indeed (26:20; compare 10:25; 54:7–8), and perfect peace will ensue (26:3–4, 12; see also 30:15; 57:19; contrast Jer 6:14; 8:11). In retrospect, all of this will be seen to have come about because of YHWH's predetermined plan (25:1; see also 14:24, 26–27; 23:8–9).

CONCLUSION

This brief survey of Isaiah 24–27 has demonstrated that its major apocalyptic themes are strikingly paralleled elsewhere — not only in apocalyptic sections of other prophetic books but also in nonapocalyptic sections (including all parts of Isaiah itself). Similar comparisons can easily be adduced for the other apocalyptic passages in the Hebrew Bible, since common typological themes provide a basic theological similarity between prophecy and apocalyptic. In short, a holistic typology informs both literary genres. G. Ladd's question of thirty years ago — "Why not prophetic-apocalyptic?"[36] — could justifiably be asked today. And with him I would respond: Why not indeed?

NOTES

1.   In this essay *prophecy* and *apocalyptic* will be understood as movements or schools of thought that attempt to comprehend and explain God's relationship to his people, theirs to him, and his expectations of them; *prophetic writing* and *apocalypse* will refer to the written expression of those schools of thought and, as such, will therefore often overlap with *prophecy* and *apocalyptic* (as commonly occurs in the literature on the subject); and *prophet(s)* and

apocalyptist(s) will be used to describe the literary protagonist(s) of the respective movements.

2. We are concerned here only with canonical Hebrew apocalyptic. Consideration of later Jewish (and other) apocalyptic would take us too far afield.

3. Bruce Vawter, "Apocalyptic: Its Relation to Prophecy," *CBQ* 22 (1960): 33.

4. Typical is the attempt by G. E. Ladd, who describes "the essence of apocalyptic religion" as a "twofold work of catastrophic judgment and of recreation by the direct activity of God, which is in turn based upon the influence of sin in the world" ("The Origin of Apocalyptic in Biblical Religion," *EvQ* 30 [1958]: 145)—a definition equally applicable to prophetic eschatology, as Ladd himself realizes. No more successful are F. B. Huey, Jr., and B. Corley, *A Student's Dictionary for Biblical and Theological Studies* (Grand Rapids, Mich.: Zondervan, 1983), 26. My intention is not to criticize such attempts but to point out their inadequacy.

5. See, for example, the definition of *apocalypticism* by M. Rist in *IDB*, 1:157: "It may be defined as the dualistic, cosmic, and eschatological belief in two opposing cosmic powers, God and Satan (or his equivalent); and in two distinct ages—the present, temporal and irretrievably evil age under Satan, who now oppresses the righteous but whose power God will soon act to overthrow; and the future, perfect and eternal age under God's own rule, when the righteous will be blessed forever." One gets the distinct impression that every such definition, however heuristically helpful, has a particular apocalypse (or small group of apocalypses) in mind, since it clearly does not describe the broader spectrum of literary productions often identified as apocalyptic in nature.

6. J. Lindblom, *Die Jesaja-Apokalypse* (Lund, Sweden: Gleerup, 1938), 102.

7. Among those who refer to Lindblom's list—some approvingly, others disapprovingly—are P. D. Hanson, *The Dawn of Apocalyptic* (Philadelphia: Fortress, 1975), 6–7; D. S. Russell, *The Method and Message of Jewish Apocalyptic* (Philadelphia: Westminster, 1964), 105; H. H. Rowley, *The Relevance of Apocalyptic*, rev. ed. (New York: Harper, 1947), 23, n. 3. Concerning the list, Rowley makes this comment: "Some of these are rather the accidents than the essence of apocalyptic, however."

8. See, for example, the chapter titles in L. Morris, *Apocalyptic* (Grand Rapids, Mich.: Wm. Eerdmans, 1972), some of which parallel the items in Lindblom's list, others of which nuance them in various directions, and still others of which supplement them. Other authors supply their own preferences, which do much the same as do those of Morris.

9. Compare, for example, Rist in *IDB*, 1:157–61.

10. George E. Ladd, "Why Not Prophetic–Apocalyptic?" *JBL* 76 (1957): 192–200; P. D. Hanson, "Old Testament Apocalyptic Reexamined," *Int* 25 (October 1971): 463; *IDBSup*, 29–34; Vawter, "Apocalyptic," 33–46.

11. See previous note, and see text following noted material.

12. Robert Dick Wilson, *A Scientific Investigation of the Old Testament* (1926; reprint, Chicago: Moody, 1959), 106.

13. For a seminal statement, see Hanson, *Dawn of Apocalyptic*, 2–31.

14. Compare, for example, Ladd, "Why Not?" 197; Vawter, "Apocalyptic," 38–39, 43. In an important article, D. L. Christensen concludes that "apocalyptic thought not only emerges in the transformation of OT prophecy as has been shown convincingly by F. M. Cross, P. D. Hanson, and others; but a number of the themes of subsequent apocalyptic literature have already begun to emerge as early as the time of Josiah, having their origin within so-called holy war traditions associated with the 'day of Yhwh,' which may well have been a rather specific setting within the cultic and political life of preexilic Israel" ("Zephaniah 2:4–15: A Theological Basis for Josiah's Program of Political Expansion," *CBQ* 46 [October 1984]: 682). The exilic period as represented by Ezekiel is the time when apocalyptic originated, according to Hanson, "Old Testament Apocalyptic," 464, 468; see also B. Erling, "Ezekiel 38–39 and the Origins of Jewish Apocalyptic," in *Ex Orbe Religionum*, ed. J. Bergman et al. (Leiden, Netherlands: Brill, 1972), 106.

15. See, for example, J. Oswalt, "Recent Studies in Old Testament Eschatology and Apocalyptic," *JETS* 24 (December 1981), 291, 294, 300–301; G. E. Ladd, "The Place of Apocalyptic in Biblical Religion," *EvQ* 30 (1958): 81; Vawter, "Apocalyptic," 33–34, 37, 41, 45; Hanson, "Old Testament Apocalyptic," 456–57, 464; Erling, "Ezekiel 38–39," 104; Russell, *Method and Message*, 218, 224. G. von Rad's attempts to relate apocalyptic rather to Israel's wisdom movement *(Old Testament Theology* [New York: Harper, 1965], 2:306–8; *Wisdom in Israel* [London: S.C.M. Press, 1970], 277–83) have attracted very few adherents.

16. Vawter, "Apocalyptic," 33. Contemporary with or perhaps later than the Book of Revelation and sharing many of its characteristics are other literary productions that we also call apocalypses, such as the Apocalypse of Baruch, the Apocalypse of Elijah, the Apocalypse of Esdras, and the Apocalypse of Zephaniah. These, however, represent only a fraction of the books post-dating the Hebrew Bible that are often classified as apocalyptic.

17. R. K. Harrison, *Introduction to the Old Testament* (Grand Rapids, Mich.: Wm. Eerdmans, 1969), 1132.

18. M. Rist, for example, defines *apocalypticism* as "a type of religious thought which apparently originated in Zoroastrianism, the ancient Persian religion" *(IDB*, 1:157). Compare also the observation of G. F. Moore, *Judaism* (Cambridge: Harvard University Press, 1927), 394–95.

19. T. W. Manson, *The Servant-Messiah* (Cambridge: Cambridge University Press, 1953), 19.

20. Vawter, "Apocalyptic," 44. See also Hanson, "Old Testament Apocalyptic," 473; Ladd, "Origin of Apocalyptic," 140.

21. L. Morris, *Apocalyptic* (Grand Rapids, Mich.: Wm. Eerdmans, 1972), 27; see also Russell, *Method and Message*, 88–91.

22. See, for example, Oswalt, "Recent Studies," 292; Ladd, "Place of Apocalyptic," 80–81.

23. We need to affirm once again that such differences between prophecy and apocalyptic are matters of emphasis, not of mutual exclusiveness. This will help to explain why there is no general agreement on the identification of apocalyptic passages in the Hebrew Bible.

24. B. W. Anderson, *The Living World of the Old Testament*, 2d ed. (New York: Longmans, 1966), 538.

25. Vawter, "Apocalyptic," 41; see further Russell, *Method and Message*, 92–100.

26. Vawter, "Apocalyptic," 34. Vawter himself, however, seems to have no problem with designating Isaiah 24–27 as apocalyptic (ibid., 42).

27. Rowley, *Relevance of Apocalyptic*, 23–24.

28. See, for example, Harrison, *Introduction*, 1132; Hanson, "Old Testament Apocalyptic," 471; *IDBSup*, 30; Rist in *IDB*, 1:158–60.

29. H. M. Wolf, *Interpreting Isaiah* (Grand Rapids, Mich.: Zondervan, 1985), 138. Wolf dates the chapters to the eighth-century Isaiah of Jerusalem; see also A. Gileadi, *The Apocalyptic Book of Isaiah* (Provo, Utah: Hebraeus Press, 1982); Y. Kaufmann, *The Religion of Israel* (Chicago: University of Chicago Press, 1960); E. Kissane, *The Book of Isaiah* (Dublin: Browne and Nolin, 1941); R. Youngblood, *Themes from Isaiah* (Ventura, Calif.: Regal/GL, 1984). In spite of structural, literary, and other evidence to the contrary, the recent study by W. R. Millar, *Isaiah 24–27 and the Origin of Apocalyptic* (HSM 11 [Missoula, Mont.: Scholars, 1976]), while affirming that the author of Isaiah 24–27 was a disciple of Isaiah (115) and referring to the section as "proto-apocalyptic" (114), nevertheless concludes that it is to be dated in the last half of the sixth century B.C. (120). Some who deny Isaianic authorship to these chapters assume further that the section, interpolated into the Book of Isaiah, is pseudonymous, since pseudonymity is a supposed characteristic of apocalyptic. Rowley, however, correctly points out that anonymity and pseudonymity are not synonymous *(Relevance of Apocalyptic*, 23, n. 1); see also R. J. Bauckham, "The Rise of Apocalyptic," *Themelios* 3 (January 1978): 12: "Apocalyptic prophecy is not pseudonymous, though it is often anonymous." In any case, it is highly unlikely that the Hebrew Bible contains pseudonymous works; compare J. G. Baldwin, "Is There Pseudonymity in the Old Testament?" *Themelios* 4 (September 1978): 6–12.

30. Wolf, *Interpreting Isaiah*, 45; see also Youngblood, *Themes from Isaiah*, 98. The apocalyptic character of Isaiah 34–35 has long been recognized; see, for example, R. H. Charles, "Apocalyptic Literature," in *Encyclopaedia Britannica*, 11th ed. (New York: Encyclopaedia Britannica Company, 1910), 2:171.
31. The phrase in each case is "in that day," and its attestations in Isaiah 27 are especially noteworthy since it appears in the first two verses and last two verses.
32. Apocalypse routinely reflects historical background contemporary with the writer's own time. Isaiah refers to the betrayal of treacherous enemies (24:16b), alternately Assyria (33:1) and Babylonia (21:2). As Edom is symbolic of God's enemies elsewhere in Isaiah (34:5–17; 63:1), so Moab performs that function in this section (25:10). The Israel of Isaiah's day is judged (27:7–11; compare 17:8 for another Isaianic reference to "Asherah poles"), as is Assyria (27:7; see 37:36). Judahite exile to Babylon is foreseen, symbolized by a blast from the east wind (27:8; see Jer 4:11; Ezek 19:12). But redemption follows judgment, and a trumpet will summon Israel's exiles from Assyria and Egypt (27:12–13; see also 11:11–12; 19:23–25).
33. See *ANET*, 137–38 (the Canaanite equivalent of Leviathan is Lotan or the like); see also H. Wallace, "Leviathan and the Beast in Revelation," in *BAR*, 1:290–98.
34. See further Pss. 49:14; 69:15; 141:7; Prov. 1:12; 27:20; 30:15b–16. Death's ravenous appetite is also a theme with mythological origins; compare, for example, *ANET*, 140, where Mot ("Death") is described as crushing Baal in his mouth. It has been proposed that Hebrew *bĕlîyaʿal* (whence the proper name Belial, 2 Cor 6:15) is derived from *blʿ*, "to swallow," but without sufficient warrant (see *TDOT*, 2:133, for brief discussion and bibliography).
35. This verse concludes Isaiah's apocalyptic song of the vineyard (27:2–6), which has obvious connections with 5:1–7—although the judgment context of the latter contrasts sharply with the restoration context of the former.
36. See n. 10.

16

The "Day of Small Things" vs. the Latter Days: Historical Fulfillment or Eschatological Hope?

Wayne O. McCready

The postexilic community of ancient Judah is often understood solely in light of the tragedies of the destruction of the Jerusalem temple and the deportation of the Jews into Babylonia. The community is viewed as the last phase in the decline of ancient Israel after the split of Solomon's empire into the two kingdoms of Israel and Judah. This appraisal suggests that the postexilic community viewed itself as the "last days" of Israel, a shadow of the preexilic era. In some Christian estimations there is a tendency to see the prophets and Jesus as representing high points of religious expression in contrast to the Judaism of the postexilic era.[1] Judaism from 522 B.C. may be referred to as the "people of God" but only by default, as they struggled to maintain some semblance of days gone by. This low estimate of the postexilic community tends to be confirmed by the fact that the writings of the postexilic community constitute the last section of the Hebrew Bible. But such an impression of the postexilic community is only true for those who do not make a close examination of the literature, who do not recognize the flow of religious writings that continued in Judaism well past the days of Haggai, Zechariah, and Malachi, as well as Ezra and Nehemiah.

The Wellhausen school has impressed on biblical scholarship that postexilic Judaism represents a decline from the moral and spiritual heights present in preexilic and exilic writings.[2] The emphasis on the temple and the sacrificial system at Jerusalem following the return has been misrepresented as a turn toward legalism and a shallow religious expression. This view often reflects modern inability or unwillingness to recognize the importance and sophistication of ancient Israel's cult or sacrificial system. G. F. Moore warns that scripture does not warrant "dividing the law into ceremonial and moral, and attributing to the latter perpetuity and superior obligation, while regarding the former as of less moment in the eyes of God."[3] The prophets' criticism of the sacrificial system was due to the conduct of the practitioners of the cult, not to the system itself. Modern scholarship should refute the ideas of a separation between the prophets and the sacrificial system and of conflict between the prophets and the priests.[4]

My thesis is that postexilic Judaism, which I will represent primarily through a consideration of the Book of Zechariah, represents a vibrant phase of Judaism as it developed into a world religion. The community that returned to the homeland viewed itself as an essential link between the days of the heroes David and Solomon and a greater Israel of the future. I propose that the postexilic writers of the Hebrew Bible deliberately directed their writing to the future and claimed a primary place for themselves in the fulfillment of expectations raised by preexilic and exilic prophets.

I also suggest that, in retrospect, the rebuilding of the Jerusalem temple was a significant factor in legitimatizing the exile as an appropriate phase of Israel's existence and in anticipating a better, more glorious future. I maintain that the postexilic writers were, in fact, successful in what they set out to do by way of implementing God's design for the times. I hold that subsequent phases of Judaism, down to and including such groups as the Pharisees, Essenes, and Christians, at the turn of the common era, inherited a religious self-concept that anticipated a more glorious day for the people of YHWH. Whether their claims to being *the* community to introduce that glorious day were correct is not relevant here. What is important is that these later communities expected a better day, and that the source of their positive outlook has its roots in the writings of the postexilic period.

THE EXILE AND THE PROPHETS

In the eighth century B.C., after the empire of David and Solomon had divided, the Northern Kingdom of Israel grew affluent and prosperous. Her army expanded her northern boundaries into ancient Syria, taking Damascus, and she gained nominal control of Judah for a short period. Both Amos and Hosea give vivid descriptions of the religious promiscuity and social injustice that prevailed in that day. Both preexilic prophets warned of the consequences of such religious and social conditions. The Northern Kingdom managed to maintain her independence until circa 732 B.C., when Tiglath-pileser attacked Israel. His successor, Sargon, seized Samaria a decade later and dispersed a large portion of Israelites throughout the Assyrian empire.[5]

Although world power shifted from the Assyrians to the Babylonians, the people of the Southern Kingdom incurred a similar fate in 597 B.C., when Judah surrendered to Nebuchadnezzar. He deported the upper strata of Judean society, along with its craftsmen, to Babylon. After Babylon discovered a Judean conspiracy, the Babylonian military might came down full force on Jerusalem. In 587 B.C., the city was devastated and Solomon's temple was destroyed. Five years later, another segment of Judean society was transported to Babylonia, while an unknown number fled into the surrounding territories of Edom, Samaria, the Transjordan, and Egypt.[6]

The exile represents a tragic phase in Judah's history and religious self-concept.[7] A fundamental tenet of the ancient Israelite faith was that YHWH had promised Israel land and statehood as signs of his special covenant relationship with her. These institutions included a capital city and a formal sanctuary where sacrificial worship was carried out. All these had been attained during the reigns of David and Solomon. The annexation of Israel to the Assyrian empire and of Judah to the Babylonian empire was a direct challenge to the professed heritage of ancient Israel.

It is clear that the prophets' response to this situation is less revolutionary than it is frequently judged to be.[8] The bulk of their writings, both before and after Israel's exile, deals with calling their audience back to allegiance to YHWH. The people are challenged to fulfill their responsibilities as his covenant people. The prophetic understanding of the "ways of the fathers" is that the Israelites have a responsibility to God and to one another because of their acceptance of the covenant (these conditions were laid down in Exod 20 and Deut 5). Part of the prophets' task was discerning YHWH's activity in the experience of the deportations of Israel and Judah. This discernment did not come solely from the experience of the exile itself but also drew on the traditions of ancient Israel. Through the lens of a specific confessional heritage, the prophets saw the exile as an act of God that was both judgmental and redemptive. (Of course, the Assyrians and Babylonians did not perceive the deportations as having a spiritual significance.)

The prophetic message possessed two aspects. First, judgment came as a consequence of Israel's not living up to her obligations as YHWH's chosen people. Second, there was hope for the future. Israel's failure to keep the covenant with YHWH ended in judgment. The deportations of both Israel and Judah were understood to be YHWH's way of dealing with the sins of his people. The experience of being uprooted from her land arrested Israel's attention. A desire and anticipation of resolving this circumstance forced Israel to come to terms with the cause of her present situation.

Jeremiah, Isaiah, Ezekiel, and the deuteronomic school determined that the tradition of deliverance in the Exodus would serve as an important model for the self-understanding of the exiled community.[9] One important difference between the Exodus and the exile is that the former is stated as a condition that the Hebrews found themselves in without reference to a reason. The latter is clearly understood to be the consequence of Israel's and Judah's not living up to the requirements of a covenantal people. The point I wish to make here in regard to the exile is that acceptance of the disaster was followed by an anticipation of something better. The appropriateness of the exile and an anticipated better day set the tone of a religious self-concept in the postexilic period. There was an acknowledged continuum between the disaster and the recovery. Hence, any community that would come after the exile would view itself as an essential development from the judgment period.

The prophets believed that the deportations were in response to the sin of YHWH's people. Israel's ultimate restoration included not merely a willingness on the part of YHWH (that is, his grace or goodness) to restore Israel. It also required that the people respond appropriately to a new covenant. This is seen specifically in the rebuilding of the temple and the reestablishment of the sacrificial system.[10] The community's vitality in responding to YHWH after the disaster was a witness to the depth of the spirituality of postexilic Judaism. The reinstitution of the cult was not merely a "works" response to YHWH's goodness; it was perceived as an appropriate and proper response to both apostasy and restoration. Such a response was only possible after coming to terms with the deportation. As such, it makes the postexilic community a vital link to a new day.

In the period immediately after the return from exile, the community established the basis for a renewed people of YHWH. What is unique about this phase of Judaism is that Judaism had experienced the exile, and this experience had produced a resolution to return to the ways of the fathers that could come only out of both exile and restoration. The exile and restoration were phases through which the people of YHWH were required to go in order that a better day might be realized. Those who returned from exile took part in a unique phase of the history of ancient Israel.

The second aspect of the prophetic message had to do with building hope for the future. Even a preexilic prophet as judgmental as Amos acknowledges a hope for a better day: "In that day I will raise up the booth of David that is fallen and repair its breaches, and raise up its ruins, and rebuild it as in the days of old" (Amos 9:11). Jer. 31:38 anticipates that the day would come when Jerusalem would be rebuilt. Restoration and reconciliation with God would be the positive consequences of the religious and national tragedy of the exile. In the deuteronomic estimation of the exile, the scattering of the people is balanced with the belief that if they return to their covenantal obligations of religious loyalty to their God (and responsibility to each other), a better day will dawn:

> If you search after him with all your heart and with all your soul. When you are in tribulation, and all these things come upon you in the latter days, you will return to YHWH your God and obey his voice.
>
> (Deut 4:29b–30)

It is this belief in the possibility of "latter days" that served as a confessional basis and inspired the exiled community to hope for a national restoration. When the opportunity to return to the homeland arose, the religious understanding of prophets such as Zechariah and Haggai was that the "latter days" were indeed more than a wish/dream. They viewed the returning exiles and the rebuilding of the Jerusalem temple as a transitional link between the former days of a golden era under David and Solomon, and the eventual latter days when Israel would return to YHWH and obey his voice.

THE RETURN

A brief historical sketch of the return of the exiled Jews indicates that when the Persians gained control of the Babylonian empire they attempted to secure peace among a large and diverse mix of nationalities and cultures. This was done by allowing deported peoples to return to their homeland. Syria–Palestine was part of a large satrapy or province in the western portion of the Persian empire, sometimes referred to as "Babylon beyond the River" (Ezra 4:11). Typical of foreign policy in this stage of antiquity was Persia's intent not to allow establishment of a political state. To prevent this possibility, Persia sponsored theocracies or political institutions that had priesthood leadership. The priesthood directed cultural, social, and religious affairs. It is therefore not surprising that the office of high priest emerged as an important national and religious role in postexilic Judaism.

Although source material on the return of exiled Jews is substantial, it is very difficult to determine the exact chronology of the postexilic restoration. Ezra 1 and 6 refer to Cyrus's edict as it relates to the Jews.[11] It appears that the edict allowed for the return of deported Jews to the homeland, as well as for the rebuilding of the city of Jerusalem and the sacrificial institution of the temple. As I suggested above, the intent was not to create an independent political state, but rather a central sacrificial/religious site. For the Persians, the presence of a temple in Jerusalem would demonstrate an official state presence in a remote region of their vast empire.

Though remote, the Syria–Palestine area was an important part of the Persian empire because of its closeness to Egypt, and it thus served as a jumping-off point for expansionist ambitions. From the Babylonian geographical standpoint, Jerusalem was in a territory "beyond the Euphrates," thus requiring increased security. The return of locals sponsored by the Persian government was a demonstration of state interest in this outer region.

The Jerusalem area was probably set up as a temple–municipality where social organization would be centered around the sacrificial site.[12] This was a typical administrative arrangement of the Persian period, and such an organization explains why the Persian government was willing to sponsor the rebuilding of the Jerusalem temple.[13] The *Bet Abot*, the house of the fathers, was the centralizing unit of social organization. State sponsorship of the Jerusalem temple's rebuilding was accepted as a normal occurrence by Jews who understood the Persian government's policies. As we will see, Zechariah and Haggai reflect this social/cultural citizenry–temple–municipality mentality in their writings, giving it a particular meaning that assisted postexilic Judaism in coming to terms with the spiritual significance of the return to the homeland.[14]

In approximately 536 B.C., a plan was set in motion for returning Jews to the homeland. Initially, few took the opportunity to return to Palestine. Life in Babylonia had become quite comfortable for Jews, and an important, influential Jewish community eventually emerged from those who elected to remain in Babylonia.[15] A Davidic prince, Sheshbazzar, led the first group of those who returned, but he was not successful in reestablishing a new Jewish community in the homeland. An ambitious nephew, Zerubbabel, followed and sought to reopen the temple at Jerusalem to be a focus for national and religious orientation.[16] Although it is difficult to make a full reconstruction of the circumstances, it appears that Zerubbabel had ambitions to establish Jerusalem as an independent political entity. He was eventually removed by the Persian governor, who took measures to discourage further displays of royal aspirations.

It was at this stage that the high priest of Jerusalem (Joshua ben Jehozadak) was vested with whatever leadership powers were deemed appropriate by the Persian governor. From the middle of the sixth century B.C. until the first century of the common era, the high priest emerged as a pivotal figure in postexilic Judaism. It is quite possible that initially Zerubbabel and Joshua ben Jehozadak functioned in some sort of dual leadership capacity. In 515 B.C. a modest temple was completed. Much of the support for Zerubbabel's ambitions to rebuild the Jerusalem temple came from the prophets Haggai and Zechariah.[17] By considering their role in rebuilding the temple, we may be able to determine how the postexilic community understood its place in the scheme that would make possible the "latter days."

HAGGAI AND ZECHARIAH AND
THE IMPORTANCE OF THE JERUSALEM TEMPLE

The books of Haggai and Zechariah are among the easiest of Hebrew Bible texts to relate to a historical context.[18] Zechariah 1–8 (the section under consideration) dates from the eighth month of emperor Darius' second year of reign in 520 B.C. Darius was the son of Cyrus and heir to his father's empire. These chapters seem to cover a two–year span. The Book of Haggai reflects the same time frame, although its concentration is restricted to a three-month period.

Zechariah's encouragement that the temple be rebuilt was a natural religious development, as it served as an essential link with the preexilic cult. From the period of David onward, the centrality and primacy of Jerusalem as the locus of YHWH's presence in Israel had increasingly gained a definitive symbolic meaning.[19] There was an integral tie between sacrificial worship and its appropriateness at the temple in Jerusalem.[20] For those returning to the homeland, it was quite reasonable to attach the possibility of a better day to the rebuilding of the Jerusalem temple. Jerusalem and the concept of the temple combined two important religious ideas. The city underscored David's role as a confirmation of YHWH's promise of a land and a nation. The reestablishment of a cult center allowed not only for a typical reenactment of religious worship but also provided a way of reinforcing religious confession demonstrated in such celebrations as the Day of Atonement and the Passover. In other words, city and temple were physical links with ideas dominant in the preexilic age.

Because Zechariah prophesied in the period immediately after the exile—
which was understood by the prophets as a necessary, correcting phase for
YHWH's people—Zechariah's primary concern was to establish a forward-looking
attitude that would not see the exile as an end in itself.

The sources indicate that from the decree of Cyrus until the time of Darius
there was no substantial progress in the rebuilding of city and temple. Possibly
there was opposition by both Jewish and gentile sectors of society to Jerusalem's
being established as a center of importance.[21] In 520 B.C., both Haggai and
Zechariah began exerting pressure for attention to be given to the building of
the temple. In a series of fiery oracles, Haggai chided Jerusalem for failing to
be concerned about temple construction.[22] He blamed misdirected priorities
for the returnees' poverty and difficulties in readjusting. Once the temple was
built, the success of the society would follow:

> For thus says YHWH of Hosts: Once again, in a little while, I will shake the heavens
> and the earth and the sea and the dry land; and I will shake all nations; so that the
> treasures of all nations shall come in, and I will fill this house with splendor, says
> YHWH of Hosts. . . . The latter splendor of this house shall be greater than the former,
> says YHWH of Hosts; and in this place I will give prosperity, says YHWH of Hosts.
>
> (Hag 2:6–7, 9)

The rebuilding of the temple as the appropriate response from a community that has learned the lesson of exile is paralleled in Zechariah:

> This is YHWH's word to Zerubbabel: Not by might, nor by power, but by my Spirit,
> says YHWH of Hosts. What are you, O great mountain? Before Zerubbabel you shall
> become a plain; and he shall bring forward the top stone amid shouts of "Grace, grace
> to it!" Moreover YHWH's word came to me, saying, "The hands of Zerubbabel have
> laid the foundation of this house, his hands shall also complete it." Then will you know
> that YHWH of Hosts has sent me to you. For whoever has despised the day of small
> things shall rejoice, and shall see the plummet in the hand of Zerubbabel.
>
> (Zech 4:6b–10a)

This portion of Zechariah is set within a group of vision oracles that make
up the core of chapters 1–8.[23] The passage cited is part of a *menorah* or
"lampstand" vision that views the temple as restored. D. L. Petersen proposes
that "Zechariah's visions stand somewhere between purely mundane concerns
and an utopian vision of renewal." Petersen suggests that the "notion of 'in-
betweenness' serves as an accurate indicator for the content of Zechariah's
visions."[24] That is, Zechariah and Haggai represent a theological response to a
new situation. On the one hand, their visions are concerned with a political,
economic, and social reality. On the other hand, it is necessary that they
inspire their fellow returnees with a vision that will give more than a survival-
for-the-moment mentality. The completed temple is the basis not only for
verifying that the prophet was divinely sent but for projecting new possibilities
for the community.[25]

THE TEMPLE AND THE "DAY OF SMALL THINGS"

The thrust of the *menorah* oracle is an emphasis on building procedures. Its first principle is that neither might *(ḥayil)* nor power *(kōaḥ)* will accomplish what is desired. The presence of YHWH itself will be the source of inspiration for a better day. Verse 7 hints that there is opposition to Zerubbabel, and there have been efforts to identify the "mountain" as Joshua ben Jehozadak, the high priest. A more reasonable reading — given the total context of the Book of Zechariah — is to identify the source of opposition as the administration in Samaria.[26]

I would like to emphasize Zerubbabel's role in building the temple. When the temple is completed the prophet's ministry will be vindicated: "Then will you know that YHWH of Hosts has sent me to you"; and those who have "despised the day of small things" will rejoice when they see the building instrument in the hand of Zerubbabel (Zech 4:9–10a). R. E. Ellis proposes that when a temple was rebuilt a brick from the earlier sacred structure was placed in the foundation of the new building as a link between the previous temple and the new.[27] The brick was a point of continuum for the community between old and new. In most cases, the king (as a representative of the deity involved) was an important functionary in the ceremony of transferring the brick from its old worship center to the new. Hence, the place of Zerubbabel as a key figure in this oracle.[28] Following A. Petitjean, as well as Ellis's proposition, that the foundation ceremony was a means of giving the temple's construction primary significance seems clear.[29] The second temple was not to be minimized, and the task of construction was worthy of the energy and dedication required to see its completion. The present age, or "day of small things," was not to be despised. The temple's construction served as the main point of continuum with the golden days of the former temple.

Hag. 2:3–7 deals with the same subject matter. Those who knew the splendor of the former structure are encouraged to take heart. Special encouragement is directed toward both Zerubbabel and Joshua ben Jehozadak. The exodus out of Egypt is a precedent for those who returned to be optimistic about present circumstances. As YHWH's presence was with their ancestors, so "my Spirit abides among you; fear not" (2:5–6). This theme of reassurance appears in the oracles of both Haggai and Zechariah. Zechariah envisions opposition to Zerubbabel but claims that the "mountain" will in fact become a plain. Zechariah anticipates that the "stone of the former sanctuary" will soon be set amid anthems of praise.

Even though those who returned would consider their present circumstance a "day of small things" in comparison to the central importance of Jerusalem before the exile, the prophet proposes that they should rejoice. The rebuilding of the temple is the necessary step toward something better. It is not a position of importance by default. Those who returned are the only people of God who can bring about the "latter days" anticipated in Deuteronomy 4. They had experienced the calamity of the exile and they had come to terms with the necessary lesson of that experience. The sign that the lesson had been learned was the rebuilding of the Jerusalem temple. In Zech. 1:16, the prophet declares that YHWH has returned to Jerusalem and that YHWH's house shall be built in it; the measuring line would be stretched out over Jerusalem. In Zech. 8:9–13, the prophet promises that there will be a substantial difference in the people's state of affairs when the temple is completed:

> But now I will not deal with the remnant of this people as in the former days, says YHWH of Hosts. . . . And as you have been a byword of cursing among the nations, O house of Judah and house of Israel, so will I save you and you shall be a blessing.
>
> (Zech 8:11, 13a)

In appraising the period after the rebuilding of the temple, we can see that its reality (and the deep religious meaning it held) became important for the ongoing religious self-definition of Jews as they returned from dispersion to the homeland. E. Bickerman suggests that there is a rewarding polarity between the dispersion and the homeland in the postexilic period. He comments that "the Dispersion saved Judaism from physical extirpation and spiritual inbreeding. Palestine united the dispersed members of the nation and gave them a sense of oneness. This counterpoise of historical forces is without analogy in antiquity."[30] The Jerusalem temple was the focus of this polarity.

The return gave birth to future possibilities. Zechariah and Haggai were aware of its importance in the scheme of things. Although they may not have envisioned the exact course of future events, their emphasis on the temple and the subsequent potentiality of greater days was integrally tied to this "day of small things." Later, rabbinic figures, such as Yohanan ben Zakkai and the academy, as well as Jesus and his journey to Jerusalem, the separatist claims at Qumran, and the Sadducees of Jerusalem ultimately defined their religious claims in relation to the Jerusalem temple. Their representation of God was cast vis-à-vis the temple. This characteristic of the time was a consequence of the religious self-concept of Jewry established by Zechariah and his contemporaries. Without the belief in the necessity of their age as an important link to a better day, Judaism, and subsequently early Christianity, would have lacked an essential religious element.

HISTORICAL FULFILLMENT
OR ESCHATOLOGICAL HOPE?

In an excellent article on Zechariah and early postexilic Judaism, R. Mason defines current views on the religious context of the prophets of the restoration.[31] O. Plöger proposes a division between concerns of a priestly nature — that centered on the temple as a way of organizing and focusing the life of those who returned — and the concerns of a group who returned with strong eschatological expectations of a new age.[32] As time passed, this latter group sharpened their views of a new age until apocalyptic thought emerged as a distinct movement. P. D. Hanson follows Plöger's model but emphasizes the separation of priest and apocalyptic.[33] He believes that Haggai and Zechariah belong to the priestly faction, as evidenced by their emphasis on rebuilding the temple. The eschatological hope is only peripheral to the main concern of resuming the Jerusalem cult.[34]

However, these biblical scholars have made an artificial separation between the sacrificial system and its importance as a directive for "better days." The cult was an essential element in the religious expression of ancient Israel. It provided for the ritualization of primary Israelite beliefs. The sacrificial system included a double strain—a liturgical expression and an appropriation of Israel's covenantal relationship to YHWH.[35] It showed the tension that exists between "action" and "reason for action." This interplay was both positive and creative. The rebuilding of the temple was understood as the action required of those who returned; its reconstruction was an appropriate religious response subsequent to the exile. However, the second temple was not an end in itself; it was built with the anticipation of a better day.

The postexilic prophets' position was that the rebuilt temple provided the foundation for a new age. Zechariah makes it clear that military action was not a prime principle for better days. He saw that the cult would permit the believer to incorporate the idea of covenant commitment in a deeper and more meaningful sense than could be expected by rallying to social causes or military ambitions. Historically, this view also proved to have greater longevity. The reestablishment of the sacrificial system provided a means for reaffirming the theme of YHWH's involvement with humanity. Haggai and Zechariah recognized the importance of providing this worship context not only for assessing the exile but also for emphasizing deliverance from exile. The rebuilt temple was a sign that his people recognized YHWH's involvement with them, both in exile and in restoration. The cult provided a touchstone for making claims about the future. In this light, the "day of small things" functioned as a springboard of renewed eschatological hope (see Hag 2:9 and Zech 3:9–10).

Petersen proposes that biblical prophecy had a great deal to do with the institution of kingship.[36] The early orientation of prophets centers on monarchy,[37] and Petersen suggests that with the fall of Israel and Judah, the prophets had to change their religious orientation. The postexilic prophets are characterized as reinterpreting earlier classical prophecy in a nonmonarchical society. This assessment of postexilic prophecy may partly explain the orientation of postexilic Jewry as the people of the "book." In his latest work, Petersen provides a wealth of material on the social, economic, and religious context of these prophets.[38] The absence of a monarchy is indeed a major religious dilemma facing the postexilic prophets. The magnitude of the Persian empire may have necessitated an alternative direction for expectations of restoration. Whether the monarchy had a cause-and-effect relationship on biblical prophecy may not, however, be as clear as Petersen has suggested. At any rate, the intent of Haggai and Zechariah is clear: the rebuilding of the temple is a mandate before YHWH's people may enjoy better days.

R. P. Carroll argues that postexilic prophecy should be viewed as a terminal stage of biblical prophecy because in the final analysis prophecy failed.[39] That is, although the predictions of judgment were realized, the promises of restoration did not match preexilic and exilic expectations. Those prophets who came after the return had to cope with the tension of earlier prophetic hopes and dreams that stood in sharp contrast to the realities of the "day of small things." Their solution was to reinterpret the earlier prophets in terms of present circumstances, placing emphasis on "delay factors" and projecting yet future events.[40] As Mason has pointed out, the term *failure* is difficult to assess.[41] What might first be viewed as failure may, in fact, become a basis for success. Carroll is correct in determining that the postexilic prophets were left with a potential "failure context." However, he has underestimated the importance of a prophet such as Zechariah.[42] To Zechariah not only was the rebuilding of the temple an appropriate response by YHWH's returning people, it was a necessary catalyst for something better. The resumption of the cult was the primary link between Israel's "former days" and YHWH's continuing presence among his people.

SUMMARY

Mason has rightly pointed out that the editorial framework of both Haggai and Zechariah indicates that the rebuilt temple will be the "first installment" of things to come.[43] Two factors exercise an important interplay in the Book of Zechariah. One is the emphasis on the actual rebuilding of the temple — with the symbolic brick that validates its importance. The other projects the rebuilt temple past a sixth-century time frame. The creative genius of the prophets was to focus the earlier prophets and their expectation of a better day on the temple. It is this interaction of an essentially religious institution (the temple) as a continuum of YHWH's presence among his people that characterizes Zechariah and leaves open the idea of a better day. That day will come when successive generations respond appropriately to the "day of small things" — Zechariah's day. This stage in the development of YHWH's people was not merely a phase of default or decline. It demanded a high degree of creativity, as well as significant intellectual and spiritual insight.

NOTES

1. See R. H. Pfeiffer, *Religion in the Old Testament* (New York: Harper & Row, 1961), 54. Compare H. G. Mitchell, *A Critical and Exegetical Commentary on Haggai and Zechariah* (New York: Charles Scribner's Sons, 1912), 36, who attempted to counter this perspective almost a century ago.
2. J. Wellhausen, *Die kleinen Propheten* (Berlin: G. Reimer, 1898). For a brief redress, see P. R. Ackroyd, *Exile and Restoration* (Philadelphia: Westminster Press, 1968), 1–7. Ackroyd

makes a telling comment in note 12 on page 5. He suggests that popular assessments of the Hebrew Bible—such as those in classroom textbooks—remain unchanged, even though scholarship has revised its position substantially. This is particularly true in the area of the cultic aspect of ancient Judaism, and yet the old way of thinking persists.

3. G. F. Moore, *Judaism in the First Centuries of the Christian Era* (Cambridge, Mass.: Harvard University Press, 1927), 2:6.

4. Compare H. H. Rowley, "Ritual and the Hebrew Prophets," *JSS* 1 (1956): 338–60. Ackroyd, *Exile and Restoration*, 84–102, has pointed out that the priesthood also was critical of abuses against the cultic system.

5. For a brief summary of this period, see D. J. Silver, *A History of Judaism* (New York: Basic Books, 1974), 1:77–171.

6. See E. J. Bickerman, "The Historical Foundations of Post-Biblical Judaism," in *The Jews: Their History*, ed. L. Finkelstein (New York: Schocken Books, 1970), 72–88.

7. See Y. Kaufmann, *The Religion of Israel*, trans. Moshe Greenberg (New York: Schocken Books, 1972), 447–51, and Ackroyd, *Exile and Restoration*, 232–56.

8. Compare N. W. Porteous, "Jerusalem-Zion: The Growth of a Symbol," in *Verbannung und Heimkehr*, ed. A. Kuschke (Tubingen, West Germany: Mohr, 1961), 235–52, and Robert de Vaux, "Jérusalem et les prophètes," *RB* 73 (1966): 481–509.

9. See R. Gordis, "The Bible As a Cultural Monument," in *The Jews: Their Religion and Culture*, ed. L. Finkelstein (New York: Schocken Books, 1971), 21–25. Compare Jer. 16:14–15; Isa. 51:9–11.

10. See John M. Lundquist, "Temple, Covenant, and Law in the Ancient Near East and in the Old Testament," in this volume.

11. See E. Bickerman, "The Edict of Cyrus in Ezra I," *JBL* 65 (1946): 249–75; K. Galling, *Studien zur Geschichte Israels im persischen Zeitalter* (Tubingen, West Germany: Mohr, 1964), 61–77; A. Kuhrt, "The Cyrus Cylinder and Achaemenid Imperial Policy," *JSOT* 25 (1983): 83–97; J. Myers, *Ezra, Nehemiah*, Anchor Bible (New York: Doubleday, 1965), 5–9; J. B. Pritchard, *The Ancient Near East* (Princeton, N.J.: Princeton University Press, 1958), 1:206–8; *ANET*, 315–16.

12. A substantial case can be made for a temple–municipality citizenry in Palestine in the early postexilic period (see H. Kreissig, *Die Sozialökonomische Situation in Juda zur Achämenidenzeit* [Berlin: Akademie-Verlag, 1973]; W. Schottroff, "Zur Sozialgeschichte Israels in der Perserzeit," *Verkündigung und Forschung* 27 [1982]: 46–48; E. Stern, *The Material Culture of the Land of the Bible in the Persian Period, 538–332 B.C.E.* [London: Aris & Phillips, 1982; Jerusalem: Israel Exploration Society, 1973]; J. Weinberg, "Die Agrarverhältnisse in der Bürger–Tempel–Gemeinde der Achämenidenzeit," in *Wirtschaft und Gesellschaft im Alten Vorderasien*, ed. J. Harmatta and G. Komoroczy [Budapest: Kiado, 1976], 473–86; S. Weinberg, "Post-Exilic Palestine: An Archaeological Report," *Proceedings of the Israel Academy of Sciences and Humanities* 4 [1971]: 78–97).

13. The administrative territory "beyond the Euphrates" probably had a Persian governor over the entire province with a low-ranked governor over the Jerusalem area (see Galling, *Studien zur Geschichte Israels*, 19–24; M. Noth, *The History of Israel* [London: Adam & Charles Black, 1965], 306–8; D. L. Petersen, *Haggai and Zechariah 1–8, a Commentary* [Philadelphia: Westminster Press, 1984], 24–25).

14. For a discussion of the Syria–Palestine political structure, see P. Ackroyd, "Archaeology, Politics and Religion: The Persian Period," *Iliff Review* (Denver) 39 (1982): 5–24, and S. McEvenue, "The Political Structure in Judah from Cyrus to Nehemiah," *CBQ* 43 (1981): 353–64.

15. See J. Neusner, *History of the Jews in Babylonia*, 5 vols. (Leiden, Netherlands: Brill, 1965–70), and J. Neusner, *There We Sat Down* (New York: Abingdon Press, 1972).

16. See S. Japhet, "Sheshbazzar and Zerubbabel," *ZAW* 94 (1982): 66–98.

17. It is possible that Zechariah may have arrived with Zerubbabel (see K. Galling, "Die Exilswende in der Sicht des Propheten Sacharja," *VT* 2 [1952]: 18–36).

18. See Petersen, *Haggai and Zechariah 1–8*, 17–31.

19. See R. E. Clements, *God and Temple: The Idea of the Divine Presence in Ancient Israel* (Oxford: Oxford University Press, 1965).

20. See J. Simons, *Jerusalem in the Old Testament* (Leiden, Netherlands: Brill, 1952); and L. H. Vincent, *Jérusalem de l'Ancien Testament*, 2 vols. (Paris: Gabalda, 1954–56).

21. For a discussion on Jewish and gentile response to the resettlement, see F. Dexinger, "Limits of Tolerance in Judaism: The Samaritan Example," in *Jewish and Christian Self-Definition*, ed. E. P. Sanders (Philadelphia: Fortress Press, 1981), 2:88–114.

22. For a discussion of the oracles of Haggai, see Petersen, *Haggai and Zechariah 1–8*, 32–37; P. Hanson, *The Dawn of Apocalyptic* (Philadelphia: Fortress Press, 1979), 106–7; R. Mason, "The Purpose of the 'Editorial Framework' of the Book of Haggai," *VT* 27 (1977): 413–21; K. Koch, "Haggais unreines Volk," *ZAW* 79 (1967): 52–66.

23. There is an identifiable literary progression of theological thought in the oracles (see B. Halpern, "The Ritual Background of Zechariah's Temple Song," *CBQ* 40 [1978]: 167–90; and Petersen, *Haggai and Zechariah 1–8*, 111–13; also compare S. Amsler, "La parole visionaire des prophètes," *VT* 31 [1981]: 359–63; and B. Long, "Reports of Visions among the Prophets," *JBL* 95 [1976]: 353–65).

24. Petersen, *Haggai and Zechariah 1–8*, 113. Also see D. L. Petersen, "Zechariah's Visions: A Theological Perspective," *VT* 34 (1984): 198.

25. See D. W. Thomas, "The Sixth Century B.C.: A Creative Epoch in the History of Israel," *JSS* 6 (1961): 33–46.

26. I am following the context of the question "What are you?" that would seem to refer to an opponent of Zerubbabel. For discussions on possible opponents of Zerubbabel, see W. Beuken, *Haggai-Sacharja 1–8. Studien zur Überlieferungsgeschichte der frühnachexilischen Prophetie*, Studia Semitica Neerlandica 10 (Assen, Netherlands: Van Gorcum, 1967), 50–63, who does not view that a priest at this period would challenge the position of Zerubbabel. Compare Petersen, *Haggai and Zechariah 1–8*, 239–40. Avraham Gileadi views the term *mountain* as a metaphor denoting Persia and her opposition to Davidic aspirations; compare Babylon as a "mountain" (Jer 51:25); the kingdom of God as a "mountain" (Dan 2:35) (by personal communication to the author).

27. See R. E. Ellis, *Foundation Deposits in Ancient Mesopotamia* (New Haven, Conn.: Yale University Press, 1968), 20–29. The *hāʾeben hārōʾšâ* (the RSV translates it as "top stone") should be thought of as "headstone" or "cornerstone" in a foundation. Petersen, *Haggai and Zechariah 1–8*, 237, translates it as "former stone" (see his comments on 240–42).

28. For a full discussion on kings involved with temples, see B. Halpern, "Ritual Background of Zechariah's Temple Sons," 167–80; A. Kapelrud, "Temple Building, a Task for Gods and Men," *Or* 32 (1962): 56–62; A. Petitjean, "La mission de Zorubabel et la reconstruction du temple," in *Ephemerides Theologicae Lovanienses* (Louvain) 42 (1966): 40–71; D. L. Petersen, "Zerubbabel and Jerusalem Temple Reconstruction," *CBQ* 36 (1974): 366–72; see also, John M. Lundquist, "Temple, Covenant, and Law in the Ancient Near East and in the Old Testament," in this volume.

29. A. Petitjean, *Les oracles du Proto-Zacharie. Un programme de restauration pour la communaute juive après l'exile* (Paris: Gabalda, 1961), 236, reads *hāʾeben habbĕdîl* of 4:10a as a metal tablet similar to Assyrian building deposits. The frequent translation is a builder's "plummet" (see Petersen, *Haggai and Zechariah 1–8*, 237–44).

30. Bickerman, "Historical Foundations," 72.

31. Rex Mason, "The Prophets of the Restoration," in *Israel's Prophetic Tradition*, ed. R. Coggins and A. Phillips, M. Knibb (Cambridge: Cambridge University Press, 1982), 137–53.

32. O. Plöger, *Theocracy and Eschatology* (Richmond, Vir.: John Knox Press, 1968).

33. Hanson, *Dawn*.

34. Hanson, *Dawn*, 251, proposes that in regard to Zechariah's prophetic vocation of integrating the vision of divine activity into structures and events of historical reality, the prophet had by and large abdicated this characteristic.

35. The attempt to make a sharp division between liturgy and interpretation of covenant and set them against one another is misguided. The liturgy (that is, the particular sacrifice offered on a designated day) is enacted with the intention of bringing out as forcibly as possible the essential meaning of such a covenantal idea as liberation through Passover.

36. D. L. Petersen, *Late Israelite Prophecy: Studies in Deutero–Prophetic Literature and in Chronicles* (Missoula, Mont.: Scholars Press, 1977).

37. See J. Holladay, "Assyrian Statecraft and the Prophets of Israel," *HTR* 63 (1970): 29–51.

38. Petersen, *Haggai and Zechariah 1–8*. The relevant passages in Zechariah are discussed on 111–25 and 237–44.

39. R. P. Carroll, "Twilight of Prophecy or Dawn of Apocalyptic," *JSOT* 14 (1979): 3–35, and R. P. Carroll, *When Prophecy Failed* (London: S.C.M. Press, 1979).

40. Carroll, *When Prophecy Failed*, 168.

41. Mason, "Prophets of Restoration," 141.

42. Carroll, *When Prophecy Failed*, comments on 212: "Yet the capacity of prophecy to survive through change reveals its inner toughness and its ability to cope with substantial dissonance." He also suggests that the role of prophecy in the future was minor.

43. See Mason, "Prophets of Restoration," 142–49, as well as his article "The Purpose of the 'Editorial Framework' of the Book of Haggai," *VT* 27 (1977): 413–28.

17

Israel's Life Cycle
from Birth to Resurrection

Joseph E. Coleson

In a work which has become a standard, R. K. Harrison's *Introduction to the Old Testament*, the author makes the point that "the prophets continually predicted the future, on the perfectly logical basis that, as Augustine and others have expressed it, what is to happen is already inherent in the present situation. They experienced little immediate difficulty in surveying both the nearer and the more distant historical scene."[1] Y. Kaufmann further observes that "the literary prophet . . . is first of all a messenger whose task is not to reveal hidden things, but to command or reprove in the name of God. To be sure, he is privy to 'the secrets' of God; he knows and reveals the future; he sees visions and symbols and interprets them. Yet all these are subordinate to his message and his mission."[2]

As with the future, so with the prophet's treatment of Israel's past history. Reciting the nation's history was not the main purpose of Israel's classical prophets. However, they did use Israel's history in their efforts to call the people back to faith and trust in YHWH. The prophets' recollections of Israel's history and their predictions regarding her future were both subordinate to their message and mission.

Because their prophetic insight extended in both directions, past and future, and because YHWH had so clearly revealed himself as a personal God to his people Israel, the metaphor of YHWH as Husband taking Israel for his wife presented itself naturally and repeatedly as the prophets sought to convey their message of reproof and warning, coupled with the invitation to repent and return to YHWH. This metaphor then easily lends itself to extension backward in time, so that Israel's early history can be described in terms of the birth of the girl-child. Similarly, Israel's apostasy, coming punishment, and eventual restoration can be accommodated within the figure by speaking in terms of marital infidelity, divorce/death, and resurrection.

Ezekiel 16 is, of course, the lengthiest and most consistent passage in carrying the figure through from beginning to end. I will use this chapter as the basis of this study, and its outline will be essentially my own. I contend that in this context the classical prophets often thought in terms of a distinct life cycle of Israel's history and that they foresaw that life cycle continuing into the future, beyond the coming exile. Israel's metaphorical representation as a female progressing from birth, through death and resurrection, is not unique to Ezekiel. The metaphor is quite common in the prophets and may even be said to be a dominant theme in Israel's classical prophetic tradition.

ISRAEL'S PARENTAGE AND BIRTH:
THE FOUNDLING GIRL-CHILD

In Ezek. 16:3 it is Jerusalem, the old Jebusite city which David captured and made his dynastic center, that is addressed directly. But Jerusalem so dominated the economic, political, and religious life of the truncated nation of Judah that no Judean hearing these words could shrug them off as not applying to him. Though Jerusalem's early history was not Israelite, to address Jerusalem at this time was to address the nation; this intensified the irony and therefore the sharpness of the rebuke of Ezekiel's opening remarks on the origins of the city.

Ezekiel had a twofold purpose in identifying Jerusalem's birth as "from the land of the Canaanite," with "an Amorite" as her father and a "Hittite" as her mother. This is an oracle of judgment and condemnation; an initial strong reaction of mingled indignation and shame is Ezekiel's intended effect. To identify the city and its people with those who, by the orthodox historical traditions, had been driven from or destroyed in the land for their shameful iniquities (Gen 15:16; Amos 2:9–10) was an attempt to shock and shame his hearers. This is underscored by Ezekiel's repeated reference, in 16:45, to Hittite and Amorite parentage. The second purpose in this identification, so odious to Ezekiel's hearers, was to remind them that YHWH's actions toward the nation had been, from the very beginning, all of beneficence. Not only Jerusalem's origins (within the land) but also Israel's (outside the land) are both so humble and so complex that neither Ezekiel nor we today could unravel them completely. Israel did arise out of an Amorite-Canaanite (and Aramaean) ethnic and cultural complex, probably with a significant remnant, culturally at least, of the old Hittite ascendency added in as well. Israel could point to no long, proud heritage of her own making. Her parentage was obscure and humble, even shameful. Beginning even here, she owed what she became to YHWH.[3]

Ezekiel presses the shock value of his opening remarks about Jerusalem's parentage by his description of her birth. Verse 4 begins with the almost sarcastic phrase "as for your birth" and continues by relating the degrading treatment and exposure of the newborn infant. The usual ministrations were purposefully omitted, and Ezekiel takes care to remind the now-grown woman that on the day of her birth, when an infant's helpless condition ought to evoke the tenderest and most loving responses, she was not only unpitied, but actively loathed.

This loathing resulted in the infant's exposure in the open field. The action could be rendered literally: "But you were cast upon the face of the open field in the abhorrence of your life." Exposure of infants, especially of girls, was not uncommon in the ancient Near Eastern and Mediterranean world. Hecataeus of Abdera, a Greek historian, notes with surprise that the Jews raised all their children, without exposing any.[4] Josephus states that the law requires that all children be raised.[5]

While the exposure of female infants in the pagan society of which Ezekiel was speaking would not have surprised his hearers, Ezekiel may also be adapting the exposed infant/foundling child folktale to his own ends here. B. Lewis has analyzed the infant exposure tale as having typically seven components.[6] In place of Lewis's first component, an explanation of the abandonment of the infant, Ezekiel substitutes a description of the ferocity of the contempt with which the child is treated as she is born and exposed. This of course underscores the reasons for the abandonment in a far more effective manner than would a dutiful setting forth of those reasons.

The second component of the tale is the revelation that the infant is of noble birth. This is present of course in Ezekiel's allegorical tale in his designation of the child's parents as Amorite and Hittite. But this is a deliberately ambiguous attribution. On the one hand, the infant is of noble birth, since both the Amorites and (especially) the Hittites possessed a long and proud heritage in the history of the ancient Near East. On the other hand, it is a reversal of the theme of noble birth. As we have seen, the Canaanite, Amorite, Hittite heritage of Jerusalem was, in the opinion of Ezekiel's hearers, emphatically not a noble heritage.

Lewis's third component, the preparation for the exposure of the infant, is also reversed in Ezekiel for heightened effect. In the classic form of the tale, elaborate precautions are often taken by the persons who actually expose the infant to increase the infant's chances of survival until its hoped-for discovery by a third party. In Ezekiel, however, all actions are mentioned only for the purpose of noting that they are neglected. The cord is not cut; the infant is not washed. By the intensive use of the infinitive absolute, it is noted that the infant was certainly neither rubbed with salt[7] nor swaddled. Thus the intended death of the infant is made more certain.

The fourth component, the exposure itself, is stated by Ezekiel in stark simplicity. The somber finality of the action is Stygian in its impact: for this infant, of all abandoned infants, there could be no hope.

To this point in his adaptation of the tale,[8] Ezekiel has carefully stressed the hopelessness of the infant's condition, which is even more precarious than in the usual exposure tale. He does this in order to accentuate the greatness of the infant's preservation and deliverance: no other abandoned infant has been rescued by YHWH himself! Lewis's fifth component is the infant's protection (or nursing) in an unusual manner. Ezekiel also presents this component of the tale straightforwardly, with no elaboration whatsoever. The protection (deliverance from death) of the infant YHWH is able to accomplish by a simple command. Ezek. 16:6–7a may be translated, "But I passed by you and I saw you writhing in your blood, and I said to you [while you lay] in your blood, 'Live! And grow up like a plant of the field.' "⁹ By YHWH's effective word, and by it alone, the child is enabled to survive and grow.

The shame and helplessness of Jerusalem in the circumstances surrounding her birth have been carefully and effectively related in this opening section of Ezekiel's indictment. None of the other prophets (nor Ezekiel elsewhere) refer to Israel's origins with such detail.¹⁰ This is probably because the major emphasis of the prophets' message falls naturally upon the history of Israel's unfaithfulness to her covenant with YHWH. Even under the figure of Israel as YHWH's bride, her covenantal dealings with him reached back only to the period of her youth.

ISRAEL'S COMING OF AGE

Ezekiel's first words about the child's growth actually represent a confirmation of the unusual protection and deliverance of the infant. Immediately after recording YHWH's command to live and grow up, Ezekiel records His observation that the child did indeed grow up and become tall (Ezek 16:7). Of course, growing up entails reaching womanhood. Ezekiel stresses this by recording the most obvious signs that a girl is becoming a young woman. Ezek. 16:7b may be translated, "And you came to the time of menstruation,¹¹ your breasts became firm, and your (pubic) hair grew."

While there is not the opprobrium attached to the young lady in this period of her life that she endured as an infant because of her shameful parentage and birth, she still is destitute. The use of the hendiadys emphasizes this; the end of verse 7 may be translated literally, "Yet you were nakedness and bareness," that is to say, "naked and bare." Everywhere Ezekiel is concerned to stress the initiative of YHWH in lifting Israel to a status she could not reach on her own.

However, Ezekiel passes over the sins of the maiden's youth here only to scrutinize them the more intensely when he returns to the theme of the nation's outrageous adulteries in chapter 23. Jerusalem, "Oholibah," and her older sister Samaria, "Oholah," are depicted as reaching womanhood in the land of Egypt. There, even before YHWH took them to wife, "they committed harlotry in their youth, there their breasts were pressed, and there their youthful nipples were squeezed" (23:3). In order that their youthful transgressions be not forgotten before they are forgiven, each of the sisters is reminded that her later adulteries in the land are but the continuation of the habits she learned as a maiden in Egypt. Samaria is so reminded once (23:8) and Jerusalem twice (23:21, 27).

Though he does not discuss it in terms of Israel's life cycle, Hosea does accuse the daughters of Israel of playing the harlot and the brides of committing adultery (Hos 4:13–14). And he does connect their individual harlotry with the nation's unfaithfulness as a whole (4:14–15). Presumably, the daughters here include unmarried daughters and so would reflect Israel and Judah in the harlotry of their own youth, as depicted in Ezekiel 23.

It would seem that the many prophetic references to the "Daughter of Zion" (and similar phrases) refer at least indirectly, and perhaps we may say on the subconscious level, to the life cycle of Israel, pictured metaphorically as a woman. It is not uncommon to refer to a loved one in terms that, strictly speaking, are more appropriate to the youth or even the childhood of the beloved. Such terms (ones that may be true only in retrospect), when used in the present as terms of endearment, take on another meaning and become all the more precious because of it. Perhaps the term *Daughter of Zion* is intended to be seen in this light. If it is, we have many more indirect references in the prophets to the young womanhood of Israel's life cycle.

YHWH'S WOOING AND WEDDING OF ISRAEL

YHWH returned, saw that the infant he had saved from death had grown to marriageable age, and married her (Ezek 16:8). This represents Lewis's sixth component in the infant exposure tale, namely the discovery and adoption of the infant. Yet here again we see Ezekiel's artistry in adapting the form to his own prophetic ends. In the classic telling of the tale, the agent of protection of the infant and the agent discovering who the infant really is and adopting him/her are two different persons. The agent of protection may even be an animal or bird, and it is also possible that the agent of discovery and the agent of adoption are themselves two different persons. But Ezekiel reveals this infant's helplessness and YHWH's beneficence all the more clearly by combining in YHWH all the roles. When she was doomed to certain death, YHWH saved her life, and that on the very day of her birth. When he came later and she was now grown, yet still without position or prospect, he adopted her, not (as is usual in the tale) as his daughter or heir, but as his bride.

Neither Ezekiel 16 nor 23 refers to YHWH's wooing of the maiden. They focus rather on his taking her as his wife and his subsequent actions on her behalf. Some of the other prophets do contain brief but moving references to YHWH's wooing and winning of his bride. Hos. 2:14–23 is the most explicit passage. The passage actually speaks of how YHWH intends to woo his erring wife to himself again. However, the promise of the new courtship is presented in terms of the way in which YHWH had wooed her when she first became his bride. The first courtship had been in the wilderness; therefore, YHWH would bring her back into the wilderness to renew his suit. Her response would be favorable as it had been "in the days of her youth." The characteristics of the renewed betrothal were to be the same as those in which YHWH had dealt with his bride from the very beginning of their relationship.

Jeremiah also preserves a memory of the young woman's loving and faithful response to YHWH's wooing. Jer. 2:2 represents YHWH as remembering the "*ḥesed* [loving-kindness/devotion] of your youth, the love of your espousals, your going after me in the wilderness, in a land not sown."

In these passages Hosea and Jeremiah are recalling the beginnings of Israel's relationship with YHWH as a time of eager response, trust, and faithfulness on her part. That there was a dark side to her nature even early on we have already seen in Ezekiel's charges of youthful debauchery while she was still growing up in Egypt (Ezek 23). In this connection, we may recall the episodes of the golden calf (Exod 32) and the sin of Baal–Peor (Num 25), among others contained in the pentateuchal record, as examples of Israel's early indiscretions. Yet, just as Ezekiel could say that Jerusalem by her grievous sins had caused Samaria and Sodom to appear righteous (Ezek 16:47–52), so by her later adulteries (by comparison) YHWH's bride had caused her early behavior to appear faithful and virtuous.

In describing the consummation of the marriage, Ezekiel uses the normal Israelite language. YHWH spread his skirt over her, entered into a covenant with her, and she became his (16:8). In Ezek. 23:4, this is not spelled out in as much detail; YHWH says simply, "And they became mine." Yet here again we are dealing with understatement for effect. Everyone knows that a man "spreads his skirt" over a woman as a sign both of possession and protection; everyone knows that YHWH spread his skirt over Israel when she was young and small and defenseless as a nation. Everyone knows that a man and a woman enter into a covenant when they marry; everyone knows that YHWH and Israel entered into a covenant at Sinai. Everyone knows that a man and woman really do *belong* to each other in a special and exclusive way when they are married; everyone knows that YHWH possesses Israel in a way that is different from his possession of the rest of the world.

However low-key the description of the marriage may be, Ezekiel has a larger purpose that requires he elaborate in some detail the generous actions YHWH performed for His bride, and the magnificent gifts He bestowed on her. YHWH personally bathed her, washed off the blood which still remained upon her, and anointed her with oil (16:9). His actions at this late date remind us again that absolutely no one else was available to help her; from her infancy until now no other individual had helped her. These actions by YHWH made her presentable in polite society.

If YHWH's actions made his bride socially acceptable, his gifts to her made her socially noticeable. Of course gifts from the groom to the bride were common in the ancient Near East, as they are in many other cultures. (I am not speaking here of dowry, or bride-price, but of personal, unencumbered gifts.) We may think of the gifts to Rebekah in Genesis 24, presented by Isaac's agent, as one example.[12] But YHWH's gifts entail the outfitting of this young woman in every aspect of her being in the manner befitting his own consort. Her clothing, her jewelry, and her food were the best obtainable, and all bestowed on her by her new husband as his wedding gifts.

Not only are YHWH's gifts splendid, they are efficacious: "So you became very, very beautiful, and you succeeded to royal status, and there went out for you a name among the nations concerning your beauty, for it was perfect through my splendor which I bestowed upon you" (Ezek 16:13b–14). YHWH's bride may have been beautiful before her marriage; we are not told that she was. In any case, her beauty was brought to perfection, not only by the bestowal of YHWH's material gifts upon her but also by the bestowal of his own splendor. She became the standard for beauty among the nations. Such a husband and such a wedding for a foundling girl-child — it beggars the imagination, as by his telling Ezekiel intends.

ISRAEL'S UNFAITHFULNESS

At this point in the tale of the exposed infant, we would expect narration of the tale's seventh and final component — the accomplishments of the hero (in this case, of the heroine). The tale should relate here those great deeds and virtuous characteristics of the now-grown foundling which mark her as preeminently worthy of the considerable effort expended in preserving her life and in bringing her to her present status. In many examples of the tale, this component actually forms the bulk of the narrative.

In fact, Ezekiel does give us the seventh component, and it comprises the bulk of his tale also. But oh, the bitter and appalling nature of Jerusalem's accomplishments! For this, her life was spared on the day of her birth? For this, her divine husband bestowed on her all his gifts and his own splendor? By her behavior, faithless Jerusalem ironically twists the tale inside out.

In his adaptation of the tale's structure to suit his own ends, Ezekiel had followed the spirit, if not the letter, of all its components. The only hint of this reversed outcome was in the ambiguity of its second component — the fact that the infant was of noble birth. (From one perspective, an Amorite–Hittite birth was a noble heritage; but presumably from the viewpoint of most of Ezekiel's hearers, such a birth was anything but noble.) However, here there is not the saving grace of even a suspected ambiguity. On the contrary, the daughter's actions are so vile that the mother, whose sins had not been named in so many words, is smeared with the daughter's record. After a lengthy indictment of Jerusalem, Ezekiel applies to her the proverb, "Like mother, like daughter" (16:44). He then lists but one sin of the mother — that she loathed her husband and her children — before returning to an even stronger indictment of Jerusalem.

Of course, there is no theme more widely present in the prophets than the unfaithfulness of Israel. The representation of this theme under the metaphor of the adulterous wife, too, is undisputed. But in no other place is the indictment of Israel for her unfaithfulness presented in such lurid, unrelenting detail as it is in Ezekiel 16 and its companion passage, Ezekiel 23. The depths of the depravity of this faithless wife can be summed up in three details contained in Ezekiel's indictment: she made her pagan neighbors ashamed of her conduct (16:27, 57); she paid her lovers, rather than being paid, as an ordinary harlot would (16:31–34); by her actions she made her older sister Samaria and her younger sister Sodom appear righteous (16:51–52).

Other passages in the prophets depict the intensity of YHWH's sorrow and wrath over Israel's unfaithfulness just as forcefully, though much more briefly.

Jeremiah, in discussing Israel's harlotry, likens her to a she-camel in heat running in all directions, looking for mates (Jer 2:23-24). Hosea compares whoring Israel to a stubborn heifer (Hos 4:15–16). Amos likens the wealthy women of Samaria to cows of Bashan (Amos 4:1).

Several times the prophets compare Israel unfavorably with the pagan nations around her; those nations, although they do not know YHWH, are more faithful to their gods (see Jer 2:10–11). Ezekiel witnessed an ironic example of this in the temple, where he saw "women sitting, weeping for Tammuz" (Ezek 8:14). The Jerusalemite women typified the unfaithfulness of Jerusalem, YHWH's bride, by weeping over the mythic death of Tammuz, the Mesopotamian god who represented the desired lover.[13] The myth, by contrast, depicts Inanna, the new bride of Tammuz, remaining loyal to her husband even in his death, lamenting over him and avenging his murder. Inanna, the pagan goddess, was more faithful than were the women of Jerusalem.

ISRAEL'S DIVORCE/DEATH

The punishment meted out by YHWH to his bride seems, on a first perusal, to be somewhat ambiguously stated by the prophets. Was YHWH threatening to divorce her, or to have her put to death as the law prescribed for an adulterous woman (Lev 20:10; Deut 22:22)? The ambiguity may be more apparent than real, and in either case the punishment is a drastic one.

Isa. 50:1 speaks briefly of the "document of divorce of your mother [by] which I sent her away," but Isaiah does not really follow up on this. Jeremiah speaks of sending Israel away and giving her a divorce document (Jer 3:8). He then holds YHWH's action up to Judah as an example from which Judah refused to take warning. Though Jeremiah continues to discuss the harlotry of Judah, and to call both Israel and Judah to a hoped-for repentance, he does not actually threaten or prophesy a divorce for Judah. Hosea pronounces the presumed formula for divorce: "She is not my wife, and I am not her husband" (Hos 2:2). We may assume that Hosea is speaking here for YHWH, as well as for himself—against Israel, as well as against Gomer. Of course, Hosea does follow up on this formula in terms of a divorce which actually was promulgated; Gomer left, only to be bought back later as a slave–wife (Hos 3:2). YHWH's promise to "bring her into the wilderness" (Hos 2:14) refers to a coming exile that will become a second exodus.

On the other hand, Hosea does represent YHWH as saying, "I will destroy your mother" (Hos 4:5). That sounds more like death than divorce!

Ezekiel is even more explicit in threatening the death of the adulterous woman as the punishment which YHWH will bring upon Jerusalem. In Ezek. 16:38–40, he says, "Then I will judge you [with] the judgments of adulteresses and shedders of blood, and I will bring upon you the blood of wrath and jealousy. . . . And they [your lovers] will bring up an assembly against you, and they will stone you with stones, and they [your lovers?] will cut you to pieces with their swords." In Ezekiel 23, holding Oholah (Samaria) as an example before her sister Oholibah (Jerusalem), he states that YHWH had delivered Oholah into the hands of her former lovers, the Assyrians, and "they slew her with the sword" (23:10). The finale of this chapter sounds very much like Ezek. 16:38–40 in its threatened punishment. Oholah and Oholibah will be judged by righteous men as adulteresses and shedders of blood; they will be stoned with stones and cut down by the sword (23:45–47).

Several observations may be pertinent. The references to death and divorce as the punishments to be meted out are not mixed within a given passage, scarcely within a given prophet. Hosea emphasizes divorce and refers to death in passing, but keeps the two well apart.

All the prophets speak in terms of a future for the faithless wife in a restored relationship with YHWH, her husband. This would seem to militate against death as the punishment to be dealt. However, in the events that would constitute the fulfillment of these threats, death became the punishment on two levels. In the destructions of both the Northern and the Southern kingdoms, a substantial portion of the populations was actually killed. This means that death was, at least partially, the punishment for the two sisters' adultery. Virtually the entire surviving populations of the two kingdoms were exiled as well, Samaria's by Assyria and Jerusalem's by Babylon. By the destruction of their cities and the depopulation of their territories, the nations ceased to exist politically — the sisters were "killed" for their adultery.

ISRAEL'S RESTORATION/RESURRECTION

The final section of Ezekiel 16 (vv 53–63) speaks of Jerusalem's restoration in terms which do not necessarily require us to think of resurrection. Verse 53 speaks of the return from captivity of all three of the sisters — Sodom, Samaria, and Jerusalem. Yet if we remember that the destruction of both the Northern Kingdom of Israel and the Southern Kingdom of Judah was spoken of in terms of their deaths, as well as in terms of YHWH's divorcing them, then we may see here the returning from captivity not only as a restoration but as a "resurrection" from the dead.

It has often been argued that there was no developed belief in resurrection from the dead in ancient Israel, that this was a development of Second Temple (intertestamental) Judaism. However, L. J. Greenspoon has recently demonstrated that the concept of bodily resurrection is an early development in Israel, derived from certain aspects of, and dependent on, the theme of YHWH as divine warrior.[14] In the light of Greenspoon's study, we may assert, with some confidence, that Ezekiel made reference, at the end of chapter 16, not only to a return from captivity seen as a national restoration (a most unusual occurrence of itself), but also to a resurrection of the unfaithful wife who had been killed (in accordance with the law) for her adulterous harlotries.

I do not argue here that Ezekiel 16 contains a clearly developed and unequivocal statement declaring the bodily resurrection of the (righteous or unrighteous) dead. However, I agree with Greenspoon that by Ezekiel's time the concept of the resurrection of at least the righteous dead was widely enough known and accepted that he could incorporate it into his depiction, in chapter 16, of Jerusalem's life cycle. That, we have seen, began with her parentage and birth. If the punishment of the unfaithful wife was death, as we believe, then for the metaphor to be extended—and Ezek. 16:53–63 certainly does seem to consti-tute a continued use of the metaphor in Ezekiel's thinking—the restoration from captivity and the establishment of an everlasting covenant with her must be seen as alluding to a real resurrection. Otherwise, Ezekiel's handling of his artistic device, the extended metaphor, becomes sloppy, and his conclusion debilitates its effectiveness rather than strengthens it.

The first element of this restoration/resurrection is a return from the exile/death by which YHWH had punished his unfaithful bride. However, great as a return from exile/death will be, YHWH's graciousness will not be limited to a mere return. Jerusalem's latter state will be more glorious than her former. Both of her sisters, Samaria and Sodom, will also be returned from their captivity, but their relationship will now be that of daughters to Jerusalem. The covenant which YHWH will establish with his bride will be an everlasting covenant. This covenant constitutes the second element of her restoration/resurrection.

All this is not without its ironically humbling overtones, however. In carrying out her adulterous actions, Jerusalem had been boldfaced, brazen, unashamed. Now, in his promise of restoration/resurrection, Ezekiel says three times (vv 54, 61, 63) that Jerusalem will remember her wickedness in order to be ashamed of it. The second reference is contrasted pointedly with YHWH's own remembrance:

> 60   And I will remember my covenant with you in the days of your youth,
>   and I will establish with you an everlasting covenant.
> 61   But you will remember your ways and be put to shame.

Probably the most widely known passage depicting resurrection of the dead is Ezekiel 37, the prophet's vision of the Valley of Dry Bones. Of course, it may be argued that this vision is only a metaphor for Israel's return from captivity into her own land and therefore cannot really be used to argue for a belief in resurrection this early in Israel's history. We agree with Greenspoon, however, that "Ezekiel was working with a concept of the resurrection of the dead well enough known to his audience to allow for the simultaneous appli-cation of this belief to a 'literal' resurrection and national restoration."[15]

Certainly the language of the vision in chapter 37 is graphic in depicting a literal resurrection. First, the dry bones come together, and then they are clothed with sinews, flesh, and skin (vv 7–8). At the prophet's prophesying, breath comes into them and they stand on their feet (v 10). In YHWH's inter-pretation of Ezekiel's vision, he speaks specifically of the individual members of the house of Israel being brought back from their graves into the land of Israel (v 12).

Isaiah is another classical prophet who speaks of resurrection in explicit terms. Isa. 26:19a should be translated, "Your dead shall live, their corpses shall rise." For Isaiah to speak so emphatically of corpses rising again implies a familiarity with the beliefs of his audience.

Isaiah also speaks of Israel's restoration in terms of the feminine life cycle. Isa. 54:1–8 recalls the shameful time before YHWH's judgment on his erring wife, but now promises her numerous progeny. Isa. 66:7–13 portrays Zion's joy and ease of childbirth at her restoration/resurrection, as well as her pleasure in nursing her newborn children. These pictures, too, imply a further revolution of the cycle to reflect an earlier point in her life.

FLUIDITY OF THE LIFE CYCLE METAPHOR

There is another aspect to Ezekiel's and the other prophets' use of the life cycle metaphor, an aspect I choose to term its fluidity. By this I mean the ease with which the prophet can shift between the metaphor itself and the thing it describes, or, better perhaps, a recognition that the metaphor and the thing it describes cannot, in the final analysis, really be distinguished. The point of many if not most metaphors is but one: two unlike objects are compared at their point of similarity. However, there are a few metaphors for which there exist many points of likeness between the metaphor and the thing it describes. This fact accounts, in large measure, for the strength and aptness of such metaphors.

We have concentrated primarily on the metaphor of the feminine life cycle as it is used in the prophets to describe Israel's existence as a nation. This extended metaphor blends at many points with the reality the prophets seek to describe. The metaphor is fluid; their descriptions may be understood metaphorically, literally, or both at once.

Compounding the already considerable force of this extended metaphor is the fact that blended into the prophets' use of it is another extended metaphor, also of great fluidity—the metaphor of Israel as bride, the wife of YHWH. YHWH has taken Israel as his bride; he has entered into a marriage covenant with her. She has borne him children; but she has also been unfaithful to him, and he is obliged to punish her. This constitutes one segment of the feminine life cycle metaphor, it is true. But it is also an extended metaphor in its own right. It is used most frequently by the prophets, but when it is taken up and incorporated by them into the life cycle metaphor, used wholly (Ezek 16) or in part (as elsewhere), it adds its own considerable force, doubling and redoubling the effectiveness of the life cycle metaphor.

An enumeration of several points within the life cycle metaphor, at which language must be understood both metaphorically and literally, will illustrate this. It will also demonstrate my contention that the prophets developed as a major theme the history of Israel under the figure of a woman from birth through death and resurrection.

Ezekiel 16 asserts twice (vv 3, 45) that Jerusalem's parentage was Amorite on the one side and Hittite on the other. This is true metaphorically (some might say spiritually), inasmuch as the Amorite and the Hittite signify for

Ezekiel's hearers a pagan, sinful, unworthy heritage. But it is almost certain on the literal level that the ethnic heritage of Jerusalem particularly, but also of all Israel, was Amorite, and perhaps Hittite, certainly Canaanite (v 3).

On the other hand, the finding of Jerusalem (Israel) may be understood metaphorically, certainly under the image of the foundling girl-child, and also of the young maiden rediscovered at the age for marriage. But who in Ezekiel's audience, knowing the stories of the Patriarchs and the Exodus, would deny that YHWH had indeed "found" Israel, not once, but several times?

Likewise, the marriage covenant with YHWH (Ezek 16:8 and many times elsewhere) is certainly metaphorical. YHWH as husband takes Israel as his bride. Yet every Israelite knew that YHWH had literally covenanted with Israel. That covenant was not a metaphor; it possessed all the attributes of royal suzerainty treaties, including blessings for adherence to and curses for disobedience of its formal stipulations.[16]

The adultery and harlotry of YHWH's bride (Ezek 16:15ff., etc.) is unquestionably metaphorical. Just as a wife may be unfaithful to her husband by lying with another man, so Israel was unfaithful to YHWH; she worshiped other gods and trusted in other nations for her protection. Yet her adultery was also literal, as Hos. 4:13–14, and many other passages make very clear. The rites of worshiping some pagan deities included adultery by every married man and woman who participated in them. Such participation by any person, married or unmarried, could fairly be characterized as harlotry.

Chasing after lovers and giving them gifts is a metaphor of Israel's unfaithfulness to YHWH. Yet it is also a realistic description of the way both the Northern Kingdom of Israel and the Southern Kingdom of Judah squandered their resources. They themselves took the initiative in forming alliances with Phoenicia, Damascus, Assyria, Egypt, and Babylonia. These alliances usually resulted in a significant drain on the national treasuries and other resources. In the end, all resources, including life itself, were forfeit, with no gain realized. Often such alliances involved recognition of other gods, even to the point of observing foreign cults simultaneously with that of YHWH within the precincts of the temple itself. That could be called literally "chasing after lovers" and giving them gifts of the things YHWH had bestowed on her.

Again, the death of the adulterous wife, threatened in Ezek. 16:38–40, and elsewhere, is metaphorical. Yet on two levels it was also literal. A sizable percentage of Judah's people (as Israel's before her) were killed during the twenty-five years or so between Josiah's death and Gedaliah's assassination. More to the point, when all its surviving population is deported, a nation is politically dead.

Similarly, the promises of Israel's restoration may be understood as portending a metaphorical resurrection of YHWH's wife and a restoration to her previous privileged position (Ezek 16:53–63, etc.). But, like her death, the promised resurrection of the nation is metaphorical on one level, and literal on another. As expressed in Ezek. 37:1–14 and Isa. 26:19, YHWH's promise is of a literal resurrection, made not only to the nation, corporately, but also to individuals, corporeally.

SUMMARY

I have taken Ezekiel 16 as my starting point and attempted to demonstrate a fairly broad use in the prophets of the metaphor of Israel as a woman, described by means of a life cycle that extends from birth through death and resurrection. I am aided in my analysis by Ezekiel's use in chapter 16 of a transformation of an extant literary pattern—the tale of the exposed infant. In this, Ezekiel used or adapted all seven components of the tale. Its adaptation to his own purposes strengthens Ezekiel's description of Israel's history in terms of the feminine life cycle. It also emphasizes the fact, and heightens its impact, that all the good that happens to her comes through YHWH's beneficence, and at his initiative.

I found that the metaphor of the feminine life cycle for the history of Jerusalem (Israel) in Ezekiel 16 comprises a description of the infant's parentage and birth, including YHWH's rescue of the infant from death, her coming of age, YHWH's wooing and wedding of her, her unfaithfulness to her husband, her punishment (death), and her restoration/resurrection. Most of these stages in her life are individually represented in other passages from the prophets; however, none is as explicitly developed in terms of an entire life cycle of Israel as Ezekiel 16. Their cumulative effect is nevertheless persuasive in identifying such a life cycle.

Also persuasive is what I have called the fluidity of the extended metaphor, that property of the metaphor which lends itself, at one and the same time, to both metaphorical and literal interpretation. The fact that this is true at several important points in the extended use of the metaphor of Ezekiel 16 strengthens considerably the argument for the cycle theme in the prophets. We may state with confidence that the prophets thought of Israel's history in terms of a life cycle and that they foresaw this continuing in a resurrection (probably both national and personal) beyond the coming exile. In their depiction of the life cycle, they used language that at key points could be applied both metaphorically and literally to Israel's existence. By clothing their themes in literary art as attractive as the themes themselves, the prophets guaranteed the interest of their hearers in their message, even down to the present day.

NOTES

1. Roland K. Harrison, *Introduction to the Old Testament* (Grand Rapids, Mich.: Wm. Eerdmans, 1969), 758.
2. Yehezkel Kaufmann, *The Religion of Israel* (Chicago: University of Chicago Press, 1960), 348.
3. For a discussion of the Amorites in Israel's history, see J. Tracy Luke, "'Your Father Was an Amorite' (Ezek 16:3, 45): An Essay on the Amorite Problem in OT Traditions," in

H. B. Huffmon, F. A. Spina, and A. R. W. Green, *The Quest for the Kingdom of God* (Winona Lake, Ind.: Eisenbrauns, 1983), 221–37.

4. *Fragm. gr. Hist.* II, 392, pars. 4, 8.
5. *C. Ap.* II, 202.
6. Brian Lewis, *The Sargon Legend* (Cambridge, Mass.: American Schools of Oriental Research, 1980), 211–53.
7. Rubbing of newborn infants with salt was probably done because of salt's antiseptic properties (see John B. Taylor, *Ezekiel* [Downers Grove, Ill.: Inter-Varsity Press, 1969], 134).
8. It may be argued that Ezekiel could not have adapted the infant exposure tale, due to paucity of examples. However, three examples, at least, of the genre would have been known to Ezekiel: the Birth of Moses; the Birth of Sargon; and the Canaanite tale, the Birth of 'El's Children, the Gracious Gods. In any event, I am not arguing that Ezekiel consciously analyzed the tale into seven components, as Lewis has, only that he was a master literary craftsman and recognized the value of adapting a familiar genre to his own prophetic purposes.
9. For the text-critical decisions implicit in this translation, compare Walther Zimmerli, *Ezekiel 1: A Commentary on the Book of the Prophet Ezekiel, Chapters 1–24* (Philadelphia: Fortress Press, 1979), 323–24.
10. Hosea does refer to "your mother," "on the day when she was born" (2:2–3).
11. Compare Zimmerli, *Ezekiel 1*, 324; also Taylor, *Ezekiel*, 135.
12. See the discussion of A. van Selms, *Marriage and Family Life in Ugaritic Literature* (London: Luzac & Company, 1954), 22–23.
13. For an excellent study of the myth of Tammuz, see Thorkild Jacobsen, *Toward the Image of Tammuz* (Cambridge: Harvard University Press, 1970), 73–101.
14. Leonard J. Greenspoon, "The Origin of the Idea of Resurrection," in *Traditions in Transformation: Turning Points in Biblical Faith*, ed. Baruch Halpern and Jon D. Levenson (Winona Lake, Ind.: Eisenbrauns, 1981), 247–321.
15. Greenspoon, "Origin of the Idea of Resurrection," 294.
16. For the covenant, see the work of George E. Mendenhall and Meredith G. Kline.

18

A New Israel:
The Righteous from among All Nations

Duane L. Christensen

The tension between nationalism and universalism in the prophetic literature of the Hebrew Bible has long been a focus of scholarly attention.[1] Some scriptural passages express Israel's narrow self-interest, and even hatred for her enemies among the nations. But other passages express an exalted vision of worldwide salvation for "the nations." In addressing this issue, D. E. Hollenberg describes the situation for Isaiah 40–55 as follows:

> The "worm Jacob" will become a threshing sledge against his enemies. . . . The nations are to come to Israel in chains . . . , lick the dust of Israel's feet . . . , and even eat their own flesh . . . , while Yahweh speaks to Israel in the most affectionate, intimate terms. . . . On the other hand the Servant is given as a "light to the nations" . . . and "the coastlands" wait for the Servant's *tôrâ* . . . and hope for Yahweh's salvation.[2]

After a summary of previous attempts to explain the observed conflict, Hollenberg offers a solution in which he sees *the nations* as an inclusive category:

> Israel's lost sons and daughters have become so swallowed up within the nations that Second Isaiah can describe them as *foster children*. . . . Could it be that on certain occasions when Second Isaiah speaks of "the nations," he is really concerned with the foster children within their ranks, foster children who may already have begun to think of themselves as children of the nations and no longer children of Israel?[3]

In short, Hollenberg sees the Servant in the Book of Isaiah as having a mission to "crypto-Israelites" scattered among the nations. Those who respond to the Servant's message constitute the new Israel of prophetic vision, making Isaiah's universalism an extension of nationalistic hope.

Hollenberg's identification of "crypto-Israelites" living among the nations is workable and makes good sense for a number of passages in Isaiah 40–55. But, as he himself notes, "Cyrus seems to be an exception to Second Isaiah's attitude toward foreigners, for Yahweh has anointed him and grasped his right hand . . . , and Cyrus calls on Yahweh's name."[4] Hollenberg further notes that the role of Cyrus here is antithetical but comparable to that of Assyria, "the rod of my anger," in an earlier part of the Book of Isaiah (10:5).[5] Cyrus is an instrument in God's hands to achieve a specific objective for Israel.

This raises an important question. How deeply rooted is the concept of universalism in Hebrew prophecy? I find it difficult to see the origins of the exalted religious concept of universalism in the narrow self-understanding of scripture Hollenberg has suggested, particularly when universalism appears in texts earlier than Isaiah 40–55. Because of limitations on the scope of this essay, I will focus on four of *the nations*, namely, Egypt, Assyria, Edom, and Moab. I will attempt to demonstrate that the roots of universalism in Hebrew prophetic tradition are deeper than Hollenberg has outlined.

EGYPT AND ASSYRIA

Perhaps the most interesting references to Egypt and Assyria in the Book of Isaiah are found at the conclusion to the oracles on Egypt in Isa. 19:24–25:

> In that day Israel will be the third with Egypt and Assyria,
>   a blessing in the midst of the earth,
>   whom YHWH of Hosts has blessed, saying:
> "Blessed be Egypt my people, Assyria the work of my hands,
>   and Israel my heritage."

Although the prophetic oracles against the nations are difficult to date, particularly in the Book of Isaiah, they are not to be interpreted as postexilic glosses to the prophetic tradition of the Hebrew Bible, as was so often done in earlier scholarly discussion.[6] Both Egypt and Assyria are, in effect, described here as YHWH's people, with Israel as the mediator and blesser of the nations (Gen 12:3).

In Isaiah we find an important contribution to the developing tradition of oracles against foreign nations in that both Egypt/Ethiopia and Assyria are incorporated into the traditional roll call of the nations. The oracle against Arabia (Isa 21:13–17), for example, does not necessarily move beyond the Davidic ideal of early tradition (witnessed by the inclusion of Arab tribes in the roll call of nations in Psalm 83). Arab groups were apparently occupying land within the idealized boundaries of the former Davidic Empire. Moreover, the agreements formulated between the Queen of Sheba and Solomon clearly placed Arabia within the sphere of influence of the united monarchy. With Egypt/Ethiopia and Assyria, no such rationalization was possible.

The new model needed for the incorporation of these nations under YHWH's suzerainty was found in the holy-war traditions of ancient Israel, especially in the war songs from the premonarchic era. The Divine Warrior was seen as the suzerain of all nations, the Lord of history, whose dominion knew no geographical bounds. Even mighty Assyria was but the "rod of YHWH's anger" as the Divine Warrior chastened his chosen people. But once he had used this unwitting servant, the Divine Warrior vented his wrath on Assyria herself: to punish "the arrogant boasting of the king of Assyria and his haughty pride" (Isa 10:5–12).

The resurgence of Assyria in the last half of the eighth century B.C. was paralleled by a dramatic recovery on the part of Egypt, which was succumbing to invasion from the south and political subjugation to Ethiopia. Although these events in Egypt did not immediately threaten Judah, Isaiah incorporated them in his model of nations under YHWH's suzerainty in a series of oracles (chaps. 18–20; 30:1–17; 31:1–3). YHWH, the Divine Warrior, comes riding on the storm cloud to Egypt where Egypt's gods tremble before him (19:1). It is YHWH who stirs up Egyptian against Egyptian in the civil struggle (19:2). It is YHWH who confounds their plans (19:3) and gives the Egyptians over to a hard master, a fierce king who will rule over them—perhaps Piye (Pi'ankhi) or his brother Shabaka, who founded the twenty-fifth Ethiopian Dynasty in Egypt, circa 710 B.C..[7]

Since the second part of this oracle against Egypt possesses transhistorical elements, it was but a short step to lift the entire oracle to the realm of eschatology.[8] Thus, YHWH's judgment on Egypt is portrayed in apocalyptic fashion as the Nile is dried up (19:5–10) and the traditional wisdom of Egypt's sages is turned into such confusion that Egypt "staggers as a drunken man in his vomit" (19:11–15). An altar and a pillar are to be erected in Egypt to YHWH, as a sign and witness of YHWH's presence there. When the Egyptians cry to YHWH for deliverance from the oppressors, YHWH will send a savior to "defend and deliver them" (19:19–20). The picture presented here is indeed remarkable: YHWH will one day send a new Moses to deliver Egypt from bondage! Moreover, YHWH will reveal himself to the Egyptians, who in turn will worship him (19:22). Then YHWH will build a highway from Egypt to Assyria, and both the Egyptians and Assyrians will be one with Israel in their worship of YHWH in the restored land of promise (19:23–25).

The idea of Assyria as "the rod of mine anger" in Isa. 10:5 must be understood in terms of its literary context. As I have argued elsewhere, the "March of Conquest" presented in Isa. 10:27c–34 is more than a description of the approach of Assyrian troops on the nations and on hapless Jerusalem.[9] It is the Divine Warrior himself who comes to threaten daughter Zion with destruction in apocalyptic fashion. The vision continues across the chapter division. In spite of the hewing down of "the thickets of the forest" (10:34), a shoot from the stump of Jesse will become an ensign to the nations (11:1, 10) for an eschatological contest. Although the focus in these passages is on the remnant of Israel, clearly YHWH is Lord of the nations. YHWH will use even wicked Assyria to pave the way for a new conquest (11:12–16) that will establish his people in a new kingdom—a kingdom described in messianic terms (11:1–9). This scenario represents a transformation of prophetic language and thought that very nearly anticipates that of apocalyptic.

In Zephaniah's oracles against the nations, we have further evidence of an apocalyptic transformation that includes the nations within the purview of YHWH's people. YHWH's terrifying might "will lay waste all the gods of the earth." They are going to "bow down before him, each in his own place—all the lands of the nations" (Zeph 2:11).[10] The picture is somewhat like that found in Jeremiah's oracle against Elam, in which YHWH declares that he will establish his throne even in that distant land (Jer 49:38). As I noted on another occasion,

> with the reference to Yahweh establishing his throne in distant Elam, replacing her king and princes, we appear to be entering a different realm of history. The prophet is projecting his message into the future where he sees a new day on the horizon, a day when pagan world powers will submit themselves to Yahweh, the suzerain of the nations.[11]

The inclusion of the righteous—those who give YHWH their allegiance— from among all nations in the new Israel of prophetic vision appears to be a specific and sustained challenge to a narrow nationalistic conception rooted in ancient legal pronouncements. This ancient nationalistic point of view surfaces in the fundamentalist reforms of Ezra and Nehemiah, which excluded all foreigners. But imbedded in the very structure of the canon is an alternate point of view, as illustrated in the Book of Jonah and its place within the so-called Book of the Twelve. The message of Jonah is clear: YHWH not only has a right to show compassion on Nineveh, the capital of wicked Assyria, but Jonah's anger over YHWH's compassion for Nineveh is dangerous. The moment Jonah's anger excludes compassion for Assyria his anger becomes a great evil that will destroy Jonah (and Israel as well).

A close look at the four central books in the Book of the Twelve shows up the canonical ambivalence which Hollenberg has sought to remove from Isaiah 40–55.

JONAH–MICAH/NAHUM–HABAKKUK

That Nahum and Habakkuk may be outlined as a single literary unit has been argued elsewhere.[12] Here a simple outline will illustrate the point.

a - Hymn of Theophany (Nah 1)
  b - Taunt Song against Nineveh (Nah 2–3)
    c - Problem of Theodicy (Hab 1)
  b - Taunt Song against the "Wicked One" (Hab 2)
a - Hymn of Theophany (Hab 3)

The close relation between the books of Jonah and Micah is demonstrated by the fact that the missing ending to the Book of Jonah has been supplied in liturgical use in Jewish tradition by the addition of Mic. 7:18–20 to the afternoon reading on the Day of Atonement to the present time. Wicked Nineveh is the subject of both Jonah and Nahum, but in sharply contrasting manner. In the Book of Jonah, Nineveh is the focus of YHWH's compassion in what some have called the greatest missionary text in the Hebrew Bible. Conversely, as R. H. Pfeiffer once put it, "Nahum's classic paean on the fall of Nineveh is one of the earliest and by far the best of these outbursts of hatred for the heathen kingdoms."[13] The conflicting attitudes of nationalism and universalism could not be put in sharper contrast.

The complimentary nature of the books of Jonah–Micah and Nahum–Habakkuk is also seen in a comparison of the second half of each of these literary constructions. Micah's prophecy on the fall of Jerusalem (Mic 3:9-12) sets the stage for Habakkuk's reflections on the profoundly disturbing problem of why a just God is "silent while the wicked swallow up those more righteous than themselves" (Hab 1:13): when YHWH has punished his people at the hands of foreign nations, then those nations, too, are punished, most often more severely (Hab 2:4-20).

It should not be surprising to find perhaps the most exalted example of universalism (outside Isaiah 40–55) in the center of Micah (4:1-3), a passage which appears in Isa. 2:2-4 as well:

> It shall come to pass in the latter days
>   that the mountain of the house of YHWH
> shall be established as the highest of the mountains,
>   and shall be raised up above the hills;
> And peoples shall flow to it,
>   and many nations shall come, and say:
> "Come, let us go up to the mountain of YHWH,
>   to the house of the God of Jacob;
> That he may teach us his ways
>   and we may walk in his paths."
> For out of Zion shall go forth the law,
>   and the word of YHWH from Jerusalem.
> He shall judge between many peoples,
>   and shall decide for strong nations afar off;
> And they shall beat their swords into plowshares,
>   and their spears into pruning hooks;
> Nation shall not lift up sword against nation,
>   neither shall they learn war any more.

These words complement the universalistic message of the Book of Jonah. YHWH's compassion for Nineveh will ultimately be extended to include all nations. As noted, this universal vision stands in stark contrast to the nationalistic invective of Nahum directed against this same Nineveh. The dialectic within the prophetic literature of the Hebrew Bible, in terms of nationalism and universalism, is thus part of the very structure of the canon. It is not to be removed by scholarly reconstruction of the biblical text, nor is it to be explained away by semantics. Even wicked Assyria is the work of YHWH's hands (Isa 19:24), and as such she enjoys the same potential relationship to YHWH as did Israel of old. As a light to the nations, servant Israel has a mission to the nations. Those who respond to YHWH's message, even among the Assyrians, will constitute YHWH's people—a new Israel. What David and Solomon accomplished politically (compare 1 Kgs 8:65–66) will be accomplished spiritually as well as politically again.

EDOM AND MOAB

That the visionary language in the prophetic oracles against the nations is
not to be relegated to the realm of postexilic glosses is evident from a close
look at Edom in the Book of Jeremiah. Embedded in the invective against
Edom is the curious command, "Abandon your orphans! I will sustain them;
and your widows may trust in me."[14] B. C. Cresson dismisses this instance of
"sweetness and light" in the midst of a picture of gloom as a "later intrusion
which is foreign to 'damn-Edom theology.' "[15] But it is difficult to explain this
verse as a late insertion. As A. W. Streane notes, the attitude portrayed runs
counter to "the attitude which later days would have assumed towards an
enemy so bitterly hated."[16] The attitude of concern for orphans and widows
who survive Edom's calamity makes better sense historically in the preexilic
period than it does after the fall of Jerusalem when the Edomites fought
Judah in league with Nebuchadnezzar.[17] What we have here is a text that
potentially includes righteous Edomites among the people of YHWH.

The structure of the patriarchal narratives in the Book of Genesis suggests
an even more remarkable role for Edom. This is illustrated in the following
diagram:

		Jacob (Israel)
Abraham	Isaac	
		Esau (Edom)

Jacob and Esau are presented as twin brothers and the eponymous ancestors of Israel and Edom respectively. Z. Weisman has recently made a strong
case for the priority of national consciousness as reflected in the Jacob stories
over that of the traditions concerning Abraham and Isaac.[18] This observation
raises new questions about the canonical process itself in ancient Israel. For
example, it has long been noted that the editorial conclusion to the Book of
Job places Job among the Patriarchs of the Genesis account:

> And after this Job lived a hundred and forty years; and he saw his sons, and his sons'
> sons—four generations. And Job died, an old man, and full of days.
>
> (Job 42:16–17)

One could argue from a literary standpoint that Job, in effect, constitutes
an adoptive Patriarch, one who takes his place in the canon of scripture alongside Abraham. In that sense Job is a "crypto-patriarch," a model of righteousness comparable to and complimentary of Israel's ancestors. The 140 years
allotted to Job after his great testing is part of a larger structural pattern that
associates that number with the Patriarchs. Abraham was 140 years old when
his son Isaac married Rebekah. Isaac and Rebekah were married for 140 years.
Jacob was 140 years old at his wrestling match at the Jabbok River when his
name was changed to Israel (Gen 32). And, of course, Jacob's twin brother
Esau/Edom was also 140 years old at the decisive reunion of the estranged
brothers. Placing Job within this schema makes him the literary counterpart of
Abraham, as suggested in the following diagram:

Job		Jacob (Israel)
	Isaac and Rebekah	
Abraham		Esau (Edom)

That the home of Job and his friends is strongly associated with Edom thus takes on deeper meaning.

At this juncture it is instructive to take a closer look at deuteronomic legislation regarding the nations. In this legislation both Egypt and Edom are given clear precedence over Moab and Ammon, the incestuous offspring of Lot. According to the deuteronomic law,

> You shall not abhor an Edomite, for he is your brother; you shall not abhor an Egyptian, for you were a sojourner in his land. The children of the third generation that are born to them may enter the assembly of YHWH. . . .
>
> (Deut 23:7–8)

The treatment of Moabites and Ammonites, on the other hand, is much harsher:

> No Ammonite or Moabite shall enter the assembly of YHWH; Even to the tenth generation none belonging to them shall enter the assembly of YHWH for ever; Because they did not meet you with bread and with water on the way, when you came forth out of Egypt,and because they hired against you Balaam the son of Beor from Pethor of Mesopotamia, to curse you. . . .You shall not seek their peace or their prosperity all your days for ever.
>
> (Deut 23:3–6)

It is possible to see a historical reason for this treatment of Egypt and Edom versus Moab and Ammon in terms of the idealized program of political expansion in the time of King Josiah. At that time Edom was within the political sphere of Egypt, and both stood outside the scope of Josiah's projected political expansion. The latter included both the territory of the former Northern Kingdom of Israel and the transjordan states of Moab and Ammon.[19] As noted previously, both Egypt and Edom are also included within a broad prophetic conception of YHWH's people.

But whether one dates the deuteronomic legislation to Moses, to the writing prophets, or to a superimposition of law reforms in the time of Josiah, it too represents but one side of the coin. A look at the canonical process in ancient Israel reveals an entirely different point of view, one that potentially includes Moab within the new Israel of prophetic vision. In a study of women of the Bible, J. G. Williams has once again challenged the early dating of the Book of Ruth.[20] But it is not really a question of how old the tale is. In its present form, the story is a rather sophisticated work of literary art with theological profundity.

J. Myers argued some years ago for the poetic base of the book.[21] J. C. de Moor has carried this discussion a good bit further in a recent article entitled "The Poetry of the Book of Ruth," involving techniques for the systematic analysis of West Semitic poetry.[22] (His article is the first installment of a long-term research project involving a number of scholars at Kempen.) If de Moor is correct in identifying the genre of Ruth as narrative poetry (as I independently believe),[23] the question of both genre and setting of the Book of Ruth is due for a new round of scholarly discussion. Williams may have anticipated these developments in his conclusion that the book's author found patriarchal religion inadequate. Or to put it another way, "Only a foreign woman could embody what he wanted to say — even a Moabite who, according to Deut. 23:4, could never enter into Yahweh's assembly."[24] As Robert Alter indicated some years earlier, "Ruth is conceived by the author as a kind of matriarch by adoption."[25]

These ideas are a literary and canonical challenge to a simplistic reading of the Book of Deuteronomy, in a manner somewhat paralleled by the Book of Job. F. M. Cross has long argued that Job challenges a superficial reading of the deuteronomic theology of history.[26] Job suffers, not because he violated the terms of the covenant but because he was "a blameless and upright man" — at least within the folktale frame of the book. Like Ruth, this man from the land of Uz is a foreigner. In essence, Job and Ruth are to the Patriarchs of earlier tradition what the nations are to Israel in the prophetic literature. While universalism can be qualified as a form of nationalism, as Hollenberg has argued, it can also stand alone. Job was admitted into the patriarchal structure of the Genesis account because he was righteous — "blameless and upright, one who feared God, and turned away from evil" (Job 1:1). Job and Ruth become part of the community of faith because of the quality of their lives. Thus, universalism need not have national roots, as the examples of Job and Ruth adequately show. But in the end, of necessity, universalism becomes national because those who swear allegiance to YHWH, as Ruth did, are Israel — they are the people of YHWH from among all nations (Isa 19:2).[27]

NOTES

1. In addition to the commentaries, see E. J. Hamlin, "The Nations in Second Isaiah" (Ph.D. Diss., Union Theological Seminary, New York, 1961); R. Davidson, "Universalism in Second Isaiah," *ScotJT* 16 (1963): 166–85; and D. E. Hollenberg, "Nationalism and 'The Nations' in Isaiah XL–LV," *VT* 19 (1969): 23–26. The larger issue beyond Isaiah 40–55 is discussed by N. K. Gottwald, *All the Kingdoms of the Earth* (New York: Harper, 1964), 330–40.

2. Hollenberg, "Nationalism and 'The Nations,'" 23; see Isa. 41:14–15; 45:14; 49:23, 26; 43:3–4, 14, 20–21; 44:1–2; 49:15–16; 54:5–17; 42:6; 49:6; 51:4–6, respectively.

3. Ibid., 25–26; see Isa. 49:22–23.

4. Ibid., 30; see Isa. 45:1; 41:25, respectively.

5. Compare Gottwald, *All the Kingdoms*, 330–40.

6. This matter is discussed in detail in my doctoral dissertation: D. L. Christensen, *Transformations of the War Oracle in Old Testament Prophecy*, Harvard Dissertations in Religion 3 (Cambridge, Mass.: Scholars Press, 1975). See in particular the section on Isaiah, 127–53.

7. For a more detailed discussion of this complex chapter in Egyptian history, see ibid., 77–86.

8. See Avraham Gileadi, *The Apocalyptic Book of Isaiah: A New Translation with Interpretive*

Key (Provo, Utah: Hebraeus Press, 1982), esp. 195. See also Alfred E. Krause, "Historical Selectivity: Prophetic Prerogative or Typological Imperative?" in this volume.

9. D. L. Christensen, "The March of Conquest in Isaiah X 27c–34," *VT* 26 (1976): 385–99.

10. See D. L. Christensen, "Zephaniah 2:4–15: A Theological Basis for Josiah's Program of Political Expansion," *CBQ* 46 (1984): 669–82.

11. Christensen, *Transformations of the War Oracle*, 223.

12. See my article on "Nahum," in *The Harper's Bible Dictionary* (San Francisco: Harper and Row, 1985), 681.

13. Robert H. Pfeiffer, *Introduction to the Old Testament* (New York: Harper & Brothers Publishers, 1941), 443.

14. Christensen, *Transformations of the War Oracle*, 228.

15. Bruce C. Cresson, "Israel and Edom: A Study of the Anti-Edom Bias in Old Testament Religion" (Ph.D. Diss., Duke University, 1963), 78.

16. A. W. Streane, *The Book of the Prophet Jeremiah* (Cambridge: Cambridge University Press, 1881), 285.

17. Christensen, *Transformations of the War Oracle*, 232.

18. Z. Weisman, "National Consciousness in the Patriarchal Promises," *JSOT* 31 (1985): 55–73.

19. See my discussion in "Josiah's Program of Political Expansion," 669–82.

20. James G. Williams, *Women Recounted: Narrative Thinking and the God of Israel*, Bible and Literature Series, 6 (Sheffield, England: Almond Press, 1982), 87.

21. J. Myers, *The Linguistic and Literary Form of the Book of Ruth* (Leiden, Netherlands, 1955), cited in R. E. Murphy, "Wisdom Literature: Job, Proverbs, Ruth, Canticles, Ecclesiastes, and Esther," in *The Forms of the Old Testament Literature* (Grand Rapids, Mich.: Wm. Eerdmans, 1981), 13:86.

22. Johannes C. de Moor, "The Poetry of the Book of Ruth," *Orientalia* 53 (1984): 262–83.

23. See my article, "Narrative Poetics and the Interpretation of the Book of Jonah," in Elaine R. Follist, ed., *Directions in Biblical Hebrew Poetry*, *JSOT* Supplement 40 (1987), where it is argued that the genre of Jonah is narrative poetry as well.

24. Williams, *Women Recounted*, 87.

25. Robert Alter, *The Art of Biblical Narrative* (New York: Harper Colophon Books, 1981), 59.

26. First published in the form of a Convocation Address, "Will You Lie for God?," delivered 24 September 1958 at the Memorial Church, Harvard Divinity School, Cambridge.

27. I owe the substance of this final paragraph to Avraham Gileadi, whose editorial assistance did much to improve this paper.

19

Pilgrimage and Procession: Motifs of Israel's Return

Eugene H. Merrill

The most traumatic event in the history of ancient Israel was the destruction of Jerusalem and the temple by the Babylonians in 586 B.C. In one crushing blow not only was the physical center of the commonwealth reduced to ashes but the cultic and theological fabric of the nation, so inextricably bound up with temple and land, was unraveled, and the national promise and hope seemed doomed. Then, as though to ensure the finality and irreparability of the destruction, the Babylonians deported the cream of Judean social, political, and religious society to Mesopotamia. Thus the land and city lay devastated, incapable of providing the leadership necessary for rebuilding.

DESTRUCTION AND RESTORATION

The prophets, having foreseen this day, interlaced their messages of doom and devastation (Lev 26:27–33) with words of hope: the nation dispersed to the ends of the earth would eventually return and rebuild the city and temple (2 Sam 7:11b–16). In fact, the glory of the restoration would far exceed that of the grandest days of Israel's long history. The nation of Israel would once more become YHWH's people and dwell securely in her land. She would resume her worship of YHWH in a temple whose magnificence would outstrip even that of Solomon's temple (Amos 9:11–15; Mic 4:1–5).

Bible scholars are virtually unanimous in their agreement that an exile of Israel did occur and that it was reversed by the return of the Jews to their homeland coincident with the decree of Cyrus in 538 B.C. There is no consensus, however, about whether or not the historical restoration completely fulfills the prophecies. But it is clear to me that the condition of the restored community and the mode and process of return fell short of the extravagant prophecies. Therefore, the only way to harmonize the prophecies with the historical event is to find their fulfillment through the church—the new Israel[1]—or to posit an eschatological fulfillment in which a literal, physical Israel will be gathered to the land and assume her role as a redemptive community functioning cultically and politically in a manner akin to that of the ancient covenant nation.[2]

THE RESTORATION AS EXODUS OR PILGRIMAGE

This paper, however, is not concerned with the question of literal versus nonliteral fulfillment—whether the restoration pertains to the church or to a new political Israel. The eschatological versus historical aspects of the restoration prophecies are, in fact, of little interest here. My concern is with the language of restoration itself. Scholars in recent years have come to understand promise and fulfillment more and more in terms of type and antitype.[3] That is, people and events of history provide paradigms against which to view the promises of God concerning future events.

Nowhere has this hermeneutical approach been more consistently applied than in the matter of Israel's postexilic restoration. And this is not surprising because the Hebrew Bible itself views the restoration as the antitype of the most significant historical and redemptive event in Israel's past—the exodus from Egypt. This is especially clear in Isaiah 40–55, wherein the prophet uses exodus language pervasively to describe the impending return of YHWH's people from Babylonian exile.[4] That return, he says, will be nothing less than another exodus—a mighty act of God in which Israel will be redeemed from tyranny, brought through impassible waters and deserts, and restored to covenant fellowship with YHWH as his kingdom of priests.

Although the exodus typology is evident in Isaiah and in other prophetic speech, it is by no means adequate to account for all the prophetic imagery. Such elements as gathering from throughout the earth (not merely from a single place of bondage) and the emphasis on Zion and the temple argue for another complex of themes and motifs—namely, those of pilgrimage and procession.[5] The exodus as type cannot be denied, but by itself it is obviously inadequate to provide a satisfying hermeneutic by which to understand the full dimension of Israel's return. The picture is not only that of a people redeemed and miraculously transported to the land of promise but also that of a redeemed people celebrating their redemption and covenant status by undertaking a pilgrimage to Zion, the city of YHWH, Sovereign of heaven and earth. In short, my thesis is that pilgrimage and procession are as much typical antecedents to the historical and eschatological acts of YHWH in the restoration of his people as the exodus itself.[6]

PILGRIMAGE AND COVENANT COMMITMENT

A corollary to Israel's covenant with YHWH was the requirement that she make periodic pilgrimages to the sanctuary where he was enthroned. Just as the suzerain–vassal treaties of the ancient Near Eastern world stipulated that the vassal kings make regular journeys to the city of the great king to render their homage and reaffirm their loyalty,[7] so the Mosaic covenant texts spelled out the need for Israel's representatives to present themselves before YHWH as an act of corporate or community affirmation that YHWH was the God of Israel and Israel was the people of YHWH.

This requirement is first articulated in the Book of the Covenant,[8] the document by which Israel's covenant relationship with YHWH was spelled out. This pericope, of course, is juxtaposed with the complex of exodus narratives and becomes both the explanation of the purpose of the exodus and the regulation for the behavior of the nation now brought into this privileged status. The covenant text consists of the Decalogue (Exod 20:1–17)—the statement of apodictic stipulation—and the Book of the Covenant proper (20:22–23:33), with its narrative introduction (20:18–21) and covenant ceremony (24:1–18), most of which is case law specifying stipulations. Within the code is the commandment that the adult males of Israel must represent the nation before YHWH three times a year—at the feasts of unleavened bread, wheat harvest, and ingathering (Exod 23:14–17).

This requirement was further elaborated from time to time (Exod 34:18–23; Deut 16:16) and festivals were added to it, thus creating complexes of commemorative activities (see Lev 23; Num 28:16–29:39). But these never required more than the three processions to the central place of worship.[9] Historical evidence that these obligations were carried out faithfully on a national scale is lacking, but there are hints in narrative texts that the pious were careful to appear before YHWH on these stated occasions to fulfill their covenant responsibilities.[10]

THE PSALMS AND PILGRIM PROCESSION

Something of the nature of pilgrim procession is seen in David's removal of the ark of the covenant from Kiriath-Jearim to Jerusalem. Though this royal activity does not appear to have coincided with any of the prescribed festival events, it ties in closely with covenant celebration (1 Chr 16:15–17) and with the later dedication of the Solomonic temple. Hence it serves adequately as an expression of pilgrimage in obedience to covenant commitment. Accompanied by priests and Levites, David made his way toward Zion with joyful abandon. Having installed the ark in the new tent–shrine he had just completed, the king, acting on behalf of the people, praised YHWH for his covenant faithfulness and rehearsed his acts of deliverance and proclaimed his sovereignty over all the earth (1 Chr 16:31).

It is not possible here to explore thoroughly the question of David's procession as a reflex of some liturgical pattern in which later kings of Israel and Judah annually celebrated the enthronement of YHWH and secured for themselves ongoing regal authority. There is no evidence for S. Mowinckel's theory of an annual enthronement festival patterned after ancient Near Eastern analogues such as the Akitu festival. However, it is likely that the Davidic procession did provide impetus to the psalms designated "Song of Zion" (Pss 46, 48, 76, 84, 87, 122), and it clearly gave inspiration for Psalm 132, a piece A. Weiser titles "Dedication of the Temple."[11]

Weiser maintains that the psalm formed part of the Covenant Festival of YHWH, which was celebrated in autumn. This seems clear from the fact that Solomon quoted a part of the psalm (132:8–10) in his dedicatory prayer (2 Chr 6:41–42), a dedication which took place precisely at the time of the Feast of Tabernacles (7:8–10). Even if David's movement of the ark to Zion originally had nothing to do with the autumnal festival, the psalm celebrating it did in Solomon's time.

The style of royal procession must have set the tone for subsequent generations of pilgrims who made their way to the holy precincts of Zion. This is most evident in Psalms 84 and 122, which the best form-critical analyses designate "Songs of Pilgrimage." Psalm 84, though cast in the form of a hymn and similar to the "Songs of Zion," is nevertheless, as Weiser points out, "a valuable testimony to the mood of the festival pilgrims" and "provides us with a graphic illustration of the Old Testament's devotion to the house of God and the spiritual aspect of its cultic piety."[12] Particularly instructive because of its exodus associations is this passage:

> Blessed are those whose strength is in you,
>   Who have set their hearts on pilgrimage.
> As they pass through the Valley of Baca,
>   They make it a place of Springs. (NIV)
>   (vv 5b–6a)

As we shall see presently, the exilic community found in these words a source of inspiration for its own pilgrimage to Zion from Babylon.

Psalm 122, the only other "Song of Pilgrimage" in the strict sense,[13] centers on the joy of being in Jerusalem, the house of YHWH "where the tribes go up" (v 4). It also portrays the holy city as a place where peace may be found for the pilgrim whose feet at last are allowed to tread in its sacred precincts (v 2). This psalm is canonically part of a larger collection designated "Pilgrim Psalms" (Pss 120–34), otherwise known as "Songs of Ascent" because they presumably were sung in order as the procession made its way to Mount Zion.[14]

In these psalms the pilgrim points out that he has come from faraway Meshech and Kedar (120:5), places whose inhabitants hate peace (120:6–7).[15] Though the journey has been long and hard, YHWH has been his keeper and shade (121:5–6). Were it not for YHWH, the pilgrim would long since have been overwhelmed in the floods (124:4–5) and fallen to the enemy (124:6–7). Instead he can rejoice in his travels and proclaim to the nations that YHWH has done great things (126:2–3). These include restoration from captivity, a restoration as miraculous as the flowing of streams in the desert (126:4).

This restoration is another redemption (130:8), a return to Zion like that in which David transported the ark in high procession (132:1–10). The very fact of David's devotion and its acceptance by YHWH attests to the eternal character of YHWH's covenant favor to Israel. Though Zion might be destroyed, she must necessarily rise again: "YHWH has chosen Zion, he has desired it for his dwelling" (132:13). His ability to do this and to effect all of his restorative, redemptive work lies in his role as Creator of heaven and earth (134:3).

It is not difficult to see in this collection the foundation of exodus language. It is easy to understand why the prophets would use the imagery of these psalms to describe appropriately the restoration of the exilic community from its widespread dispersion and the return to Zion in pilgrim procession.

The so-called "Hallel-psalms" (Pss 113–18)[16] are also related to the three pilgrimage feasts. Psalms 113 and 114 are traditionally sung prior to the Passover meal; Psalms 115 through 118 are sung afterward.[17] But their relation to the three festivals is unclear. The incomparability of YHWH—a major theme also of Isaiah 40–55—is celebrated lavishly in Psalm 113. It is he who is above all things (113:4–5) and who is able to elevate the poor and weak to positions of eminence (113:7–9). This was demonstrated in his redemption of Israel from Egypt, an act which included his subjugation of sea and mountain alike (114:3–6).

In a work of superb irony and polemic, the author of Psalm 115 compares YHWH to the manufactured idols of the pagans which, he says, cannot speak, see, hear, smell, handle, or walk (115:5–7). Though many scholars claim "Second Isaiah" has priority over this psalm and argue that the unknown prophet provided inspiration for the Psalmist in his discussion of idolatry,[18] there is no real basis for doing so because anti-idolatry polemic can be traced back to Israel's earliest times (see Josh 24). Rather, Isaiah must have had this very psalm in mind (as well as similar passages) when he inveighed against the Babylonian gods of the exilic period, describing them in terms almost identical to those in the psalm.

The link between exilic restoration and pilgrim processional is apparently not coincidental, but rather is made deliberately by Isaiah, who connects the pilgrimage festival song to the return of the Babylonian exiles to Zion. The allusion to cult and temple (Ps 115:9–12) and to creation theology (115:15–16) confirms this connection, because the prophet makes clear that it is the Creator—YHWH—who is able to restore his people to the land and to reestablish worship in the new temple in Zion (see Isa 40:26–31; 42:5–9; 44:24–28; 51:9–16). Pilgrimage themes appear less dominantly in Psalms 116 and 117, but Psalm 118, a composition associated in tradition with the autumnal feast of ingathering,[19] abounds with restoration overtones. YHWH's ḥesed (covenant loyalty) is stressed repeatedly (118:1, 2, 3, 4, 29), as is his help against overwhelming odds (118:6–12). As a result of his faithfulness to them, his people are able to approach the holy temple and offer their tribute and thanksgiving to him there (118:27–29).

Pilgrimage and processional themes are also found throughout the Psalter in compositions not specifically identified as "Songs of Pilgrimage," "Pilgrim Psalms," or "Hallel-psalms."[20] Limits of space preclude attention to them here. Indeed, such attention is unnecessary, because enough data can be culled from the psalms cited above to make the case that the prophets, in appropriating themes and clichés relevant to the exilic restoration as pilgrimage and procession, did so from their own hymnic traditions.[21] The remainder of this paper attempts to demonstrate this point.

THE PROPHETS AND PILGRIM PROCESSION

No prophet more comprehensively brings the motifs of pilgrimage and procession to bear on the exilic restoration than Isaiah. The bulk of my discussion will refer to Isaiah, but for the sake of completeness, I must give cursory attention to the words of the other prophets first.

The earliest prophetic works come from Amos, who, in his famous prophecy concerning the "tabernacle of David," speaks of the restoration of Israel as another exodus (Amos 9:7). Yet this exodus is different in that the godly remnant will be gathered from among all nations (9:9) to reconstitute a new tabernacle of David (9:11). *Tabernacle* is a metaphor for the Davidic dynasty, the kingdom of Judah, the whole Davidic empire, or the city of Jerusalem alone. The terms *breaches* and *ruins* (9:11) might seem to favor the last of these choices, but the use of *bānâ* ("build") calls to mind the prophecy of Nathan (2 Sam 7:11–16) and prayerful response of David (2 Sam 7:27), the latter of which uses this verb in referring to dynasty. This exodus–restoration will be accompanied by a marvelous renewal of the land and the firm and final settlement of YHWH's people on it (Amos 9:13–15). Return from throughout the earth and emphasis on the tabernacle are sufficient to indicate a strong flavor of pilgrimage language.

Exodus and wilderness imagery also informs the restoration oracles of Hosea (Hos 2:14–23). YHWH will bring his people back to the land but, more important, will restore them to covenant fellowship (2:18–19), a renewal that will bring productivity of land and soil as well (2:22). As with Amos, however, the exodus of Hosea transcends that of the Mosaic era in that it is universal in its point of origin. The remnant will come from both Egypt and Assyria (that is, everywhere; 11:11). Thus their coming is more than redemption. It takes on the character of joyful procession, of pilgrimage from the distant parts of the earth to the dwelling place of YHWH (2:15, 23).

Micah, too, speaks of procession to Zion but includes within his purview the ascent[22] of the nations along with that of the remnant of Israel (Mic 4:1–8). Jerusalem is clearly identified as the city of the great king (4:2).[23] From there YHWH will reign over the earth. This reign will be concentrated in the reconstituted Israel (4:7). That the regathering will take the form of a new exodus is spelled out in Mic. 7:14–17. But it is not merely an exodus, for it will originate from all the points of the compass (7:12–13). It will therefore be a procession to Jerusalem,[24] to YHWH, who will pardon his people and renew his covenant with them (7:17–20).

If the language of Micah is somewhat veiled in terms of the pilgrimage motif, that of Zephaniah is unambiguous. He speaks of the purification of the remnant that will make a happy pilgrimage from distant lands in order to present offerings to YHWH (Zeph 3:9–10). In the language of the Enthronement

Psalm,[25] YHWH is described once more as Sovereign (3:15), he who inhabits Zion (3:16–17). The regathering of those who sorrow for the solemn assembly (3:18)[26] will result in their praise and exaltation among the nations of the earth (3:19–20).

The idea of a pilgrimage to Zion of both the remnant of Israel and the nations is stressed also by Jeremiah. References of gathering to Zion (Jer 3:14), to the throne of YHWH (3:17), and a return of Judah and Israel from the north (3:18) suggest that this gathering is not so much a new exodus as a procession to the temple in order to render homage to YHWH.

The contrast between exodus and pilgrimage is highlighted in Jer. 16:14–15; 23:7–8, where the prophet proclaims that it will no more be said, "'As surely as YHWH lives, who brought the Israelites up out of Egypt,' but they will say 'As surely as YHWH lives, who brought the descendants of Israel up out of the land of the north and out of all countries where he had banished them.'" (NIV) They will come in joyous procession (Jer 31:8–9), making their way to YHWH in Zion (31:6). That this is not merely a second exodus is evident from the fact that the return is characterized by the elements of pilgrim procession: song, offering of grain and livestock, and unbridled joy (31:10–14).

Ezekiel, the great prophet of the exile, also refers to Israel's return in terms of pilgrimage. Nowhere is this clearer than in chapter 20, where, following a description of the return couched in language of a new exodus (vv 33–39),[27] Ezekiel speaks of YHWH's holy mountain, the seat of YHWH's dominion, where he will receive the offerings of his returning people (vv 40–41).[28] They will know that he is YHWH and will confess him before all nations (vv 42–44; compare 28:25–26; 36:32–38).

That all the prophecies are not fulfilled by the return of 538 B.C. is most evident from the testimony of the late postexilic prophets Haggai and Zechariah. The return as an exodus must have appeared to be a reality by their time (520 B.C.), but the restoration of cult and ceremony, centered in the temple, was unfulfilled. Haggai thus chided the people for not rebuilding the temple (Hag 1:7–8), and when the meager edifice was finished, he spoke of a day when the house would be filled with YHWH's glory and become the repository of the sacrificial gifts of his pilgrim people, Israel and the nations alike (2:6–9).[29]

Zechariah also writes of a day of glory subsequent to the building of the second temple. It will be a day in which YHWH again chooses Zion as his dwelling place (Zech 1:16–17). The nations will assemble there and become, with Israel, his own people (2:8–13). Israel herself will be gathered from the whole earth (8:1–8) and will undertake the celebration of the stated festivals (8:19).[30] Devotion to YHWH will spread, and the nations will join in joyful procession to make their way to Zion (8:22–23).[31] In an unmistakable reference to pilgrim journey, Zechariah speaks of the nations undertaking annual observance of the Feast of Tabernacles, a procession that is mandatory if they are to enjoy divine favor and blessing (14:16–19).[32]

ISAIAH AND PILGRIM PROCESSION

Isaiah employs the motifs of pilgrimage and procession most pervasively, capitalizing at the same time on exilic restoration as a second exodus. Often the two ideas are interwoven in the same passage. The very recognition of these two strands, and not that of an exodus only, will aid the hermeneutical process.

A. L. Merrill draws attention to the fact that the two strands were already interwoven in the exodus accounts: Moses had requested of Pharaoh that the people be allowed to leave Egypt for the express purpose of undertaking a pilgrimage to the desert, there to hold a feast to YHWH.[33] The merging of the exodus and pilgrimage themes in the prophets' writings should not, therefore, be surprising. When the interpreter sees that Isaiah frequently abandons exodus terminology in favor of pilgrimage terminology, or mingles the two, he does not have the problem of trying to explain elements which seem to be disharmonious to a strictly exodus type and antitype.

This juxtaposition of themes appears first in Isa. 11:11–16. Here the prophet bases the exilic return of the remnant on a second exodus deliverance (11:16b). However, the point of origin is the whole world, not Egypt alone (11:11–12). Moreover, the way will be prepared through water and desert, so that the exiles will be able to make their way with ease from Assyria—symbolic of the entire hostile world (11:16). But the Isaianic return transcends an exodus redemption because Assyria and Egypt themselves are included in the return (19:23–25). Isaiah thus joins the other prophets in affirming the universal dimensions of YHWH's salvation.

The festal and the cultic character of the return to Zion is spelled out in Isaiah 25. YHWH will make a feast in Zion for all nations (25:6);[34] there they will rejoice in his protection and provision (25:9–10). His redeemed ones will undertake their homeward trek at the blast of the trumpet (27:13), a signal associated with the commencement of holy procession (Lev 25:9).[35] Their way home will be prepared by YHWH (Isa 35:8–9); they will come to the holy city with joy and singing (35:10).[36]

In the part of his work commonly known as "Second Isaiah" (chaps. 40–55), Isaiah describes the special preparation of the way of return: the valleys are exalted and the mountains leveled. As many scholars have observed, exodus language and themes appear throughout. But not enough attention has been paid to the thread of pilgrimage and procession as restoration imagery. In Isa. 41:17–20, a piece that has been described as a "Proclamation of Salvation,"[37] the prophet speaks of the pilgrim way as one whose desert route will be rejuvenated by springs of water and an abundance of flora. In a similar proclamation (42:14–17)[38] he describes the process of road-building YHWH undertakes in order to facilitate the return of his people. Though blind, they will easily find their way.

In the Oracle of Salvation of Isa. 43:1–7, we find an obvious juxtaposition of the exodus and pilgrimage themes. Here the redemption of Israel is predicated on the powerful intervention of the Creator–YHWH. Deliverance, however, is not from Egypt but from the ends of the earth (43:5–6). This, as the prophet goes on to say, is "a new thing" (43:19), not just a repetition of the exodus of old. YHWH's redeemed will not only return from the extremities of the earth but will come to the accompaniment of cosmic singing and rejoicing (49:13; compare 51:3).

Similarly, in the pericope of Isa. 51:9–11, the prophet, having described the expected redemption from Babylon in terms of mythic creation,[39] adds to it exodus imagery (51:10) and a scene of joyous procession to Zion (51:11). The latter is reminiscent of the colorful vocabulary of pilgrim psalms.

This added pilgrimage dimension is reinforced in the passage of 52:7–12. After introducing the messenger of good tidings who comes to the exilic community at his behest, YHWH commands his redeemed ones to flee their bondage. The remarkable thing, however, is that they must not do so in haste, as was the case in the exodus from Egypt (Isa 52:12; compare Exod 12:11). Rather, they must go with deliberation, resting in the knowledge of YHWH's presence and protection. Furthermore, they must leave only after having become ceremonially purified. The cultic associations here are obvious. These are not prisoners escaping for their lives but pilgrims about to embark on a joyous procession to Zion.[40]

Isaiah, too, is well aware that the pilgrim path is not exclusively Israel's. In the day of YHWH's redemption, the foreigner and stranger will be brought to the holy mountain, to YHWH's house of prayer (Isa 56:6–7). They, with Israel, will constitute YHWH's gathered ones (56:8). As an expression of homage to Israel's great king, they will come from afar with YHWH's elect, bearing tribute of every kind (60:4–7).[41] Their offerings will be accepted as a contribution to the ineffable glory of YHWH's temple (60:7). In effect, the remnant of Israel will itself be a kind of offering to YHWH, brought to him by the nations among whom his people had been scattered (66:20). The entire process of origination, movement, gifts, and acceptance is clearly that of pilgrimage, of holy procession of YHWH's redeemed people to his dwelling place in a transformed Jerusalem (66:22–23).

CONCLUSION

Bible scholars have long recognized that the prophets, particularly Isaiah, described the return of Israel from Babylonian exile in terms of a second exodus. That is, they viewed the Mosaic exodus as a paradigm or type of divine deliverance from Babylonian captivity. That same interpretation permits one to understand all divine deliverances, including those of eschatological times, as redemptive events patterned after the pristine exodus from Egypt.

While this understanding has been immensely helpful in providing insight into the sources of prophetic imagery and literary form, it has drawn attention away from the discontinuities between the Exodus and postexilic fulfillment of prophecies. It is true that the prophets describe the return of the remnant of Israel to their homeland as a process predicated on a great redemptive act of

YHWH akin to that of the Exodus. It is likewise true, however, that the return itself is not merely a wandering through wilderness toward a land flowing with milk and honey. It is, rather, a pilgrimage, a solemn and yet joyous procession of YHWH's redeemed to the high and holy precincts of Zion. The language of the prophets in describing this procession becomes transmuted from that of exodus and redemption to that of pilgrimage and worship.

Evidence for this is the fact that the language finds its vocabulary, themes, and motifs in cultic texts, particularly the so-called "Songs of Pilgrimage," "Pilgrim Psalms," and "Hallel-psalms," all of which appear to be hymnic expressions of the experience of the pious approaching Zion at the times of the stated festivals. For the prophets to appropriate the imagery of processional and pilgrimage literature in describing Israel's historical and eschatological return to Zion suggests, therefore, that modern interpreters of those prophets must look not only to exodus contexts for their meaning but to pilgrimage and procession as motifs of Israel's return.

NOTES

1. This is the classical amillennial position. For an excellent exposition, see Dirk H. Odendaal, *The Eschatological Expectation of Isaiah 40–66 with Special Reference to Israel and the Nations* (Nutley, N.J.: Presbyterian and Reformed Publishing Company, 1970), esp. 172–80.

2. J. Dwight Pentecost, *Things to Come* (Findlay, Ohio: Dunham Publishing Company, 1958), 441–45.

3. The literature in this area is voluminous. See especially D. L. Baker, *Two Testaments, One Bible* (Downers Grove, Ill.: Inter-Varsity Press, 1977), 239–70, and the literature cited there.

4. B. W. Anderson, "Exodus and Covenant in Second Isaiah and Prophetic Tradition," in *Magnalia Dei: The Mighty Acts of God*, ed. F. M. Cross et al. (Garden City, N.Y.: Doubleday, 1976), 339–60.

5. For pilgrimage as a religious phenomenon in general, see Victor Turner, "The Center Out There: Pilgrim's Goal," *History of Religions* 12 (1973): 191–230, esp. 197.

6. A. L. Merrill, while conceding that the pilgrimage process is not prominent in the Hebrew Bible, does emphasize that "much of the Old Testament has been written using the paradigms that have arisen from the life and worship of Israel" (see his "Pilgrimage in the Old Testament: A Study in Cult and Tradition," *Theological Markings* 4 [1974]: 6).

7. George E. Mendenhall, "Covenant Forms in Israelite Tradition," *BA* 17 (1954): 59.

8. For helpful studies on the pericope commonly designated as the "Book of the Covenant" (Exod 20:22–23:33 plus introductory theophany and concluding ceremony narrative), see J. Morgenstern, "The Book of the Covenant," Part 1, *HUCA* 5 (1928): 1–151; Part 2, *HUCA* 7 (1930): 19–258; Part 3, *HUCA* 8–9 (1931–32): 1–150; Part 4, *HUCA* 33 (1962): 59–105; S. M. Paul, *Studies in the Book of the Covenant in the Light of Cuneiform and Biblical Law* (Leiden, Netherlands: E. J. Brill, 1970), 43–98; G. J. Wenham, "Legal Forms in the Book of the Covenant," *Tyndale Bulletin* 22 (1971): 95–102.

9. R. de Vaux, *Ancient Israel*, Vol. 2: *Religious Institutions* (New York: McGraw-Hill, 1961), 471–74.

10. See, for example, Elkanah (1 Sam 1:3); Doeg? (1 Sam 21:7); and Absalom (2 Sam 15:7-12). Merrill reminds us, however, that the pilgrimage process itself is never described in the Hebrew Bible. Even the examples cited here refer more to religious festivals than to pilgrimage ("Pilgrimage in the Old Testament," 6).

11. A. Weiser, *The Psalms* (Philadelphia: Westminster Press, 1962), 778-79.

12. Ibid., 566.

13. Leslie C. Allen, *Psalms 101-150*, Word Biblical Commentary, vol. 21 (Waco, Tex.: Word Book Publishers, 1983), 157.

14. For discussion of this terminology, see Leopold Sabourin, *The Psalms: Their Origin and Meaning* (New York: Alba House, 1974), 9-11.

15. These place names constitute a merism, namely, "everywhere" (see M. Dahood, *Psalms III 101-150*, Anchor Bible [Garden City, N.Y.: Doubleday, 1970], 197).

16. Sabourin, *Psalms*, 188-89.

17. Allen, *Psalms 101-150*, 99-100.

18. H. J. Kraus, *Psalmen* (Neukirchen-Vluyn, West Germany: Neukirchener Verlag, 1978), 964.

19. Weiser, *Psalms*, 724-25.

20. See, for example, Pss. 42:1-5; 43:3-4; 48; 68:4-5, 15-18; 87; 96; 99; 100; 102:12-22; 107:1-9; 146; 147:1-3.

21. For the sake of convenience these major elements of pilgrimage and procession, derived from the three most relevant categories of psalms—"Songs of Pilgrimage," "Pilgrim Psalms," and "Hallel-psalms"—are here listed with the passages from the prophets that appear to show dependence on them, or at least concepts shared with them.
    A. Goal of Pilgrimage
       1. Zion/Jerusalem (Pss 84:5, 7; 122:3, 6; 125:1; 126:1; 128:5; 129:5; 132:13; 133:3; 134:3; compare Zeph 3:16-17; Jer 3:14; 31:6; Zech 1:16-17)
       2. The Temple (Pss 84:2, 10; 122:1; 116:28-29; 132:5-7)
    B. Purpose of Pilgrimage: Payment of Offerings/Vows/Tribute (Pss 116:14, 18-19; 118:27; 126:6; compare Zeph 3:9-10; Jer 31:8-9; Ezek 20:40-41; Hag 2:6-9; Isa 60:4-7; 66:20)
    C. Universal and Scattered Origins of Pilgrimage (Ps 120:5; compare Amos 9:9; Hos 11:11; Mic 7:12-13; Jer 3:18; Zech 8:1-8; Isa 11:11-12; 19:23-25; 43:5-6)
    D. Path of Pilgrimage
       1. Building of the Highway (Ps 84:5; compare Isa 35:8-9; 40:3-4; 42:14-17; 62:10)
       2. Irrigation of the Desert (Pss 84:6; 114:8; compare Isa 11:15; 41:17-20)
       3. Drying of the Rivers (Ps 124:4-5; compare Isa 11:16)
       4. As an Ascent (Ps 122:4; compare Mic 4:1-8; Isa 2:1-4)
    E. Mode of Pilgrimage
       1. As a Stream (Ps 126:4; compare Mic 4:1-8; Isa 2:1-4)
       2. With Divine Protection (Pss 84:11; 113:7-9; 115:9-11; 116:6, 8; 118:5-14; 121:3-8; 124:1-3, 6-8; 125:1-2; compare Isa 25:9-10; 52:7-12)
       3. With Song and Rejoicing (Ps 118:15, 24; 126:5-6; 132:9; compare Jer 31:10-14; Zech 8:22-23; Isa 30:29; 35:10; 49:13; 51:11)

22. The verb *let us go up* (Mic 4:2) is a form of the Hebrew verb ʿālâ, a common term for pilgrimage to Jerusalem (Pss 24:3; 122:4; Isa 2:3; Jer 31:6; see Delbert R. Hillers, *Micah* [Philadelphia: Fortress Press, 1984], 50).

23. Leslie Allen sees the pilgrimage theme clearly here when he says, "Year by year bands of pilgrims would make their way to Jerusalem to engage in festive worship, in the course of which they would receive instruction in the moral traditions of the covenant" (*The Books of Joel, Obadiah, Jonah and Micah* [Grand Rapids, Mich.: Wm. Eerdmans, 1976], 323).

24. See Hillers, *Micah*, 91.

25. Ralph L. Smith, *Micah-Malachi*, Word Biblical Commentary, vol. 32 (Waco, Tex.: Word Books Publishers, 1984), 143.

26. Smith (ibid., 143) translates verse 18: "Those who went away from the festival I have swept

away from you. They were heaping disgrace upon her." The textual difficulties he alleges are not at all as insuperable as his translation would suggest. "The sorrows for the appointed feast" (NIV) or "I will gather those who grieve about the appointed feasts" (NASB) seems to be reasonable.

27. As Walther Zimmerli shows, however, the exodus of the exiles will transcend that of Moses because of its widespread points of origin (*A Commentary on the Book of the Prophet Ezekiel, Chapters 1–24* [Philadelphia: Fortress Press, 1979], 415).

28. Here occurs a mingling of exodus and Zion themes, a prime characteristic of the exilic restoration as viewed in terms of pilgrimage and procession (ibid., 417).

29. Haggai teaches that "they will come with the wealth of all nations" (2:7 NASB); that is, the nations will bring their treasures as tribute to YHWH. Despite D. L. Petersen's reservations, this should be compared to Isa. 60:5–11, a passage to be taken without question as a pilgrimage text (see David L. Petersen, *Haggai and Zechariah 1–8* [Philadelphia: Westminster Press, 1984], 68).

30. The fasts of Zech. 8:10 refer to the commemoration of the tragic events surrounding the fall of Jerusalem and destruction of the temple (see respectively Jer 39:2; 52:12–14; 2 Chr 25:25; Jer 52:4). They will be turned into ritual feasts associated with pilgrimage to Zion (see Petersen, *Haggai and Zechariah 1–8*), 314–15.

31. As Petersen observes (ibid., 316), "The majority of commentators understand this oracle to be part of a larger tradition, the pilgrimage of nations to Jerusalem" (see especially Isa. 2:1–4; see also Smith [*Micah–Malachi*, 239], who speaks of this promise of pilgrimage as "a part of the continuing strand of the Zion traditions").

32. Smith (*Micah–Malachi*, 291–93) describes this entire passage as the "The Pilgrimage of the Nations to Jerusalem."

33. Merrill, "Pilgrimage in the Old Testament," 12–13; compare Exod. 3:12; 5:1.

34. The reference here to a feast of YHWH clearly roots the passage in pilgrimage thought, though usually the pilgrimage of the nations involves their presentation of gifts to Zion (see Pss 68:29–30; 72:10; 96:7–8; Isa 45:14; 60:3–4; 66:12; see also Otto Kaiser, *Isaiah 13–39* [Philadelphia: Westminster Press, 1974], 199–200).

35. Kaiser, *Isaiah 13–39*, 232–33.

36. That this is the language of pilgrim procession is shown by E. J. Young, *The Book of Isaiah* (Grand Rapids, Mich.: Wm. Eerdmans, 1969), 2:452–56.

37. See Claus Westermann, *Isaiah 40–66* (Philadelphia: Westminster Press, 1969), 79.

38. Westermann (ibid., 106–7) draws helpful parallels between this passage and Isa. 41:18–20. He shows how YHWH's opposite works of irrigation and drying up in the respective texts are two sides of his preparation of the pilgrim way to Zion.

39. This, of course, means only that Isaiah used mythopoeic language well known to his hearers/leaders in order to communicate YHWH's sovereignty over natural and political chaos (see J. Muilenburg, "The Book of Isaiah: Chapters 40–66," *IB* [New York: Abingdon, 1956], 5:401; F. M. Cross, *Canaanite Myth and Hebrew Epic* [Cambridge: Harvard University Press, 1973], 107–8).

40. The idea of YHWH going before them to lead and behind them to guard (Isa 52:12; compare 58:8) not only suggests procession as opposed to the haste of exodus, but highlights the caricature of Babylonian procession seen in Isa. 46:1–2. There, in an obvious reference to the Akitu festival, but in the language of deportation, the prophet describes the humiliation of Marduk and Nabu, who do not lead but are themselves led by their captors (see Walter Brueggemann, *The Prophetic Imagination* [Philadelphia: Fortress Press, 1978], 73–74).

41. John L. McKenzie, *Second Isaiah* (Garden City, N.Y.: Doubleday, 1968), 177.

20

The Prophetic Literality of
Tribal Reconstruction

Stephen D. Ricks

A persistent theme and concern in the Hebrew Bible, particularly in the prophetic literature, is the land.[1] Another theme that permeates the prophetic writings, one intimately connected with the motif of the land, is forebodings of national catastrophe—with the consequent dissolution of the tribes and the loss of their territory. Equally persistent (and frequently placed as a thematic countercurrent to oracles of dispossession) are prophetic promises of reenfranchise-ment: a cleansed and chastened Israel will be reunified and restored to its land.[2] Reenfranchisement and tribal reconstruction, too, are inextricably connected. Although Israel may exist and worship outside of the land, reconstruction of the tribes is never described as taking place outside of it. Conversely, in prophetic thought no meaningful return is possible without some form of tribal reconstruction. Although some prophetic writings are unclear about the extent of tribal reconstruction—or they mention only Judah or Israel in their descriptions of it—others explicitly include all the tribes, those of the north as well as Judah. This study, then, will examine the prophetic promises of the restoration and reconstruction of Israel's tribes, with particular attention paid to the relationship between tribal reconstruction and the return to the land.

It has been suggested that the oracles heralding the restoration of Israel and Judah represent secondary scribal efforts to "domesticate the prophets"—to take the biting edge off pronouncements of national disaster—or that these oracles have their origin in the euphoria occasioned by the historical return from exile.[3] That some oracles are not original with the prophet to whom they are ascribed is, of course, possible. But whether a prophecy derives from the prophet himself, from one of his followers, or from a later redactor does not affect its value for providing insight into the Israelite hope for reenfranchise-ment and tribal restoration.

R. P. Carroll's remark about the "new covenant" passage in Jer. 31:31-34 is relevant to the question of the source and dating of all pronouncements concerning tribal reconstruction, and indeed to all so-called "secondary additions" in the biblical text:

> Granted that in religious contexts, the authority issuing a statement can contribute to the significance of that statement, . . . the meaning of texts is not changed by regarding them as secondary. If the new covenant passage is a fundamentally important concept, then it remains an important concept no matter who penned it or when it was written. . . . The old practice of dismissing as unimportant (or not warranting exposition) the secondary material in the biblical traditions is on the wane, and a more responsible attitude is beginning to be taken towards all the elements in the text.[4]

Of course, that certain of the prophecies (for example, Ezekiel) have an exilic or postexilic date is uncontested. Still, it can be disputed that all the oracles of restoration have their origin in hopes and expectations occasioned by the historical return. Further, even where these prophecies may have had their source there, they cannot all have had their complete fulfillment in the postexilic period.

LAND LOSS AND TRIBAL DISSOLUTION IN THE PROPHETIC WRITINGS

Of the sixteen canonical "writing prophets," ten—Amos, Hosea, Isaiah, Micah, Zephaniah, Jeremiah, Ezekiel, Obadiah, Zechariah, Joel—write about Israel's future hopes of reconstruction and reenfranchisement. Without exception, each one writing in the preexilic period also reflects on Israel's exile and tribal dissolution. Among the exilic and postexilic prophets who mention the subject of tribal reconstruction—Jeremiah, Ezekiel, Obadiah, Zechariah, and Joel—the "scattering of Israel" is already an accomplished fact. Thus, if their works contain no explicit mention of Israel's dissolution and disenfranchisement, that is doubtless because it was a presupposition for them.

Amos, the earliest of the prophets whose oracles contain reflections on Israel's future hopes (Amos 9:15; compare 3:12; 5:3), writes in stark detail about Israel's destruction:

> Therefore this is what YHWH says: Your wife will become a prostitute in the city, and your sons and daughters will fall by the sword. Your land will be measured and divided up, and you yourself will die in a pagan country. And Israel will certainly go into exile, away from their native land.
>
> (Amos 7:17)

The harshness of Amos' saying is set in sharper relief when it is recalled that this was uttered at the height of Israel's prosperity and self-confidence. However, it sets the tone for the prophecies of later, more troubled times.

Hosea's juxtaposition of the two themes of tribal dissolution and reconstitution is embedded in his cyclical and patterned reflections on Israel's history, past, present, and future. The first part of each cycle treats Israel's imminent fall and subsequent exile (Hos 1:2–9; 2:2–14; 4:1–10:15), in which the certain discomfiture of YHWH's people is foretold: "For I will be like a lion to Ephraim, like a great lion to Judah. I will tear them to pieces and go away; I will carry them off, with no one to rescue them" (5:14). The sense of tribal disintegration is strengthened by the simile in Hos. 13:3, where Ephraim is likened to "the morning mist, like the early dew that disappears, like chaff swirling from a threshing floor, like smoke escaping through a window." Isaiah similarly indicts Israel and Judah and portends their inescapable judgment despite their self-confident assertion: "The bricks have fallen down, but we will rebuild with dressed stone; the sycamores have been felled, but we will replace them with cedars!" (Isa 9:10). YHWH's message to arrogant Israel is simple and certain: "It [YHWH's judgment] will fall on Israel" (9:8).

More than any other prophet, Jeremiah expresses the fear and inevitability of exile. In his writings there is "an extraordinary coming together of external upheaval, poetic articulation in power, and the irresistible coming of the Holy One in terror."[5] "I will uproot Judah from among them" is YHWH's judgment on his people (Jer 12:14). Because they have forgotten him, YHWH will "throw you out of this land into a land neither you nor your fathers have known, and there you will serve other gods day and night" (16:13). But Jeremiah's reflections do not cease with an affirmation of Judah's demise at the hands of Nebuchadnezzar (21:7; 22:25; 28:14; 29:21). In stunning contrast to the oracles of his predecessors, Jeremiah asserts that the exile accords with YHWH's divine intention and represents a positive good:

> Like these good figs, I regard as good the exiles from Judah, whom I sent away from this place to the land of the Babylonians. . . . But like the poor figs, which are so bad they cannot be eaten, says YHWH, so will I deal with Zedekiah king of Judah, his officials and the survivors from Jerusalem, whether they remain in this land or live in Egypt. I will make them abhorrent and an offense to all kingdoms of the earth, a reproach and a byword, an object of ridicule and a cursing, wherever I banish them. I will send the sword, famine, and plague against them until they are destroyed from the land I gave to them and to their fathers.
>
> (Jer 24:5, 8–10)

Given Jeremiah's repeated insistence that Nebuchadnezzar was acting as YHWH's agent in overthrowing Judah (as well as his direct reference to exiles among the good figs and to Zedekiah and his court among the evil figs), it is little wonder that Jeremiah encountered hatred and animosity at court. But, as J. Paterson points out, a view of landlessness as God-ordained was necessary in order to perpetuate Israel's faith: were worship inexorably bound to the land, it would have been impossible for Israel to practice her religion outside it.[6]

Unlike the exilic and postexilic prophets Obadiah, Zechariah, and Joel— none of whom explicitly comments on the fact of the exile—Ezekiel frequently reflects on its causes and on Israel's future hope. Ezek. 36:16–37 contains an epitome of the theology of the entire book. The passage is perhaps the most sustained statement of YHWH's reasons for exiling his people as well as his grounds for embarking on their return. As elsewhere in the book, the prophet cites YHWH's abhorrence of Israel's actions to be the cause of her exile: "When the people of Israel were living in their own land, they defiled it by their conduct and their actions" (36:17; compare 20:9, 22; 36:5; 39:25). As a consequence, says YHWH, "I dispersed them among the nations, and they were scattered through the countries" (36:19).

But the exile "profaned" YHWH's name, not because of the scandalous lives of the exiled Israelites but because of the disrepute into which YHWH's name had fallen in the dissolution of the triad of people, land, and God. YHWH therefore swears he will end the exile and restore his people to their land: "For the sake of my holy name. . . . I will show the holiness of my great name which has been profaned among the nations" (36:22–23). The reassembled nation will be purified in heart and spirit, and there will be one flock with one shepherd. Thus YHWH promises his people: "I will take you out of the nations; I will gather you from all the countries and bring you back into your own land" (36:24). This restoration would include a renewal of the land and its products (36:34–35). Just as vital, YHWH promises a chastened Israel a new covenant: "I will cleanse you from all your impurities and from all your idols. . . . I will put my Spirit in you and move you to follow my decrees and be careful to keep my laws" (36:24, 27).

REENFRANCHISEMENT AND TRIBAL RECONSTRUCTION IN THE WRITINGS OF THE PREEXILIC PROPHETS

If exile and tribal dissolution are the inescapable result of Israel's abandoning of YHWH, Israel's future condition represents a reversal of the consequences of her fall. Juxtaposed with the oracles of judgment that comprise much of Amos is a prophecy which delineates the shape of her future hope: YHWH promises the restoration of "David's fallen tent," the return of "my exiled people Israel" to the land, and the reconstruction of "broken places" and "ruined cities" for YHWH's people to dwell in. Israel's repossession of the land will be permanent: "I will plant Israel in their own land, never again to be uprooted from the land I have given them" (Amos 9:15).[7] While no other passages in Amos are as positive in their portrayal of Israel's future, some hold out hope for a remnant. The theme of a remnant is widely used and developed by later prophets, particularly Isaiah and Jeremiah.[8] After lamenting that "the city that marches out a thousand strong for Israel will have only a hundred left" (5:3), Amos continues: "Hate evil, love good; maintain justice in the courts. Perhaps YHWH God Almighty will have mercy on the remnant of Joseph" (5:15).

In Hosea's writings all the major themes relating to Israel's reconstruction are adumbrated: the return to the land, the restoration of the tribes, and cultic and spiritual renewal. Where Israel's lands had been lost to invaders, YHWH promises: "I will give her back her vineyards, and I will make the Valley of Achor [trouble] a door of hope" (Hos 2:15). Where before the people had rejected YHWH, and consequently had been rejected by him, "they will be called sons of the living God" (1:10). Where previously Israel and Judah had been a house divided, "the people of Judah and the people of Israel will be reunited, and they will appoint one leader" (1:11). The juxtaposition of Judah and Israel in this oracle is significant in defining the parameters of the restoration: both the Northern and Southern kingdoms would take part in the return, and both kingdoms would be united—as in the days of David and Solomon—under a single ruler (compare Isa 11:12; Jer 3:11, 18; 23:6; Zech 8:13 for other examples of the pair Judah/Israel).

Elsewhere in the prophetic literature, the pairs Jacob/Joseph (Obad 18; compare Ps 77:15), Judah/Joseph (Ezek 37:16, 19; Zech 10:6), and Judah/Ephraim (Isa 11:13; Zech 9:13; compare Ezek 37:16, 19) are used to indicate the kingdoms of the south and north.[9] The ideal of a single leader over the tribes is similarly a theme of subsequent prophets. In their reflections on this leader, his Davidic ancestry is made explicit: "The days are coming, declares YHWH, when I will raise up to David a righteous branch, a king who will rule wisely and do what is just in the land. In his days Judah will be saved and Israel will live safely" (Jer 23:5).

The promises of restoration and future blessing given in the final chapter of Hosea (chap. 14) are inextricably linked to repentance and righteousness: "Return, O Israel, to YHWH your God. Your sins have been your downfall: Take words with you and return to YHWH. Say to him: Forgive all our sins and receive us graciously. . . . Assyria cannot save; we will not mount war-horses. . . . I will heal their waywardness and love them freely, for my anger has turned away from them" (14:1–3a, 4). Hosea sees that if Ephraim's fall created new opportunities, the realization of these opportunities was contingent on Ephraim's willingness to confess and forsake sins and to exercise faith.[10] Hosea's "theology of return"—with its emphasis on repentance as a precondition for tribal reconstruction—contrasts markedly with Ezekiel's reflections cited above. To Ezekiel, Israel's return is "for the sake of God's holy name" (Ezek 36:22); no preconditions of repentance or righteousness are set: the return is strikingly certain and *sola gratia*, to use Walther Zimmerli's suggestive phrase.[11]

By making YHWH's restoration of Israel and return to the land his final act of loving kindness, Zephaniah highlights its centrality in God's design. Following pronouncements of YHWH's judgment against Judah (Zeph 1:4–13) and Jerusalem (3:1–5), against the nations (2:4–15; 3:6–8), and against all the unrighteous; and an announcement of the terrors of the day of YHWH (1:7–2:3), Zephaniah ends with a message of hope. To the nations, YHWH will give pure lips—"that all of them may call on the name of YHWH and serve him shoulder to shoulder" (3:9). He will also restore the fortunes of a meek and submissive Israel: enemies will be turned back (3:15) and sorrows removed (3:18). Then, in language reminiscent of the restoration oracle in Mic. 2:11, YHWH promises: "I will rescue the lame and gather those who have been scattered" (3:19). But YHWH's ultimate act of mercy and loving kindness lies in gathering his scattered people to their land: "At that time I will bring you home. I will give you honor and praise among all the peoples of the earth when I restore your fortunes before your very eyes" (3:20).

Zephaniah's message underscores the central importance of Israel's restoration in her land. No greater sign of YHWH's power can be given to the nations than in Israel's unexpected return to the land. Further, no spiritual restoration of Israel is complete if it does not include Israel's reconstruction in her own land.

TRIBAL RECONSTRUCTION IN THE WRITINGS OF THE EXILIC AND POSTEXILIC PROPHETS

A subtly reticulated picture that forbodes catastrophe dominates the writings of the preexilic prophets. Still, many of the major themes associated with tribal reconstruction — the return to the land of a remnant, the reunion of the tribes of the north with Judah, the land allocation of the tribes — appear there also. But the so-called theology of exile and return receives its most thorough development and nuancing in the writings of the exilic and postexilic prophets, particularly Jeremiah and Ezekiel.

If the Book of Jeremiah is laden with reflections on the terror and inevitability of exile, it is not wanting in oracles holding out a hope for return.[12] The theme of return receives its richest treatment in chapters 30–31, where prophecies of doom are interspersed with oracles of salvation, arranged so as to maintain a dynamic tension between judgment and hope. Thus, YHWH promises that "the days are coming . . . when I will bring my people Israel and Judah back from captivity and restore them to the land I gave their forefathers to possess" (Jer 30:3). The oracle of salvation continues by promising Israel and Judah a return from distant lands where they have been scattered, freedom from enslavement, and liberation to serve YHWH:

> They will serve YHWH their God and David their king whom I will raise up for them. . . .
> I will surely save you out of a distant place, your descendants from the land of their exile. Jacob will again have peace and security, and no one will make him afraid. I am with you and will save you, declares YHWH. Though I completely destroy all the nations among whom I scatter you, I will not completely destroy you.
>
> (Jer 30:9–11)

In Jeremiah's deliverance oracles the promise of a Davidic king is included as a specific element within prophecies of Israel's future restoration and reenfranchisement (Jer 23:5; 33:15, 17, 22, 26, 30). This theme is also taken up by Ezekiel (Ezek 34:23; 37:24–25; compare Hos 3:5); and Isa. 11:1–5, too, alludes to a Davidic ruler in a restoration context. In addition, according to Jeremiah, YHWH promises the restored tribes a renewal of the blessings they had formerly enjoyed:

> I will restore the fortunes of Jacob's tents, and have compassion on his dwellings; the city will be rebuilt on its ruins, and the palace will stand in its proper place. . . . Their children will be as in days of old, and their community will be established before me; I will punish all who oppress them.
>
> (Jer 30:18, 20)

The people of Judah and Israel, thus restored to their territory and to the worship of their God, ruled by a Davidic monarch rather than by foreigners, their land renewed and their cities rebuilt, are ready for the renewal of the covenant. This covenant is "not like the covenant I made with their fore-fathers, when I took them by the hand to lead them out of Egypt" (Jer 31:31). Here, for the first time, the idea of covenant in oracles of restoration is linked with reenlandisement and the reunification of Israel. The radical newness of the covenant is emphasized by its contrast with the Sinaitic covenant: whereas the former covenant was written on tablets of stone, the new covenant would reside in the hearts of the participants in a "redeemed society"; it would be "formulated on the basis of individuals who responded to the free expression of divine love."[13]

In the vision of Ezekiel 37, the themes of return, restoration, and renewal appear again: Israel and Judah, "in that day," will return from exile, be restored to their land, and become renewed in spirit. Thereafter—when both Judah and Israel are restored—a Davidic king will rule over them, and YHWH will make an everlasting covenant with them.[14]

The exact nature of the reconstitution of the tribes is described with unparalleled thoroughness in the final chapters of Ezekiel. The restored temple (Ezek 40:1–47:12) and the allotments of the tribes (Ezek 47:13–48:35) are delineated in painstaking detail. Ezekiel's description of tribal land allocations diverges significantly from the historical record of any period in Israelite history. Whereas the northern and southern borders of the land, as described in Ezekiel's account, are somewhat difficult to determine because of relatively obscure geographical terms, the Jordan River and the Mediterranean Sea clearly form the eastern and western boundaries.[15] No Israelite territory is envisioned east of the Jordan. The three historically transjordan tribes—Reuben, Gad, and half of Manasseh—are all granted territory west of the Jordan, territory which had not been theirs in the biblical period. According to Ezek. 47:14, the tribes are each to receive an equal allotment: "You are to divide it [the land] equally among them." Similarly, the order of the allotments to the tribes (from north to south) does not accord with any period in Israelite history: Dan, Asher, Naphtali, Manasseh, Ephraim, Reuben, Judah, Levi, Benjamin, Simeon, Issachar, Zebulon, Gad.

No longer is the priestly tribe of Levi landless; it has been assigned the temple area. Jerusalem's name has been changed to "YHWH Is There"— probably to eliminate former historical, political, and secular associations. The tribes descended from the maidservants—Dan, Asher, Naphtali, and Gad— are placed farthest from the temple, perhaps to reflect their inferior status in the sacred history. Dan, Asher, and Naphtali appear in the same order they usually do in the histories. However, Zebulon and Issachar have been transferred to the south, probably to place the temple closer to the center of the land. The tribe of Judah is north of Levi's allotment, while Benjamin is to the south of it—the reverse of their positions historically. The intention of this reversal may have been to associate Judah more closely with the northern tribes and to depoliticize the Davidic king who would rule over all Israel.[16] All of the tribes are again mentioned explicitly in the final passage of Ezekiel (48:30–35), where each of the twelve gates of the city "YHWH Is There" (Jerusalem) is named after one of the tribes.

Other passages that deal with tribal reconstruction might (in my opinion, often only with difficulty) be construed to have had their fulfillment in the postexilic period or (according to some Christian exegetes) in the church. Ezekiel 47–48, on the other hand, if construed in any sense literally, defies such an interpretation. I am inclined to agree with J. B. Taylor, who sees in this restoration oracle — as also in most of the final third of Ezekiel, with its references to Judah and Joseph reunited in their land, a Davidic monarch on the throne, and a rebuilt temple — a reference to an eschatological "messianic kingdom."[17]

CONCLUSION

Although the recorded extent of each prophet's reflections on tribal reconstruction varies, and although these oracles are presented with different emphases and nuances, a pattern emerges in these reflections: (1) coupled with a return to the land, there would be a reunification of the northern and southern tribes; (2) a Davidic king would rule over YHWH's people; (3) the land would be rebuilt and renewed and would have a restored temple at its center; and (4) a covenant that is "new" and "everlasting" would be made with a transformed people, Israel.

It may be argued that the church or some historical or current political configuration may correspond to certain elements in this portrait. However, nothing past or present fully conforms to this vision. Its realization belongs to a "redeemed people" (to borrow R. K. Harrison's remark on Jeremiah's restoration vision) in the messianic age.[18]

NOTES

1. Walter Brueggemann, *The Land: Place As Gift, Promise, and Challenge in Biblical Faith* (Philadelphia: Fortress Press, 1977), 3, sees in land "a central, if not *the central theme* of biblical faith." Elmer A. Martens, *God's Design: A Focus on Old Testament Theology* (Grand Rapids, Mich.: Baker Book House, 1981), 19, views land as one of the four fundamental categories of "God's design." According to Peter Diepold, *Israels Land* (Stuttgart: W. Kohlhammer, 1972), 187, the land is "*konstitutiv für Israels Existenz.*"

2. Thomas M. Raitt, *A Theology of Exile: Judgment/Deliverance in Jeremiah and Ezekiel* (Philadelphia: Fortress Press, 1977), 3.

3. W. D. Davies, *The Territorial Dimension of Judaism* (Berkeley and Los Angeles: University of California Press, 1982), 23–24.

4. Robert P. Carroll, *From Chaos to Covenant: Uses of Prophecy in the Book of Jeremiah* (London: S.C.M. Press, 1981), 216.

5. Brueggemann, *The Land*, 108.

6. John Paterson, "Jeremiah," in *Peake's Commentary on the Bible*, ed. Matthew Black (London and New York: Thomas Nelson, 1962), 555. There is a danger, as David N. Freedman

points out in "'Son of Man, Can These Bones Live?'" *Int* 29 (1975): 181, that the exile could result in the Judahites' "complete assimilation to Mesopotamian culture and ultimate loss of the Yahwist heritage." The resolution for Jeremiah of the tension between the peril and promise of the exile lies in the establishment of a "new covenant," with a transformed people who have been restored to their lands (outlined in Jer 30–33).

7. The genuineness of these verses has been widely questioned, often with compelling arguments. J. A. Motyer's response in "Amos," in *The Illustrated Bible Dictionary*, 3 vols. (Wheaton, Ill.: Tyndale House Publishers, 1980), 1:45, to this line of argumentation is much to the point: "The prevailing fashion for refusing these verses to Amos ought to be resisted. It is not out of place for a Judahite to assert the Davidic hope nor inappropriate for Amos (notwithstanding his stress on judgment) to crown the negative, ruling out of final loss, with a matching positive statement of final glory."

8. Compare, for example, Isa. 10:20–21; 37:31–32; 46:3; Jer. 6:9; 24:8; 31:7; 40:11, 15; 44:12, 14, 28; Mic. 2:12; 4:7; 5:7–8; Zeph. 2:9.

9. On the other hand, Zech. 11:14 speaks of a time when the brotherhood between Judah and Israel would be broken.

10. James M. Ward, *Hosea: A Theological Commentary* (New York: Harper and Row, 1966), 233.

11. Walther Zimmerli, "The Word of God in the Book of Ezekiel," in *History and Hermeneutic*, ed. Robert Funk (New York: Harper and Row, 1967), 13. Similarly, as Raitt, *Theology of Exile*, 185–89, shows, in this "deliverance oracle," as well as the oracle of Jer. 24:7 (compare Isa 44:22), prerequisites for forgiveness are absent—in striking contrast to the requirements for forgiveness in the preexilic period (compare Deut 4:26–31; 30:1–10; 1 Kgs 8:46–53; Jer 26:3).

12. According to Raitt, *Theology of Exile*, 124, Ezekiel "is further into the mentality of deliverance than Jeremiah," whose oracles tend to stress judgment themes.

13. R. K. Harrison, *Introduction to the Old Testament* (Grand Rapids, Mich.: Wm. Eerdmans, 1971), 853.

14. While the final third of Ezekiel is devoted almost exclusively to a description of a restored Israel, there are several oracles dealing with tribal reconstruction in the first two-thirds of the work (for example, Ezek 11:14–21; 12:15–16; 20:39–41).

15. Peter C. Craigie, *Ezekiel* (Philadelphia: Westminster Press, 1983), 314.

16. Jon D. Levenson, *Theology of the Program of Restoration of Ezekiel 40–48* (Missoula, Mont.: Scholars Press, 1976), 115–18.

17. John B. Taylor, *Ezekiel: An Introduction and Commentary* (Downers Grove, Ill.: Inter-Varsity Press, 1969), 239–40, 284–85.

18. Harrison, *Introduction to the Old Testament*, 853.

21

The Prophetic Ideal
of Government
in the Restoration Era

Douglas K. Stuart

The Hebrew prophets who predict a postexilic ideal era for Israel or other nations are consistent in describing this era as one in which YHWH will establish a rule of justice under a Davidic king.[1] Thus, in general, monarchy is the expected form of government in the restoration era. But how exactly will this rule of justice be implemented? Do the prophets foresee a monarchy with exclusive administrative powers, or is governmental authority to be shared with priests, judges, and other officials who themselves will exercise a measure of autonomy?

The question of who will or will not share power in the restoration government is important; the nature of a society is molded by its leadership institutions. Prophetic descriptions of a future glorious age may also reveal something about contemporary conditions, conditions which may parallel or contrast future expectations. Moreover, a society's relationship to its God can involve mediation of the relationship itself.

For example, prophetic descriptions of the new age that consistently portray the presence and leadership of YHWH without any intermediary other than the divinely appointed king would tend to emphasize YHWH's direct sovereignty. Conversely, predictions of a system of government in which judges and priests, too, are given independent powers or executive authority would emphasize an indirect, apportioned sovereignty. On the other hand, prophetic expectations of a government in the hands of a divinely appointed king, but involving other officials in societal leadership roles delegated by that king, would combine elements from both models. Further, such expectations might correlate aspects of the future age with those of the present age. The preexilic prophets and their immediate audiences, for example, witnessed this latter system of rule in Israel and Judah.

Evidently, judges and priests, where they function legitimately, exercise a measure of divine power or authority. We should therefore expect that prophetic descriptions of Israelite society which include roles for judges and priests would acknowledge that authority. My interest here lies chiefly in the extent of their power and authority. Do the prophets expect that in the restoration era officials such as judges and priests will exercise power not delegated to them by the king? Or, to put it more succinctly, will the divinely appointed monarchy of the restoration era be absolute or limited? By absolute monarchy I mean a kingship in which all executive, legislative, and judicial powers are ultimately vested in the king, even if many of those powers are routinely exercised by subordinate functionaries. By limited monarchy I mean a kingship in which the king cannot act entirely at will because he does not possess full power and authority. In that case, other officials would exercise authority independent of his, powers assigned to them either directly by Israel's God, without regard to the king, or by some perceived natural right or popular election or other means.

This question of whether a restoration era monarchy would be absolute or limited unfortunately has been addressed only rarely by scholars. That is partly so because the relevant prophetic passages are few and scattered but also because in such passages the relationship of nonroyal officials to the king is a matter treated incidentally rather than centrally.

THE PROPHETIC FUTURE

That the prophets expect a monarchy in the restoration era is undisputed. Kingship is not only represented widely in restoration-promise contexts among the Hebrew prophets (as in the prior references), it also features prominently in the intertestamental literature,[2] the targums, and the Talmud. The biblical evidence, however, is somewhat ambiguous and requires careful interpretation. Most prophetic descriptions of and allusions to the restoration era do not concern themselves with how the monarchy functions and thus do not relate directly to this essay. I will therefore focus on the few passages in which the prophets address more or less directly the question of *how* government is implemented, specifically in terms of power and authority exercised in the restoration era. I admit that the selection of these passages may be subjective; some may consider additional prophecies germane to the issue. However, to take the reader through all of the passages would be impossible. Those I have examined but rejected on the basis of being insufficiently informative on the function of government I have excluded from this discussion.

In my assessment there are only five prophetic passages that directly relate to the question of absolute versus limited monarchy:[3]

1. I will restore your judges [*šōpṭayik*] as at first, your counselors [*yōʿăṣayik*] as in the beginning.   (Isa 1:26)

2. Behold, a king will reign in righteousness and rulers [*śārîm*] will rule with justice.
                                                                                    (Isa 32:1)

3. David will never fail to have a man to sit on the throne of the house of Israel, nor will the priests *[kōhănîm]*, the Levites, ever fail to have a man [to stand] before me.   (Jer 33:17–18)

4. If you can break my covenant with the day and my covenant with the night . . . then my covenant with David my servant . . . and with the Levites, the priests *[kōhănîm]* ministering unto me can be broken. . . . I will make the descendants of David my servant and the Levites who minister unto me as countless as the stars.   (Jer 33:20–22)

5. In any dispute [the priests] are to serve judgment *[ya'amdû lĕmišpaṭ]* and decide *[yišpĕṭūhû]* according to my ordinances.   (Ezek 44:24)

These passages provide strong indications that some Hebrew prophets taught that power in the eschatological government would be shared. The two passages from Isaiah (Isa 1:26; 32:1) have engendered most of the scholarly speculation that shared government forms a prophetic ideal. The following commentaries on Isaiah demonstrate that the concept of a shared eschatological government is not a new one.

F. Delitzsch, in his 1889 commentary, interprets Isa. 1:26 as predicting a return of "the judges and counsellors which [Jerusalem] had in the . . . times of the monarchy." He adds: "Under such God-given leaders Jerusalem would become what it had once been and what it ought to be." He goes on to describe this form of multiple leadership as "the fundamental principle of the government of God," that is, the ideal government organization. Delitzsch's view does not exclude the notion that officials under the king would hold their authority by delegation, but neither does it exclude a measure of independent authority for judges and counselors.[4]

F. Feldmann interprets Isa. 32:1 similarly, concluding that it implies a genuinely shared power in which "the kings of the coming better era, *together with their* שרים . . . will exercise their rule with righteousness and justice" (emphasis added).[5]

O. Kaiser finds evidence in the wording of Isa. 1:26 for a view that the judges and counselors of whom Isaiah speaks were to be so close to the king in authority that "the judges and perhaps even the counsellors should be seen as members of the renewed dynasty . . . future masters of Jerusalem."[6] R. Clements follows a similar line of reasoning, seeing Isa. 1:26 as promising a special status separate from delegated power for the judges of the restoration era: "The *judges*, therefore, would be leaders chosen by the people themselves, rather than officials appointed by the crown."[7] With regard to Isa. 32:1 and its mention of "rulers" alongside "kings," Clements seems to believe that here, too, the prediction is intended to include more than just the king in the position of independent authority, this being the "picture of the true nature of godly government."[8]

Such interpretations are plausible. But are they ultimately sustainable? Unfortunately, those commentators who have disagreed with the notion of limited monarchy as a restoration ideal—and there are many—have tended not to argue against the concept but rather to dismiss it by not mentioning it. We must, nevertheless, consider the possibility seriously. But before examining the relevant passages we should understand the broader context of the restoration in terms of Israel's history of salvation. Here a look at the prophetic definition of the restoration era will be helpful.

THE PROPHETIC RESTORATION

In the Mosaic period, the broad outlines of Israel's history had already been revealed. From texts such as Lev. 26:14–45; Deut. 4:22–31; 28:1–32:43 (texts antedating the prophets,[9]) it is clear that Israel would experience a cycle of events that can be described easily as blessing/curse/blessing. The first period of blessing was to take place during Israel's first occupation of the promised land (see, for example, Deut 4:25), known to us as the period between Joshua's conquest and the fall of Jerusalem. The covenant curses would be unleashed, and the exile would ensue (4:26–28). But the curse era would be finite, brought to an end by the renewed obedience of a remnant. These would then receive the unending blessings of the new age (4:29–31).

The Hebrew writers thus view Israel as a continuum. This is evident from the way Moses addresses the Israelite community before the conquest of Canaan, as well as future generations through the exile and the restoration, simply as "you" in Deut. 4:25–31: "you" will have lived in the land a long time (v 25); "you" will be scattered among the nations (v 27); and "you" will return in the latter days (v 30). This observation is important. The language of the prophets reflects the assumption of a continuing of national identity. We cannot expect a prophet to suggest that those who live or rule in the new age are somehow not Israel, or that their God is not YHWH, or that their societal structures are not generally comparable to those of the prophet's immediate audience. For the predictions of the prophets to be comprehensible, they had to have reference points within the institutions of the society already known. We would not expect to hear a prophet say, "In the new age there will be a new kind of prosperity, but I cannot describe it for you, for you would not understand." Or, "In the new age you will be governed differently, but it is not easy to explain because it will be so different."

The future is necessarily described by analogy to the past and present; the unknown is portrayed by means of images of what is already familiar. And Israel as a continuum in the purview of the Hebrew prophets virtually guarantees such analogical description. It is therefore not surprising to find that the prophets describe the governmental authority of the future in terms of the governmental offices of the past and present. Thus, if we can determine that prophecies of the restoration era clearly envision a governmental authority shared among kings, priests, judges, and others, then we may assume that such predictions are not merely analogies to the past but are intended as independent descriptions of the future—using the contemporary terminology of the prophets' audiences. If, on the other hand, we determine that such prophecies about government make no claim that a king will actually *share* authority with other officials, then we must conclude that sole and ultimate human authority will reside with the king.

Let us now examine the five prophetic passages, cited earlier, to determine whether they should be understood as reflecting the expected continuum of societal structures or whether they actually envision a government of shared power.

THE PASSAGES

I will restore your judges *[šōpṭayik]* as at first, your counselors *[yōʿăṣayik]* as in the beginning.

(Isa 1:26ab)

The context of this poetic couplet is a rather lengthy pericope (Isa 1:2–31) in which a description of Israel's coming desolation as a punishment for her sin is the stimulus for an appeal for conversion (vv 2–20). Israel has a choice: obedience will result in blessing in the coming new age (vv 19, 25–27), but rebellion will result in destruction (vv 20, 28–31) when YHWH cleanses his people (v 25).

This theme of the need for cleansing from unrighteousness provides clues needed to place verse 26 in proper perspective. The passage does not, in actuality, address the mode of government in the restoration as much as it gives examples of eschatological reversals, that is, changes from the corrupt present to a righteous future. Indeed, when were judges not corrupt originally *(bāriʾšōnǎ)*? Only at the beginning of Israel's history—in the wilderness theocracy—when they were first appointed not as corulers but as judicatories to assist Moses in handling legal appeals were they not corrupt (Exod 18:17–26).

This historical type, then, provides the grounds for interpreting the passage. Its concern is with a restoration of official purity for the sake of a just society (compare also Zeph 3:1–5 with 3:9–13). It looks forward to divinely imposed righteousness in government, in accordance with the Mosaic promises of uprightness in the restoration era (see, for example, Deut 30:6, 8). We should also note that the structure of the pericope does not allow us to make too much of the word *šōpēṭ*, "judge." Its parallel in the second half of the couplet, *yōʿēṣ*, "counselor," is a term that denotes little about governmental authority. Isaiah sometimes uses it as a significant term for "ruler," as in Isa. 9:6; but he employs the word also in contexts that indicate only minor, subservient governing power, as in Isa. 3:3, in a list between "man of rank" *(nĕśûʾ pānîm)* and "skilled craftsman" *(ḥăkam ḥărāšîm)*.

In the broader context, Isa. 1:26 functions as part of a contrast between the present corruption (vv 21–23) and the future righteousness of Jerusalem. Jerusalem in Isaiah's day was ruled by a corrupt government that included rebellious officials *(śārîm)* who were "companions of thieves," who "all love bribes and chase after gifts" (v 23). Of their injustice, Isaiah says, "They do not defend the cause of the orphan; the widow's case does not come before them"(v 23). In his description of the cleansed, righteous Jerusalem of the future (vv 25–27), Isaiah does what he and other prophets do routinely, choosing parallel terminology to describe things or persons already known or referred to. In Hebrew poetry, variety may be its own justification, and parallelism serves the interests of variety. Having illustrated Jerusalem's corruption by describing the covenant violations of its officials, Isaiah contrasts this corruption to the purity of Zion, emphasizing the pristine integrity of its future judges and counselors. The mode of government in either case is not strictly in focus.

> Behold a king [melek] will reign in righteousness and rulers [śārîm][10] will rule with justice.
>
> (Isa 32:1)

This poetic couplet is an example of a tautological synonymous parallelism, one that does not necessarily make two separate points but a single point stated with two different wordings. In the logic of the parallelism, the different wordings do not necessarily imply two things independent of one another.[11] Accordingly, this pairing of "king" and "rulers/officials" should have no more significance than the subsequent pairings of "shelter" and "refuge" (v 2), "eyes" and "ears" (v 3), "mind" and "tongue" (v 4), and "fool" and "scoundrel" (v 5) in Isaiah's eloquent context of reversals the new age will bring. In other words, Isa. 32:1 makes the point that the restoration rule will be a just rule, but it does not necessarily describe how governmental power will be allocated. The king may rule through his officials, or what the king does may also be what the officials do. In neither case is the idea of shared authority directly envisioned.

The Davidic monarchy is here the historical type to which Isaiah refers. David administered in part through his officials, and actions that he did not carry out alone or in person are still attributable to him (see 2 Sam 5:9, 20, 25; 8:1–6; 21:13; 24:25; compare 1 Kgs 6:1–7:8). The biblical record gives no hint that any legitimate exercise of authority on the part of David's officials is other than a delegated one.

> David will never fail to have a man to sit on the throne of the house of Israel, nor will the priests, the Levites,[12] ever fail to have a man [to stand] before me to offer burnt offerings, to burn grain offerings, and to present sacrifices continually.
>
> (Jer 33:17-18)

At first glance, this passage might portray the official functioning of priests/Levites to be as essential to government in the restoration era as the Davidic monarchy will be. The language, while prose, is nevertheless somewhat parallelistic and thus may give the impression that authoritative priestly leadership will complement authoritative monarchical leadership, and perhaps even function independently of it. However, this possibility cannot be sustained, because of the difference of the two expressions "sit on the throne" (yōšēb 'al-kissē') and "before me/in my presence" (millēpānāy). The former, applied to the king, is part of the language of rule.[13] The latter, on the other hand, is part of the language of service (compare 1 Kgs 21:29; Ezek 30:9), especially temple worship.

The structure of the pericope reflects two complements. There is no hint that the functions of the priests/Levites are in fact comparable in governmental authority to that of the king. Indeed, it is conceivable that Jeremiah intends a merism of sorts here, expressing the totality of divinely controlled governmental function by citing the highest (David's son) and the lowest (priests/Levites), or the one (the king) and the many (an entire tribe). Obviously this passage also does not refer to the style of government in the coming era. The oracle's emphasis is clearly directed toward permanence, consistency, and continuity with the original covenantal promises to Israel and Judah (Jer 33:14). This emphasis is carried through in the following text as well, which is from the same chapter:

> If you can break my covenant with the day and my covenant with the night . . . then my covenant with David my servant . . . and with the Levites, the priests ministering unto me can be broken. . . . I will make the descendants of David my servant and the Levites who minister unto me as countless as the stars.
>
> (Jer 33:20–22)

Like that quoted previously, the passage employs the unusual terminology "the Levites, the priests." It also uses the same sort of language for the relationship of the Levites/priests to YHWH: "ministering unto me" *(měšārtāy)* and "who minister unto me" *(měšārtê ʾōtî)*. Interestingly, however, servant language is used of David: "my servant" *(ʿabdî)*. Can this be an indication that the priests in the new era will be on the same level with the son of David, the covenantally promised king? (2 Sam 7:12–16). Here again, the answer must be no. While the Levites/priests are to be simply functionaries, the expression "my servant" has a far more important connotation.

The Hebrew Bible lists ten individuals whom YHWH calls "my servant": David (twenty-one times); Israel (seven times); Jacob (six times); Moses (six times); Job (five times); Nebuchadnezzar (three times); Abraham (once); Caleb (once); Isaiah (once); and Zerubbabel (once). In addition, one must note that Isa. 52:13 and 53:11 refer to "my servant." The Israelite origin of the elevated title traces back to Abraham (Gen 26:24), Moses (Num 12:7), and David (2 Sam 3:18). The term "servant" *(ʿebed)*, whether singular or plural, can refer to both the lowliest slave (Exod 21:2) and the highest official (1 Kgs 8:24-25). It is, however, clearly used in the elevated sense in Jeremiah's reference to David. The Levites/priests are not considered in the same league with those whom YHWH designates "my servant." YHWH calls only two groups "my servants" *(ʿăbāday)*: Israelites (twice in Leviticus 25 and seven times in Isaiah 65) and prophets (twice in 2 Kings, five times in Jeremiah, once in Ezekiel, and once in Zechariah). None of these contexts concerns the prophets of the restoration; and nowhere are the Levites or priests called "my servants" by YHWH.

There is a single historical type for the passage: the system of government and religious observance of the Davidic era. In the final revelation of Jeremiah 33 (vv 23–26), which parallels the others in form and theme, YHWH assures Jeremiah that the sort of unity that prevailed in David's day would exist again under the future king's rule (v 26). "Jacob," in verse 26, is an unambiguous referent for all Israel rather than just for the Northern Kingdom (compare

Amos 9:8). To the prophets, Davidic rule meant unified rule and a return to the benefits enjoyed in a blessed era (Jer 33:26b; compare Hos 3:5). In that time, David controlled the priesthood, as Israelite kings did generally.[14] There is thus no reason to conclude that Jeremiah portrays an independent clergy functioning in the restoration era, but rather a subservient and dependent one, whose authority would derive from rather than compete with or challenge the authority of the king.

> In any dispute the priests are to serve judgment and decide according to my ordinances.
> (Ezek 44:24)

This last pericope, from chapter 44 of the Book of Ezekiel, is part of an elaborate prescription for clerical duties and deportment in the new temple order in the restoration era (chaps. 40–48). For the Levites, such duties and deportment were to include screening of worshipers at the temple gates (vv 44:1–3, 9, 11), ritual slaughter of animals for sacrifice (v 11), and maintenance of the temple (v 14). For the priests, the chapter prescribes the correct process of sacrifice (vv 15–16), proper (ritual) dress and grooming (vv 17–20), incumbant life-style (vv 21–22), teaching duties (v 23), juridical functions (v 24), ritual purity standards (vv 25–27), priestly economic support (vv 28–30), and essential food laws (v 31). Because the text gives "judging" authority *(špṭ)* to priests, it may appear to suggest some sort of independent societal powers, perhaps in a line of authority not answerable to the king or his appointed judges. This, however, is not the case.

In the fuller context of the passage, only the leader *(nāśîʾ)* has the administrative authority in the new temple order (see 44:3; 45:16; 46:2; 46:17). Clearly, this *nāśîʾ* is the king (compare the term in 12:10), who will lead the nation's worship and be supreme over its priests. This was, in fact, the situation historically.[15] The kings of Israel and Judah not only established and maintained altars and temples[16] but also appointed the priesthood, who served at the kings' pleasure.[17] Thus there already existed a historical type for the delegation of royal authority to the priesthood that Ezekiel and his audience would have been prepared to acknowledge.

The question remains what judging a "dispute/controversy" *(rîb)* would entail. Since *rîb* can theoretically refer to virtually any legal dispute (Deut 25:1; 2 Sam 15:2), one might conclude that the passage means that priests should judge in the sense of taking over the judiciary, or some of its functions, in the restoration era. Further analysis, however, shows this conclusion to be unsustainable on two grounds. First, Ezekiel is known to employ the root *špṭ* and its derivatives more frequently than any other prophet, often metaphorically. In the Oholah–Oholibah allegory of chapter 23, the nations are to "judge" Israel (v 24); Ezekiel is to "judge" Israel and Judah (v 36); and an unnamed righteous people are to "judge" Israel and Judah as well (v 45). In short, the functioning of a judiciary is not the subject every time Ezekiel uses *špṭ*. Second, Ezek. 44:24 is undoubtedly dependent on 44:23 in the sense that "controversies" (v 24) may refer to issues arising out of attempts to comply with the ritual purity laws which the priests are to teach the people (v 23). The latter part of verse 24 seems to refer to this topic, with its concern for "laws and decrees for all my appointed feasts and . . . sabbaths." If this is the case, verse 24 makes no reference specifically to priestly judges but merely to priestly interpreters of ritual law.

CONCLUSION

While not all prophets address explicitly the issue of the structure of a restoration government, those who do are consistent in limiting true governmental power and authority to the divinely appointed king. There will certainly be priests, judges, and other officials in the restoration era who will exercise societal leadership and serve YHWH's purpose of restoring his nation. They will not, however, govern, either independently or on equal terms, with the king. Rather, as in historical examples, they will derive their power and authority as functionaries from the king.

This conclusion should not be surprising. Israel's written history is in part a chronicle of failed leadership; much of it describes rebellion against YHWH and his authorized leaders. Many past leaders were so disloyal that the hope for the new age lay in a system radically purified and streamlined—in one righteous individual who would keep all other leaders in line (compare Isa 53:11-12; Hos 3:5; Amos 9:11-12; Ezek 37:24). The wilderness rebellions of Korah, Dathan, and Abiram, or of Miriam and Aaron against Moses (Num 12, 16); the nearly disastrous era of the judges (compare, for example, Judg 16:24; 19-21); the long line of aberrant monarchs (only two of forty kings during the divided monarchy were termed "good," in 1 and 2 Kgs),[18] and the frequent infidelity of the priesthood (for example, Lev 10; 1 Sam 2:27-36; 2 Kgs 12:7-8; 23:8; Jer 2:8; Hos 5:1)—all these pointed to a need for societal leadership and a government modeled on the divinely ordained pattern of the single, authoritative, and obedient ruler. We might reason that such an autocracy forms a restoration ideal because of its efficiency and greater possibility of pure government. Thus, Moses and David constituted paradigms of this kind of leadership (Deut 34:10-12; 2 Sam 7:8-16; 1 Kgs 2:1-4). YHWH must reign supreme if true righteousness is to prevail on the earth. YHWH will delegate unchallenged authority to his anointed, his chosen. This leader, in turn, can delegate, but does not give away, divine authority.

The prophetic view of the divinely appointed government of the restoration era, then, is a positive one. It envisions lasting stability, with a kingship so closely under YHWH's authority—and other societal leaders (priests, judges, counselors) so closely under the king's authority—that political intrigue, corruption, etc., would, by implication, be nonexistent. The prophetic expectation may also be seen to anticipate efficiency in government, since full executive powers and authority will rest in the divinely approved monarch. Finally, it looks as well to a happy continuity with the past, inasmuch as the traditional institutions of leadership, free from the corruptions of the past, will again be in place to function for the lasting benefit of all.

NOTES

1. For example, Isa. 9:7; 49:7; Jer. 30:9; Ezek. 37:24; Dan. 7:14; Hos. 3:5; Amos 9:11; Mic. 2:13; 5:2; Zech. 12:9.
2. Enoch 37–71; 2 Esdr. 7:28–29; 12:32; 2 Bar. 39:7; 40:1; 70:9; 72:2; Pss. Sol. 17:21–32; 18:5–9; 1 QS 1x.11; 1 QSa II.11–13.; CDC XII.23; XIV.19; XIX.10; XX.1; 4 Q Patriarchal Blessings I.3; 1QM V.1, etc.
3. It might be tempting to add to such a list the prediction of tribal divisions in Ezekiel 48, in which the Levites and priests share inheritance with the chief *(nāśî')* and the other tribes; Zechariah 4 and 6, in which Zerubbabel as governor and Joshua as high priest are to share authority (not exactly a restoration prediction, however); and perhaps Mal. 3:3–4, in which the role of the Levites seems to complement that of the Messiah in the purification of the restoration community. However, in each of these instances careful examination shows that the functioning of government is not the topic under consideration. I have therefore excluded these and similar texts as ultimately inconclusive for my analysis.
4. F. Delitzsch, *Biblical Commentary on the Prophecies of Isaiah*, trans. J. Martin (Grand Rapids, Mich.: Wm. Eerdmans, 1967), 1:106.
5. F. Feldmann, *Das Buch Isaias* (Muenster, West Germany: Aschendorffschen Verlagsbuchhandlung, 1925), 2:380.
6. O. Kaiser, *Isaiah 1–12*, trans. J. Bowden, OTL (Philadelphia: Westminster Press, 1983), 45.
7. R. Clements, *Isaiah 1–39*, New Century Bible Commentary (London: Morgan and Scott, 1980), 36.
8. Ibid., 259.
9. See, for example, W. Kuhnigk, *Nordwestsemitische Studien zum Hoseabuch*, BibOr (Rome: Biblical Institute Press, 1974), 24:35–39; Peter C. Craigie, *The Book of Deuteronomy*, in New International Commentary of the Old Testament (Grand Rapids, Mich.: Wm. Eerdmans, 1967), 24–29, 138–41.
10. MT *lĕśārîm* has no support among the important versions; the *lamedh* is a dittography via homoioarchton and is not original to the text.
11. On the subject of parallelism and its implications, see S. Geller, *Parallelism in Early Biblical Poetry*, in HSM 20 (Missoula, Mont.: Scholar's Press, 1979), esp. 31–42.
12. Priests and Levites seem to be in apposition here, as if Jeremiah did not wish to distinguish between them at this point. Some of the versions, however, translate "priests *and* Levites." Jeremiah's style may have been influenced by Deut. 17:9, with which he was surely familiar.
13. Compare Exod. 11:5; 2 Sam. 7:13, 16; 1 Kgs. 1:13, 17, 24, 30, 35, 48; 2:12, 19, 24; 2 Kgs. 10:3; 1 Chr. 29:23; Pss. 9:4; 47:8; Jer. 13:13; 17:25; Zech. 6:3; etc.
14. R. de Vaux, *Ancient Israel* (New York: McGraw–Hill, 1961), 1:113–14.
15. Ibid.
16. See 2 Sam. 24:25; 1 Kgs. 11:7–8; 2 Sam. 7:2–3; 1 Kgs. 5–8; 12:26–33; 2 Kgs. 12:5–9; 22:3–7; Amos 7:13.
17. See 2 Sam. 8:17; 20:25; 1 Kgs. 2:26–27; 4:2; 12:31–32.
18. See R. K. Harrison, *Introduction to the Old Testament* (Grand Rapids, Mich.: Wm. Eerdmans, 1968), 724–25.

22

Temple, Covenant, and Law in the Ancient Near East and in the Old Testament

John M. Lundquist

The following is an attempt to extend our understanding of the role of covenant and law in ancient Israel and to show their intimate relationship to the temple. To begin, I will review the historical process of temple restoration. A victorious king (or a prophet) builds or restores a temple. The building or restoration of the temple legitimizes the state or the society (in cases that do not deal with the political state in the formal sense). The act of legitimization is ritually celebrated in and through the covenant process. The content of the covenant ceremony is law. Thus it is my contention that the building or restoration of temples served as the impetus in the ancient Near East for the "codification" of customary law. Let me put it more succinctly: The temple founds (legitimizes) the state; covenant binds the foundation; law underlies the covenant. Just as this ideological/ritual complex flourished—and in its ideal form was supported by Israel's prophets—so in prophetic constructions of restoration, the same complex is found to be central.

DEFINITIONS

Temple

Let me first define the main terms of the argument. By *temple* I mean an association of symbols and practices that we find connected in the ancient world with both natural mountains/high places[1] (the *temple* par excellence) and edifices. The set of symbols and practices include, but are not exhausted by, the following: the cosmic mountain, the primordial mound, waters of life, the tree of life, sacral space, and the celestial prototype of the earthly. These emphasize spatial orientation and the ritual calendar; the height of the mountain/building; revelation of the divine prototype to the king or prophet by deity; the concept of "center," according to which the temple is the ideological, and in many cases the physical, center of the community; the dependency of the well-being of society on the proper attention to the temple and to its rituals; initiation, including dramatic portrayal of the cosmogonic myth; extensive concern for death and the afterlife, including the practice of burial within the temple precincts; sacral (covenant-associated) meals; revelation in the holy of holies through the means of the tablets of destiny; formal covenant ceremonies in connection with the promulgation of law; animal sacrifice; secrecy; and the extensive economic and political impact of the temple in society.[2]

State

By *state* I mean a highly centralized and socially stratified polity which exercises a monopoly of force, has the power to enforce its own laws, and possesses a common ideology that legitimizes a ruling hierarchy around a temple/covenant religious system.[3] At its most succinct, as far as the ancient Near East is concerned, the state, I believe, can be defined as a king (invested with kingship by the gods in a temple) plus a capital city.[4] I am here distinguishing between the formal state and the nonstate polities in the ancient Near East. I firmly believe that the previously outlined "temple ideology"[5] is found, with appropriate and predictable exceptions, in each stage of the social/evolutionary process—tribe, chiefdom, and state[6]—and throughout Israelite history. What I call the "primordial" ancient Near Eastern conception of the temple, and what is called the "chaos–cosmos ideology" by F. Willesen,[7] is in fact present both at the Sinai experience, as recorded in Exodus 19–25, and in the Solomonic temple construction. In terms of biblical scholarship, we may say that a "pre-deuteronomistic" temple ideology informs both Sinai and Jerusalem. For our purposes, let us distinguish between the temple as the dwelling place of deity (Isa 6) and as a house of prayer (Isa 56).[8] But note that both an exilic prophet, Ezekiel, and a postexilic prophet, Zechariah, reflect the older, common ancient Near Eastern temple ideology.[9]

The central difference between Mosaic and Solomonic Israel is that the former was not a state polity, while the latter was. To use G. E. Mendenhall's terminology, we are dealing with the difference between a "community" and a "political monopoly of force."[10] Even though the common ancient Near Eastern temple symbolism underlay both societies, the "political" element was missing in the Mosaic, while it was central in the Solomonic. The temple experience legitimized both societies through a covenant ceremony: at the mountain in the Mosaic, and at the temple of Solomon in the Solomonic. As I have written elsewhere, "the ideology of kingship in the archaic state is indelibly and incontrovertibly connected with temple building and with temple ideology."[11] "The ideology of kingship" is present at both Sinai and Jerusalem. In Sinai, YHWH is the king; in Jerusalem, Solomon is the king. This kind

of formal distinction, I feel, is so important in understanding the central differences and similarities in ancient Israel at various stages of her development.

Covenant

By the term *covenant* I mean a formal, ritually enacted ceremony mediated by the prophet or king in (more exactly "in front of," or "on," in case of
the mountain) the temple, a ceremony in which the community is founded
through the people's "indexical" acceptance of the revealed law.[12] Mendenhall's
definition of the covenant process at Sinai bears an interesting resemblance to
my definition:

> The covenant at Sinai was the formal means by which the seminomadic clans, recently
> emerged from state slavery in Egypt, were bound together in a religious and political
> community. The text of that covenant is the Decalogue. Since a covenant is essentially
> a promissory oath, it is only in this way that a social group could be made responsible
> to new obligation.[13]

Law

By *law* I mean the existing body of customary judicial precedents—the
so-called "just laws" in the Mesopotamian tradition—that reflect "what might
be called the sense of justice in a community,"[14] along with the community's
traditions of law court procedures which state that the ideals of justice enshrined
by the community are actually applied in specific situations. This latter,
Mendenhall calls "techniques."[15] I am speaking, in other words, of the combination of the "constitution" and the "case law." By *codification* I mean the
promulgation by a king or prophet of the "policy and techniques"—the laws—
of restoring and building temples as part of a covenant ceremony.[16]

STATE FORMATIONS AND LAW CODE ORIGINS

In each ancient tradition a first promulgation typically occurs early in the
history of that particular society. Subsequent "state renewal" covenant ceremonies at the temple will promulgate new laws but will also repromulgate the
old, hallowed, canonical tradition. This is brought out most clearly in the
Israelite tradition through a consideration of the first promulgation at the
mountain through Moses, with subsequent renewals recorded under Joshua,
Solomon, and Josiah, and during the time of Ezra. We are dealing in these
instances with very different polities, in the technical sense, and can thus see
that the temple ideology persists over time at different stages of political
development/evolution.

> The central position of temple building/rebuilding/restoring in the royal inscriptions
> of the kings of ancient western Asia is well known. In general the pattern for these
> kingdoms would seem to be similar, a pattern that would also fit the Israelite state
> under Solomon: the state is not necessarily fully formed immediately upon the acces-
> sion to kingship of a given charismatic figure. As with Israel in the time of David, state

formation began in that time but was not finalized until the reign of his successor. Further, the process of temple building/rebuilding/restoring does not necessarily take up the king's main attention in the first year or two of his reign. If we may take the Babylonian Year names as an example of this, in most cases the first few years were taken up with building/rebuilding walls, defeating remaining enemies, in general solidifying their control over their kingdom. Then, in the case of Sumuabum, the first king of the First Dynasty of Babylon, for example, it is the fourth year that bears a name connected with temple building; in the case of his successor, Sumulael, it is the seventh; in the case of his successor Sabium, the eighth; in the case of Hammurapi, it is the third. In the case of Solomon, it is his fourth year in which he began the temple construction.[17]

LAW CODES AND TEMPLES

In connecting the promulgation of the law codes with the building of temples, we should consider the ancient Near Eastern king's or prophet's role as a "righter of wrongs." The core of social legislation in the ancient Near East is expressed by Hammurapi in the Epilogue: help the widow, right wrongs, etc. Indeed, this pattern goes back in attested form to Urukagina, who gives us "our first evidence of the king's right, at the beginning of his reign to issue a set of decrees — often abrogating existing traditional law — aimed at righting social wrongs."[18] It was this that the king (or the prophet, in the case of Moses — but recall that "Moses is to a great extent depicted in royal categories")[19] — decreed in the temple or that he received as a result of incubation, visitation, revelation, etc.[20] The "law codes" are an elaboration of this motif.

The true nature of the codes is spelled out at the moment of revelatory expression following the exit of the king/prophet from the temple: do justice, protect the widow and orphan. It would be after this that royal scribes would elaborate the revelatory utterances, along with the central core of the received tradition, into a full-fledged code. The king's essential role can be understood by the phrase "righter of wrongs." Law, or the "royal judgments," as F. R. Kraus characterizes the Code of Hammurapi, is a natural extension of this essential role;[21] law comes into being at its implementation.

I suggest the following as the succession of events early in the history of a society that give us what we commonly designate *law*. The king/prophet ascends to leadership over a community that is at one of the well-defined stages of political development; he issues a decree (the *mišarum* in Babylonia, the *yašar* in Israel), an interim legislation showing him to be a "king of justice," having "done justice in the eyes of YHWH." Of course, in the meantime society continues much as before on the basis of law already decreed by earlier kings and on the basis of the common jurisprudence built on common law. Next, the king builds, renovates, or rededicates the main temple of his city, at which time the fuller version of the laws is decreed and elaborated into a stele by royal scribes. In the case of Hammurapi's code, we must distinguish between the prologue and epilogue and the laws themselves, both of which might have been constructed by different sets of scribes, working under different stylistic and religious/political directives.[22] Again, the issuance of the *mišarum* decree (usually in the first full year of the Babylonian king)[23] and the building of the temple do not occur in the same year. But as I have stated, we are dealing with a process that sees the gradual development of the community into a full-fledged formation during the first several years of its existence.

Even though it is not possible to associate explicitly the promulgation of law with the building of a temple, the two are definitely closely associated in the Gudea Cylinders, the Code of Urukagina, and the Code of Hammurapi.[24] The origin of law and of legal traditions must be sought in a ritual setting. More importantly, *law is introduced and mediated ritually* in a temple setting. Failure to understand the full implications of this fact has led occidental scholarship into the trap of animosity toward the temple.[25] A glance at the scene illustrating the stele on which the Code of Hammurapi is inscribed, and at statements in its prologue, clearly illustrates this point. Certainly, this association of law and temple is the message the majority of the ancient Near Eastern community that actually saw the stele would have received. According to J. Klima, because the majority of the population were illiterate, what they would have taken away from a view of the stele could have been the scene showing Hammurapi receiving the sceptre of authority from Šamaš.[26]

Of course, it is also necessary to point out here another important fact we learn from the stele of the Code of Hammurapi: the temple legitimizes authority. This is also the case with Moses and with other Israelite leaders, such as Solomon and Josiah. As Mendenhall has expressed it, the temple is "the ritual functioning system that establishes the connection between deity and king."[27]

THE SINAI EXPERIENCE

The primary example of what I am trying to demonstrate comes from the Sinai experience (Exod 19–26). Even though there is no political state at Sinai, we nevertheless find that what I call the temple ideology is central to that society's functioning. While I will not go into the problem of dating per se, I will focus on seven motifs found in the Sinai narratives, motifs that I think can justifiably be shown to be early, probably dating back to the time of Moses himself and to the Sinai experience.[28] It does not matter that the Sinai covenant lacks treaty curses,[29] or even that it possibly lacks the historical prologue.[30] We are not dealing here with the treaty covenant at all, but with the temple covenant system that founds and legitimizes the state.[31]

I would even predict that the treaty-covenant form is secondary to and derivative from the temple covenant system. The motifs are the mountain, law, covenant, pillars, sacrifice, covenant meal, and cosmic sanctuary. The evidence produced here from the ritual/belief systems of Israel's neighbors is not introduced to "prove" that any one of such customs or their totality provides us with an "origin" of a similar practice in the Sinai narratives or elsewhere in the Hebrew Bible. I have attempted elsewhere to delineate a common ancient Near Eastern temple ideology[32] and here simply attempt to further demonstrate ancient Israel's participation in that ideology.

MOUNTAINS

To begin with, natural mountains serve as symbols of, and in fact are, sacred places to which kings and prophets go to receive instruction from deities. According to K. Bittel, "Mountains . . . were considered, from early Hittite times onwards, to be the place where the deities were believed to be present, and where special ceremonies devoted to their worship were performed."[33] It did not particularly matter whether or not there were actual structures built on the mountains. In some cases the Hittite inscriptions specifically state that once the king arrived at the location a tent was constructed in which the king would carry out a ritual in front of a *ḫuwaši*-stone.[34] Thus the king or prophet ascends the mountain to carry out ritual obligations and, in the thesis developed here, to commune with deity. What is the content of the communication? It is law.

That the content of the revelation received on the mountain is law is shown in several sources. The clearest expression of this concept appears in the Code of Hammurapi. The prologue to the Code is virtually one continuous litany of Hammurapi's temple-related bequests, cleansings, rebuildings, and rededications. The Hammurapi stele depicts Hammurapi standing before Šamaš in a clearly ritual setting, receiving the tokens of authority; this indicates that the Babylonian scribes compiled the laws of the Code, as well as the prologue and epilogue, in the chief temple complex of Babylon, Esagila.

LAW AND SACRED MOUNTAINS

The chief evidence for the proposition that law originates in the temple or on the sacred mountain is the Sinai account itself. Moses ascends the mountain amid extensive ritual preparations by the people waiting below. The content of the revelation received by Moses on the mountain is law. These laws serve as the foundation pattern by which the society will live for many generations. Even though that society undergoes political transformations, the original promulgation of revealed law in the temple serves as the basis for future developments. Let us consider four well-attested instances of recovenanting in a temple setting in Israelite society: Joshua 24, Solomon's prayer of dedication of the Jerusalem temple, Josiah's covenant at the conclusion of the reform, and the recovenanting of Jews returned from Babylonian exile in the time of Ezra. In each of these cases, the people were recovenanted in a temple setting, but no new law was promulgated. Why? Because the code of Sinai, which had been revealed by deity in a temple setting, was still the religious and social basis of the society.

As part of the system I call state renewal, covenant ceremonies were carried out yearly at the New Year's festival when the temple was cleansed and rededicated. The state would be renewed during this time, and a new covenant would be enacted. The king would go into the temple, but a new set of laws would not be revealed; the old set would be repromulgated. The juristic content of each covenant ceremony is generally evident, but in some cases, as in 1 Kgs. 8:57, the legal content is very ambiguous.

CODIFICATION AND THE TEMPLE

Codification, by which I mean the promulgation of the ideals of justice of a given society within the context of temple building, refurbishing, or dedication, cannot be properly understood outside of this ritual setting. Law itself, of course, comprehending customary law, simply exists, with no identifiable origin in historical times. But the ancient community's concept of justice is formally enthroned within that community through a temple covenant ceremony. It is in this sense that law cannot be said to exist outside of an ordered, cosmic community. A community is made cosmic through the foundation of the temple. The elaborate ritual, architectural, and building traditions that lie behind temple construction and dedication are what allow the authoritative, validating transformation of a set of customary laws into a *code*.[35]

The temple creates law and makes law possible. It allows for the transformation of a chaotic universe into a cosmos. It is the very capstone of universal order and by logic and definition creates the conditions under which law is possible. This connection is brought out most dramatically in a tradition which may turn out to be not far removed from that of the ancient Near Eastern states, namely Hinduism.[36] According to Hindu traditions, the most important ritual action performed at the temple building site just before the metaphysical plan is laid out on the ground is the levelling of the ground. The process of levelling the ground by the king—repeated by each new temple builder—is seen as establishing order itself in the world. According to one tradition, the Buddha, "as soon as born, stepped forth upon the earth and beneath his steps [seen as achieving the process of levelling] the earth lay smooth and even, for by his footfalls the Law (dharma) was carried throughout the world and became universal. The leveled earth became its substratum."[37] In this instance, the ritual preparation of the temple site is seen as the means of cosmicizing the world, at which point law immediately comes into existence.

COVENANT AND PILLARS

The concept of covenant, as it exists in the Sinai narratives and in many other ancient settings, must be expanded to include the pillar. Covenant ceremonies are carried out at temples in front of stone or wooden pillars. "Covenants are sealed in temples or near pillars standing near temples, and thus derive their binding efficacy on the ancient society from the temple's authoritative, legitimizing position within the society."[38]

One important type of pillar, the previously mentioned *ḫuwaši*-stone, played a significant role in Hittite religion. One instance, for example, records that after arriving at the mountain and setting up his tent the king, "attended by his servants," performed "a ritual in an ordinary way, culminating in a libation in front of a *ḫuwaši*-stone."[39] According to O. R. Gurney, "In most cult-centers the deity had a stela or *ḫuwaši*-stone set up not only in his temple but also in a locality outside the town, in the open country, usually by a grove or a spring, or on a mountain."[40] Numerous texts depict the sacrifice of animals and the sharing of a communal meal at these stones.[41]

Pillars are known to have been associated with temples in Mesopotamia and Palestine since at least Chalcolithic times.[42] It is probable that the practice of erecting bronze pillars, as in Jerusalem, developed from the practice of erecting wooden pillars that were sheathed with bronze. We have examples of this practice in the Gudea inscriptions and at Khorsabad.[43] The bronze pillars thus represent the ubiquitous trees of life that flank temple entrances and that border scenes of temple ritual (Khorsabad in the former case, Mari in the latter).[44] Like the *djed* pillar in Egyptian architecture,[45] the pillar symbolizes strength, solidity, binding efficacy, endurance, continuity, cosmic order.

The pillar must play the same legitimizing role that I have described for the temple itself. The process of state renewal in Israel, which is after all what the covenant-making process is in the period of the Monarchy, derived its power from the temple. The pillar symbolizes the sanctity within which the state envelops itself. The king or the prophet enters the temple (or ascends the mountain); the law is revealed to him there; he is given the tablets of the law (or the "tablets of the decrees" in Mesopotamia—see the expositions of this point, as it relates to Mesopotamian and Israelite traditions, by G. Widengren and T. Jacobsen);[46] he then returns to a ritually prepared community and writes the law in some form. In the case of historical temples, the pillars would already stand as part of the temple construction. In the case of the "primordial" experience at Sinai, Moses erected pillars in front of which he covenanted the people.[47]

ANIMAL SACRIFICE

The next point that is central to the Sinai experience (Exod 24:5–8), and to temple ritual in general, is animal sacrifice. Animals are as ubiquitous a feature of temple symbolism as trees of life and waters of life.[48] Animals flank the trees of life not only in the famous Mari temple reliefs but also on the facades of the Khorsabad temples. The bloody sacrifice of animals in connection with temples/shrines is so ancient and so widespread that it requires little further documentation here. In the great inner Asian hierocentric states, people would come from all over the empire to the great year rites, driving herds of tribute animals before them.[49] A visit to a temple, as the facades on the Khorsabad temples imply, means bringing, or having supplied, animals for sacrifice. The purpose of the sacrifice is to seal and to sanctify the covenant.

Gurney translates a most interesting Hittite text, roughly contemporary with the historically attested aspects of the Sinai narratives, in which the themes of blood sacrifice, covenant, and covenant meal are conjoined:

> They lead in a goat and the master of the house consecrates the goat in front of the table to Sanda with wine. Then he holds out a bronze axe and says: "Come, Sanda, and let the Violent Gods come with you, who are clothed in blood-stained garments and girt with the cords (?) of Lulahhi men, who have a dagger in the belt, draw bows and hold arrows. Come and eat! And we will take the oath." When he has finished speaking he puts the bronze axe down on the table and they slaughter the goat. He takes the blood and smears the drinking tube which is inserted into the tankard with the blood. They bring the raw liver and the heart and the master of the house offers them to the god and takes a bite. They do an imitation (?). Then he puts his lip to the tube and sips and says: "Behold, Sanda and Violent Gods, we have taken oath. Since we have bitten the raw liver and drunk from one (?) tube, therefore Sanda and Violent Ones, do not again approach my gate." Then they cook the liver and the heart with fire and cut up all the rest of the goat. . . . He takes the shoulder and breast. . . . Then they surround the table and eat up the shoulder and breast. Then [just as they wish (?)] to eat and drink, so he brings, and they eat [up (?) . . .] and they drink [. . .] the tankard.[50]

Gurney states that this text "is the clearest expression of the belief in the efficacy of this solemn rite" [that is, "killing an animal to sanctify a covenant or treaty."][51] The conjunction of animal sacrifice and temple for the Akkad period is found at the north Syrian site of Tell Chuera and, in strikingly similar pictorial fashion, on the White Obelisk of Assurnasirpal I. In the former case, the excavations uncovered, from in front of the Akkad period Nord-Temple, evidence of an offertory stairway at the east entrance. Found near the stairway were what appear to be an offering table and an adjacent *Wanne*, which would have received the blood of the offerings.[52] The White Obelisk, from a time period much closer to that of Moses, shows an elaborate cult installation in front of a pillared temple before which a lowing bovine is being led to the slaughter. This latter sacrifice was performed by Assurbanipal at the *bīt Natḫi* of the temple of Ishtar in Nineveh.[53]

It has sometimes been the custom among scholars to look at recent Bedouin customs to explain the origins and meaning of animal sacrifice in connection with covenant making in the Hebrew Bible. However, the practice of sacrificing animals in front of temples as part of covenant ceremonies is extremely ancient, as my examples show.

THE COVENANT MEAL

The covenant meal of Exod. 24:9–11, seen by many scholars as an alternative and editorially distinct mode of covenant sealing, is seen by E. W. Nicholson as an integral part of the entire ceremony of Exod. 24:3–8.[54] And indeed, as the previously quoted Hittite text shows, communal meals are an integral part of temple-related covenant ceremonies, being the final installment in the whole process. Again, one need not look to recent Bedouin customs for an explanation of this practice. It is extremely ancient and widespread. The temple ritual described in the Gudea Cylinders ends with a festive meal and the fixing of the destinies for the coming year. The *akîtu* festival in Babylon was concluded by an extraordinary sacrificial meal attended by both gods and people. The annual temple rededicatory festival in Egypt during the Greco–Roman period was concluded by a communal meal, as was the dedicatory festival at the New Year in Jerusalem in the time of Solomon. Further examples could continue indefinitely.

Given the inherent aspect of secrecy in the ancient world in relation to temple ceremony, the covenant meal was the one instance, in many cases, in which common people could be present and actually partake of the blessings of renewal that the temple ceremonies promised.[55] In the context of Exodus 24, we have a people, formerly unsanctified (Exod 19) and unqualified to enter the presence of deity, now ritually sanctified and covenanted on the basis of the revealed law and permitted to attend a sacral meal in the deity's presence.

THE COSMIC SANCTUARY

Finally, the concept of the cosmic sanctuary, of which the earthly sanctuary is but a patterning (Exod 25:8), is central to the thesis presented here. Only such a sanctuary, built after the cosmic model, can properly serve as the locus of a legitimizing covenant system. Central to temple covenant systems all over the ancient Near East is the idea that the temple plan is revealed to the king or the prophet by deity. Again, many examples could be enumerated. Gudea of Lagash was visited in a dream in a temple of Lagash and shown the plan of the temple by a goddess, who gave him a lapis lazuli tablet on which the plan of the temple was written. Perhaps the best example of this aspect of temple building is the Sinai episode itself, in which, according to D. N. Freedman, "this heavenly temple or sanctuary with its throne room or holy of holies where the deity was seated on his cherubim throne constituted the *tabnît* or structure seen by Moses during his sojourn on the same mountain, cf. Exod. 25:8."[56] Likewise at Ras Shamra, where, according to F. M. Cross, "Ba'l founded his temple on Mount Sapon in order to make manifest his establishment of order, especially kingship among the gods. The earthly temple of Ba'l manifested not only Ba'l's creation of order, but at the same time established the rule of the earthly king."[57]

Thus order cannot exist, the earth cannot be made cosmic, society cannot function properly, law cannot be decreed, except in a temple established on earth that is the authentic and divinely revealed counterpart of a heavenly prototype. As J. Z. Smith has written so cogently for the *Enuma elish*, it is "not so much a cosmogony as it is a myth of the creation of a temple."[58] It is the creation of the temple, with its cosmic overtones, that founds and legitimizes the state or the society, which, in turn, makes possible the formal promulgation of law. Once promulgated in the ritual manner described, the law serves as the text of a covenant process carried out in front of the temple's pillars, accompanied by animal sacrifice and a communal meal. All these features, so characteristic of ancient Near Eastern temple practice from earliest times, are embedded within the earliest traditions of Late Bronze Age community formation in biblical Israel.

THE TEMPLE AND THE PROPHETIC FUTURE

Given the sanctity and the authority of the temple and its legal system, which were revealed by YHWH to Moses on Sinai, we will not be surprised to find that the temple system is an integral part of prophetic Israel's view of the future. This is revealed most clearly in Ezekiel's temple vision of Ezekiel 40–48. M. Greenberg, in his recent study of this section of Ezekiel, sees the importance of its temple centeredness in, among other things, his "lofty conception of a prophet's responsibility in an age of ruin."[59] At the moment of greatest ruin, of deepest despair, "the hand of the Lord came upon me and brought me in divine visions to the land of Israel, where he sat me down on a very high mountain" (Ezek 40:1–2, NAB). And thus we enter again the realm of the temple ideology that I have attempted to explicate.

Similarly, Qumran, a community that viewed itself as authoritative Israel, held at its communal heart a divinely revealed, temple-centered legal system, complete with the plan of an idealized future temple.[60]

NOTES

1. David Noel Freedman, "Temple without Hands," in *Temples and High Places in Biblical Times*, ed. Avraham Biran (Jerusalem: Nelson Glueck School of Biblical Archaeology, 1981), 21–30.
2. John M. Lundquist, "The Legitimizing Role of the Temple in the Origin of the State," *Society of Biblical Literature 1982 Seminar Papers*, 21, ed. Kent Harold Richards (Chico, Calif: Scholars Press/Society of Biblical Literature, 1982), 271–97; John M. Lundquist, "What Is a Temple? A Preliminary Typology," in *The Quest for the Kingdom of God*, ed. A. R. W. Green, Herbert Huffmon, and Frank A. Spina (Winona Lake, Ind.: Eisenbrauns, 1983), 205–19; John M. Lundquist "The Common Temple Ideology of the Ancient Near East," in *The Temple in Antiquity*, ed. Truman G. Madsen, Religious Studies Center Monograph Series (Provo, Utah: Brigham Young University Press, 1984), 53–76.
3. Lundquist, "Legitimizing Role of the Temple."
4. Ibid., 273.
5. Lundquist, "What Is a Temple?"
6. Kent V. Flannery, "The Cultural Evolution of Civilizations," *Annual Review of Ecology and Systematics* 3 (1972): 399–426.
7. Folker Willésen, "The Cultic Situation of Psalm LXXIV," *VT* 2 (1952): 289–306.

8. Jon D. Levenson, "From Temple to Synagogue: I Kings 8," in *Traditions in Transformation, Turning Points in Biblical Faith*, ed. Baruch Halpern and Jon D. Levenson (Winona Lake, Ind.: Eisenbrauns, 1981), 146–66.

9. Baruch Halpern, "The Ritual Background of Zechariah's Temple Song," *CBQ* 40 (1978): 167–90.

10. George E. Mendenhall, "The Monarchy," *Int* 29 (1975): 159.

11. Lundquist, "Legitimizing Role of the Temple," 272.

12. The term *indexical* comes from R. Rappaport and refers to both verbal and physical response during a ritual ceremony in which a participant signals to a coparticipant "that he accepts whatever is encoded in the canons of the liturgical order in which he is participating." Rappaport further writes: "Physical acts (such as kneeling, raising the hands, etc.) carry indexical messages more convincingly than does language" (see Roy Rappaport, "The Obvious Aspects of Ritual," in *Ecology, Meaning and Religion* [Richmond, Vir.: North Atlantic Books, 1979], 193, 199). For evidence of "indexicality" in biblical covenant ceremonies, see, for example, Exod. 19:8; Josh. 24:16; 1 Kgs. 8:22; 2 Chr. 6:13; 2 Kgs. 23:3; Neh. 8:5–6.

13. George E. Mendenhall, "Ancient Oriental and Biblical Law," *BAR* 3 (1970): 6.

14. F. R. Kraus, "Ein Zentrales Problem des altmesopotamischen Rechtes: Was ist der Codex Hammu-rabi?" *Genava* 8 (1960): 283–96.

15. Mendenhall, "Ancient Oriental and Biblical Law," 3.

16. Mendenhall, "Ancient Oriental and Biblical Law," 9–12; Kraus, "Ein Zentrales Problem des altmesopotamischen Rechtes"; J. Klima, "Gesetze," *RLA* 3 (1966): 243–55; Jorgen Laessoe, "On the Fragments of the Hammurabi Code," *JCS* 4 (1950): 173–87; J. J. Finkelstein, "Ammisaduqa's Edict and the Babylonian 'Law Codes,' " *JCS* 15 (1961): 91–104.

17. Lundquist, "Legitimizing Role of the Temple," 286.

18. Thorkild Jacobsen, *Toward the Image of Tammuz and Other Essays on Mesopotamian History and Culture*, ed. William L. Moran (Cambridge: Harvard University Press, 1970), 150–51.

19. Ivan Engnell, *Studies in Divine Kingship in the Ancient Near East* (Uppsala, Sweden: 1943), 174, quoted in Arvid S. Kapelrud, "Temple Building, a Task for Gods and Kings," *Or* 32 (1963): 61.

20. Gudea in Cylinder A XII–XIII, following the revelation to him in a dream; Hammurapi in Esagila, as expressed in the prologue and the epilogue to the Code of Hammurapi; Moses on Sinai; Solomon in his dedicatory prayer. In Gudea Cylinder B XVIII, we read that his work was carried out "according to the decrees of Nana and Ningirsu."

21. Kraus, "Ein Zentrales Problem des altmesopotamischen Rechtes."

22. D. J. Wiseman, "The Laws of Hammurabi Again," *JSS* 7 (1962): 162, 168; Klima, "Gesetze"; Jacobsen, *Toward the Image of Tammuz.*

23. Finkelstein, "Ammisaduqa's Edict and the Babylonian 'Law Codes.' "

24. Lundquist, "What Is a Temple?"; Samuel Noah Kramer, *The Sumerians: Their History, Culture and Character* (Chicago: University of Chicago Press, 1963); *ANET*, 165, 178.

25. See Mendenhall, "Monarchy," 155–70; Hugh W. Nibley, "Christian Envy of the Temple," *JQR* 50 (1959–60): 97–123, 229–40.

26. Klima, "Gesetze," 244.

27. Quoted in Lundquist, "Legitimizing Role of the Temple," 276.

28. E. W. Nicholson, "Covenant Ritual in Ex. 24:3–8," *VT* 32 (1982): 74–86; Frank Moore Cross, "The Priestly Tabernacle in the Light of Recent Research," in *Temples and High Places in Biblical Times*, 169–80; James Philip Hyatt, *Exodus*, New Century Bible Commentary (Grand Rapids, Mich.: Wm. Eerdmans, 1980); Mendenhall, "Ancient Oriental and Biblical Law."

29. George E. Mendenhall, "Covenant Forms in Israelite Tradition," *BAR* 3 (1970): 40–41; Dennis J. McCarthy, *Treaty and Covenant*, rev. ed., *AnBib*, 21a (Rome: Biblical Institute Press, 1978), 249.

30. McCarthy, *Treaty and Covenant*, 248–50.

31. Moshe Weinfeld, "Berîth," *TDOT*, 2:266.
32. Lundquist, "Common Temple Ideology of the Ancient Near East."
33. Kurt Bittel, "Hittite Temples and High Places," in *Temples and High Places in Biblical Times*, 66.
34. Ibid.
35. Lundquist, "Legitimizing Role of the Temple."
36. Karl–Heinz Golzio, *Der Temple im alten Mesopotamien und seine Parallelen in Indien*, *ZRGG*, Beiheft 25 (Leiden, Netherlands: E. J. Brill, 1983).
37. Stella Kramrisch, *The Hindu Temple* (Delhi: Motilal Banarsidass, 1976), 1:16–17.
38. Lundquist, "Legitimizing Role of the Temple," 295.
39. Bittel, "Hittite Temples and High Places," 66.
40. O. R. Gurney, *Some Aspects of Hittite Religion*, The Schweich Lectures of the British Academy 1976 (Oxford: Oxford University Press, 1977), 27.
41. Ibid., 27–28, 36–38.
42. Claire Epstein, "Aspects of Symbolism in Chalcolithic Palestine," in *Archeology in the Levant, Essays for Kathleen Kenyon*, ed. Roger Moorey and Peter Parr (Warminster, England: Aris and Phillips, 1978), 29.
43. Lundquist, "Legitimizing Role of the Temple," 289; H. York, "Heiliger Baum," *RLA* 4 (1975): 274.
44. Lundquist, "Common Temple Ideology of the Ancient Near East"; Yasin M. Al-Khalesi, *The Court of the Palms: A Functional Interpretation of the Mari Palace*, Bibliotheca Mesopotamica, 8, ed. Giorgio Buccellati (Malibu, Calif.: Undena Publications, 1978); York, "Heiliger Baum."
45. William Foxwell Albright, *Archeology and the Religion of Israel*, 5th ed. (Garden City, N.Y.: Doubleday and Company, 1968), 143.
46. George Widengren, *The Ascension of the Apostle and the Heavenly Book*, King and Savior, III (Uppsala, Sweden: A. B. Lundequistska Bokhandeln, 1950), 7–21; Thorkild Jacobsen, *The Treasures of Darkness* (New Haven/London: Yale University Press, 1976), 178–79.
47. Carol L. Myers, "Jachin and Boaz in Religious and Political Perspective," *CBQ* 45 (1983): 167–78.
48. Lundquist, "What Is a Temple?"; Lundquist, "Common Temple Ideology of the Ancient Near East."
49. Hugh Nibley, "The Hierocentric State," *Western Political Quarterly* 4 (1951): 226–53.
50. Quoted in Gurney, *Some Aspects of Hittite Religion*, 29–30.
51. Ibid., 30.
52. Anton Moortgat, *Tell Chuera in Nordost Syrien, Vorläufiger Bericht über die dritte Grabungskampagne 1960*, Wissenschaftliche Abhandlungen der Arbeitsgemeinschaft für Forschung des Landes Nordrhein-Westfalen, 24 (Koln/Opladen: Westdeutscher Verlag, 1962).
53. J. E. Reade, "Assurnasirpal I and the White Obelisk," *Iraq* 37 (1975): 129–50.
54. Nicholson, "Covenant Ritual in Ex. 24:3–8," 85.
55. Lundquist, "What Is a Temple?"
56. Freedman, "Temple without Hands," 174.
57. Cross, "Priestly Tabernacle in the Light of Recent Research," 174.
58. Jonathan Z. Smith, *Map Is Not Territory, SJLA* (Leiden, Netherlands: E. J. Brill, 1978), 23:99.
59. Moshe Greenberg, "The Design and Themes of Ezekiel's Program of Restoration," *Int* 38 (1984): 208.
60. Ben Zion Wacholder, "The Dawn of Qumran: 11Q Temple and the Teacher of Righteousness," *Society of Biblical Literature 1980 Abstracts*, ed. Charles E. Winquist and Paul J. Achtemeier (Chico, Calif.: Scholar's Press, 1980), #S111; Daniel R. Schwartz, "The Three Temples of 4Q Florilegium," *RevQ* 37 (1979): 83–91.

23

Theophanies Cultic and Cosmic:
"Prepare to Meet Thy God!"

Victor H. Matthews

Theophany in the Hebrew Bible serves a variety of theological roles—
depending on context, on the site of the manifestation, and on the form of
the epiphany. In every case there is the essence of power barely held in check
by the deity and a recognized danger to the mortal involved. The setting for
these divine/human encounters also adds to the awe of the moment and the
importance of the message being conveyed.

A sense of place is very much a part of Israelite tradition, but former
places of theophany sometimes lose their importance as new sites and new
concerns dominate the people's attention. Individual cultic spots like Bethel
and Shechem were supplanted by Sinai and the overriding theophanic event
that was portrayed there. In turn, as the temple cult community gained in
importance, the temple mount of Zion emerged as the site associated with
YHWH's presence. Finally, the temple mount was overshadowed in the postexilic
period by the identification of the holy mount of Zion as the place of future
sanctuary and the place of the ultimate revelation of YHWH's power.

Hand in hand with this phenomenon, keyed to the political and religious
development of the nation, was the shift in emphasis in the portrayal of
theophanies. There is a clear progression in theophonic texts from individual
encounters, with their etymological and time-limited importance, to a more
universal manifestation within an eschatological framework. This paper will
attempt to follow this evolutionary process through the texts, pointing out
developments as they occur and documenting the transformation of the cultic-
based theophanies at Sinai into the cosmically oriented theophanies in the
Book of Isaiah.

THE GLORY OF THE LORD

First, I will point out the basic elements which separate the deity from
the mortal and thereby make any encounter between them of particular

importance. The deity is immortal, omniscient, immensely strong, and capable of generating a radiance so dazzling that mortal flesh cannot gaze upon it and live. This latter quality, visually the most spectacular, is the basis for a number of stories in ancient religious history. The Mesopotamian epics often describe the "glory" *(melammu)* of the gods as a part of their armament, used to defeat their enemies or displayed as a sign of their power.[1] Similarly, the "glory" *(kābôd)* of YHWH serves as both a sign and a means of generating power which can awe and destroy the beholder.

A certain measure of the nimbus generated by the glory of the god would be transferred to or embodied in objects or sacred precincts associated with the deity. Indeed, power by association is a fairly common feature in religious traditions. By this means, certain images, sacred sites (especially mountains), temples, and leaders could acquire power as extensions of the gods whom they served. For instance, the glory of YHWH was made evident to the people after their departure from Sinai through the tabernacle and the ark, the cloudy pillar, and Moses' shining face.[2]

The Hebrew writers describe many sacred places and objects associated with YHWH's presence or power. In the patriarchal narratives this usually involved cultic sites where altars were built to signal the entrance of YHWH into the promised land.[3] During the exodus/conquest period, Sinai/Horeb and the ark of the covenant dominate the narrative as well as the theological emphasis on the law. And finally, during the monarchy the temple in Jerusalem and the temple mount of Zion form the basis for discussion of YHWH's presence with his people.

MIRACULOUS SURVIVAL MOTIF

Regardless of the place of the theophanic occurrence in the narrative, the element of danger in the divine/human encounter is present in some form. This possibility of annihilation makes the face-to-face encounter between a god and a mortal suspenseful. A theophany of any kind is a particularly remarkable event, and when it involves the chance of experiencing a glimpse of the full majesty of God, the moment is heightened to pivotal significance.

In the biblical narratives, the motif of unexpected survival after a theophany is used as a means of introducing a long-range relationship or a particularly momentous event. Many times these meetings form the basis of a "call narrative" of an individual leader or the people. The miraculous survival, then, serves in several instances as a complementary motif.

This motif is found twice in the Jacob narrative (Gen 28:10–17; 32:24–30). In the first instance, Jacob, on his way to seek a wife and a fortune from his relatives in Haran, stops at the cultic site of Bethel. Because his theophany is in the form of a dream and is received at a known cultic site, some scholars have interpreted this as an incubation or incited experience.[4] However, it should be noted that in verse 16 Jacob expresses surprise at both the visit and his survival of it. R. K. Gnuse, comparing this "unintentional incubation" with that in 1 Samuel 3, concludes that the active role of God in initiating the event and the lack of an incubation ritual both point to a desire of the biblical writers (possibly an expression of the deuteronomic reform movement) to eliminate any suggestion that YHWH could be manipulated.[5]

In the second instance, in Genesis 32, Jacob is on his way back to Canaan to have a confrontation with his brother Esau. Realizing that this could prove to be a difficult encounter, Jacob sends delegations with propitiatory messages and presents to his brother. He then divides his encampment and waits alone beside a stream (again a place of importance for those engaged in pastoralism, and one of the main sources of life). There he is accosted by a "man" (most likely a place numen in the original version of this story)[6] with whom he wrestles until dawn. The purpose of the visit is fulfilled when the divine being blesses Jacob and gives him a new name (and thus a tie to the covenant) and a prophecy that could be interpreted as a signal of success in his confrontation with Esau the next day.[7] The final certification of the theophanic event is added when Jacob/Israel testifies: "For I have seen God face to face and yet my life is preserved."

Whether an encounter with God himself, or with his envoy, the survival motif is constant. This is illustrated in Hagar's encounter with the "angel of the Lord" in Gen. 16:7–13. The passage demonstrates the effectiveness of the survival motif, even when that encounter is with an agent of the deity.[8] Hagar has fled from her abusive mistress into the desert and is found near a spring (a source of life and probably a meeting place for the tribes in the area) by the divine messenger. Her fate and that of her child is proclaimed,[9] and she is instructed to return to the authority she has fled. Once Hagar understands the message, she acknowledges the remarkable nature of her vision by exclaiming: "Have I really seen God and remained alive after seeing him?"

Two passages in the Book of Judges complete this survey of the motif of miraculous escape from harm. In the first of these, Judg. 6:22–23, occurs the call narrative of Gideon.[10] This reluctant hero fears his announced commission to go to war against the Midianites and attempts to test YHWH's resolve in the matter.[11] The test takes place on a threshing floor, which, in the Hebrew Bible is often associated with the dispensing of justice and the making of community-related decisions (see Ruth 3:14 and 1 Kgs 22:10).[12]

Once YHWH has "proven" himself, Gideon acknowledges his obligations and the validity of this theophanic experience: "Oh no! Lord YHWH! I have seen YHWH's envoy face to face!" The escape motif is completed with this assurance to Gideon: "You are safe. Do not panic. You will not die."

The other passage, Judges 13, points up the practicalities involved in meetings between man and God. In this birth announcement,[13] the future parents of Samson are informed of the prospect of their son's conception by "a man of God," whose "countenance was like the countenance of the angel of God, very terrible" (Judg 13:6).[14] As in other cases, the protocol of the theophany includes asking the name of the messenger (13:17–18) and the witnessing of a fiery ascension of the angel in the flames of a burnt offering.[15] This unexpected event generates fear: "We shall surely die, for we have seen God" (13:22).

However, it becomes evident that God's intention is not to destroy, but rather to signal a new stage of life (13:23–24).

THE SINAI PERICOPE

Another form of the theophany is found in the narratives comprising the Sinai pericope. While there are some difficulties in piecing together a chronological sequence of events, the common tie in all the stories is the holy mountain (either Sinai or Horeb) and the presence of YHWH's *kābôd* in or on this place. This will be portrayed in the text as the place of law and covenant, a place of introductions between YHWH and the Israelites, and the place at which Moses receives his special position and authority over the people. As in the instances of theophanic occurrence I have already discussed, these events are all initiated by the deity, and the mortals have the relatively passive roles of following instructions and affirming covenantal terms.

The large number of traditions generated about the mountain of YHWH and the mountain's varying name (Deut 33:2 mentions Sinai, Seir, and Paran) indicate that several group memories are being drawn upon.[16] One sign of the blending of traditions is the use in Exodus 19 of the earlier storm god imagery (thunder and lightning, smoke and fire),[17] coupled with the attempts by later redactors to center the narrative on Moses' role as mediator (Exod 20:18–21; 24:3ff.).[18]

The establishment of Moses' authority in conjunction with these manifestations of power (fire and smoke) is echoed in the theophanic experience of Elijah at Horeb (1 Kgs 19). This episode contains clear parallels to the Moses story in terms of the stubborn apostasy of the people that has driven the prophet to the holy site of YHWH's presence, the granting of authority to the prophet, and the establishment of a legal framework that serves as the chief message of the prophet.[19] There is, however, a difference in the use of the visual effects of the theophany in that these effects serve as a test of Elijah's perception of the presence of YHWH in a form other than the images associated with the storm god Baal.

Another example of use of the theophany to commission Moses as mediator of his people is found in the retelling of this episode in Deuteronomy 5 (see also Deut 18:16), in which the fear of the people in dealing with YHWH directly is the basis of their request that Moses speak to YHWH for them.[20] As in other examples, the people acknowledge the validity of YHWH's appearance and commands: "For who is there of all flesh, that has heard the voice of the living God speaking out of the midst of fire, as we have, and has still lived?" (v 26).

Yet another divergent tradition within this set of episodes at Sinai involves the meal shared by seventy elders, Moses, Aaron, Nadab, and Abihu with YHWH on the mountain as depicted in Exod. 24:9–11. This chapter, joining material originally independent, is concerned with those representatives of the people who could deal with God directly. E. W. Nicholson suggests that Moses and Aaron were not a part of the original version of this sacred meal but were added later by the priestly writers.[21] This is apparently an example of the weaving together of divergent strands of tradition to make Moses' role supreme.[22]

The degree of anthropomorphism in this passage is remarkable, and the reference to the sapphire-like pavement under God's feet suggests the sacred ground motif in Exod. 3:5 and Josh. 5:15. Those partaking in the meal were allowed to see God, and he "did not lay his hand on the chief men of the people of Israel." This is clearly an example of a covenant meal, such as that in Gen. 31:54 between Jacob and Laban (also on a mountain), which parallels the laws of hospitality. Just as one who shares a meal with you in your home cannot be harmed, the elders of Israel survived this encounter with the divine unscathed, thus receiving an implied promise of divine care for the entire nation.[23]

One final instance of confrontation with God within this narrative occurs in Exodus 33. In this text, Moses has had the singular honor of speaking with YHWH "face to face, as one man speaks to another" (v 11). However, if Moses is to become the unquestioned spokesman for YHWH to an occasionally anarchic group of Israelites, he must have a clear demonstration of YHWH's favor toward him. Thus, in Exod. 33:18–23, Moses requests, "Let me see your glory," an act similar to his request in Exod. 3:13 for YHWH's name.[24]

As in Exodus 3, Moses is given an assurance of guidance, but not what he has requested. YHWH replies that it is impossible to fulfill Moses' desire, "for no mortal man can see me and live."[25] The implication is that man cannot withstand the full radiance of God's glory and that this glory has been held in check during their previous meetings.[26] YHWH does, however, want to provide Moses with an assurance of future aid and thus arranges a partial viewing for his favored servant. Moses stands in a rocky crevice while YHWH's hand shields him from the dangerous full frontal view of the kābôd. YHWH then gives him a brief glimpse of His divine person, allowing Moses to see His back (v 23).[27]

The difference between this text and those discussed earlier is the complete lack of surprise or fear. Moses knew exactly what he wanted and what was happening throughout the episode. This may be a further reflection of the unique relationship between YHWH and Moses, or it may be a hint of a later understanding of the theophanic event as an opportunity to draw closer to the divine and perhaps even to gain a glimpse of the divine glory.

This concept is particularly evident in the parallel situation in Exod. 34:29–35. Through Moses' close contact with YHWH, Moses' face has acquired a measure of the deity's glory. The people are afraid to approach their leader's shining face, just as they would have been afraid to approach YHWH directly. Moses' continuing role as mediator was solidified by this new sign of favor, and the veil he wore when not speaking to YHWH added to the mystery. However, the fact that YHWH's glory was merely reflected from Moses' face, rather than projected from it, demonstrates that he was a man and could—unlike YHWH—be seen without ill effect.[28]

TRANSFORMATION OF DIVINE PRESENCE AND PLACE

As a result of the institution of monarchy and of subsequent political events that centralized the cult in Jerusalem, the concept of the place of divine presence and of theophanic occurrence moved from Sinai to Zion and from miraculous survival of the individual mortal and the establishment of law to security and deliverance in times to come for the faithful community.

The increasing importance of Jerusalem as the site for theophanic manifestations begins with its establishment as David's capital and the movement of the ark of the covenant to Zion (2 Sam 6).[29] Its preeminent position is solidified with the dedication of the temple and the installation of the ark and the tent of meeting in the holy of holies (2 Kgs 8). Of particular interest in this latter narrative, in terms of its parallels to the Sinai experience, is the presence of the elders of Israel and other leaders of the nation, an emphasis on maintaining the covenant made at Horeb, and the inclusion of a feast lasting seven days.

All these elements are similar to events in Exodus 24. However, there is no mention of the theophanic storm images which dominate the Sinai experience. Nor is there any direct mention of the events which took place there, other than the giving of the tablets of the law. Particularly striking, in fact, is Solomon's dedicatory prayer (1 Kgs 8:22-53). In this long recital of calamities caused by the sins of the people, the theme is that prayer and supplication done in or in the direction of the temple will draw YHWH's attention to the people's plight and repentance and thus effect an end to their difficulties.[30]

This is possible because of transference to the temple of the symbols of YHWH's presence (just as the movement of the pillar of cloud from the mountain to the tabernacle in Num 11:11-13 marks the transference of YHWH's guidance from his mountain to his people).[31] Through this action the temple becomes the new focal point of Israel's worship and of YHWH's awareness of that worship. Furthermore, the striving for holiness (exemplified in the establishment of the cultic community and the reiteration of the need for obedience to the law) is a means of making YHWH's *kābôd* apparent in the sanctuary.[32]

Thereafter, as the cult in Jerusalem grew in importance, it was impressed upon the people that YHWH's presence and the covenantal obligations had been transferred from Sinai to Zion.[33] Temple worship (as noted by S. Mowinckel in his study of the psalms) expressed a confidence in a Sinai-like epiphany in Jerusalem.[34] This idea is presented most clearly in Ps. 50:2-3: "Out of Zion, the perfection of beauty, God shines forth. Our God comes, he does not keep silence, before him is a devouring fire, round about him a mighty tempest." R. J. Clifford suggests that this is an attempt to revive a primal event or experience, perhaps as a way of legitimizing the adoption of a new sacred place for God.[35] In any event, this transference through the actions of king and cult became set in the minds and traditions of the people, and thereafter Zion became the place of ultimate safety and power, even in the face of the political calamities of the seventh and sixth centuries B.C.[36]

This is best exemplified in the theophanic experiences and images of Isaiah. His call narrative in Isaiah 6 contains some of the classic elements of the theophanic event that I have already pointed out: "Woe is me! For I am lost; for I am man of unclean lips, and I dwell in the midst of a people of unclean lips; for my eyes have seen the King, the Lord of Hosts!" (v 5). Isaiah's experience takes place in the temple, a sacred spot. It involves physical and visible signs of power: an earthquake and smoke.[37] There is also the mortal's fear of the encounter—in this instance perhaps more a fear of ritual impurity than of death. As in previous cases of theophany, his survival is based on the fact that the encounter is initiated by the deity, and the intent of that deity is to establish a mutually beneficial relationship with Isaiah.[38]

It is clear, however, that the implications of Isaiah's call vision are not limited merely to one man. Rather, Isaiah's theophanic experience portends the experience of the entire community, which, like Isaiah, is also in need of cleansing. This cleansing can be effected only by YHWH's intervention. Isaiah's vision thus prefigures his people's "seeing" and "hearing" of YHWH, even as he saw and heard.[39] Their expiation of sin, spoken of in Isa. 40:2, is predicated on divine intervention (40:10) and will lead to a return to YHWH and to a new covenantal relationship (43:1–7).

A similar shift in this theme of miraculous survival is found in the visions of Isaiah 24–26 and 40:5.[40] In these instances, the theophanic images of Sinai are invoked but are set in Zion. Isa. 24:23 describes a gathering of the elders at some point in the future, when they are permitted to view the full glory of YHWH. In Isa. 40:5 we find that this privilege will be accorded to "all flesh." These references have been interpreted by C. Westermann and others as elements pertaining to a processional vision, again echoing the journey to Sinai; YHWH's glory will be revealed in "his action in history."[41]

Very evidently this transformation of the theophany to a universal event refers to a time when the people will reach a state of ritual purity in which they can (contra Exod 20:18–20) see God and not die. Unlike Moses, they will not have to be shielded from the kābôd, and a mediator will be unnecessary. YHWH will take control of events, reestablishing his rule and law.[42] This is understood from Isa. 40:9, in which the people are instructed to "Behold your God!" Just as Moses' shining (literally, horned) face was a visual sign of YHWH's presence,[43] so YHWH's presence and power will now (in Isa 40) be made known in his restoration of his people. Idols (40:19), like those of Jeroboam's shrines at Dan and Bethel (where the people were also told to "Behold your gods!" [1 Kgs 12:28]), and the nations that produce them have no power over the God of creation (Isa 40:12–14).

A further comparison can be made by examining Isa. 26:11. The unexpectedness of the theophanic manifestation is implied: "O Lord, thy hand is lifted up, but they see it not. Let them see thy zeal for thy people, and be ashamed. Let the fire of thy adversaries consume them." The visible kābôd is imminent but unperceived, and this lack of perception is the danger.[44] For the theophanic experience to be of benefit to mortal participants, they must recognize the imminent danger that this creates. Job's statement, "Now my eyes see you" (Job 42:5), acknowledges the presence of the deity and comes as a recognition of Job's proper place in his relationship with God. This perception causes him to "repudiate and forswear dust and ashes."[45]

Those who recognize and fear the power of God can expect a restoration of the primal moment of their relationship with the deity and the banishing of all their enemies. The hand that shielded Moses from the fulness of the *kābôd* (Isa 25:10–12) now rests protectively on the mountain of YHWH,[46] while YHWH's unrestrained glory is loosed on Israel's enemies (compare 41:10). This can be compared with von Rad's concept of the "holy war" in which YHWH makes a personal appearance on behalf of his people in their struggle against their enemies. The resulting "fright and confusion" leads to ultimate victory.[47]

These events are climaxed by a feast of celebration (25:6–8),[48] certifying a new relationship with a people whose formerly clouded vision has been clarified. The fear of direct encounter is dissipated; the laws governing it, the ritual establishment of covenant obligations at Sinai, are reshaped to accommodate an expanded assemblage who will worship "on the holy mountain at Jerusalem" (27:13).

CONCLUSION

In the Hebrew Bible a developmental process informs the theophanic experience. While every encounter between human and divine is of paramount importance, a shift occurs in the importance of the sites of such encounters. In the people's early history, theophanies took place in cultic spots and were associated with the individual family and clan needs of individuals. Much later, as the Jerusalem temple community came to dominate the worship of Israel, the presence of God — and thus the theophanic experience — came to be an attribute of the holy mount, Zion.

Another element in this transference of God's presence is the motif of miraculous survival. Throughout most of the biblical text, the danger implicit in seeing God face to face forms an integral part of every theophanic narrative. In Isaiah's description of the time of restoration, however, this motif is reversed: a time is projected in which the danger is eliminated; the experience of the fulness of YHWH's *kābôd* (now for the entire community of faith, not just an individual) forms the ultimate expression of the covenantal relationship with YHWH. Moreover, the dangers associated with this confrontation with deity are transferred to Israel's enemies. This new prospect of a divine encounter for YHWH's people, then, reflects not a change in the deity vis-à-vis man, but a transformation of the people Israel and an upgrading of their spirituality vis-à-vis God.

NOTES

1. A. L. Oppenheim, "Akkadian *pul(u)ḫ(t)u* and *melammu*," *JAOS* 63 (1943): 34.
2. T. Jacobsen, *Treasures of Darkness: A History of Mesopotamian Religion* (New Haven, Conn.: Yale University Press, 1976), 16, describes how there exists a complete extension of the "awesome nimbus" or "aura" of the god to his temple. Through this association, it acquires all of the divine manifestations — "tremendum," "fascinosum," and "mysterium."
3. William McKane, *Studies in the Patriarchal Narratives* (Edinburgh: Handsel Press, 1979), 106.
4. Rudolph Smend, *Lehrbuch der alttestamentlichen Religionsgeschichte* (Leipzig, Germany, 1893), 39, and T. H. Gaster, *Thespis: Ritual, Myth and Drama in the Ancient Near East* (New York: Norton, 1950), 271.
5. Robert K. Gnuse, *The Dream Theophany of Samuel: Its Structure in Relation to Ancient Near Eastern Dreams and Its Theological Significance* (Lanham, Md.: University Press of America, 1984), 151–52. On this "unwitting" incubation, see also R. J. Clifford, "The Word of God in the Ugaritic Epics and in the Patriarchal Narratives," in R. J. Clifford and G. W. MacRae, eds., *The Word in the World: Essays in Honor of Frederick L. Moriarty* (Cambridge, Mass.: Weston College Press, 1973), 13.
6. J. Lindblom, "Theophanies in Holy Places in Hebrew Religion," *HUCA* 32 (1961): 97–98.
7. W. M. W. Roth, "The Text Is the Medium: An Interpretation of the Jacob Stories in Genesis," in M. Buss et al., eds., *Encounter with the Text* (Philadelphia: Fortress Press, 1979), 106, sees the encounter with the divine as the "touch points" combining the arches of tension between Jacob, Esau, and Laban (Gen 28:13–15; 32:23–31). T. L. Thompson, "Conflict of Themes in the Jacob Narrative," *Semeia* 15 (1979): 18, 21, describes this meeting as a chiastic balance with the theophany of Gen. 28:11–15.
8. See E. Jacob, *Theology of the Old Testament* (New York: Harper, 1958), 75–77, for the source study of angels or messengers serving as substitutes for YHWH. J. Skinner, *A Critical and Exegetical Commentary on Genesis* (Edinburgh: T. and T. Clark, 1910), 287, 411, points in this regard to an increasing sensitivity by the Old Testament editors to anthropomorphism in the text.
9. R. W. Neff, "The Annunciation in the Birth Narrative of Ishmael," *BR* 17 (1972): 51. See also the sequel of this episode in Gen. 21:9–21 and Hugh C. White's treatment in "The Initiation Legend of Ishmael," *ZAW* 87 (1975): 267–306.
10. Z. Weisman, "Charismatic Leaders in the Era of the Judges," *ZAW* 89 (1977): 402.
11. T. E. Fretheim, *The Suffering of God, an Old Testament Perspective* (Philadelphia: Fortress Press, 1984), 106, suggests that the "incredulity" of Gideon in his encounter with a divine messenger is evidence of the human character (state) that YHWH is taking as a part of the theophany and demonstrates YHWH's "vulnerability" when he does appear in human form. I cannot agree with this position since it removes the meaning from the motif of surprise at miraculous survival.
12. M. M. Aranov, *The Biblical Threshing-Floor in the Light of the Ancient Near Eastern Evidence: Evolution of an Institution* (Ph.D. diss., New York University, 1977), 166–70.
13. J. C. Exum, "Promise and Fulfillment: Narrative Art in Judges 13," *JBL* 99 (1980): 43–59, traces the literary pattern of this birth announcement.
14. Compare "Hymnal Prayer of Enheduanna: The Adoration of Inanna in Ur," in J. B. Pritchard, *Ancient Near Eastern Texts Relating to the Old Testament* (Princeton, N.J.: Princeton University Press, 1969), 581, lines 128–30, where the goddess is described as having a "fierce countenance."
15. See S. A. Cook, "The Theophanies of Gideon and Manoah," *JTS* 28 (1926/27): 368–83, for a tie to cult legend in these two passages.
16. M. Z. Soleh, "Revelation—Not Only at Sinai," *Bet Mikra* 29 (1983/84): 285–86.
17. E. C. Kingsbury, "The Theophany *Topos* and the Mountain of God," *JBL* 68 (1967): 208.

18. Compare Hans Joachim Kraus, *Die prophetische Verkundigung des Rechts in Israel,* *Theologische Studien* Heft 51 (Zollikon, Switzerland: Evangelischer Verlag, 1957), restated in *Worship in Israel* (Richmond, Va.: John Knox Press, 1966), 102–12, on the "covenant mediator" role with R. R. Wilson's position in *Prophecy and Society in Ancient Israel* (Philadelphia: Fortress Press, 1980), 158–59.

19. Wilson, *Prophecy and Society,* 198–99; see also R. P. Carroll, "The Elijah–Elisha Sagas: Some Remarks on Prophetic Succession in Ancient Israel," *VT* 19 (1969): 400–15.

20. G. G. Harrop, " 'But Now Mine Eyes Seeth Thee,' " *Canadian Journal of Theology* 12 (1966): 82; and Martin Noth, *The Deuteronomistic History* (Philadelphia: Westminster Press, 1966), 60.

21. E. W. Nicholson, *Exodus and Sinai in History and Tradition* (Richmond, Va.: John Knox Press, 1973), 81.

22. T. W. Mann, *Divine Presence and Guidance in Israelite Traditions: The Typology of Exaltation* (Baltimore: Johns Hopkins University Press, 1977), 154.

23. E. W. Nicholson, "The Origin of the Tradition in Exodus XXIV 9–11," *VT* 26 (1976): 150.

24. T. E. Fretheim, *The Suffering of God,* 99–100, notes the extreme position of vulnerability which YHWH places himself in when his name is disclosed. He notes the commandments (Exod 30:7; Deut 5:11) against taking his "name in vain."

25. U. Cassuto, *A Commentary on the Book of Exodus* (Jerusalem: Magnes Press, 1967), 435–36, denies that bodily harm is implied here since man cannot comprehend God's majesty or see beyond the finite.

26. G. H. Davies, *Interpreters' Dictionary of the Bible,* ed. George A. Buttrick (Nashville: Abingdon, 1962), 2:401–2, explores the implications of just how close a connection there is between God and his glory (see on this Lev 9:4, 6; Ps 113:4; and Zech 2:8).

27. Brevard S. Childs, *Book of Exodus* (Philadelphia: Westminster Press, 1974), 598, lists the opinions of commentators on what Moses saw of YHWH's glory.

28. R. W. L. Moberly, "At the Mountain of God, Story and Theology in Exodus 32–34," *JSOT* Supplement Series 22 (1983): 106.

29. A. F. Campbell, *The Ark Narrative: A Form-Critical and Traditio-Historical Study* (Missoula, Mont.: Scholars Press, 1975), 197–204.

30. R. J. Clifford, *The Cosmic Mountain in Canaan and the Old Testament* (Cambridge: Harvard University Press, 1972), 178, notes that "the Israelites were careful . . . to make distinctions between God enthroned in his dwelling in heaven and his Name which is in the Temple."

31. Mann, *Divine Presence and Guidance,* 165–66.

32. J. Barr, "Theophany and Anthropomorphism in the Old Testament," VTSup 7 (1959): 35.

33. Clifford, *Cosmic Mountain,* 154.

34. S. Mowinckel, *The Psalms in Israel's Worship* (Oxford: Blackwell, 1967), 156–58.

35. Clifford, *Cosmic Mountain,* 155.

36. T. Booij, "Mountain and Theophany in the Sinai Narrative," *Bib* 65 (1984): 25, suggests that the Sinai traditions do not acquire "canonical authority" until after the Exile, but it is apparent that the Sinai motif was used for theophanic descriptions both before and after the exilic period.

37. Kingsbury, "The Theophany *Topos,*" 209. See also Mic. 1:2 and Ps. 18:7 for earthquake imagery.

38. O. Kaiser, *Isaiah 1–12* (Philadelphia: Westminster Press, 1972), 76–77.

39. Avraham Gileadi has kindly let me see a section of his forthcoming volume, *The Literary Message of Isaiah,* in which he makes a comparison between the paradigm of Isaiah's role and mission and the people's fulfilled condition of healing found in Isaiah 40.

40. P. Hanson, *The Dawn of Apocalyptic* (Philadelphia: Fortress Press, 1975), 163, points to the "salvation–judgment oracle" in Isa. 59:7–16 and its promised demonstration of power as a sign of judgment and the "final deliverance of the oppressed community" in a theophanic appearance of YHWH when "there was no man . . . , no one to intervene" to reestablish justice (v 16).

41. C. Westermann, *Isaiah 40–66* (Philadelphia: Westminster Press, 1969), 39; and Hanson, *Dawn*, 127.

42. Compare Phillips's suggestion in "A Fresh Look at the Sinai Pericope," *VT* 34 (1984): 282–94, that the mention in Exod. 34:23ff. "that Moses rather than Yahweh appears to have written the laws on the second set of tablets may indicate that the reader is to identify King Hezekiah 'as a second Moses' who interceded for his people and introduced the reform which saved Judah from Samaria's fate."

43. Moberly, *At the Mountain of God*, 109.

44. Barr, "Theophany and Anthropomorphism," 34–35.

45. D. Patrick, *Arguing with God: The Angry Prayers of Job* (St. Louis: Bethany Press, 1977), 60.

46. William R. Millar, *Isaiah 24–27 and the Origin of Apocalyptic* (Missoula, Mont.: Scholars Press, 1976), 68, depicts the theme of this passage as warfare.

47. G. von Rad, "The Origin of the Concept of the Day of Yahweh," *JSS* 4 (1959): 104.

48. Clifford, *Cosmic Mountain*, 152–53, n. 72, compares this to the feasting gods celebrating Baal's victory over Mot (Death); he notes how the Canaanite deity has been "depersonalized" in Isaiah 25.

24

The Transcendent Nature of Covenant Curse Reversals

Herbert M. Wolf

One of the most remarkable things about the Hebrew prophets is the exuberant way in which they describe the restoration of the nation of Israel. The people, the buildings, and even the fields and crops—all share in a renewal which transforms a deserted wasteland into a prosperous nation. Although YHWH judges the people because they break his covenant, he restores their fortunes after a time of punishment.

THE REALITY OF COVENANT CURSES

There exists an ominous element in ancient Near Eastern treaties: a list of curses comprises an integral part of the treaty form. The latter part of these agreements lists a series of blessings and curses designed to encourage the cooperation of the vassal with the stipulations spelled out by the suzerain. The benefits are expressed as part of the blessings, but in order to strike fear into the heart of a vassal who might be inclined toward rebellion, a large number of curses is included. In the ancient world, even if a nation had little enthusiasm for her overlord, the curses were sometimes enough to ensure compliance with a treaty.

The Hebrew Bible describes Israel's covenant with YHWH in terms similar to those in the ancient treaty form. The consequences of obedience or disobedience are delineated in an impressive list of blessings and curses.[1] Leviticus 26 and Deuteronomy 28 summarize most fully the blessings and curses associated with the Sinai covenant. Following a comparatively short section outlining the blessings of obedience appears a lengthy discourse (26 verses in Leviticus; 54 in Deuteronomy) on the calamities sure to result from disobedience. If Israel abandons YHWH, he will send drought and crop failure, pestilence and disease. Israel's armies will be defeated in battle, and the people will die or be carried away into captivity. Beautiful cities will be destroyed and lie abandoned for decades, while the exiles languish in foreign lands, diminished in number and broken in spirit.

If these curses go back to the time of Moses,[2] their fulfillment was delayed for centuries until the powerful armies of Assyria and Babylon ravaged the Near East. When Israel's idolatry increased, YHWH "delivered Jacob to utter destruction ḥērem" (Isa 43:28), just as he had destroyed Canaan by the armies of Joshua. When Nebuchadnezzar's armies breached the walls of Jerusalem in 587/586 B.C., the temple, the palace, and "all the houses of Jerusalem" were burned down (2 Kgs 25:9).

The prophet Isaiah had warned the nation of the imminent fulfillment of the covenant curses. He began his prophecy, "Hear, O heavens, and give ear, O earth," thus calling heaven and earth as witnesses against the people (compare Deut 30:19). Isa. 1:5–9 goes on to describe the disease and desolation associated with the curses. M. Deroche argues that because Israel had violated the covenant, Hosea announced that YHWH would punish the nation with a reversal of creation. Animals, birds, and "even the fish of the sea" would be eliminated (Hos 4:3).[3]

EXAMPLES OF CURSE REVERSALS

Although the prophets emphasize YHWH's judgment on a sinful Israel, they also describe the restoration of the land to a paradise-like condition as the covenant curses are reversed.[4] Such a reversal of curses is not documented outside of Israel and thus signifies an important variation from usual Near Eastern treaty patterns.[5]

Curse reversal of another kind can be demonstrated, however, and this was usually accomplished by pronouncing a blessing to nullify the effects of the curse. In the Gilgamesh Epic, the doomed hero Enkidu curses the city of Erech and the woman who has introduced him to civilization, but he changes this curse to blessing when Gilgamesh points out the benefits of civilized society.[6] In a bizarre episode recorded in Judg. 17:1–2, a man named Micah steals eleven hundred pieces of silver from his mother but confesses to the theft when he hears the curse she pronounces upon the thief. When the woman realizes she has cursed her own son, she quickly tries to reverse the curse by saying, "Blessed be my son by YHWH."[7] But then she uses the money to make an idol, an act sure to provoke YHWH's anger as much as that of stealing.

In describing an equally strange incident, Numbers 22–24 records the ill-fated attempts of the prophet Balaam to curse Israel. Hired by Balak, king of Moab, for that very purpose, Balaam makes several attempts to curse the Israelites, but each time YHWH instructs him to bless Israel instead. Deut. 23:5 sums up the incident by saying, God turns "the curse into a blessing for you." In spite of Balaam's eagerness to curse Israel he utters four remarkable blessings before Balak gives up in disgust. Not long after, however, the Moabites follow Balaam's advice to involve the Israelites in the worship of the Baal of Peor (Num 25:1–2; 31:16). This clever suggestion leads to idolatry and immorality and brings a plague that kills twenty-four thousand Israelites (Num 25:8–9). Thus Balaam has been able to curse Israel after all. Yet the only curses Balaam was permitted to utter were directed against enemies of Israel, such as Moab and Edom, who were intent on seeing Israel cursed (Num 24:17–24).[8]

Another example of curse reversal results from the harsh words expressed by Jacob when he predicts the future of his son Levi in Gen. 49:5–7. Levi and Simeon are guilty of treacherously slaying all the males of the city of Shechem after their sister Dinah is raped by Prince Shechem himself. Because of their violent behavior, Jacob curses their anger and declares that they will be scattered in Israel. Although Jacob curses the anger rather than the individuals, his words constitute an indirect curse on Simeon and Levi.[9] In subsequent years, however, the descendants of Levi rally to Moses' side as he pronounces judgment on Israel at Sinai for worshiping the golden calf (Exod 32:25–29). As a reward of their covenant zeal, the tribe of Levi is designated to fill a priestly role for the whole nation, and the scattering predicted by Jacob turns out to be an honorable dispersion to forty-eight cities to take care of the spiritual needs of all the tribes (Josh 21:1–42).

A MARVELOUS TRANSFORMATION

The most remarkable descriptions of curse reversals in the Hebrew Bible appear in those passages in the prophets that deal with the restoration and rebuilding of Israel after a long period of shame and disgrace in exile. The once-battered nation now achieves a level of prosperity and blessedness that more than compensates for her great suffering and degradation. The curses of famine, disease, and war give way to unprecedented blessings of health, fruitfulness, and peace.

A Glorious Return from Captivity

According to Deut. 28:49, YHWH's anger at his people's apostasy would lead him to bring against Israel a nation "from the end of the earth, . . . a nation whose language you do not understand," which would destroy animals and crops, besiege cities, and take captive those who survived the ordeal. The prospect of living in a foreign country filled the Israelites with fear and uncertainty (Deut 28:65–67). Separation from the promised land and from the beloved city of Jerusalem meant sorrow and an aching heart (Ps 137:1–6).

The announcement in the prophets that Israel would one day return home, therefore, was a welcome word indeed. YHWH had not abandoned his people, for once again cities would be inhabited and young men and maidens would rejoice together (Jer 31:13, 16–17; 32:37). Through Hosea, YHWH says that Israel would be called "not my people" (Hos 1:9), but YHWH also has pity on the nation and will again declare, "You are my people" (Hos 2:23).[10]

As YHWH had redeemed his people from Egypt, so he would again display his redeeming power in their release from Babylon. When Israel left Egypt, the people traversed a wide and dangerous wilderness. YHWH promises that in the return from Babylon the valleys will be lifted up and mountains made low, enabling the exiles to travel on a straight highway (Isa 40:3–4). There will be "rivers in the desert" (43:19) so that the people will not thirst along the way. YHWH himself will go before them (52:12), as he did in the pillar of cloud and fire during the exodus out of Egypt (Exod 13:21). Isaiah calls the regathering of the exiles, "YHWH's return to Zion"; YHWH will again be the Sovereign One, ruling as king over his people (Isa 52:7–8).

The years of exile are a fulfillment of the curse that Israel would be taken captive to a foreign land. Isa. 55:5, however, reverses this situation as nations that know little about Israel are attracted to her and to her God. A similar picture is given in Isa. 2:2–4, in which the nations stream to Mount Zion to learn about the God of Jacob. Kings and queens will bow down and acknowledge the greatness of Israel and her God, and her people will become "renowned among the nations" (Isa 61:9; compare 14:2; 49:23). Those who once held her captive will submit to her; Israel will posses the nations (54:3). Similarly, "the wealth of the nations" will come to her who was stripped of wealth (60:5).[11] This constitutes a marvelous change from the condition of slavery that humbled the Northern Kingdom of Samaria in 722–721 B.C. and the Southern Kingdom of Judah in 587/586 B.C. The enemies of Israel would tread her down no more.

A Growing Population

As a result of foreign invasion, the population of Israel steadily decreased as young men fell in battle. Conditions worsened as cities were besieged and the inhabitants died of starvation, disease, or plague. When the walls were breached, enemy troops poured into the cities to kill the weak and the ill and to engage the soldiers in battle. Those who survived were taken away as captives. By the time Jerusalem was captured, the population of Judah had been severely decimated, as the list of captives given in Jer. 52:28–30 indicates.[12] Of the several million who lived in Judah in the seventh century B.C., only a small percentage—a remnant—was taken to Babylon. The Israelites had disobeyed YHWH and were "left few in number" (Deut 28:62).

When the exiles were free to return to Judea, a relatively small number, about fifty thousand, accompanied Zerubbabel in 538 B.C. (see Ezra 2:64–65). Yet the prophets speak of the day when the borders of Israel will not be able to hold the returning population. During the exile, Judea was like a barren woman (Isa 54:1) or a widow bereaved of her children (Isa 49:21), but eventually the land will not be large enough to hold Israel's descendants. Amazed, she will wonder where everyone has come from and who it was that gave birth to so many children (49:21). Recalling the words of the Abrahamic covenant (Gen 22:17), Hosea says that the Israelites will then be as numerous as grains of sand on the seashore (compare Hos 1:10).

To insure the safety of the growing population, YHWH will remove wild animals from the land, a blessing promised in Lev. 26:6. Ezekiel combines this removal of wild animals with the absence of foreign armies when he speaks of peace restored to the land (Ezek 34:25, 28). Even on the return road no lion or "ravenous beast" will attack the redeemed of YHWH (Isa 35:8–10).

Super–Abundant Crops

The most frequently mentioned curse reversal in the prophets is the change from barren, unproductive soil to fertile earth that produces abundantly. The Book of Deuteronomy warns about drought and famine (Deut 28:23), and throughout the Hebrew Bible disobedience preceded years of little or no rain (compare 1 Kgs 17:1). To underscore the return of YHWH's blessing upon the restored nation, the prophets speak of plentiful harvests unlike any seen before the exile. Jeremiah lived at a time when the land had become a desolate wilderness (Jer 12:10–11), but he looked forward to a day when men would rejoice "over the grain, the wine, and the oil" (Jer 31:12). According to Hosea, vines and fig trees would be laid waste, but in that day crops would again be plentiful (Hos 2:12, 21–23). Joel prophesies that "the mountains shall drip sweet wine, and the hills shall flow with milk" and none of the stream beds will run dry (Joel 3:18). Ezekiel refers to trees that will then yield their fruit; and the earth will yield its increase when YHWH ensures a regular rainfall (Ezek 34:26–27).

The Book of Isaiah contains several passages that depict the transformation of Israel's soil from barrenness to fertility. One of the most dramatic of these includes a strong denunciation of complacent women who will shudder and beat their breasts when the vintage fails and the ground yields only thorns and briers (Isa 32:9–14). Immediately after this announcement of doom, however, Isaiah predicts that some day a Spirit from on high will be poured out and the wilderness will be changed into a fruitful field (32:15). Once again YHWH's people will live in safety, and justice and righteousness will prevail (32:16). According to F. C. Fensham, this swift movement from curse to blessing is unknown in other ancient Near Eastern literature; curses abound, but they are not so reversed.[13] The fruitful fields will also produce enough feed for animals. Cattle will enjoy wide pastures, and oxen and donkeys will eat a rich provender (30:23–24; compare 32:20). So great will be Israel's fruitfulness, her wilderness will be "like Eden," her desert "like the garden of YHWH" (51:3).

Although Amos wrote long before the collapse of either the Northern Kingdom or the Southern Kingdom, he too spoke about the calamities the nation would endure and the glorious restoration that would follow. At the end of his book, Amos says that sowing and reaping will then be continuous, and vineyards and gardens will produce abundant harvests: "The plowman will overtake the reaper and the treader of grapes him who sows the seed" (Amos 9:13).

The Spectacular Rebuilding of Jerusalem and Its Walls

When YHWH abandoned his people and permitted foreign armies to invade Israel, cities were besieged and fortified walls knocked down (Deut 28:52). In 2 Kgs. 25:9, we learn that after Jerusalem's walls were breached, the temple, the palace, and all houses were burned down. The holy city, renowned for its beauty and splendor, was laid in ruins. In the decades that followed, the exiles mourned the collapse of Jerusalem and forgot its glorious past (Ps 137:5-6).

After the Persians captured Babylon, King Cyrus issued the famous decree that allowed YHWH's people to return home and rebuild the temple in Jerusalem (see Ezra 1:2-4).[14] Isaiah predicts that through Cyrus Jerusalem would be rebuilt and its temple foundations laid (Isa 44:28). Amos predicts that the people will "rebuild the ruined cities and inhabit them" (Amos 9:14), and Jeremiah describes the day when the walls of Jerusalem will be rebuilt (Jer 31:38-40).

In a remarkable picture of the restored Jerusalem, Isaiah speaks about the precious stones that will be used in the construction process. YHWH will lay the foundations with sapphires; the pinnacles will be adorned with rubies, the gates with carbuncles. The very walls of the city will be made of valuable stones (Isa 54:11-12). Nothing of such beauty and magnitude has ever been featured in the building of Jerusalem, although several kinds of precious stones were used in Solomon's temple (1 Chr 29:2). The restored Jerusalem will be a prosperous and peaceful city whose gates will never be shut (Isa 60:11, 18).

The Reign of a Righteous King

With the collapse of Jerusalem and the deportation of the young King Jehoiachin in 598/597 B.C. and his uncle Zedekiah in 587/586 B.C., the nation wondered whether the Davidic dynasty would be restored. Had the terms of the Davidic covenant been shattered beyond repair and brought an end to the rule of David's descendants? In answer to this question, Jeremiah promises that in some future day Israel's prince will be one of their own people (Jer 30:21). He will be a "righteous branch" of the line of David and will rule his people with justice and righteousness. YHWH's covenant with David cannot be broken (33:15, 21-22). Isaiah likewise speaks of a "shoot from the stump of Jesse" (Isa 11:1); he, too, predicts that a descendant of David will one day sit on the throne and faithfully execute justice and righteousness (9:7; 16:5). Ezekiel speaks of this king as "my servant David," a shepherd who feeds his flock (Ezek 34:23; 37:24). The name *David* may mean that the king would be a descendant of David and would rule with the same power and authority.

As an indication that the Davidic dynasty was not dead, the prophet Haggai designates Zerubbabel, governor of postexilic Judah, as "a signet ring" (Hag 2:23). A signet ring was a seal that could validate the authority behind the contents of a letter (1 Kgs 21:8) or be used as a pledge to guarantee future payment (Gen 38:18). In Jer. 22:24, YHWH compares King Coniah (another name for Jehoiachin) to a signet ring torn from the finger of his right hand

and given to Nebuchadnezzar. YHWH then curses Coniah's family by announcing that none of his descendants will ever rule over Judah again (Jer 22:30). Since Zerubbabel was Coniah's grandson, it may be that Haggai was trying to reverse the curse against the deported king. By comparing Zerubbabel to a signet ring, Haggai may be saying that Zerubbabel is a pledge that a king will come from David's descendants.[15]

With the raising up of the righteous king, the restoration of Israel will be consummated. Once again Jerusalem will become the center of a prosperous kingdom, filled with people enjoying plentiful crops, a city safe and secure. In spite of the harsh realities of judgment, a gracious YHWH delights in reversing the curses that covenant disobedience had made necessary. Indeed, in a concrete sense Israel's restoration consists of a transcendent reversal of these divine curses—a miraculous and marvelous healing of the effects of transgression. As a result of this reversal, Israel's final state will surpass in glory any to which she had attained formerly.

NOTES

1. See F. C. Fensham, "Malediction and Benediction in Ancient Near Eastern Vassal-Treaties and the Old Testament," *ZAW* 74 (1962): 1–9.

2. Roland K. Harrison, *Introduction to the Old Testament* (Grand Rapids, Mich.: Wm. Eerdmans, 1969), 648–49.

3. In Gen. 1:20–24, these creatures were created in reverse order (see Michael Deroche, "The Reversal of Creation in Hosea," *VT* 31 [1981]: 400–409).

4. See Avraham Gileadi, *The Apocalyptic Book of Isaiah* (Provo, Utah: Hebraeus Press, 1982), 205.

5. Ibid., 177.

6. See H. W. F. Saggs, *The Greatness That Was Babylon* (New York: Hawthorn Books, 1962), 396–97.

7. See Arthur E. Cundall, *Judges*, ed. D. J. Wiseman (Chicago: Inter-Varsity Press, 1968), 183.

8. Ronald B. Allen, "The Theology of the Balaam Oracles," in *Tradition and Testament*, ed. John S. Feinberg and Paul D. Feinberg (Chicago: Moody Press, 1981), 85–86.

9. Josef Scharbert, *TDOT*, 1:411.

10. See Frances I. Andersen and David Noel Freedman, *Hosea* (Garden City, N.Y.: Doubleday, 1980), 264.

11. Herbert M. Wolf, *Interpreting Isaiah* (Grand Rapids, Mich.: Zondervan Publishing House, 1985), 222, 298–99.

12. See John Bright, *Jeremiah* (Garden City, N.Y.: Doubleday, 1965), 369.

13. F. C. Fensham, "Common Trends in Curses of the Near Eastern Treaties and Kudurru Inscriptions Compared with Maledictions of Amos and Isaiah," *ZAW* 75 (1963): 174. Note the way the promises of Hos. 2:14–23 reverse the threats made in 2:2–13; compare Andersen and Freedman, *Hosea*, 264.

14. *ANET*, 316.

15. See Herbert M. Wolf, *Haggai and Malachi* (Chicago: Moody Press, 1976), 54–55; R. T. Siebeneck, "The Messianism of Aggeus and Proto-Zecharias," *CBQ* 19 (1957): 318.